INDIAN KĀVYA LITERATURE

Volume Two

INDIAN KĀVYA LITERATURE

The Origins and Formation of Classical Kāvya

A.K. WARDER

VOLUME TWO

SINCE 1903

MOTILAL BANARSIDASS
PUBLISHING HOUSE

*3rd Reprint: Delhi, **2025***
Second Revised Edition: Delhi, 1990
First Edition: Delhi, 1974

Also available at:
MOTILAL BANARSIDASS PUBLISHING HOUSE

- 4637/20, F-2, Hari Sadan, First Floor, Ansari Road, Darya Ganj Delhi–110 002 *Tel.*: (+91-11) 4559 7999
- 1st Floor, 1/2 Rathnavilas Road, Basvanagudi, Next to Pai Vista Convention Hall, South End Circle, Bengaluru–560004 (India) *Tel.*: +91-80-41275911

ISBN: 978-93-9321-481-2 (Hardcover)
ISBN: 978-93-9321-486-7 (Paperback)

Printed & Published by
Rajendra P Jain *for*
Motilal Banarsidass Publishing House
A-44, Naraina Industrial Area, Phase I, New Delhi–110 028 (INDIA)
Email: naraina@mlbd.in Website: www.mlbd.in
Tel.: (+91-11) 4751 1592

CONTENTS OF VOLUME TWO

Chapter IX

PRE-KĀVYA LITERATURE : THE VEDA

500. The 'origin' of literature in India is hidden in a remote antiquity, of which the hardly reconcilable testimonies of archaeology and ancient legends give us at present but a very shadowy idea. One can merely take for granted that story telling and song are as ancient as human society, and regard the earliest extant Indian specimens of these arts, which antedate *kāvya* by a thousand years, as belonging to a tradition, or a complex of traditions, of incalculable age.

501. To obtain an idea of the literature of pre-*kāvya* India, as a background to the rise of *kāvya*, we may begin with a glance at the earliest archaeological evidence for literature, that is for attestation of particular stories and legends. This is found in the ruins of the great cities of the Indus valley civilisation, at levels belonging to the —3rd millennium. Though we have inscriptions from these cities, they have not yet been convincingly deciphered; hence we cannot yet infer from them anything about literature, and the language itself remains unidentified. Pictures in relief, mostly on seals, do however suggest something about the literature of these cities. A hero is shown fighting two tigers (Mackay Plate LXXXIV. 75, 86; XCV.454), gods and goddesses as well as humans appear with hints of myths and stories (Mackay LXIX. 23; XC. 23, 24: XCII. 10; XCIV. 401, 430; CIII. 16; LXXXII.1), there are, besides ordinary Indian animals, monsters, composite beasts, sometimes partly human (Mackay LXXXIX. 347; XCIII. 13, 14; XCIV. 411; XCV. 450; XCVI. 521; XCVII. 554).

502. The great hero resembles his Mesopotamian (Sumerian) contemporary Gilgamesh, who wandered over the earth, fought monsters and performed various superhuman feats, as well as later Indian heroes, especially the incarnations of Viṣṇu (including Rāma). The Sumerian 'minotaur' Eabani (Enkidu), first the enemy, then the ally, of Gilgamesh, has been compared with an Indus valley representation of a similar monster fighting a horned tiger (Marshall Plate III. 375). Clear parallelisms with Sumerian literature are occasionally found in

India in the Vedic literature, for example the legend of the Flood, which we shall consider in a moment.

503. A story recalling a later Indian fable (the cock and the cat—e.g. *Jātaka* No. 383) is suggested by representations of a man up a tree, escaping from a tiger which walks away disappointed (Mackay XCVI.522). Footprints on a seal resemble those symbolising Viṣṇu (and Rāma) in later Indian art (Mackay XCI. 4 b; XCII.12 c). Sculptured and relief representations of a great god, simultaneously ascetic and symbolic of fertility, strongly suggest the Great God (Mahādeva) Śiva of later ages, around whom many antique myths are clustered, some of which are retold in *kāvyas* (Mackay LXXXVII.222, 235; XCIV. 420). Śiva himself later takes a particular interest in *kāvya*, and is one of its presiding deities frequently invoked by *kavis*.

504. We seem able to infer that later Indian literature is in some significant elements continuous with that of the Indus valley in the --3rd millennium.

505. Vedic literature, representing a period of about a thousand years, following the collapse of the ancient empire in the Indus valley (which took place *c.* —1600), is preserved in a Canon of varied though restricted content. The restriction is due to the purpose of the priests who compiled it, which was to make a collection of sacred texts for use in religious ritual, together with descriptions and explanations of the rituals. In the latter part of the period, philosophical dialogues were added as a kind of appendix, intended to govern meditation as a substitute for ritual. This Canon, the *Veda*, includes both verse and prose, and lyrics, songs, heroic poetry, ballads, dialogues, myths, legends, historical narratives and stories. There is tragedy and farce, philosophy and comedy.

506. Many poems, the *Indragāthās*, belong to what may be regarded as an epic or cycle celebrating the feats of the war-god Indra, who led the Aryan people to victory and to the conquest of the Indus valley (he 'gave the land to the Ārya'—*ṚVS* IV. 26. 2.). We do not expect to find in the most ancient literature of these conquerors much trace of that of the conquered people, yet in the later parts of the Canon there appear to be myths and stories of the Indus valley, as suggested above, and gradually gods new to the *Veda*, apparently of Indian origin (especially Śiva) make their way into the pantheon. Unimportant at first,

Śiva in the post-Vedic period becomes more dominant than any Vedic god except Viṣṇu, and Viṣṇu too seems to be either an originally Indian god or an amalgam of a minor Aryan deity with a great god of India. As the Aryans—barbarian nomads from the steppes of Central Asia—spread across Northern India they gradually settled down and adopted the civilised life. Having previously destroyed the Indian cities and the irrigation systems, they later built cities of their own and began to use the waters of the great rivers. As the archaeological investigation of this period of transition has hardly yet begun, we can say little of the beginnings of the civilisation of the Aryans. They appear to have destroyed almost everything of the Indus civilisation and left the cities abandoned, yet the ancient culture seems to show through the Aryan culture a few centuries later, and we may suppose that the reborn civilisation owed much to its predecessor: the Aryans were, to a degree not yet clear, assimilated to the Indians.

507. At the time of the conquest, however, the barbarians saw the Indian civilisation as an evil, the work of demons, which should be erased from the Earth, restoring nature to its free, wild state. In the numerous Indra poems, which belong to the early phase of Vedic literature, the god smashes the citadels of the enemy, overcomes demons and releases the waters, or rivers, and cattle from captivity (*ṚVS* II. 11, 12, 13, 14, 15, 19 and 20 are good examples). In the eyes of nomads the herding of cattle in enclosures perhaps appeared as an oppressive captivity; as for the waters, it has convincingly been suggested that the irrigation works on which agriculture in the dry Indus region depended, the dams and canals, were detested and destroyed by the nomads as an atrocious imprisonment of the sacred rivers. At the same time, it is clear that the annual monsoon, the rainy season inaugurated by thunder and the massing of clouds, was also associated with the beneficient activity of Indra: shattering the demon Vṛtra with his thunderbolt and bringing back the clouds which also had been made captive (*ṚVS* IV.19). This latter aspect of Indra's work, which remained topical, seeming to be re-enacted every year, eclipsed the historical aspect of dam-breaking, which was gradually forgotten although traces of it remain in a few of the poems. A few poems commemorate the human leaders who won battles during the conquest

(*ṚVS* I. 51, 53, 54, 112; VI. 27). Others are concerned with later events, such as those on the *Dāśarajña*, the Battle of the Ten Kings, where the glorification of the brahman minister who guides the victor tends to take precedence over that of the warrior himself (*ṚVS* VII.18, 33).

508. Among the lyrical poems may be mentioned those in which natural phenomena are personified, for example Dawn (*ṚVS* I.124) and Night (*ṚVS* X.127) as goddesses, the Sun (*ṚVS* I.115) and the Thunderstorm (*ṚVS* V.83) as gods, as well as more direct descriptions of nature scattered in many places. Since most of the poems in the *Veda* are in honour of particular deities, personification is frequent--any phenomenon may be regarded as the work of, or as a manifestation of, the appropriate deity.

509. The metres used (all of which are 'syllabic') are well suited to the types of poetry: a heroic sounding, strongly articulated line of 11 syllables predominates in the epic type, whilst in the lyrics a variety of metres and strophe structures is found. The principles of construction are very different from those of *kāvya*, and even from Tradition. The eight syllable line, which may be regarded as the ancestor of the narrative *vaktra* of Tradition, is here a lyric metre constructed in various kinds of strophe (most characteristically in a strophe of three lines of eight syllables, all having the same cadence), whereas in the epic *vaktra* form, though it derived from the eight syllable line, we have in effect a line of sixteen syllables—since the two halves have opposed and balancing cadences. A further characteristic of Vedic metre is that in lyric verse two different metrical lines may be combined, for example the eight line and the twelve line in various arrangements. These peculiar Vedic strophes are sometimes of considerable complexity, and it was by variety of strophes, not of metrical lines, that the repertoire of Vedic lyric metres was enlarged. Many Vedic poems were set as songs, but the metres do not reflect musical organisation as later do the 'musical metres' of *kāvya*.

510. The Vedic ballads and dialogues may be considered together. They are not numerous, but they may represent a form more popular than their extant number suggests. Their chief interest for us is that we may see in them a forerunner of the *kāvya* drama, a transition from simple epic recitation by one narrator towards the impersonation of the characters of the story by more than one. We lack clear evidence for a 'performance' of these dialogues by two or more narrator-actors, though the presence in the ritual of several priests, uttering different verses or prayers, might suggest a dramatic performance. The extant dialogues are rather terse and fragmentary, having probably been cut to fit the ritual purpose for which alone they were preserved: this might suggest they had a non-ritual origin, and a performance for dramatic entertainment (*ṚVS* X. 108). The stories of the ballad-dialogues are myths (e.g. *ṚVS* IV.42, conflict of Varuṇa and Indra; X.86, Indra and his consort) and legends, one of which at least (Purūravas and the nymph—see *ṚVS* X. 95) was actually made into a full scale drama (a *toṭaka*) by Kālidāsa in the +5 [1402].

511. Comedy and farce are found in a number of poems and dialogues. Some of those concerning Indra show him comically intoxicated (*ṚVS* X.119). The comparison of frogs croaking in the rain with groups of brahmans chanting, in the poem of the frogs (*ṚVS* VII.103), seems now satirical, though its humour may have been quite harmless in the Vedic period (mild humour, not felt to be satirical, is quite characteristic of Indian religious legends, which are as a rule exceedingly good-natured and full of human touches, suggesting the view of an amused but benevolent spectator). More serious satire, mysteriously included in the scriptures (for its didactic purpose or as a prayer for the release of the victim?), is the poem of the gambler who complains of the magical power of the dice, which he cannot resist though it has separated him from his wife and left him homeless and in debt, a beggar (*ṚVS* X. 34).

512. In the prose books of the *Veda* (which form its later stratum) we find mythical or legendary narratives more fully expressed than in their verse counterparts. A few examples of ancient story telling in prose (sometimes interspersed with verse) have been vouchsafed us because they seemed to explain features of the ritual. The prose style is most terse and abrupt, with short sentences and a severe absence of any ornamentation such as variation of words or phrases to avoid repetition. Later prose writers used such uncompromising directness only for technical or philosophical works: it did not provide a 'classical' standard for prose literature, and in the *kāvya* period very different styles were evolved. The narratives *ākhyānas* in prose of the *Veda*, which purport to be historical (as giving precedents, for example), are clearly the forerunners of the biographies or histories *ākhyāyikās* of *kāvya*. There are a few prose narratives in Tradition also, showing a somewhat less heavy style. The term *ākhyāna*, however, was used for verse narratives as well as prose, if they purported to be historical, thus the main story of the Great Epic is an *ākhyāna*. The Vedic ritual also directs that an *ākhyāna* on famous ancient kings, the *Pāriplava* (*ŚBr.* XIII.4.3), is to be chanted in verse, accompanied on a lute *viṇā*, as part of the preparation of a certain rite. This is to be extemporised by the chanter (who belongs to the warrior class, a professional bard, not a priest), no doubt in the then fluid epic tradition. The later Vedic texts (*AVS* XV.6.4ff.; *ŚBr.* XI.5.6.8, XIII.4.3.12, etc.) refer already to *Itihāsa* (Tradition) and *Purāṇa* (Antiquity: cosmogony and history), so that the great age of these in some form is certain, though the texts now extant are many centuries later than the Vedic period. Their tradition was evidently oral and fluid and reflected changing fashions until at last they were written down well after the beginning of the *kāvya* period.

513. The myths and legends of the prose phase of Vedic literature include the wars between the gods and the demons as an evidently popular subject (*ŚBr.* I.2.4.8ff.; 5.4.6ff; V.1.1; IX.2.3; 5.1.12ff.; XI.1.6,8; 5.9; XIII.8.1.5; 8.2). Sometimes the gods hold heaven, sometimes the demons, and men also seek the way there—which the gods try to block in order to keep it to themselves (*Aitareya Br.* II.1; III.42). At one time the demons, in the ascendant, made the Three Worlds (Earth, atmosphere and sky = Heaven) into three citadels *puras*—which reminds us of those of the Indus valley smashed by Indra (*ŚBr.* III.4.4; *Aitareya Br.* I.23). A variant of this myth appears later as a subject for *kāvyas* celebrating Śiva's victory over the demons [333]. On another occasion a truce is arranged in the struggle for the worlds (again when the demons have the advantage), and it is agreed that the universe shall be divided, the gods taking only as much as Viṣṇu, a dwarf, can cover in three steps. With these three famous steps Viṣṇu then covers all three worlds, and so the demons are driven below the Earth (*Aitareya Br.* VI.15; *ŚBr.* I.1.2.13; 2.5; 9.3.8ff.). In later Tradition this feat by which Viṣṇu saved the worlds is a popular *avatāra* legend: that of the Dwarf, for in this disguise he deceived the demons as to his powers [1074]. In these stories the gods seem relatively unimportant and unimpressive. Prajāpati (the 'Lord of Creation'), usually identified as Brahmā, now appears as the creator of them all, and of the demons and the Three Worlds. Somehow he evolved out of nothing (*ṚVS* X.72), or in another version (*ṚVS* X.129) out of neither being nor nothing, became immortal and created everything.

514. In another myth the boar Emūṣa raises the Earth (*ŚBr*. XIV.1.2.11): here Emūṣa is identified with Prajāpati, but in Tradition the boar who raises the Earth from the cosmic ocean, killing a demon who tries to prevent him, thus making it a place habitable by human beings, is an incarnation of Viṣṇu [381]. More famous, perhaps, is the story of the Flood, when Manu Vaivasvata escaped to restart the human race (*ŚBr*. I.8.1). He was saved by the advice and aid of a fish, which he found in his washing water. The fish warned him of the coming flood and advised him to build a ship. Manu looked after the fish, which grew rapidly. When the flood came Manu embarked, and the fish, now enormous, towed the ship to the Himālaya. According to Tradition this fish was an incarnation of Viṣṇu [1331].

515. The legend of Purūravas and the nymph appears in a prose book in a fuller form (*ŚBr*. XI.5.1). Lastly we may glance at the curious story of Śunaḥśepa as an example of an old narrative (*Aitareya Br*. VII.13-8—this time in mixed verse and prose, the verse being perhaps more original). It brings in one of the favourite heroes of Tradition and *kāvya*, Hariścandra, paragon of truthfulness. Hariścandra (an emperor of the Solar Dynasty) gets a son through the favour of the god Varuṇa (the greatest of the original Aryan gods, the just ruler of the universe), but Varuṇa asks him to sacrifice the son to him. Hariścandra procrastinates, at last refuses and goes off into the forest. Varuṇa seizes him. The son, Rohita, wanders about and meets a certain Ajīgarta, who has three sons. He asks to buy one of them, and is sold the middle one—Śunaḥśepa. Rohita takes Śunaḥśepa to Hariścandra, who prepares, with Varuṇa's consent, to sacrifice him as a substitute. Śunaḥśepa takes refuge with (appeals to) the gods and is released. The priest Viśvāmitra, who is officiating at the sacrifice as *hotṛ* (reciting the poems invoking the god), takes Śunaḥśepa on his lap. Ajīgarta, filled with remorse, asks for his son back, but Viśvāmitra adopts him instead, Ajīgarta's deed being irreparable.

516. The philosophical poems (showing the development of speculative philosophy from cosmogony—above all *ṚVS* X.129) and prose dialogues of famous teachers (in the *Upaniṣads*, especially the *Chāndogya*, of the *Sāmaveda*) are of interest here only as a testimony of the sophisticated intellectual life and the habit of analytical enquiry which grew up in the latter half of the Vedic period, giving a promise of elaborate theoretical accompaniment to the rise of *kāvya*—the aesthetics and poetics outlined above—and suggesting the rationalistic and intellectually sophisticated mental environment in which *kāvya* will be born. The development of astronomy, mathematics (e.g. *ŚBr*. VIII—X) and the physical sciences (e.g. *Chāndogya Up*. VI) as well as scientific linguistics is strongly reflected in some of the prose books of the *Veda*, and it is from these early examples of technical literature that we can trace the method and style of the handbooks *śāstras* on a great variety of subjects, preserved from about the —5 onwards (beginning with the *Vedāṅgas*). It would be difficult to exaggerate the rationalistic outlook of Indian culture in this transitional period from *Veda* to *kāvya*. The ritual itself had developed (*ŚBr.*) as an attempt to construct a model of the universe, through which it could be understood and manipulated. This does not differ in principle from science and in its creative phase stimulated truly scientific enquiry, which became independent as the ritual proper became fossilised. The widespread rejection of dogma and the growth of free enquiry gave rise to many schools of philosophy between about the —8 and the —3, including the materialist Lokāyata, the philosophies of the Ājīvakas and Jainas and of the Buddha which became new religions, and eventually the Vaiśeṣika which developed a metaphysics on the basis of a physics and a theory of knowledge. The Buddhists appear to have been the pioneers of logic from at least the —3. Though in later ages the rationalistic spirit in India struggled in vain for many centuries against a gradually solidifying scholasticism, appropriate to the development of a society fixed in the hierarchical order of the medieval or feudalistic system, the *kāvya* tradition most happily reflects in its practice, and especially in its ever changing theory, the critical and analytical outlook of the period of its origin.

Chapter X

THE EPIC TRADITION: ITIHĀSA

517. As we have just noticed, by the latter part of the Vedic period there had grown up a new kind of epic literature, the *Itihāsa* or Tradition, replacing the older epic poetry and historical narrative of which fragments are preserved in the Vedic Canon. The language of this Tradition, though perhaps not very authentically represented in the texts as eventually written down and preserved for us, was certainly very different from that of the Vedic poetry and even Vedic prose. It was apparently, as suggested in discussing the languages above [9], the language—probably modified by poetic archaisms and epic conventions—of the Pañcāla Empire from *c.* —900 onwards, when the earlier parts of the *Veda* were already incomprehensible to many people and a difficult study even for scholars. New legends eclipsed the old. This new epic literature grew in part around a kernel of ancient cosmogony and legend, but later heroes dominate it and those of the period of the conquest of Northern India and immediately after are nearly all forgotten, or if they are remembered their deeds fade into oblivion, leaving them cyphers in a genealogy, to whom any heroic value might be attached.

518. The event which above all dominated this Tradition was the Bhārata War. It made a uniquely deep and tragic impression on the minds of the people, especially on the aristocracy who chiefly patronised the epic minstrels (*sūtas*, rhapsodes). The war took place most probably some time between —950 and—900, though this date is disputed. Nearly all the historical details also are disputed. According to the extant Great Epic, the vast outcome of many centuries of epic improvisation, the war was a family feud between two branches of the Bhārata (=Paurava or Lunar) Dynasty of the Aryans, which claimed imperial hegemony over all the Aryan peoples. In this war of succession for the throne at Hastināpura, princes from all parts of Northern India joined. In the culminating battle of their massed forces there was enormous slaughter on both sides, and the victorious Yudhiṣṭhira, the claimant of the Pāṇḍava branch, succeeded to the throne in tragic circumstances which turned his mind towards the renunciation of the world. Eventually he placed his brother's grandson, Parīkṣit (orphaned by the war), on the throne and retired into the Himālaya Mountains to end his days as an ascetic.

519. Tradition, the *Veda* of the people (the forerunner of drama as 'Fifth *Veda*'), as it has come down to us consists of the Great Epic and the *Purāṇas*, with which certain *śāstras* (sometimes called *Upapurāṇas*) are later associated (there were differences of opinion as to exactly what constitutes this department of literature, but these do not affect our present purpose; see *An Introduction to Indian Historiography* pp. 17-19). As sources of 'well known' subjects for *kāvyas* we need concern ourselves only with the Great Epic and the *Purāṇas*. The Great Epic is basically the story of the Bhārata War; the *Purāṇas* narrated originally the evolution of the world: cosmogony, myth, legend and history. It appears (according to the *Purāṇas* themselves— see Pargiter pp. 21ff.) that at first there was only one *Purāṇa*: now there are many, but most bear the traces of this common original subject matter. They could be regarded as so many different recensions of the story of evolution. Sometimes, and anciently, the title *Jaya*, 'The Victory',is used for this department of literature, referring to the Bhārata battle which was considered the heart of it, but including the *Purāṇas*.

520. The 'well known' stories of *kāvya* are derived chiefly from Tradition, which for this purpose, as remarked above, consists of the Great Epic and the *Purāṇas*. This is not the exclusive source, but it is the source of the overwhelming majority of extant *kāvyas* having well known subjects. Some of the stories of Tradition were retold again and again in *kāvyas*, with new interpretations, new characterisations of the heroes and heroines, and often fresh, invented, episodes [284-5, 301]. The possibilities of interpretation of these stories and their many sided significance could not be exhausted. The *kavi* must be original, but this originality is to be found in the details, especially those expressing character and delineating finely the complex operations of the emotions. It will be convenient to review here the narratives of Tradition, with special attention to those favoured by the *kavis*. We cannot dwell on their stories, but may mention the most famous heroes, assigning them their place in chronological order. The most convenient source is Pargiter's compendium *Ancient Indian Historical Tradition*, most carefully constructed out of the matter of the available texts, which we have taken as a basis.

521. To begin with there are the myths of the gods, partly taken up from the *Veda* though often differing from it on details. In theory all these belong to the evolution of the universe, are regarded as 'historical', but we may note them separately, particularly as we have already touched on some of them. They include stories of Śiva and his consort Caṇḍī (the Great Goddess, immensely popular during the *kāvya* period, who goes by many different names, such as Umā, Durgā, Pārvatī and Devī) [1422], and of Indra [1148], all of them usually in conflict with the demons. Viṣṇu with his incarnations on Earth is more 'historical', some of these being quite recent [1331]. The Churning of the Ocean by the gods and demons united was discussed above in describing the types of drama [331].

522. Human history, according to Brahmanical Tradition, proceeds in cycles dependent on the evolutions and dissolutions of the world, which are short episodes in the lives of the gods [37-8]. The Buddhists and Jainas agree that evolution is cyclic, but diverge very widely on the details [609, 861]. However, the Brahmanical Tradition still preserves some accounts close to the Buddhist version, indicating a common origin (see especially *Mahābhārata*, *Śānti Parvan*, *adhyāya* 224 and the *Vāyu Purāṇa*, VIII). It appears that Tradition was generally revised at the beginning of the feudalistic period (+4), in line with monarchical conceptions. In Tradition, in each cycle the first man, who is also the first king, is called 'Manu', but with an individual patronymic ('our' Manu, who lived nearly a hundred generations before the Bhārata War, is Manu Vaivasvata, since his father was the Sun God, Vivasvant). From this ancestor of all humanity (apart from those stemming from unions of women with gods, or other divine irruptions into the world), who is also the original lawgiver, all the ancient dynasties of kings are descended, and the several royal lines in our cycle are traced in Tradition from Manu Vaivasvata's sons and daughter (he produced this 'daughter' by means of the ritual; she became his wife according to the *ŚBr.*). The 'history' of previous cycles also is briefly described : here we may note, as a famous king, Pṛthu, the great grandson of the Manu before ours, who levelled the earth, developed agriculture and trade, and built cities and villages (this tradition is found already in *AVS* [*Śaunaka*] VIII. 10.24: Pṛthī [sic] invented ploughing, etc.; cf. also *ŚBr.* V.3.5.4). That cycle ended after only eight more generations with the great Flood referred to already, in which Manu Vaivasvata alone escaped, guided by Viṣṇu in the Fish incarnation, to repopulate the earth for the next cycle. In the eventual system each cycle *manvantara* is divided into four ages *yugas* and these cyles themselves are segments of a greater cycle called a *kalpa*, 'our' segment being the seventh. The first segment of the *kalpa* was that of Manu I Svāyambhuva; the second that of Manu II Svārociṣa, described at some length in the *Mārkaṇḍeya Purāṇa*, especially its unfortunate King Suratha of the Caitra Dynasty (named after one of the Manu's sons; see *adhyāya* 78, Veṅkaṭeśvara edition); and so on.

523. The most important dynasties descended from Manu Vaivasvata, which ruled simultaneously in different parts of India (the centre of the world—the barbarian outer regions hardly come into the story), from time to time reducing one another to vassalage, are the Solar and the Lunar. According to the *Nāṭyaśāstra* (I.8 in its apparent and probably original meaning) the Kṛta Yuga preceded Manu Vaivasvata (but Abhinavagupta gives a forced interpretation following late Purāṇic doctrine and extant Purāṇic Tradition continues that happy Age until Sagara) and he inaugurated the Tretā Yuga. The Solar Dynasty (after Manu's patronymic) is the direct line through Manu's eldest son, Ikṣvāku. Among the most famous of this line are Hariścandra (for his truthfulness and generosity, severely tested by Viśvāmitra, also a descendant of Iksvāku, but who had become a priest), Bhagīratha (four generations after Sagara, for bringing down the divine river Ganges from heaven to earth [1150], Raghu [1391] and Rāma (most famous and popular of all heroes in *kāvya*). After Rāma, with whom the Dvāpara Yuga begins, the dynasty went into permanent decline. The historicity of this dynasty is doubtful, and its Traditional geographical location in Eastern India difficult to reconcile with some other traditions. Its basis may have been the traditions of pre-Aryan tribes in the Ganges region (its antiquity placing it before the Aryan settlement of this region), or—more appropriate for the supposed rulers of a great empire—it may have been a dynasty of the pre-Aryan Indus Empire. Its kings are not mentioned in the earlier stratum of Vedic literature, the poems of the *Ṛgveda*, except for coincidences (presumably) of some names with rulers of the Pūru (Lunar) tribe and one mention (*ṚVS* VIII.52.1) of Manu as 'Vivasvant', which offered a starting point for either the construction or the grafting on of the Solar Dynasty. It is very attractive to suggest that this great dynasty represents the tradition of the Indus valley civilisation, fused with those of the conquering Aryans in the period of assimilation, but until the Indus inscriptions are deciphered this is pure conjecture contrary to the geographical statements of Tradition. (Migration of a dynasty from one country to another is fairly common in Indian history, however, and the Ikṣvākus in Kośala, if historically attested, might have been emigrants from a lost Western kingdom.)

524. The Lunar Dynasty resulted from the union of Manu's daughter Ilā with Budha the son of the Moon God, whose offspring was the romantic Purūravas (who loved the nymph Urvaśī [1402]. His grandson Nahuṣa deserves to be remembered as having established the first theatre on earth, after a visit to Heaven, where he saw a performance of Bharata's *Śarmiṣṭhāyayāti*, a tragic play about his own son! (as we have seen, the drama originated in Heaven) [1581]. Nahuṣa's son Yayāti (both father and son are known to the earliest Vedic literature) is a famous emperor, whose five sons bear the names of five Aryan *tribes* well known in the earliest Vedic poems. From them various dynasties traced their descent, the main line being usually called Pauravas after the eldest son, Pūru [1145]. The references in the most ancient Vedic sources corroborate the tradition that these Lunar kings, or originally tribes, ruled in the North West of India, from (including) modern Afghanistan to the upper reaches (only) of the Ganges, though there is a tendency in Tradition to shift them slightly to the East. Evidently they were the early descendants of the Aryan invaders who appear to have overthrown the Indus Empire, and the curious manner of connecting their ancestor Yayāti to Manu and the Solar Dynasty may be suspected of being an assimilation to Indian traditions (in the Aryan tradition the first man or mortal was originally called Yama, not Manu, and these two were never completely assimilated—*ṚVS* X.14, *Vīdaēvadāta* II, etc.).

525. The Pauravas long suffered eclipse (corresponding in Tradition to the ascendancy of the Solar Dynasty), until Duṣyanta restored their power (he lived in the same period as Bhagīratha, but the exact relationship between the dynasties, chronological and political, is not recorded) [1419]. His son Bharata gave his name (in the derived form Bhārata) to the dynasty, to the Great War among his descendants, and to India. His descendant Saṃvaraṇa (somewhat later than Rāma) married Tapatī, a daughter of the Sun, and their son Kuru added the name Kaurava to his descendants. Their story has long been familiar in the theatre through the success of Kulaśekhara's play *Tapatīsaṃvaraṇa*, *c*. +900. The line eventually continues through Kuru's second son Jahnu and grandson Suratha. It was a feud between the families of the sons of the latter's descendant Vicitravīrya—Dhṛtarāṣṭra (elder, but born blind, hence legally unfit to rule) and Pāṇḍu (consecrated king)— which culminated in appalling (for those days) slaughter in the Bhārata War and with it the beginning of the present depraved Kali Yuga. The sons of Dhṛtarāṣṭra seized the throne after Pāṇḍu's death and ruled as Kauravas (thus claiming legitimacy as the senior line: with them this dynastic name ends). Pāṇḍu's five sons, the Pāṇḍavas, of whom the most famous are Yudhiṣṭhira (the truthful hero), Bhīma (bold but rash and irascible) [949] and Arjuna (the type of the brave hero) [1493], finally triumphed, and the dynasty continued under the older name Paurava through the grandson of Arjuna, Parīkṣit. Of the later descendants we need mention only Udayana, the most romantic of all kings and almost the last of the dynasty before its extinction in the Magadhan Empire [964]. He ruled in the first half of the —5, at Kauśāmbī on the lower Yamunā river, the ancient capital Hastināpura on the Ganges having been destroyed by a flood three centuries earlier.

526. Only the Yādava branch of the Lunar dynasty is comparable in importance to the Pauravas. Tracing their descent from Yayāti's son Yadu, they established themselves at Mathurā on the upper Yamunā (the home of the Śaurasenī Prakrit language) and extended their rule over all the country to the South as far as the borders of what was to become Mahārāṣṭra. In the time of the Bhārata feud the Yādava tyrant Kaṃsa, who had imprisoned his father and usurped the throne, was killed by his nephew Kṛṣṇa and the old king restored (but there are good reasons for supposing the constitution of the Yādavas to have been in fact republican, for references see Jayaswal, *Hindu Polity*, 34-6, 75-6, 355-60) [1044]. Miraculous stories are told of the divine Kṛṣṇa's infancy and youth, since in later times he came to be regarded as an incarnation of Viṣṇu. Before the Bhārata war took place the Yādavas were attacked by Jarāsandha, king of Magadha (descended from Kuru's third son), and moved their capital to Dvāravatī (Dvārakā) on the West coast. In later life Kṛṣṇa became the friend of the Pāṇḍavas (though the other Yādavas favoured the Kaurava cause) and just before the Battle he exhorted Arjuna to do his duty in the *Bhagavadgītā* (an episode in the Great Epic which has attained independent status as a Vaiṣṇava scripture, or which alternatively was an old scripture later inserted into the Epic when the hero Kṛṣṇa was identified with the incarnation of Viṣṇu who had revealed it). In the Battle the ruses of Kṛṣṇa enabled the hard pressed Pāṇḍavas to win [951-2]. Subsequently the Yādavas were themselves engulfed in civil war, and Kṛṣṇa withdrew to the life of an ascetic in the forest (as Yudhiṣṭhira withdrew to the mountains). Here he was accidentally shot and killed by a hunter. His grandson was re-established at Mathurā by the Pāṇḍavas. The *Viṣṇu Purāṇa* (V.26f.) narrates the story of Kṛṣṇa's abduction of Rukmiṇī from Vidarbha, defeating her brother, and the birth of Pradyumna to them as a partial incarnation of Kāma, the God of Love (Pleasure), who previously had lost his body when burned by Śiva. The myth of Kāma's wife's incarnation as Māyāvatī and their eventual reunion follows. The same *Purāṇa* narrates (V.32f.) the story of Pradyumna's son Aniruddha, loved by Uṣā [1581].

527. A few other famous heroes may be very briefly mentioned. The compassionate hero Śivi, a descendant of Yayāti's son Anu, ruled at Mūlasthāna on the middle Indus over the whole Indus valley. His self-sacrificing generosity endeared him to Buddhist writers as well as brahmans [919, 1642]. Kārtavīrya Arjuna, a Haihaya king (a branch of the

Yādavas which ruled on the West coast—Ānarta or modern Gujarāt—in very ancient times), defeated Rāvaṇa, the 'demon' king of Laṅkā (originally Ceylon) who frequently raided Southern India. Demons being long lived, like gods, this Rāvaṇa could be the same as the one killed long afterwards by Rāma. The Haihayas had quarrelled with their family priests, the Bhṛgus or Bhārgavas. One of these, named Rāma (Paraśu Rāma, Rāma of the Axe, to distinguish him from the Solar emperor), killed Kārtavīrya Arjuna, whereupon Kārtavīrya's sons killed Rāma's father Jamadagni. In terrible revenge the priest resolved to slaughter the entire class of warriors (*kṣatriyas*, aristocrats), and so far succeeded that only five survived to continue the great dynasties [1144]. Paraśu Rāma founded Bhṛgukaccha and other important ports on the West coast. The chronology of this period is confused, as perhaps indicated by the appearance of Rāvaṇa, and Tradition is obliged to make Paraśu Rāma also exceptionally long lived, since he reappears to meet his Solar namesake [1589]. Both Rāmas were eventually deified as incarnations of Viṣṇu. Lastly, among the heroes of Tradition celebrated in *kāvyas*, should be mentioned the mysterious Nala, king of Niṣadha (of uncertain descent and probably not Aryan) [1580]. The delightful story of his marriage with Damayantī, daughter of Bhīma (a Yādava emperor who ruled a century later than Bhagīratha, with his capital at Vidarbha in the far South of the empire—which later gave its name to the *vaidarbha* style of *kāvya*), and the unhappy sequel of his subsequent temporary loss of his kingdom and destitution through gambling, is in the Great Epic told to Yudhiṣṭhira suffering in similar circumstances.

528. The Buddhists naturally preferred to draw stories for *kāvyas* from the life of the Buddha and his contemporaries, as recorded in the Buddhist Canon [610, 714]. They also used their collections of stories of former lives of the Buddha, Śivi being claimed as one of these[579, 919], and apocryphal additions to the *Tripiṭaka* such as the *Avadānas* (e.g. for Śivasvāmin's *Kapphiṇābhyudaya*) [1276].

529. The Jainas had their own version of traditional history, brought into line with their legends of the twenty four Jinas who from time to time have refounded their religion on earth. At least eighteen of these Jinas and perhaps all of them, from Ṛṣabha, the first, to Mahāvīra, the latest, have served as the heroes of separate *kāvyas* now extant. Rāma, whom the Jainas call Padma, appears as a divine hero (a Baladeva —though the Jainas make no real distinction between gods and men), in a variant version of his life, whilst Kṛṣṇa is similarly a Vāsudeva (and his brother Balarāma a Baladeva) [854, 1449]. There are nine each of these Baladeva and Vāsudeva heroes, and their nine enemies (Prativāsudevas), including Rāvaṇa and Jarāsandha [862]. With the Jinas and the twelve universal emperors *cakravartins* this makes up the sixty three 'great men' of their tradition. The emperors include Bharata and Sagara, and Brahmadeva or Brahmadatta who is familiar also to the Buddhists, but the others are not familiar elsewhere. Three of them, including Śānti, became Jinas also. The Jaina traditions seem to draw in part on ancient sources independent of those of the brahmans, as do the Buddhist also, and are not merely corruptions of Brahmanical Tradition. It is noticeable that their legends are much more schematic and regular than the others. Many other characters appear, some of whom are immortalised in independent *kāvyas* (for example there are twenty four Kāmadevas—from Kāma, the God of Pleasure or Love).

530. All these heroes, in so far as they are historical, lived before the rise of *kāvya*, which begins to appear immediately after Udayana's reign (and may perhaps antedate him, if we could trace its origin more closely). Later historical heroes celebrated in *kāvya* may be left until we come upon them in following its history, though for nearly a thousand years after Udayana their annals were inserted in Tradition. The *Purāṇas* as now extant—our sources for the dynastic lists—appear to be basically a recension made in the +4 (with many later interpolations in several of them, but the dynastic lists seem to have been left as they then were, not going further than the beginning of the +4).

531. At that time of the definitive establishment of feudalistic monarchy all over India, and the disappearance of more ancient political systems, especially of the republics, it seems clear that history was largely rewritten with a view to consolidating the new outlook. We know that in the ancient period republican government was widespread at various times, and most, perhaps all, of the countries of Northern India were under republican rule at some time in their history. Some republics (for example the Yaudheya Gaṇa) flourished from an indefinite period before (probably long before) the -4 down to the +4, with an interval in the middle when they were under Magadhan hegemony (but apparently able to preserve their own institutions in spite of this). A Vedic text (the *Aitareya Brāhmaṇa*, VIII.14) implies that at the time of the Kaurava kingdom in the central part of Northern India (*c*.—11?) monarchy prevailed only in the Centre and the East, the greater part of the Aryan people being republican (in the North, West and South). As we have seen, the five great tribes of the Aryans have been converted into five sons of Yayāti and the dynasties of kings supposed to be their descendants. Thus the Kaurava kingdom established by Saṃvaraṇa would appear to have been preceded by a Paurava republic. Several sources confirm that the Yādavas in the South had a republic [526]. By the —5 several countries had reverted from monarchical to republican rule, including the Kuru people in the Centre, who were no longer under the rule of the so-called Paurava kings now at Kauśāmbī (*Arthaśāstra* XI). All these republics, so offensive to feudal notions, have been suppressed in Tradition, which allows only an initial period of 'anarchy' before Manu was elected as the first king. The *Purāṇas* have artificially extended the monarchies back into the mythical past, converted republics into kingdoms—making famous heroes such as Kṛṣṇa kings—and substituted fictitious lines of kings for intervals of republican government. Being over-zealous in this they have given us far too many kings for the period available and upset the chronology, pushing the Bhārata War, for instance, from the —10 back to —3102.

Chapter XI

THE ORIGINS OF THE KĀVYA MOVEMENT (*c.*—500)

532. In the period when *kāvya* was well developed we have usually no difficulty in distinguishing which works belong to it. The generalisations we can make about its content and form amount to a reasonably clear definition [1]. It is not scripture or Tradition, but the work of individual writers. So no doubt was Brahmanical scripture in origin, but it came to be regarded as revelation of transcendental, non-human, words. Buddhist and Jaina scripture no less came to be regarded as not the work of an individual Buddha or Jina but a statement of eternal truths revealed by all Buddhas or Jinas at different times. Tradition, or genuine epic, was handed down and gradually modified by lines of bards or minstrels or rhapsodes, though on the other hand a view grew up later which ascribed its enormous works to an individual sage, Kṛṣṇa Dvaipāyana (= 'Vyāsa', the 'Arranger'—a title which conceded the main point in relation to some of his activities at least: see Pargiter 21f.), and placed this mythical author in the ranks of the *kavis* (Ānandavardhana, p. 365). Again and primarily, *kāvya* is a form of art, in contrast to technical books *śāstra* [34-5].

533. Alternatively, as regards form, *kāvya* when in verse uses a range of sophisticated metres, compared with which the verses of some *śāstra* works are crude doggerel, those of scripture different in structure and rhythm, those of Tradition in some ways transitional but still archaic and primitive [422]. In prose, it is fond of long sentences and long compounds, whereas the prose of all other kinds of literature tends to be opposite in both respects [429, 442, 461]. Finally *kāvya* is invariably adorned with figurative speech, though the simpler and more primitive figures, such as simile and metaphor, occur fairly frequently in scripture and Tradition also [184]. We need not go further into the distinction of styles and other qualities of *kāvya*, though we must note as characteristic that *kāvya* should produce *rasa*, have aesthetic value (the Great Epic also has this quality, the main reason for later placing it among the *kāvyas* —Ānandavardhana pp. 530f.).

534. When we look for the origin of *kāvya*, however, wishing to pick out its earliest extant examples, we do not find in the earliest period where we seek it the full conscious array of formal techniques springing up simultaneously. We have rather to look for a variety of significant prototypes. Our quest is made extremely difficult by the paucity of materials from this early period and by the accident (from the *kāvya* point of view) of the preservation of certain texts which interest us in the canonical collections of the Buddhists and Jainas—contrary to our definitions. The relationship to the epic poetry of Tradition is naturally complex: *kāvya* represents a break with this, an innovating movement, yet also a continuation of epic art, the creation of a new type of epic (the *sargabandha*) as well as of the prose epic, the novel. One can make formal distinctions on the statistical ground of the structure of the ancient narrative metre (the *vaktra*) as it grew out of the much more ancient Vedic *anuṣṭubh*, a distinction made long ago by the theorists who attributed to Vālmīki, the 'First *Kavi*', the invention of the true *vaktra*, but in practice we are forced to draw a rather arbitrary line across an apparently gradual sequence of development (see *Pali Metre*, pp. 199f., 173). Vālmīki himself, as we shall see in Chapter XIII, is known to us as a purely mythical figure. In fact we find the decisive beginning of *kāvya* in lyric poetry, not in epic, and the stamp of this origin has always remained on it (for example the quatrain as unit, even in epic, not the line, or the manner of narrating an epic [403-4]).

535. As to the terms *kāvya* and *kavi*, which became specialised in connection with literature as an art, *kavi* at least had been current throughout the Vedic period as a designation of those, later regarded as 'seers' *ṛṣis*, who in fact composed the poetry of the Vedic Canon. It thus at first sight seems to mean a 'poet', but a consideration of its Vedic contexts (and also of the Avestan, for the term appears there too and so goes back to the Indo-Iranian people of the Oxus valley of the—3rd millennium—see Gershevitch: *The Avestan Hymn to Mithra*, pp. 185f.; *Yasna* XXXII.14; etc.) shows that these ancient *kavis* were regarded as inspired seers, even as priests able to influence the supernatural. The word *kavi* never lost the suggestion of one having the power of a kind of supersensory vision of the things he writes about but often could not have experienced directly. Thus the *kavi* was expected to fill the lacunae of Tradition by means of this insight, and his recreation of the character of an ancient hero with psychological details unknown to Tradition was accepted (if it was accepted) as a kind of truth. The ancient *kavis* of the *Veda* were perhaps more priests than poets, but their poetic art (which they themselves describe as a craft) was highly developed and conscious. The Vedic poetry was the art-literature of its day, only later regarded as scripture, as not composed but merely 'seen' by (revealed to) its *kavis*. Its techniques, the 'craft' of its authors, and particularly the basic technique of metre, are decisively different from those of *kāvya*, the wide gap between them being to some extent bridged by Tradition and the scriptures of the Buddhists and Jainas.

536. In the post-Vedic period and at the time of the origin of *kāvya* the term *kavi* was used to denote secular poets as well as religious ones, and it was applied also to the rhapsodes of Tradition. The best source now available for this period is the Buddhist Canon *Tripiṭaka*, of which the fullest and most authentic recension now extant is the Pali Canon. This Canon, though strictly speaking an *āgama*, happens to include a substantial amount of poetry and some prose stories in addition to its central prose dialogues (Pali *suttas* = Sanskrit *sūtras*) expounding the teaching of the Buddha. Though these are applied to propaganda purposes, they are clearly adaptations or applications of the techniques of the secular poetry and story-telling of their day, which we are thus fortunately able to study through them. The Pali Canon also contains some brief allusions to current poetic theory.

537. This Canon came to be regarded as consisting primarily of a record of the actual words of the Buddha (—566 to —486), together with some contributions by his followers. Against its literal authenticity in detail we have to observe (1) that the present Canon can be shown to have grown through several centuries of developing literary techniques, changing ideas and new needs as Buddhism spread, (2) that the Pali Canon is in a language of Western India, despite many borrowings from an Eastern language, whereas Buddhism originated in the East (though it spread rapidly)—it is thus, if not a translation, a distinct Western recension of the proto-Buddhist collection of the Buddha's literary heritage, and (3) that the growth of the Canon is to some extent recognised even by the tradition of its own (Sthaviravāda) school, which records a series of 'rehearsals' for establishing the received text as well as the inclusion in the text of certain later compositions (some of which, for example, it ascribes to the Mauryan period, i.e. after —320). In a separate work (*Pali Metre*) the present writer has studied the problems of the chronology of the metrical parts of the Pali Canon, and here we may simply take up the conclusions there worked out.

538. In brief, the verse parts of the Canon seem to cover the period approximately —500 to —100 in successive phases distinguishable on the ground of the development of the metres, and, which is most interesting, this development saw in its early phase the appearance of quite new metres (the 'musical' metres briefly discussed above in Chapter VI [413-4, 422]), opposed in structure to the older ones of *Veda* and Tradition (see *Pali Metre*, pp. 84ff.). It is this new metrical technique which appears as the decisive step in bringing into existence the new form of literature which we now call *kāvya*. Through the Pali recension of the Buddhist scriptures we can discern the beginnings of *kāvya* in the popular secular literature of Eastern India in the—5, apparently in the Māgadhī language. Magadha was then still a small state, and its language may not have been used much outside its borders, though the dialects of the rest of Eastern India, which are unknown to us, were probably very similar to it. With the growth of the Empire of Magadha, the spread of the language and its literature was assured. The best evidence for Māgadhī being the original *kāvya* language, however, is perhaps that the first of the new metres, the *vaitālīya*, is also called *māgadhikā*.

539. In this period of the origin of *kāvya*, literary theory, as reported in the Pali Canon, was conscious of *kāveyya* (the Pali for *kāvya*) as covering an area of literature not entirely coinciding with *kāvya* as later defined, and with rather different classifications within it. Prose story-telling is seemingly not included, and we are concerned with poetry only: prose narrative alternating with or occupying the place of epic poetry was probably not yet regarded as *kāvya* but as ordinary language, and *kāvya* would mean precisely 'poetry', which seems to be its original meaning. Drama, as dramatised episodes with verses uttered by the characters expressing the climaxes of conflict, but apparently embedded in prose dialogue, is not separately mentioned in the earliest Pali classification, but was certainly associated with *kāvya* from a very early stage, perhaps from the beginning. Actors appear, as poets, in the Pali Canon. The basic classification of this early theory is in fact of four kinds of *kavi* (*Aṅguttara Nikāya*, II 230).

540. The first kind of *kavi* is the epic poet or bard, the traditional poet (*suta-kavi* in the Pali) or poet of what he has heard handed down in a tradition. This is in fact the poet of Tradition reciting *ākhyānas*, and the somewhat later commentaries on the Canon specify the *Bhārata* as an example of the latter (*Sumaṅgalavilāsinī* I 84). The Canon itself contains evident examples of the form belonging to the Buddhist tradition, some of them going back to a pre-Buddhist tradition modified by the Buddhists [561, 564]. The *Sumaṅgalavilāsinī* (I 95) thus names the Vessantara legend as an example of the form [579].

541. The second is the 'improvisor-poet' (Pali *paṭibhāna-kavi*) who describes in spontaneous verses what he has just seen. He is primarily a lyric poet, a descriptive poet of the beauties of nature and of the manners of society. The presumed examples of this form in the Pali Canon include a rich sample of the new metres: it is here especially that we see the impulse which produced *kāvya*. The Commentary (*Manorathapūraṇī* III 211) names Vāgīsa (see below [547]) as a poet of this kind.

542. The 'didactic poet' (Pali *attha-kavi*) is hardly discussed theoretically in the Pali sources, but we may suppose that he was the most important for the Buddhists: the poet who uses his skill to convey philosophical or other teaching in easily palatable form. We can illustrate this copiously from the Canon, and also from later *kāvya*, but as a peripheral application of the techniques of the other kinds of *kavi* its interest is secondary.

543. Lastly we have the 'reflective poet' *cintā-kavi*, who, as opposed to the 'improvisor' describing what he sees in impromptu verses, composes more deliberately and in seclusion. In some ways he appears a truer forerunner of the great *kavis* whose masterpieces we now most admire than is the 'improvisor', though we know that the improvisation of verses has been expected of *kavis* (indeed of educated people generally) at most periods. It is difficult to pick out any examples of this form in the Pali Canon, since we have no poem actually labelled *cintā* either in the text or in the commentaries, and no example is mentioned to elucidate the term. In fact the likely candidates for the title in the Canon would be 'didactic' poems as well. It is hard to distinguish any techniques specific to the 'reflective' poet, as the epic poet has his archaic metres and conventions and the 'improvisor' experiments with the new metres and other devices. We seem to be left in this classification (evidently more empirical, relating to existing persons and schools, than theoretical) with two main kinds of poetry, the epic and the improvised lyric, with the 'reflective' as a studied development probably of the latter and the 'didactic' as a secondary application.

544. Nothing in the Pali Canon is actually labelled drama, and it contains nothing in the forms of drama established in later *kāvya* [570, 588]. On the other hand we do find a considerable number of dramatic episodes, all very short: dramatic dialogues and brief scenes in which often the Buddha appears and exchanges verses with another character, such as a god who praises him, which suggest visual performance. The Buddhists at first were averse to any kind of public show, and could be expected to be tardy in taking up such a medium for propaganda, but their Canon is definitely aware of 'shows' *pekkhās*, which very likely included some form of drama (the Sanskrit equivalent, *prekṣā*, is certainly applied to the theatre [365]), and of actors (see *Dīgha Nikāya* I 6, where the Commentary explains *pekkhā* as *naṭasamajjā*, 'assembly with actors'—*Sumaṅgalavilāsinī* I 84; the monk Tālapuṭa is recorded to have been an actor [588]). In any case the existence of the drama by the —4 is also attested by the grammarian Pāṇini (*c.*—350), as we have seen [45], who was familiar with actors and even with text books on acting. We may therefore examine these possible dramatic pieces, despite the silence of the commentaries as to their purpose (which would probably have lapsed before the commentaries were written, since by then we have full fledged Buddhist dramas of the later standard types), as belonging to a world familiar with the drama and as likely to reflect dramatic characteristics. A possible confirmation of actual performance of pieces like these may be seen in references in the inscriptions (of —257: 'Rock Edicts' I and IV) of the Buddhist emperor Aśoka (—268 to—232) to public assemblies *samājas* both good and bad (we know of course that dramas were performed at *samājas* [28]) and to public displays of 'divine forms', including the heavenly mansions, elephants (supposed to be the mounts of divine beings) and the celestial bodies (consisting of the substance fire, i.e. the stars, etc.). The latter could be identified with scenes in the Pali Canon, where the traditional Brahmanical gods are made to subserve Buddhist edification, often in a dramatic manner (struggles between the gods and the demons, visits of gods to the Buddha, rebirth as a god as fruit of a good action by a human being).

545. The data of the Buddhist Canon are to some extent confirmed and extended by the Jaina Canon, though the latter has been much less successfully preserved and contains little which is early enough to serve our present purpose. Moreover the few texts that may be of the—4 to—2 are handbooks for monks, not propaganda for spreading Jainism, and rarely adopt the techniques of *kāvya*.

546. The chronology of the Pali *kāvya* pieces indicated in rough outline as part of the conclusions of *Pali Metre* still leaves much uncertain. Thus we cannot say which poems were composed during the Buddha's lifetime, or even that any were then composed, but only that certain pieces in the *anuṣṭubh* metre belong statistically, on grounds of rhythmic structure, to the period *c.*-500. This date cannot be guaranteed to be within 50 years of the true date, though it is probably not as much as 100 years wrong. As to pieces in the 'new' metres, the uncertainty is greater since we have no pre-Buddhist examples to confirm the period of their evolution: this might have been in the – 6, in the Buddha's lifetime, but it may have begun only in the – 5. For the other terminus of the Pali development we have greater certainty from comparative metrical studies and from the history of the schools of Buddhism, moreover a few poems are actually dated by the commentaries (these dates, which lie within the first half of the – 3, agree with whatever other evidence exists and seem to be authentic—they are recorded quite incidentally and no great importance is attached to them: the fact that they did not fall in the Buddha's own time and so could not be connected with him reduced their interest for the commentators).

547. The name of the poet Vāgīsa (written also Vaṅgīsa), who became a Buddhist monk, is prominent in early Pali lyric poetry and famous in the tradition of the Sthaviravāda school. The Canon represents him as a contemporary of the Buddha, who asked him to extemporise verses, improvisation being his special skill, on various occasions. On examining these improvisations we find what appears to be an ancient kernel mostly in the old metres, whilst a number of poems mostly in the new metres look like work of later times ascribed to the famous Buddhist poet. If this impression is false, the evolution of the new metres was practically complete by *c.*-500; if not, then the *paṭibhāna* style of improvisation—which we have associated with the origin of *kāvya*—began within the framework of the old metres and the new metres were evolved for it gradually afterwards.

548. To illustrate the verses most likely to be original Vāgīsa, and contemporary with the Buddha, we may look first at the following extempore verses in praise of Sāriputta (the leading disciple of the Buddha, who did much to systematise the Master's teaching):

> Profound and wise, learned in the Way and the wrong way,
> Sāriputta of great understanding teaches the monks the doctrine;
>
> He teaches briefly, also speaks in detail,
> pours out his improvisation like the song of the mynah bird;
>
> By his beautiful voice, soft and exciting,
> the thoughts of the monks are elated and gladdened as they listen intently.
>
> (*Theragāthā* 1231-3 = *Saṃyutta Nikāya* I 190)

'Improvisation' here translates *paṭibhāna*, and the simile of the mynah is interesting as relating to it. We may note that the verses are not separate, as they usually are in *kāvya*, but seem more continuous—which one might perhaps expect in improvisation—as in the older poetry.

549. Nearby are these verses in praise of the Buddha himself:

More than a thousand monks attend on the Well-gone
as he teaches the clear doctrine, Nirvāṇa which knows
no fear from any source.

They listen to the abundant doctrine taught by the
Perfectly Enlightened One;
How glorious the Buddha is, facing the community of
monks !

O Master, your name is 'Dragon' (*nāga*), best of sages,
for, like a great cloud, you rain on your pupils.

Leaving the afternoon rest from a wish to see the teacher,
O great hero, your pupil Vāgīsa salutes your feet.
(ib. 1238-41 = 192-3)

550. In the following the first verse is in the *vaitālīya*, the first new metre (the rest are in *vaktra*, like the preceding poems):

Today being the full moon, five hundred monks have
met for purification,
cutting the fetters of union (which cause transmigra-
tion), peaceful sages who have exhausted rebirth:

As an emperor with his retinue of ministers,
circles all round this earth whose limit is the ocean;

So the supreme caravan leader, having conquered in
battle,
is attended by his pupils, who have the triple
knowledge and have eliminated death.

All are sons of the Master; here no futile talk is found;
I salute the destroyer of the arrow of desire, the kinsman
of the Sun.
(ib. 1234-7 = 191-2)

A good many words are here used metaphorically: 'fetters' (but this is general Buddhist usage), 'caravan leader', 'conquered', 'battle', 'sons', 'arrow'. As to the Sun, the Buddha was believed to be a descendant of a branch of the Solar Dynasty, and there is also allusion to his metaphorical powers of illumination. In all these poems we can pick out similes and metaphors appropriate for *kāvya*, though by themselves they might not differentiate this poetry from the more poetic parts of the *Veda* or the *Itihāsa*. Ambiguity, which underlies many of the 'characteristics' listed in the *Nāṭyaśāstra* [185], is prominent here and perhaps generally in the early Buddhist literature, where worldly imagery is used to convey the ideas of liberation from the world. Of the 'aesthetic experience' in the *Tripiṭaka* one can almost always say it is the 'calmed', but touches of the heroic, sensitive, comic, compassionate, etc., will also be found.

551. Another poem begins with a reference to Vāgīsa's previous way of life:

> Intoxicated with *kāveyya* we wandered from village to village, from city to city,
> then I saw the Buddha who had gone beyond all phenomena... (ib. 1253 = 196)

This indicates that the poets made a livelihood by touring, as also did companies of actors mentioned in the Pali Canon, and these two groups were not mutually exclusive.

552. A poem in which Vāgīsa asks the Buddha whether his lately deceased preceptor, Nigrodhakappa, has in fact attained Nirvāṇa, which like the above occurs in two books of the Canon (the *Theragāthā*, 1263-79, and the *Suttanipāta*, 343-58, with minor variations), may be authentic. It contains some striking similes: the blowing away of defilements, as dark storms covering the earth by the wind; the compelling voice of the Buddha as of a wild goose *haṃsa*, his words like cool rain which relieves us from the overpowering heat of summer (cf. the 'Dragon' above).

553. Of the same early period as these verses of Vāgīsa is perhaps the poem which contains the following. It is in another old metre, the *triṣṭubh*:

As a man who has gone down into a river
—a stream in spate, swiftly flowing—
is borne along with the stream,
—how can he help others across ?—

So one who has not discovered the true doctrine,
nor listened to the discourse of the learned,
ignorant himself, not yet across doubt,
—how can he make others see ?

And as one who has boarded a strong boat,
equipped with paddles and poles,
would bring many others across,
—wise, good at finding out the means—

So one who had knowledge, and developed it,
learned, intrepid,
he, knowing, would make others see
—as they transmigrate—who listen intently.

(*Suttanipāta* 319-22)

554. Let us add a few more verses by the monks, apparently of the earliest period. First some attributed to Sāriputta himself:

The great ocean, the earth, a mountain, or the wind,
are not fit for comparison with the excellent liberation
of the teacher;

The elder monk who follows the wheel (of the doctrine),
great in knowledge, concentrating,
he is earth, water, fire—he is not gladdened or
offended;

He has attained the perfection of understanding, the
great sage of great intelligence,
(he is) not dull, though he seems dull, (for) he is
always calm.

(*Theragāthā* 1013ff.—the great elements mentioned are not easily influenced or contaminated and are regarded as essentially pure)

555. Then by Godhika (not well known), in one of the early new metres, the *aupacchandasika*, a single verse (or 'strophe'):

It rains like good singing—my hut is thatched, pleasant, calm,
my mind is well concentrated—so let it rain if it likes!
(*Theragāthā* 51)

556. In the following poem by Mahākassapa we are nearer to established *kāvya*, with some of the specifically poetic vocabulary, description of mountains, and another subject very proper to *kāvya*—the rains, with such a characteristically *kāvya* touch as the peacocks welcoming them [815, 1240]—though with a Buddhist turn: the use of refrain, however, common in Pali poetry, is archaic:

Spread with garlands of *kareri* (a creeper), those are the places which delight the mind,
resounding delightfully with elephants those crags delight me.

Splendid with the colour of blue clouds, with cool clear waters,
covered with 'Indra's herdsmen' (a red insect, probably ladybirds) those crags delight me.

Resembling ridges of blue clouds, like a fine barrel-vaulted house,
resounding delightfully with elephants those crags delight me.

Mountains whose delightful surfaces are rained on as the sages seek them out,
echoing the peacocks' cries those crags delight me.

Perfect for me when I wish to meditate, exerting myself and self-possessed,
perfect for me wishing for well being, for a monk exerting himself,

Perfect for me wishing to be comfortable, for a monk exerting himself,

perfect for me wishing to concentrate, for such a one
exerting himself.

Clothed in *ummā* flowers, like the sky covered with clouds,
strewn with various flocks of birds those crags delight me.

Not full of worldly people, but sought out by herds of
wild animals,
strewn with various flocks of birds those crags delight me.
With clear waters and broad rocks, full of yaks,
their pools covered with *sevāla* (weed) those crags delight
me.

I do not get such pleasure from the five kinds of musical
instrument,
as when with concentrated mind I gain insight rightly
into the doctrine.

(*Theragāthā* 1062-71)

As to the vocabulary here, the words for 'elephant' and 'waters' are not the common Pali prose words, further there are two for each, unlike the translation; also 'places', 'clouds', 'peacocks', 'resounding', 'full of' and other words are not the prose synonyms, and in their Sanskrit forms they are familiar in later *kāvya*.

557. This old poem ascribed to Moggallāna is all refrains, a monks' chorus:

Forest dwellers, alms collectors, pleased with gleanings
in our bowls,
we split the army of death, well concentrated in ourselves.

Forest dwellers, alms collectors, pleased with gleanings
in our bowls,
we shake the army of death as an elephant a reed hut.

Living under trees, persevering, pleased with gleanings
in our bowls,
we split the army of death, well concentrated in ourselves.

Living under trees, persevering, pleased with gleanings
in our bowls,
we shake the army of death as an elephant a reed hut.

(*Theragāthā* 1146-9)

This is certainly a negative example: nothing like it is found in *kāvya* afterwards.

558. The nuns also composed verses. The following are from a long poem attributed to Subhā, a blacksmith's daughter who joined the Community:

> Let me not associate with passions, among which there is no shelter,
> —passions are enemies, executioners, painful like masses of fire;
>
> This is an ambush, dangerous, bringing remorse, a bandits' lair;
> this is greed, a very rough (path), a great opening to delusion ..
>
> (*Therīgāthā* 351-2)

559. To the nun Dantikā is attributed this short poem:

> Having gone out from the afternoon rest to Mount Gijjhakūṭa (Vulture's Peak, in Magadha, outside the old capital),
> I saw an elephant on the bank of the river, coming out after he had plunged in.
>
> A man took his hook and asked: 'Give me your foot!'
> the elephant stretched out his foot and the man mounted him.
>
> Through seeing the wild beast tamed, controlled by human beings,
> I concentrated my mind and went into the forest (to meditate).
>
> (*Therīgāthā* 48-50)

Here what might later be called a *jāti* or 'genre' lyric [419, 1345] is applied to illustrate Buddhist training, and the actions of the elephant coming out after refreshing himself in the river are made to allude to those of Dantikā herself.

560. To conclude this group of early lyrics, and perhaps to illustrate what was meant by 'reflective' rather than 'improvised' poetry (this might be illustrated also by the 'Boat' poem above), we have a poem attributed to the monk Pārāpariya:

> The philosopher-monk Pārāpariya had these reflections (*cintā*),
> as he sat alone, isolated, meditating:
>
> By what system, what vow, what conduct, can a man
> do what he should for himself but not harass anyone else?
>
> The faculties of man are for welfare, and for disadvantage,
> —unguarded they bring disadvantage, guarded they bring welfare;
>
> Guarding his faculties, protecting them,
> he does what he should for himself but does not harm anyone else;
>
> If his faculty of sight goes unchecked among objects,
> not seeing disadvantages he is unhappy and does not get free...,
>
> ...As a strong man doing carpentry knocks down a nail with another nail,
> so one who is skilful knocks down his faculties with other faculties:
>
> Developing confidence, energy, concentration, self-possession and understanding,
> with these five he strikes the other five (sight and the other senses), then a 'brahman' becomes peaceful.
>
> Having gained his welfare, remaining in a good mental state, that man has applied in practice the verbal instructions
> of the Buddha, completely,—he increases happiness.
>
> (*Theragāthā* 726ff.)

(The Buddhists tried to take over the term 'brahman' and apply it not to the brahman by birth but to the 'true' brahman who developed virtue.)

561. In most of these poems we are not far from the earlier tradition of poetry, and if we look at the oldest epic poetry in Pali we are still closer to Tradition. Some of the earliest pieces in the Canon are short episodes in the biography of the Buddha. One begins like this:

> I will sing the famous going forth, how the man with insight went forth,
> how, investigating, he made the going-forth splendid.
>
> 'Confined is this household life, a dusty sphere', he said,
> 'But going-forth is open'—seeing this he went forth.
>
> And having gone forth he avoided bad actions,
> abandoning bad speech he purified his way of life.

(the narrator plunges straight into the episode of the Buddha's meeting with King Bimbisāra of Magadha, after he went forth but before he attained enlightenment:)

> The Buddha went to Rājagaha, the Mountain Capital of Magadha,
> to gather alms, he who was full of excellent marks,
>
> Bimbisāra saw him from his palace,
> having seen him with those marks he spoke like this:

(the King comments on the noble appearance of the wanderer, and orders messengers to go and ask him where he is going; told he has gone to Mount Paṇḍava after collecting alms, the King drives out in his chariot to see him, and after some polite talk to start the conversation he goes on:)

> 'You are young, youthful, newly fledged,
> handsome and tall like a well-born warrior
>
> Making the vanguard glorious, leading a troop of elephants!
> —I'll give you lands, enjoy them!—Now tell me who you are'.
>
> 'In truth, O king, my country is on the slopes of the Himālaya,

endowed with wealth and energy, in Kosala,

My clan is the Solar one, by tribe I am a Sākiya,
—from that tribe I have gone forth, not yearning for pleasures;

Having seen disadvantage in pleasures, security in renunciation,
I am going for exertion—this excites my mind'.
(*Suttanipāta* 405-9 and 420-4)

562. In another piece the Buddha himself describes his 'exertion' to attain enlightenment on the banks of the river Nerañjara (*Suttanipāta* 425-49). The scene develops into a dialogue with Namuci or Māra, the personification of 'death' (= transmigration, i.e. repeated deaths and rebirths), who urges him to give up the hard struggle, the asceticism and fasting, and make the most of his life—by all means doing good, but not exerting himself. The Buddha rejects these words of temptation and hypocrisy, since the life recommended is only death postponed, and sticks to his asceticism, to the drying up of his flesh and blood (like the nearby river, since it is the dry season) which makes his mind clearer and strengthens his self-possession, understanding and concentration. He rejects the 'armies' of Namuci—passion, loneliness, hunger and thirst and all the others. The god, as he is here called, goes off dejected—like a crow which mistook a stone for a piece of fat—letting his lute *vīṇā* fall from under his arm in his depression. As we shall see, episodes like this are of great interest as showing how the drama could grow out of epic, by staging a dialogue of conflict, a crucial scene in a struggle. This 'temptation by Death' remained a most popular subject among the Buddhists for every medium of art [600,714].

563. The monk Sunīta tells his story as follows in another autobiographical piece:

I was born in a low family, poor and starving,
my work was low— I was a sweeper,

Disgusting to men, despised, treated with contempt;
humbling my mind I would pay respect to many people.

Then I saw the Buddha leading the community of monks,
the great hero, entering the capital of Magadha;

I put down my carrying pole and approached to pay respect
—the highest of men waited, through compassion for me.

I saluted the teacher's feet, then waiting on one side
I asked the highest of all beings to let me go forth.

'Come, monk!' he said to me—that was my entrance (to the community)...

—he follows the admonitions of the teacher and attains liberation when meditating at night, then:

As the night ended and the Sun rose,
Indra and Brahmā came and bowed to me with joined hands:

'Hail to thee, learned among men! Hail to thee, highest of men!
As the influences are exhausted in you, dear sir, you are one worthy of gifts'...

(i.e. he is as good as any brahman, or god. The teacher, seeing this, remarks that one is a 'brahman' through leading the highest way of life, asceticism.)

(*Theragāthā* 620ff.)

564. A curious piece of old epic legend, in the most archaic form of Pali *vaktra*, or of *anuṣṭubh* still in transition to *vaktra*, must be quoted from as a final example of the earliest Pali poetry. It is perhaps pre-Buddhist legend, folklore of very ancient times, which chanced to be taken up into the Buddhist Canon. It contains more poetic vocabulary than the preceding epic pieces. Here are some excerpts:.

In delightful Uttarakuru, near beautiful Mount Neru,
men are born unselfish, without any possessions.

They sow no seed, draw no ploughs,
men enjoy rice growing wild, uncultivated.

The rice grains have no husk or dust, are clean and fragrant,
—they cook them in a gourd, and then enjoy a meal...

...There the trees are always in fruit, full of various flocks of birds,
resounding with peacocks and herons and soft cuckoos.

Here there is the cry of partridges, and the *oṭṭhavacittakas*,
wild cocks, *kuḷīrakas* and *pokkharasātakas* in the wood.

Here there is the cry of parrots and mynahs, and the *daṇḍamānavakas*,
Kuvera's lotus pool is glorious all the time, always.

People describe it as North of here,
and the famous king who protects that region, he

The lord of the gods (*yakkhas*) is called Kuvera, he
enjoys himself leading the gods in dancing and singing.

(*Dīgha Nikāya* III 199ff.)

565. These early epic pieces show none of the characteristics of *kāvya* epic; the 'traditional poet' has not changed his style but the Buddhists have sometimes applied it to new subjects. Examples from the Great Epic would show the same non-*kāvya* style (provided we avoided late interpolations), but their chronology is hard to settle and it would be hazardous to attempt to relate them to the period of origin of *kāvya*. In the Pali, on the other hand, we have a mixed collection in various styles, where we can identify chronological strata. Here we see that the characteristics of *kāvya* appear first in lyric poetry. We find some of the metres, the specific vocabulary, the more figurative language, even the method of indirect allusion instead of direct statement. The separation in meaning of the individual verses or quatrains hardly appears, but it was probably implicit in the new metres (see *Pali Metre*, p. 136).

Chapter XII

NEW TECHNIQUES IN POETRY AND CONTEMPORARY TRENDS IN DRAMATIC LITERATURE AND NARRATIVE PROSE IN PALI
(c. —450 TO —200)

566. The following examples of Pali poetry belong to a somewhat later stratum, datable probably within 50 years of —400. First a brief extract from a poem in one of the musical metres (*aupacchandasika*):

Who disciplines his anger when it arises, as a serpent's
poison is dispersed by medicines,
that monk abandons both here and beyond, as a snake
its old withered skin.

Who has absolutely annihilated passion, as plunging in
(one gathers) lotus flowers growing in a lake,
that monk abandons both here and beyond, as a snake
its old withered skin.

(*Suttanipāta* 1-2)

This lyric uses the ancient technique of refrain, whilst further exploring possible similes for ascetic poetry.

567. At about this time a further development in metre took place. The musical organisation is now carried as far as possible, whereas in the early 'musical' metres (such as *vaitālīya* and *aupacchandasika*) we have a hybrid type of verse, the cadences being fixed. In the fully musical metres which now appear, the entire verse, or 'strophe' *gāthā*, is variable on musical principles (see *Pali Metre*, pp. 139ff.). It corresponds rhythmically to an eight bar musical phrase (more rarely to a twelve bar phrase), in which within quite broad limits any rhythmic patterns may be used provided the total quantity of each 'bar' *gaṇa* is equivalent to four short syllables and the bar lines are not infringed by a long syllable crossing them. First an example in rather simple language, with hardly any poetic atmosphere except the remarkable metre, but expressing the highest ideals. The metre, the earliest variety of this 'bar metre' *gaṇacchandas*, is called *gīti*, which incidentally means 'song'.

> One should act with skill in welfare, having understood
> the calmed state,
> one should be capable, straight, very straight, using good
> words, soft, not arrogant.
>
> Contented and easily satisfied, having little business and
> frugal habits,
> with calm faculties and wise, not proud among the people,
> not covetous;
>
> One should do nothing mean, which others, discerning,
> would blame;
> let all beings be happy and secure, —let all be happy!
>
> Whatever living beings there are, timid or strong, without
> exception,
> the tall or large, medium or small, minute or gross,
>
> Those seen or unseen, living far away or nearby,
> those already born and those yet seeking birth, let all
> beings be happy!
>
> None should deceive another, or despise any, anywhere,
> or, being angry, feeling repulsion, wish unhappiness
> for another.
>
> As a mother would look after her only son, sacrificing
> her life,
> even so one should develop one's thoughts, without limit,
> towards all beings.
>
> Thoughts of benevolence towards all beings one should
> develop without limit,
> above, below, all round, unconfined, without hatred,
> without rivalry.
>
> Whether staying or going, sitting, lying down, one should
> be without stupidity,

one should resolve on this self-possession (through benevolence)—this, they say, is the best way of life.

(*Suttanipāta* 143ff.)

(In connection with benevolence *maitrī* as described here cf. the *Daśarūpaka* theory of the 'calmed' [93]).

568. A few such *gīti* verses are ascribed to Vāgīsa and described as 'improvised'; they include:

For the purpose of crossing the flood he explains the Way by many methods,
when that 'immortality' is explained we remain imperturbable, seeing the doctrine.

The 'lamp-maker', having penetrated, has seen the transcending of all stations (of opinion or of consciousness—Cy.),
having known and observed he teaches the highest path of insight.

(*Theragāthā* 1243-4 = *Saṃyutta Nikāya* I 193)

569. The following extracts are from a poem in *gīti* organised in twelve bar strophes:

Of the wise, without delusion, who has broken the fallow land, gained the victory,
peaceful, of most impartial thoughts, old in virtue, of good understanding,
gone beyond the rough ways (of passion), pure—of that master I am the pupil.

Of the calm, of wide understanding, of great understanding, without greed,
of the thus-gone, the well-gone, the incomparable person, unequalled,
of the confident, subtle master, his pupil am I.

(*Majjhima Nikāya* I 386)

There are ten of these strophes praising the Buddha, and ascribed to Upāli, a lay follower this time. The Commentary observes with some justification that the fault of redundancy (of later poetic theory) may be found in some of these hundred epithets, but says that for the sake of praise a good quality may be mentioned repeatedly. The hazard is difficult to avoid in the 'hymn' *stotra* [418] division of lyric *kāvya*, of which this is a very early example, though amongst the countless later *stotras* a poet of genius has on occasion deliberately courted it to display his skill.

570. To this period seems to belong a piece of the epic or *ākhyāna* type, but with verses which for perhaps the first time in epic are in one of the musical metres (*aupacchandasika*). It is found in the vast *Jātaka* collection (of about 550 stories), from the epic riches of which we have not yet quoted. The *Jātaka* stories are basically in verse, and as handed down in ancient times the verses were the only fixed text (with one exception). Many of them require further narrative, to be elaborated by the story teller probably as in a *parikathā* [449]—or by the 'traditional poet' –to suit the occasion, and all of them now have prose narratives added later as 'commentary'. They would yield, then, further light on the old epic tradition. Here we are interested in an episode in a longer epic, that of the future Buddha in a previous life as the great minister Mahosadha, whose brilliance at court arouses deadly resentment from the four other leading ministers. They insinuate to the king ('Vedeha' of Mithilā), who is very fond of him, that Mahosadha is a traitor, and suggest that he can be tested by an apparently innocuous question about secrecy. If he says a secret should never be revealed to anybody he should not be trusted. The following scene is in the musical metre, and is in dialogue form:

King: The five wise men have met—a question occurs to me,
listen to it:
whether a blameworthy matter or a praiseworthy one,
to whom may a secret be revealed ?

Senaka: Even you must reveal this, protector of the Earth, lord
and endurer of burdens, tell us this;
reflecting on your will and pleasure, O king of men,
the five wise men will speak.

King: If she is virtuous, inaccessible to others,
controlled by her husband's will, pleasing,
whether a blameworthy matter or a praiseworthy
one, a secret may be revealed to a wife.

Senaka: If he is a refuge to one in difficulty and afflicted, a
resource, a support,
whether...a secret may be revealed to a friend.

Pukkusa: (to a virtuous brother)

Kāvinda: (to a good son)

Devinda: (to a loving mother)

Mahosadha: The secrecy of a secret is good, the revealing
of a secret is not praised,
a wise man should bear it whilst it has not borne
fruit, but when the matter is accomplished he
may speak at pleasure.

(Later:)

Queen: Why are you perplexed, O king ? This that we
hear is not the speech of the king of men !
thinking of what are you depressed ? O king I
am not at fault (in asking).

King: 'The wise Mahosadha must be executed'—because
I have ordered the execution of the sage,
I am depressed thinking of it. O queen you are
not at fault.

(Mahosadha disappeared to evade arrest, despite the secrecy of the order. According to the 'Commentary' he seized control of the city the next day and then faced the king. In any case he secures another assembly with the other ministers present, the king dissembling:)

King: You disappeared in the evening and now you
come—hearing what was your mind apprehensive?
who said what to you, O wise one ? Now we shall
hear those words, tell me that !

Mahosadha: 'The wise Mahosadha must be executed'—if,
O king, in the evening you discussed this confidentally,
privately told it to your wife, this secret, being revealed, was heard by me.

The wicked deed of Senaka in the *sāla* wood, the low thing he did,
he told in private to a friend, this secret, being revealed, was heard by me.
(Senaka admits this and is arrested)

Your man Pukkusa, O king, has a disease which makes him unfit for the royal service,
he told this in private to his brother...
(Arrest of Pukkusa)

Kāvinda is ill, possessed...
he told this in private to his son...
(Arrest of Kāvinda)

That eight-faceted noble jewel—now Devinda has it!
he told this in private to his mother...
(Arrest of Devinda)

--The secrecy of a secret is good, the revealing of a secret is not praised,
a wise man should bear it whilst it has not borne fruit, but when the matter is accomplished he may speak at pleasure!

(*Jātaka* VI, 379ff.)

Thus the use of the new metres begins to encroach on the field of epic, but for a dramatic episode showing 'wisdom' [42], which would be more effective on the stage than when read. Epic begins to be reorganised as a form of *kāvya*.

571. The following dialogue belongs to the same period and is in a similar metre:

Dhaniya (a cowherd):

My rice is cooked, my milk is milked, my dwelling place is near the bank of the Mahī,
my hut is thatched, my fire is lit—so let it rain if it likes!

The Master:

My anger is gone, my mind is broken in, I stay for one night only near the bank of the Mahī,
my 'hut' is open, my 'fire' is out—so let it rain if it likes!

(*Suttanipāta* 18f.)

The dialogue continues for some time with such pairs of opposed verses, the Buddha capping the advantages claimed by the cowherd for his quiet domestic life with those of homeless wandering. At the end, when it actually does rain violently and alarmingly, Dhaniya acknowledges the Buddha as teacher and takes 'refuge' with him. In the last verses Namuci (here called Māra, his more usual name) appears for a single exchange with the Buddha, but this is probably a secondary addition, the metre being different (the *Netti* in any case attributes Māra's verse to Dhaniya). The original ending of this little drama is more appropriately the settling of the encounter between Dhaniya and the Buddha, brought to its conclusion by the storm. The Buddha with his non-attachment to anything fears nothing, the cowherd with his possessions, family and comforts, and probably superstitious belief in supernatural powers, is thoroughly alarmed at a thunderstorm and glad to hear reassuring, confident words from a philosopher.

572. Round about (perhaps a little before) —300 may be dated a number of poems, for example another dialogue in the *Suttanipāta* (510ff.) in the same metre as the Dhaniya (*vaitālīya* and *aupacchandasika* mixed) and similar in content (the metre seems to represent a later stratum). In this case a wanderer named Sabhiya puts questions to the Buddha concerning the ascetic life both lead. He is convinced by the answers and enters the Buddhist community.

573. At this time we can perhaps fix the invention of the metre called *rathoddhatā* (*Pali Metre*, p. 124). The significance of this for *kāvya* is that it is apparently the first of the new series of metres we have above called 'fixed quatrain metres' [422], which are both syllabic (fixed number and quantity of syllables) and strictly musical (in rhythm) at the same time. These form by far the largest group of *kāvya* metres, and are most characteristic of this branch of literature. It is clear from the structure of the *rathoddhatā* and many other 'fixed' metres (*akṣaracchandas* is the technical term for them) that they derive from the musical metres, typical rhythms from the structure of which appear as their basis. In the musical metres these rhythm patterns are variants alternating freely within the musical scheme, but now for a fixed metre a particular pattern is taken for a line and then four rhythmically identical lines—in most of them—are taken as a quatrain (in a few metres the lines, though fixed, are not all identical). The *rathoddhatā* itself is a derivative from the early musical metres (other fixed metres are derived from the later 'bar' metres) with four identical lines. It is used for example in a poem ascribed to Ambapālī, celebrated in Buddhist tradition as a very beautiful geisha who was a lay follower of the Buddha, whose community she richly endowed. Eventually she is supposed to have become a nun, and then to have composed these verses (which is not historically possible if our chronology is even remotely correct).

> Black like the colour of bees, and wavy was my hair,
> through age it's like coarse hemp, truthful are these words, not false!
>
> Scented like a fragrant casket, full of flowers was my coiffure,
> through age it smells like rabbit's hair, truthful are these words, not false!...
>
> Drawn as if by a painter, my brows were once lustrous,
> through age they are wrinkled and flabby, truthful are these words, not false!...
>
> Smooth like a conch shell well polished, my throat was once lustrous,
> through age it's ruined, destroyed, truthful are these words, not false!...

Full and round, firm and high, my breasts were
 once lustrous,
in age which is like a drought (*iti*) they hang dry,
 truthful are these words, not false !...

Like two elephant's trunks, my thighs were once
 lustrous,
through age they're like bamboo stems, truthful
 are these words, not false !

...Such was this body—shattered, the home of much
 suffering,
it's become like an old house with falling stucco,
 truthful are these words, not false!

(*Therīgāthā* 252-70)

574. If we turn for a moment to the earliest stratum of Jaina Ardhamāgadhī literature, the Canonical text called *Sūyagaḍa* contains a section in the *vaitālīya* metre which can be placed slightly later than the Sabhiya dialogue. This has a striking pun on the name of the metre itself, which in the Ardhamāgadhī language is *veyāliya*, since *veyāliya* means also 'destruction' (Sanskrit *vaidālika*): 'He who has entered the Way to the destruction (of transmigration) = the Way (described) in the *vaitālīya* metre' (*Sūy.* 1.2.1). The section consists of ascetic poetry which directly recalls the Pali snake poem quoted above, where the snake leaves its slough, and gives other similes for the transience of life and for purification from the world.

575. Returning to the Pali, the very popular *Dhammapada* can be dated by the average structure of its mostly *vaktra* verses to the first half of the—3 (*Pali Metre* pp. 118, 135, 172f., 225; the individual verses naturally may vary widely from this average date, since the book appears to be a compilation, yet a certain homogeneity of outlook, which agrees with other evidence for the trend of that period, suggests that the chronological spread is not completely random). There are a few verses in the musical metres. Some verses from the *Dhammapada* will illustrate the spirit of the —3, and of the emperor Aśoka who tried to persuade the whole world to follow these Buddhist ideals:

Hatreds are never settled by hatred in this world,

by non-hatred they are settled, this is an eternal truth (*dhamma*) (5).

Who will conquer this earth, with the worlds of Death and the gods ?
who will recognise a verse of truth (*dhamma-pada*), as an expert a flower ? (44).

As a bee takes nectar from a flower and flies away
not spoiling the colour or scent, so should a recluse beg alms in a village (49).

As one may make many garlands from a heap of flowers,
so in human life one should do much good (53).

The scent of flowers doesn't go against the wind,
—not that of sandalwood nor *tagara* nor white jasmine;
—but the scent of the good goes against the wind,
the good man becomes known in all regions (54).

Hydraulic engineers guide water, fletchers point their arrows,
carpenters bend wood—wise men tame themselves (80).

Like a solid rock unmoved by the wind,
wise men are not bent by praise or blame (81).

Better than a thousand futile verses
is one verse by hearing which one becomes calm (101).

Better than living a hundred years indolent, without energy,
is a single day of life carried on with firm energy (112).

Don't despise evil—'It won't happen to me'—
a water jar is filled by tiny drops,
so a fool is gradually filled with evil (121).

Who harms a harmless man,
a man pure and blameless,
the evil comes back to that fool,
like fine dust thrown against the wind (125).

Not in the sky, not in the middle of the ocean, not
hidden in a mountain cave,
there is no place in the world Death cannot force (128).

Everyone dreads violence, life is dear to all,
comparing others with oneself do not kill or
cause to kill (130).

This ignorant man grows old like an ox,
his flesh increases but not his understanding! (152).

Tolerance, forbearance, is the highest asceticism;
the Buddhas say Nirvāṇa is highest,
he has not 'gone forth' who harms others, he is not
a philosopher who harasses another.

(184, from the *Dīgha Nikāya*).

Let us live very happy, not hating among the haters !
among hating men let us live not hating ! (197).

Let us live very happy, who have no possessions,
let us feed on joy like the radiant gods ! (200).

Conquering one generates hatred, the conquered remains
in misery,
the calm one remains happy, having abandoned victory
and defeat (201).

Health is the highest gain, contentment the highest
wealth,

trust the highest kinsman, Nirvāṇa the highest happiness (204).

Good men can be seen from afar like the Himālaya mountain,
the bad cannot be seen even here like arrows shot in the night (304).

As water on a lotus leaf, as a mustard seed on the point of a needle;
who does not cling to pleasures—him I call a brahman (401).

Besides similes one may find the 'characteristics' 'illustrating' and 'example' among these verses [186].

576. In the same period we have some poems dated by the commentaries. The monk Tekicchakāni is said to have composed this during the reign of Bindusāra, Aśoka's father and predecessor [653] :

The paddy's harvested, the rice is in the barn,
I get no alms, what shall I do? (*Theragāthā* 381).

(this lament is supposed to be inspired, in fact spoken, by Māra—the first part refers to the lack of gleanings in the fields, which ascetics were allowed to take. The monk thinks of the Buddha, the doctrine and the community to take his mind off hunger, then Māra says :)

You live in the open, these winter nights are cold!
don't be distressed, overcome by cold, enter a dwelling and close the latch.

But Tekicchakāni refuses to give way and settles down to meditate. The poetic interest of these verses lies in the metres, which are forms of bar-metre otherwise unknown to us. This confirms the hypothesis that this series of metres originated before the—3.

577. Aśoka's brother, Prince Tissa, became a monk and

was then called 'Ekavihāriya' ('Lone-dweller'), perhaps from the theme of his poem :

> ...Alone and master of my welfare I'll enter the delightful grove quickly,
> which creates joy for ascetics and is frequented by wild elephants.
>
> Having splashed my limbs in the cool mountain ravine
> I'll walk about alone in the well-flowered cool wood.
>
> When shall I live alone, with no companion, in the delightful great wood,
> having done what I had to do and being without influences?
>
> Thus let my intention prosper, since I wish to act,
> I will accomplish it myself—no one can act for another.
>
> Here I bind on my armour, I will enter the grove
> and I will not leave it without having attained the elimination of the influences.
>
> I'll pierce through ignorance, sitting on the peak of a mountain
> as the cool fragrant wind blows by.
>
> I'll certainly enjoy myself, happy with the happiness of liberation, on (Mount) Giribbaja
> —on the cool slope in the wood covered with flowers...
>
> (*Theragāthā* 539-545)

This poem, though short for statistical purposes, has the same *anuṣṭubh* structure as the *Dhammapada* (80% *pathyā*), thus confirming the approximate dates suggested for both. The specifically poetic vocabulary here is noteworthy (e.g. : *ramma* = 'delightful' and the verb *ram* generally, *su* = 'well', 'very', *māluta* = 'wind', *surabhi* = 'fragrant', *naga* = 'mountain', *kusuma* = 'flower' : these are not the ordinary prose words of Pali, they ought perhaps to be translated by such words as 'zephyr' and 'blossom', but poetic words are in essence untranslatable). The often repeated word 'cool' suggests the cooling of the passions in Nirvāṇa as well as its literal meaning.

578. Tissa was governor of a province in his brother's empire before he left the world: several members of the royal family became monks or nuns at about this time, and a short poem by another of Aśoka's brothers, Vītaśoka, has also been included in the *Theragāthā* (169f.).

579. It should be noted in passing that in this period of the growth of the Buddhist Canon many epic poems were composed and included, mostly in the *Jātaka* collection. The long *Vessantara Jātaka* (*Jātaka* VI 481ff.) [540] is probably the best known among these, in which the Bodhisattva, the future Buddha in his previous lives, sacrifices everything for his ideals. These legends provided popular subjects for later dramas and other kinds of *kāvya* among the Buddhists, alongside the story of the Buddha himself and those of his best known followers. We cannot here trace the transition from early epic to *kāvya* epic in detail—its beginnings were indicated in the last chapter and a further stage in this—but we may remark that the use of the poetic vocabulary associated with *kāvya* increases. The *Jātaka*, though with a single exception its stories are in verse, occupies also an important place in the history of story-telling in India, in the history of the short story [443, 451] which came to be subsumed under the *kāvya* category of *kathā* and—also under that category—of the novel, the earliest known examples of which clearly belong to the same tradition of story-telling as the *Jātaka* [650 ?, 671, 841]. This tradition combines two conflicting elements : realism and criticism of social evils on the one hand and the growth of fantasy, of the acquisition of superhuman powers, in connection with extraordinary adventures, on the other. Travel in distant countries—the tales of merchants and sailors—is a fruitful source of fantasy, which is found already in the *Jātaka* and grows strongly afterwards. In the *Jātaka*, however, it is rather the powers of sages and of the Bodhisattva's idealism that come into play, not yet so often those of 'wizards' and alchemists.

580. Short epic pieces in Pali are sometimes discussed separately as 'ballads'. They show particularly well the fusion of the epic and *kāvya* traditions, the tendency to increased lyricism in the course of a narrative in principle epic. Three good examples in the *Therīgāthā* can be placed in the – 3 : the poems of the second Subhā, of Isidāsī and of Sumedhā (*Pali Metre* pp. 130-5, 153, 225). Subhā's poem is a particularly good example of early *kāvya*, in metre (*vaitālīya*), vocabulary, 'characteristics' [184-7] and figurative speech. Here is an extract :

> The trees (*duma*) waft sweetness all around, diffusing the pollen of their blossoms,
> the beginning of spring is a happy season—come !—let us enjoy ourselves in the flowery forest !
>
> The trees (*pādapa*) are crested with blossoms, they rustle as the wind stirs them,
> but what pleasure will there be for you, if you plunge alone into the forest ?
>
> —It is full of wild animals, wanton elephants, eager she-elephants,
> and you want to go without a companion, into the great forest deserted and terrifying !
>
> Like a doll made of pure gold, you wander like a nymph in Cittaratha,
> O incomparable one ! You will look wonderful in beautiful clothes, of soft, fine Banāras silk !—
>
> I would be completely in your power, if we were to enjoy ourselves in the woods:
> no living being is dearer to me than you, O lady with gentle eyes like a fairy's !
>
> (*Therīgāthā* 371-5)

(Cittaratha is the god Kuvera's garden, in which Gandharvas, celestial musicians, live.)

581. In Isidāsī's poem we find a fresh metre, derived from the *gīti*. This is the *āryā*, which became very popular in Prakrit and Sanskrit *kāvya* and was long the standard form of 'bar metre' *gaṇacchandas*. It is distinguished from the *gīti*, which it soon supplanted, chiefly by a syncopated final cadence. Here it is used as a narrative metre, a rôle which it maintained in Prakrit though not in Sanskrit, where it is used only for songs. Thus we see here in Pali the establishment of a new epic metre for Prakrit and of a narrative tradition for *mahākāvyas*, parallel to that of Sanskrit but using *gaṇacchandas*, which continued with later derivatives of *gaṇacchandas* in the Apabhraṃśa epics and in those of the modern languages [413].

582. After the *rathoddhatā* mentioned above, a number of other metres of the same *akṣaracchandas* class appear to have been invented during the – 3 [573]. In principle these metres have both the number and the quantity of their syllables fixed, whereas the 'old' metres had only the number fixed and the 'musical' metres only the total quantity (see *Pali Metre*, pp. 140 and 213ff.). The wholly fixed—save for the last syllable of each line, as a rule—metre is thus a new type, combining the characteristics of both the older types. The 'fixed' metres are the most widely used in *kāvya* literature: they are—balancing what might otherwise be the monotony of fixed rhythms—extremely numerous and most varied in structure. The quatrain may consist of similar or different lines, lines of up to twenty one syllables are frequently used, and occasionally even longer ones. The rhythmical effect depends on almost every possible combination of long and short syllables being available, with a preference for rhythms arising from musical construction. The fixed metres clearly evolved out of the musical metres (of both the *mātrācchandas* and *gaṇacchandas* varieties), but some of the old metres were assimilated to fixed forms too, only the *anuṣṭubh-vaktra* continuing its independent development. Consequently we find early, transitional stages in which some alternation, of two short syllables in place of one long, or vice versa, is still practised.

583. A few examples of verses in these metres may be translated here, though with no attempt to imitate the rhythms:

Breaking out, breaking the bar, knocking out the royal
  boundary post, the imperturbable ones
Go on their mission pure and spotless, young
  elephants tamed by the man with insight.

(here by metaphor the Buddhist monks freed from the confinements of worldly life are the elephants and the Buddha is their driver)

(*svāgatā* metre, not quite fixed as yet; *Dīgha Nikāya* II 254 = *Saṃyutta Nikāya* I 27)

I hear, elated, your varied discourse comprehending welfare,
speak and dispel my grief, philosopher! bringer of happiness! live long for my sake!

(*aparavaktra* metre; *Jātaka* IV 443)

Hard indeed is going forth—hard is living in the world,
the doctrine is profound—property is hard to acquire!

Difficult for us is either way of life!
—it is proper to think constantly of impermanence.

(unnamed and otherwise unknown metre; *Theragāthā* 111)

584. The most remarkable metre of the Pali Canon is the *upasthitapracupita*, in which each of the four lines of the quatrain has a different structure and there is a most complex system of interlocking rhythms derived from both varieties of musical metre. It is probably the most complicated of all Indian metres, and was not in fact much used in the literature now available: the favourite *śārdūlavikrīḍita* of Sanskrit poetry has the same opening rhythm (first nine syllables) and probably replaced it with its simpler structure of four identical but longer lines. Two Pali quatrains translate as follows:

He resolved on freedom from anger, he gave alms
and fine clothes pleasant to the skin;
In that previous life
he dispensed gifts, as the god rain on the earth.

Having done that, when his life here ended he was reborn in heaver,

and experienced the ripening of the fruit of good
action;
(Then,) his skin having the lustre of a body of gold,
he becomes an Indra (king) here like the greatest of
the gods.

(*Dīgha Nikāya* III 159f., *Lakkhaṇasuttanta*)

585. The ancient *triṣṭubh* was assimilated to the fixed metres and became the *upajāti*:

The sky extends far, far too spreads the earth,
the other side of the ocean they say is far.
Yet farther than these they say, O king,
extends the influence of doctrines, whether true or
false.

(*Jātaka* V 483)

586. Another derivative from the *triṣṭubh* (from a variant *triṣṭubh* line and with the musical substitution of two short syllables for an original long one) did not find favour after these early Buddhist texts and was not described or named by the theorists. Elsewhere (*Pali Metre* p. 213) we have proposed to call it the *ānandajāta*. The following two quatrains are from a prologue to a much older Pali text. It may be compared with the ancient episodes of biography of the Buddha quoted in the preceding chapter. This biography was naturally of great interest to the Buddhists, but the more original Pali texts contain very little to satisfy anyone desiring a general life of the Buddha. Only through the post-canonical tradition of the commentators was a comprehensive biography gradually built up, by a kind of inferential system where direct evidence was largely lacking, and this gave the fullest scope for miraculous events and superhuman manifestations. Our present text is still comparatively restrained:

Then to him called Asita (a sage) the Sakyas showed
the son,
a boy flaming like gold

In a crucible, gladdening the expert smith,
brilliant with good fortune, unequalled in beauty.

Seeing the boy brightening as a flame,
like the pure bull of stars, the sky-goer,
The Sun radiant as in autumn when the clouds have gone,
he rejoiced and was filled with affection.

(*Suttanipāta* 686-7)

587. Some of these verses, particularly those in *upasthitapracupita* (which are associated with *vaktra* verses which are 85% *pathyā*), bring us probably to about −200. We may now turn to a group of poems, and of pieces in mixed prose and verse, which also seem mostly to belong to the −3, though there are anticipations of their form which are probably of the −4. This group consists of dialogues between two or more speakers, many of which have the characteristics of dramatised episodes. It has been conjectured that these pieces were intended for performance at public assemblies, such as festivals, just as we know the drama was, but as Buddhist scenes inculcating Buddhist values [544]. Earlier in this chapter we looked at some dialogues or dramatised episodes which are probably to be dated in the −4, and which are scattered in the texts of that period (*Jātaka*, *Suttanipāta* [570-2]). Those we are now concerned with are found in a collection of generally similar pieces in the first volume of the *Saṃyutta Nikāya*.

588. This collection contains about 300 pieces, all in a mixture of prose and verse and assigned on that account to a special category of literature by the later commentaries. The name of this category, *geyya*, meaning literally 'to be sung,' does not seem to fit particularly well, except for the verses—if these can be regarded as songs. We might, however, bearing in mind also that the drama is in mixed prose and verse, suggest that in this context *geyya* meant rather 'to be performed'—though this is a pure conjecture. Some support for it may be found in the *Kāvyānuśāsana* (p. 18) of the Jaina writer Vāgbhaṭa (+12), who calls the group of dances which Dhanika describes as *nṛtyas* [375ff.], of which he names eleven (adding from Abhinavagupta's group, plus the *goṣṭhī*, 'etc.'), *geya rūpakas*, explained as acting of the meanings of words (which is Dhanika's *nṛtya*). In theory other texts in mixed prose and verse may be classified as *geyya*, but nowhere else in the Pali Canon do we find such a large collection of purely *geyya* pieces. Practically all these pieces have the form of dialogues, the verses in particular being uttered by different characters. In the majority of them a god utters a verse and the Buddha then caps it with one that is better, at least from the Buddhist standpoint, as in the dialogue with Dhaniya already quoted [571]. About sixty pieces are of more serious dramatic interest than such simple illustrations of the new ideas supplanting the older religion of the Brahmanical tradition, whose very gods thus attest the higher value of Buddhism. In these sixty an actual conflict is presented with dramatic movement, instead of the simple fact of the submission of the gods to new ideals. Here we have true dramatic content, not merely the formal characteristics of dialogue and of mixed prose and verse. The bulk of these pieces probably belong to the −3, consequently it seems legitimate to compare them with the performances implied by Aśoka in his inscriptions of the middle of that century, noted in the last chapter [544]. It may not be irrelevant here to add that the verses ascribed to the monk Tālapuṭa in the *Theragāthā* (1091-1145) appear to belong to a late stratum of that text, very likely of the −3. This Tālapuṭa is recorded to have been the leader of a company of actors before he joined the Buddhist order. The verses ascribed to him are lyric—the frequent *Theragāthā* theme: the soliloquy of a monk,—but since there were ex-professional actors in the Buddhist order it is not improbable that they applied their skill, perhaps within narrow limits in order not to alarm their colleagues, to the purpose of propaganda for their new ideals. As in the old epic tradition, the usual metre in the dramatic episodes of the *Saṃyutta Nikāya* is the *anuṣṭubh-vaktra*.

589. We may begin our selection from these episodes with some which illustrate the adaptation of traditional mythology to Buddhist ends. First the popular stories of the wars between the gods and the demons [513]. One episode opens in prose as follows:

> Once upon a time the gods and demons were deployed in battle. Then Vepacitti [658], the king of the demons,

addressed the demons: 'My friends, if the demons conquer the gods...then bind Sakka (Śakra, Indra), the king of the gods, by his hands, feet and neck and bring him to me in the Demon City.' And Sakka, the king of the gods, addressed the Tāvatiṃsa gods (the gods of the Vedic tradition): 'My friends, if the gods conquer the demons...bind Vepacitti...and bring him to me in the Sudhammā Palace.'

In that battle the gods conquered...Then the Tāvatiṃsa gods bound Vepacitti...Vepacitti...bound... entering and leaving the Sudhammā Palace...abused and slandered Sakka, the king of the gods, with rude and harsh words (Commentary supplies examples: 'Thief! Fool ! Ox! Donkey! We'll win next time!' etc.—*Sāratthappakāsinī* I 342).

Then Mātali, the charioteer (of Sakka), upbraided Sakka with this verse:

'Is it from fear, Sakka, or rather from weakness that you forbear,
Hearing harsh words from Vepacitti?'

(S.) 'Not from fear nor from weakness do I tolerate Vepacitti,
How could a discerning person like myself bandy words with a fool?'

(M.) 'Fools get angrier if no ones tops them,
Therefore a wise man should check a fool with violent punishment.'

(S.) 'I think just this is the way to stop a fool:
That one who knows the other is enraged should be self-possessed and calm.'

(M.) 'This forbearance seems to me a fault, O Vāsava (Sakka),
—When a fool thinks: "From fear he forbears with me",
The blockhead will bully you more, like a bull if you run away.'

(S.) 'He may well think so, or not: "From fear he forbears with me",

—There is no advantage greater than toleration, the
highest of all good advantages.

Who, indeed, being strong, forbears with one who is weak,
His is called the highest toleration—the weak always
forbear !

That strength is called weakness, whose strength is the
strength of a fool;
There is no denier of strength which is guarded by truth.

The worse of the two, therefore, is he who counters
anger with anger;
He who does not counter anger with anger wins a
battle which is hard to win.

He brings about the advantage of both, his own and
the other's,
Who knows the other is enraged and yet is self-possessed
and calm.

This is the healing of both, of oneself and the other;
People think "He is a fool"—if they know nothing of
truth.'

(*Saṃyutta Nikāya* I 221-2)

590. It is curious that in the piece which follows this one we find identical verses except for the first two, whilst the prose introduction is different. In that second piece the gods and demons are again deployed in battle, but Vepacitti challenges Sakka to a contest in 'good speech' instead, to decide the victory. The 'assemblies' (it is not clear whom these include) of the gods and demons are brought together to judge the contest, the gods and demons themselves applaud the speeches of their own side and greet the other side's with silence. Sakka persuades Vepacitti to open the contest, on the ground that he is senior, and he utters the second of the verses above ascribed to Mātali. The verse dialogue then continues as before, but between Sakka and Vepacitti and punctuated by prose statements of the applause or silence of the supporters on both sides. At the end the 'assemblies of the gods and demons' pronounce judgment: 'Vepacitti...has spoken his verses, and they have force as their scope, the sword as their scope; this is disputing, strife, quarrelling. Sakka...has spoken his...and they do not have force as their scope...The victory by good speech is Sakka's.

591. Since the verses are constant, except that the first two are missing in the second version, it appears as if originally just the verse dialogue were handed down in fixed form, and that we now have in the *Saṃyutta* records of, or directions for, two 'productions' of the piece, differently realised.

592. Instead of thus adapting myths by ascribing Buddhist ideals, such as non-violence, to a god, other pieces in this collection bring the Buddha himself on the scene among the gods and demons. According to the ancient mythology a demon named Rāhu causes eclipses by pursuing and swallowing the Sun and Moon. Fortunately no permanent harm is done because the demon has no body, but only a head (only the head became immortal: at the Churning of the Ocean, when Rāhu took a mouthful of the ambrosia of immortality his head was cut off before he could swallow it [331, 1337], so that the oppressed Sun and Moon gods reemerge after each ordeal. In the Buddhist version of this it is the Buddha who saves the two gods: when the Sun is seized by Rāhu he calls (in a verse) upon the Buddha to help him. The Buddha upbraids Rāhu, who is unable to resist this appeal and releases the Sun. The discomfited Rāhu returns to Vepacitti and there is a further exchange of verses between the demons, in which Rāhu says his head would split in seven pieces if he did not obey the Buddha (*Saṃyutta Nikāya* I 51). In other words the supernatural power of the Buddha is said to be greater than that of the demon (the Buddha himself invokes his compassion when upbraiding Rāhu: the Buddhists held that this compassion was a real force in the universe). A parallel piece (p. 50) brings in the Moon in place of the Sun.

593. In a number of scenes the Buddhist ideal (Nirvāṇa, 'extinction', or peace or calm) is dramatically opposed to the heaven of the gods, or the virtues of the two doctrines are contrasted (the virtues which lead to attainment of the ideals). A deity speaks a verse to the Buddha:

'Time passes, the nights drive (people) along,
The stages of life gradually abandon (them);
Observing this danger of (approaching) death,
One should do good actions which bring happiness.'

(The Bu.) 'Time passes, the nights drive along,
The stages of life gradually abandon;
Observing this danger of death,
One hoping for peace should abandon the meat of the world'.

(*Saṃyutta Nikāya* I 3)

(Good actions would lead to heaven, but for final peace one must abandon attachment to any kind of life—here heaven is just part of the world, another region of the universe.)

594. Once upon a time one of the Tāvatiṃsa gods was enjoying himself in the Nandana Park (in Heaven) with a group of nymphs, regaled and supplied with divine pleasures of the five classes (corresponding to the five senses). At that time he spoke this verse:

"They do not understand happiness, who do not see Nandana !
—Dwelling place of the glorious Thirty Gods."

When he said this, another deity replied:

"Fool ! You don't understand the saying of the worthy ones,
That all forces are impermanent, having the nature of occurrence and decay,
After happening, they cease,—happiness is the calming of them."

(*Saṃyutta Nikāya* I 5f.)

595. In another scene Sakka appears in his ancient rôle of God of War, called in the verses Vatrabhū (conqueror of Vatra, Sanskrit Vṛtra, a demon prominent in Vedic literature as Indra's opponent [507]. He accosts the Buddha:

'What must one destroy, to rest happily? What must
one cut off in order not to grieve?
Of what one phenomenon does the killing please you,
Gotama?'

The Buddha replies:

'Anger must be destroyed to rest happily, anger must
be cut off in order not to grieve,
Of anger, the base of poison yet supremely sweet,
O Vatrabhū!
The noble ones praise the killing, cutting that off one
will not grieve.'

(*Saṃyutta Nikāya* I 47)

596. This is brief and simple, but might be effectively produced, and humorously, by showing the War God armed and ready for battle with his accustomed foes, but told instead to destroy anger. It seems Sakka learnt the lesson well (besides cultivating forbearance, as we saw), and applied it in the following curious allegory:

> Once upon a time an ugly deformed demon sat down in the seat of Sakka, the king of the gods. On account of that the Tāvatiṃsa gods were annoyed, indignant and angry...and the more annoyed, indignant and angry they became the more the demon became handsome, beautiful and lovely. Then the Tāvatiṃsa gods went to Sakka and reported the matter..."He must be a demon who feeds on anger." Then Sakka, king of the gods, approached that anger-eating demon, put his cloak on one shoulder, knelt down on his right knee, joined his hands in salutation and announced his name three times: "I am Sakka, king of the gods, sir..." And the more Sakka announced his name the more the demon became ugly and deformed, and after becoming ugly and deformed he vanished. Then Sakka sat down in his own seat and spoke these verses to conciliate the gods:
>
> "My mind is not easily disturbed, nor am I easily
> brought on by provocation,

For a long time I have not been angry, anger does
not remain in me.

I do not speak angrily or harshly, nor praise archers,
I check myself well, seeing my own advantage."

(*Saṃyutta Nikāya* I 237-8)

597. The opposition of different kinds of values is brought out most clearly through the figure of Māra, a deity who symbolises death (his origin was in the old God of Death) together with all the worldly values, especially (sexual) love, which the Buddhists regard as interdependent (the world as the universe of transmigration, of death and rebirth, with love and other forms of attachment as its driving force) [562]. At the same time Māra incorporates the values of the Brahmanical tradition, with heaven as the highest: and heaven for the Buddhists is equally part of the universe of transmigration, a temporary abode only.

598. Māra approaches the nun Upacālā: 'Where do you wish to be reborn?' She replies: 'I do not wish to be reborn anywhere, sir.' He speaks this verse:

'There are the Tāvatiṃsa, Yāma and Tusita deities,
The Nimmānarati and Vasavatti gods;
Let your mind aspire there, where you will experi-
ence pleasure (*rati*, especially love).'

(Upacālā:)

'The Tāvatiṃsa, Yāma and Tusita deities,
The Nimmānarati and Vasavatti gods,
Are bound by you with the fetters of pleasure (*kāma*)
and come again and again into Māra's power.

The whole universe is blazing, burning,
The whole universe is flaming, shaking:

The unshaken, immovable, not pursued by many people,
Where Māra cannot go—my mind is devoted to that.'

Then Māra, the evil one, was unhappy and depressed, thinking
'The nun Upacālā knows me !', and he vanished.

(*Saṃyutta Nikāya* I 133)

599. Elsewhere we have equally brief encounters where the Buddha repudiates statements by gods that men rejoice in sons and cattle, or society, or a home—in other words the various values of the world (cf. the dialogue with Dhaniya above [571]). The Buddha says these cause unhappiness, and we should look for real advantages, peace of mind, non-attachment, knowledge. Māra is several times the exponent of worldly values: men live long and should enjoy themselves innocently like babes—to which the Buddha objects that life is short and one should seek peace at once (*Saṃyutta Nikāya* I 108).

600. The popular theme of the 'temptation' of the Buddha by Māra is represented in this collection, where we find for example the following allegory of the temptation by 'Māra's daughters' :

Then (after Māra's unsuccessful attempts to tempt the Buddha with worldly values, or at least to persuade him not to teach others renunciation) Māra's daughters, Desire, Discontent and Passion, approached Māra and accosted him with this verse:

"Why are you depressed, dear father ? Over what man do you grieve ?
We will bind him with the snare of passion, like a forest elephant (caught by a decoy),
And bring him—he will be in your power."

(M.) "There is a worthy one, well-gone, in the world, not easily lured by passion,
He has passed beyond the Māra-world, that is why I am greatly grieved."

Then Desire, Discontent and Passion approached the Buddha and said to him: "Philosopher ! Let us enjoy your feet ! (i.e. massage them, be your servants)"

But the Buddha did not pay any attention, as he was liberated in the ultimate destruction of attachments. Then Desire, Discontent and Passion withdrew to one side and conferred thus : "Men's wishes vary. Suppose we each create a hundred maidens ?"—They do so, and try sending to him women of all ages, but without any success, so they conclude : "What father said is true !... For if we attacked in this way a philosopher or *brāhmaṇa* who was not without passion his heart would burst, or hot blood would spout from his mouth, or he would go mad or mentally deranged. Just as a green shoot when mown dries up, dries out and withers, so he would dry up, dry out and wither." Then they approached the Buddha and stood on one side, and Desire accosted him with this verse:

"Are you sunk in grief, since you meditate in the forest ?
Or have you lost your wealth, and are wishing for it ?
Have you committed some offence in the village ?
Why are you not friendly with people ?
Won't you be friendly with any one ?"

(B.) "The attainment of welfare, peace of heart,
Having defeated the army of dear and sweet appearances,
Meditating alone on this, understanding happiness,
—Therefore I am not friendly with people,
I will have friendship with no one."

Then Discontent accosted the Buddha with this verse:

"What way of life should a monk cultivate,
Who has crossed the five 'floods' (senses), in order to cross the sixth (the mind) ?
How, meditating much, are the perceptions of pleasure
Kept out so that they do not get him ?"

—The Buddha replies: by calmness of the body, freedom of the mind, etc.; after which Passion, standing near him, speaks this verse:

"Having robbed Desire he is followed by groups and communities.
Certainly many beings will follow,
Having robbed the King of Death of many people
This homeless one will lead them beyond (to Nirvāṇa)!"

...Afterwards they return to Māra and he upbraids them :

"Fools ! Will you crush a mountain with water-lily stalks ?
Will you dig away the crags with your nails ? Will you chew iron with your teeth ?
Having knocked out the solid rock with your heads will you try to fathom the underworld ?
Having embraced a stake with your breasts will you make Gotama lose heart ?"

(*Saṃyutta Nikāya* I 124-7)

The final verse above is a good example of the characteristic '(rhetorical) question' [186]. There is a concluding verse here, which the commentary says is a later addition to the text:

All radiant they came, Desire, Discontent and Passion,
—The Teacher dispelled them as the wind fallen cotton.

(The reference is to the cotton from cotton-producing trees.) If this tells us little about the 'production' of such a drama, we have plenty of reliefs and paintings of the scene.

601. Though the gods of the old religion, including Brahmā himself, are often shown as in effect good Buddhists, adhering to Buddhist values or attending on the Buddha, there are other, more polemical, episodes which directly attack the Brahmanical or Vedic religion. As in the prose dialogues of the Pali (e.g. *Dīgha Nikāya* I 17ff., 215ff.), satire is sometimes employed against the supreme being, the creator god, of Brahmanism. His omniscience and omnipotence are exploded. In one scene the relationship of Brahmā with the Buddha is shown as most cordial: the Buddha goes to visit Brahmā and is received as an old friend (*Saṃyutta Nikāya* I 142-4):

> Come, my friend, welcome to you! It is a long time, my friend, since you came here. This world (the heaven of Brahmā), my friend, is permanent, fixed, eternal, whole, not subject to passing away. Here there is no being born, growing old, dying, passing away and being reborn. There is no liberation higher than this.

The Buddha replies:

> Brahmā is in a state of ignorance! He is ignorant in that he insists on saying that the impermanent is permanent, the not-fixed fixed, the non-eternal eternal ...that there is no liberation higher than this—when there is a higher liberation.

Brahmā here utters a verse:

> The seventy two (presumably Brahmā's retinue),
> O Gotama, as a result of good actions,
> Wielding power, having gone beyond birth and old age,
> Have this final existence in the Brahmā world, which they have attained by means of the *Veda*;
> Many people pray to us!

The Buddha:

> This is short, not a long life,
> What you think is a long life, O Brahmā,
> Is a hundred thousand *nirabbudhas*:
> I know how long your life is, O Brahmā!

After this Brahmā asks for instruction, especially about his former good conduct and observances. The Buddha tells him the good actions which had resulted in this relatively happy life in heaven, and finally Brahmā admits he is a Buddha, whose magnificence illuminates the Brahmā World.

602. In another scene (pp. 144-6) one of the retinue of Brahmā holds another kind of erroneous opinion: No philosopher or priest can come here (to the Brahmā world). The Buddha becomes aware of this through his telepathic power and proceeds, by attaining the heat element (i.e. using a radiant body), to the Brahmā world, sitting in the sky above the Brahmā. Four of the Buddha's followers are able to see where the Buddha has gone and follow him there, stationing themselves round him in their radiant bodies. One of the latter, Moggallāna, upbraids the Brahmā with a verse:

> Do you even now have that opinion which you had before?
> Look at this radiance in the Brahmā World surpassing all the other radiance there!

The Brahmā admits that he was wrong, and that he cannot now think that he is permanent and eternal. He further goes to tell the supreme Brahmā of the incident, and the latter is very pleased.

603. Elsewhere the *brāhmaṇas*, the priests of Brahmā, confront the Buddha. In one scene the Buddha rejects the doctrine that it is by the Vedic 'science' and conduct, not by virtue and asceticism, that a man becomes pure:

> Though muttering many prayers a brahman is not (pure) because of his birth,
> When he is rotten inside, defiled, depending on deceit.
>
> A *kṣatriya* (warrior, aristocrat), *brāhmaṇa*, *vaiśya* (peasant or bourgeois), *śūdra* (helot), *caṇḍāla* or *pukkasa* (the lowest classes),
> Putting forth energy, exerting himself, always having firm courage,
> Attains the highest purification; know this, O *brāhmaṇa*!
>
> (*Saṃyutta Nikāya* I 166)

Several scenes end with the conversion of a *brāhmaṇa* to become a follower of the Buddha.

604. In connection with the dramatic opposition of ethical values in these pieces we find that, under the heading of generosity, the point is made—familiar elsewhere in Buddhist poetry—that the gift of the doctrine *dhamma*, the Buddhist teaching, is the greatest of all gifts. This, the ideal of spreading the truth, will continue to be prominent in Buddhist *kāvya*, and the theme of 'conversion' (if this term is acceptable) which we have just noted is closely related to it. In one of our present pieces (*Saṃyutta Nikāya* I 20-22) a group of deities approach the Buddha, and six of them recite verses beginning with the words 'Good, my friend, is generosity...' and continuing with variations on this theme, contrasting it with meanness and negligence, praising even a small gift—which if out of small resources is worth thousands,—bringing in the surprising parallel of a battle (a few, but confident, may conquer many), adding that it should have been justly acquired and that the giving should be 'inscrutable' (or 'discreet')—each god caps the other's verses. Another deity then asks the Buddha which he likes of these. He approves them all, but adds his own verse:

> Generosity is praised in many ways by those who trust in it,
> But a verse of truth is better than such a gift;
> For formerly, long ago, good people
> With understanding attained Nirvāṇa itself.

605. It is natural, then, that the decision of the Buddha to teach, after his attainment of enlightenment, should be dramatised. At least three of our pieces represent this theme. Of the three stories, the best known, and probably most ancient in origin, is that of Brahmā persuading the Buddha to teach. Immediately after the enlightenment, the Buddha reflected that his doctrine (or truth) was difficult and profound and unlikely to be appreciated by the world. Brahmā became aware of this and was alarmed: 'Alas! The world perishes... as the Buddha...is not inclined to teach the truth'. He goes down and urges the Buddha to look at the people sunk in grief: '...Let the Master teach the truth, there will be some who will grasp it.' The Buddha sees that people vary in degrees of ignorance and ability and agrees to teach (*Saṃyutta Nikāya* I 136-8). In a very brief scene Māra attempts to persuade the Buddha not to teach, as it would lead to contention. To this objection the Buddha opposes his compassion for welfare (ibid. I 111). Similar is the third scene, but with Sakka suggesting it is not a good thing for a philosopher, who is supposed to be liberated from all ties, to instruct others. Again the Buddha replies that one must teach out of compassion, and says that if one teaches with a confident (or trusting) mind there will be no 'connecting' (with the world—the ties referred to by Sakka) (ibid. I 206).

606. One more scene in which Māra appears should be mentioned. A number of gods carry on a kind of contest in verses in the presence of the Buddha, as he sits one night meditating in a thicket of bamboos. These verses praise the doctrines of various philosophers of the time of the Buddha: three of the leaders of the Ājīvakas and the founder of Jainism. Another god intervenes and says that, however loudly he howls, a jackal will never be like a lion. Then Māra speaks, upholding these philosophers—their instruction is right and leads to the other world. Here the Buddha intervenes with a verse: Namuci (Death, Māra) praises those who serve his deadly purpose, like bait for fish. Another god concludes the scene with a verse praising the Buddha (*Saṃyutta Nikāya* I 65-7).

607. Finally let us look at a scene in which the attempt is made to dramatise the Parinirvāṇa (final Nirvāṇa) of the Buddha: hardly a dramatic subject, since it is difficult to see how there could be any conflict. The later critics of the drama, as we have seen [90-4], debated whether the attainment of peace or calm, as an end of human life, was an appropriate subject for drama, some holding that there are plays which may be said to have the calmed *śānta* as their main *rasa*. The calmed was recognised as a ninth *rasa* by an increasing number of them. This scene shows the Buddha in the wood near Kusinārā, lying on his right side and surrounded by his followers. Most of it agrees verbatim with an account given elsewhere in the Buddhist canon, and it was probably extracted from this (it is a brief extract from a long narrative [610]) for the purpose we have supposed for these scenes. It begins with the Buddha uttering his last words: 'Well, now monks I am addressing you. You should succeed, through care. The forces have the nature of cessation (the 'forces' are all the forces of the universe, natural forces, animal instincts, etc.).' He then enters into a series of meditations, at the end of which he 'attains extinction'. When he had attained extinction Brahmā spoke a verse:

'All beings in the world will discard their bodies,
Just as this teacher without an equal in the world;
The Thus-gone who was strong, the Buddha has attained extinction.'

Sakka spoke a verse:

'Alas ! The forces are impermanent, having the nature of occurrence and decay,
Having occurred, they cease—the calming of them is happiness.'

The monk Ānanda spoke a verse:

'Then there was what is terrifying, then it was hairraising,
When the Buddha, who had all excellent qualities, attained extinction !'

Finally the monk Anuruddha spoke two verses:

'There was no breathing in or out, of the one whose mind was firm;
Imperturbable because of his calm, the man with insight attained extinction.

His mind unflinching, he accepted pain (of his final illness);
Like the extinction of a lamp was the liberation of his mind.'

(*Saṃyutta Nikāya* I 157-9)

It seems legitimate, in view of the human weaknesses ascribed to Ānanda's character by the Buddhist tradition and contrasted with the intellectual strength and moral firmness of more advanced monks, to see here a deliberate opposition of Ānanda's reaction of fear and sorrow to the correct Buddhist view of the situation, optimistic and detached, which is finally asserted.

608. The progress of the art of story telling in prose can be documented from the Pali Canon, which preserves more varied examples than the prose Vedic texts. The style is a little less abrupt and heavy, but still with no concern at all to avoid verbal repetition and hardly ever any to ornament the language. Many short stories could be quoted from the *Nikāyas*, which are told to make a particular point, to exemplify the opinion of the teller. They are often humorous (see particularly those in the *Pāyāsi Suttanta* of the *Dīgha Nikāya*—II 316ff.), satirising stupidity or obstinacy, for example.

609. Quite different in content are a number of longer narratives, which might be called prose *ākhyānas* (cf. those of the *Veda* and Tradition) on account of their legendary or semi-(or pseudo-) historical nature [38]. From some of these (especially in the *Dīgha Nikāya*, again, Vol. III 84ff., 58ff.) a Buddhist 'Tradition' of the evolution of the universe and more especially of human society appears, more logical than historical and all the more social-critical for that. We have the story of the election of the first king (familiar to Brahmanical Tradition as well, with divergent details) and traditions of great and generally just emperors of ancient times. Most interesting is the social history, which shows many of the admitted evils of society arising from greed and acquisitiveness, which do not seem evil as a rule to their subject and are sometimes widely accepted in human societies and held to be beneficial. Thus at first all food was gathered daily from naturally occurring sources—until someone thought of making a store for himself. When many people laid in stores a shortage resulted. To ensure fair distribution property in land was invented: the places where food (especially rice) grew wild were shared out as private holdings. The result of this was the invention of theft. To maintain order the first king was then elected. Another narrative shows the kingship already established and a just emperor maintaining harmony by gifts to anyone who became poor. His successor, through ignorance, stops the grants to the poor. Poverty becomes widespread and theft is invented or rediscovered, followed inevitably by punishment and then by robbery with murder. All subsequent attempts of kings to prevent crime fail, resulting instead in the further degeneration of civilisation.

610. Out of the accounts of episodes in the life and particularly the teaching activities of the Buddha, mostly in the form of dialogues in prose, a tradition of Buddhist historical writing developed. The narrative of the last few months of the life of the Buddha (to which we alluded in connection with the scene of the Parinirvāṇa) was supplemented by accounts of events in the Buddhist community of monks afterwards and has been continued from time to time since then. For the present we may merely note the existence of this Buddhist tradition of historical writing (later we shall be, if briefly, concerned with its partial absorption into the fully developed *kāvya* literature). On the other hand the Parinirvāṇa narrative itself, the *Mahāparinibbāna Suttanta* of the *Dīgha Nikāya* (II 72ff.; and its Sanskrit version, for that matter, edited by Waldschmidt; though the latter is later it agrees closely with the Pali and is simply a translation of some ancient version in an unknown dialect) is a relatively sophisticated piece of narrative, in six chapters, more elevated in style and vocabulary than most of the Pali dialogues and seemingly composed with conscious intent to make it impressive. One might see the development of the biography *ākhyāyikā* here, as a *kāvya* form [423]. The setting out of the parallelism between the conditions for welfare of the Vajjī Republic and of the Buddhist Community; the intertwining of the Buddha's progress from Rajagaha to Kusinārā with the major political events of the time; the predictions about Pāṭaliputra; the occasional verses uttered by the Buddha and bringing in metaphors; the Buddha's illness and his comparison of his body with an old cart barely held together with straps; his insistence on the impermanence of all 'forces', reinforced by his own case; his equal and dramatic insistence that there is nothing else he can do for his followers and that they must go their own way, with only his teaching as a provisional guide; the pathos introduced by the Buddha's last look at the city of Vaiśālī as he leaves it—to these touches of the story teller's art a Buddhist narrator has further added a background of miracles, of the marvellous, such as flowers blooming out of season, muddy water clarified and the attendance of deities: for the Parinirvāṇa is no ordinary event to be told in a matter of fact manner, it is an event of cosmic importance and the whole universe must be concerned in it.

611. It is almost an anticlimax to our notes on Pali prose to add that in the *Kuṇāla Jātaka* (*Jātaka* V 416-56), the only exception to the rule that the ancient *Jātaka* text is exclusively in verse, we find much greater elaborations of actual prose style than in the above narratives, with very long compounds and a most elaborate description of the slopes of the Himālaya Mountains. The prose alternates with verse (in *vaitālīya*, *rathoddhatā* and other metres) and the work is a true *campū kāvya* in form. The content is mostly criticism of women through a discussion among birds, with reference to various old legends. The hero Kuṇāla, the bird who mostly lectures against women, bears the name of the son of the emperor Aśoka, who is recorded to have been persecuted and blinded by his anti-Buddhist stepmother Tiṣyarakṣā, when he rejected her love. Probably this *campū* was designed as a bitter response to the actions of Aśoka's last empress, who tried to undo her husband's good works after gaining influence over him in his old age: one should never trust a woman.

612. We need not pursue the development of the Pali Canon into the –2, since at this point we can pick up the earliest threads of strictly secular *kāvya* and attempt to place the 'First *Kavi*'.

Chapter XIII

THE EARLIEST KĀVYA LITERATURE IN SANSKRIT

(*c.* −400 to −150); VĀLMĪKI

613. Turning now to the earliest *kāvya* of the main, secular tradition, and at the same time to the use of Sanskrit as a medium for *kāvya*, we may examine the following evidence. Vālmīki, author of the *Rāmāyaṇa*, was, according to later *kavis*, the 'First *Kavi*' (Bhavabhūti: *Uttararāmacarita* II, after verse 5; Ānandavardhana 542f.). According to Aśvaghoṣa (+ 1; *Buddhacarita* I. 43) on the other hand he was the first to compose in verse *padya*. There is an apparent quotation from the *Rāmāyaṇa* by the grammarian Patañjali (−2?) in his *Mahābhāṣya*, on Pāṇini III.1.67. The grammarian Pāṇini (−4) attests the existence by his time of the drama and of schools of actors (such as Śailālin's) and even of theoretical works on it, but without giving any details (IV.3.110). A Pāṇini, not necessarily the same, was a major poet and the author of an epic *kāvya*, the *Jāmbavatījaya*, no longer available, it seems, apart from about twenty quotations. Kauṭalya (end of −4) refers to biographies *ākhyāyikās* (I.5). Patañjali refers to a *kāvya* by Vararuci (*Mahābhāṣya* on Pāṇini IV.3.101). There are traditions of the grammarian Vararuci, author of the 'Supplement' *Vārttika*, which suggest he was a junior contemporary of Pāṇini (on those traditions see below). No authentic *kāvyas* by a Vararuci of this period appear to have survived. A dramatist named Subandhu is recorded by much later writers on drama to have lived at the beginning of the −3, and to have had a play performed before the Mauryan emperor Bindusāra, from which a brief extract has been preserved (Abhinavagupta III p. 172). Finally Patañjali quotes about forty verses in the *kāvya* style and refers to three biographies *ākhyāyikās*, giving their titles (*Mahābhāṣya* on Pāṇini IV.2.60 and 3.87—one work of Vararuci named in later sources, to be discussed below [650], may be either a biography or a novel). Patañjali also refers to dramas, and explains a word *vāsavadattika* as meaning someone who studies a *kāvya* on the story of Vāsavadattā. We have already discussed [317-9] the question of the earliest dramas on the basis of the traditions of the *Nāṭyaśāstra*, concluding that there were in the earliest period religious plays, plays taken from Tradition and comedies and satires: we can now add that the Subandhu just mentioned took a subject from history, from the –5; history is of course included in Tradition.

614. It is not known whether Vālmīki is a historical person, or whether, like the Vyāsa of Tradition, he is a theoretical amalgam of a series of traditional poets. Like the Great Epic, the *Rāmāyaṇa* has been much revised, being treated rather as a work of Tradition than as a *kāvya*. In other words, instead of being accepted as a fixed text by a given poet it became the property of the popular reciters of Tradition, who were concerned not with meticulous accuracy and faithful interpretation but with inspiring their mass audiences. The need to carry such audiences with them probably resulted in modifications, expansions, and more rarely cuts in the received text, and in time such alterations as satisfied the reciters became permanent revisions widely, sometimes universally, accepted. On the whole the style of the original was maintained, but not in every detail.

615. It can be stated that this style is more homogeneous than that of the Great Epic, that it agrees in language and metre with the later parts of the latter, and hence that it reflects the usages of a period of transition between the old epic tradition and epic *kāvya*. The metrical analysis of the text as we now have it indicates about – 100 as its average period (see discussions in *Pali Metre*, following Oldenberg, Edgerton, etc.), and we know that substantial additions have been made since the +1. Though the analysis of the separate parts of the poem, which might lead to fairly precise chronology, has not yet been carried out, we can already estimate that there existed sometime before – 100 a poem of perhaps less than a quarter the length of the extant text, which narrated the story in the main as we now have it but with the important differences that the last Book was entirely missing, together with most of the first (for these Books being apocryphal, see Johnston, Introduction to his translation of Aśvaghoṣa's *Buddhacarita*, xlviiiff.).

616. This version of the story, which seems to be a combination of two or even three old legends, has the appearance of being the creation of an individual *kavi* of genius, whom we might provisionally call 'Vālmīki'. It is difficult to push the date back far enough to make it literally the 'First *Kāvya*', but it could very well be from a later standpoint the first great masterpiece of *kāvya*. Further, since *kāvya* seems to have originated in lyric poetry, though we cannot place the *Rāmāyaṇa* in the period of the earliest known *kāvya* lyrics and hence of the continuing old Epic tradition, we can regard it as marking a new departure, in epic *kāvya*. The question is further complicated by the tradition that Vālmīki was a metrical innovator, who invented the new form of *anuṣṭubh* called the *vaktra* (this derives from the current *Rāmāyaṇa* itself, I. II. 17). We noted this in an earlier chapter, where we saw also that this innovation seems from the available evidence to have been in fact a gradual and smooth development, so that to assign a starting point for the *vaktra* appears arbitrary [534]. As to the tradition about Vālmīki, this makes him an ancient sage contemporary with Rāma himself (he so appears in the current text and in other *kāvyas* from a fairly early period on [1127-8]). The extant *Rāmāyaṇa*, even when shorn of immense accretions as just noted, may not be as early as the *kavis* Vararuci and Subandhu. As to the *kavi* Pāṇini, there is reason to believe that he was a different person from the grammarian and lived a good deal later. On stylistic grounds, from what we know of his epic we should place it rather later than the *Rāmāyaṇa*, since it appears to have the characteristics of *kāvya* epic fully developed. To admit the reverse chronological order would be to make 'Vālmīki' the reverse of an innovator, clinging to a style closer to the old Epic tradition after epic *kāvya* was well established. We must remember that this is quite possible: the tradition of Vālmīki as innovator and even as a *kavi* in the new sense may misrepresent his true position. However, as a working hypothesis we may follow the tradition and discuss the *Rāmāyaṇa* first, in its presumed more original form.

617. The story of the *Rāmāyaṇa* is one of the finest things in the world's literature. It was adapted again and again for the Indian stage and became almost a hackneyed theme [285]; though it was with good reason that one of the adapters said:

If they abandon the story of Rāma because it has been used by predecessors, then who else with such qualities will conquer in the world?

Are there authors possessing the Absolute Speech, vibrating profound and sweet with the weight of such qualities, who can help themselves?

(Only Vālmīki was such a divine incarnation of authorship, capable of independent creation—Murāri: *Anargharāghava* I.9).

618. In the hands of a succession of poets and dramatists the story has shown many variations of detail, and indeed it seems capable of infinite variation, especially in the psychological interpretation of the main characters [285]. Perhaps the uniqueness of the story of Rāma lies in this unfathomable psychological depth, the inexhaustible complexity of the characters, which demands and receives new interpretation in each generation. 'Vālmīki' himself (if we apply this name to the creator of the archetype of the extant *Rāmāyaṇa*, without the last Book and other less important accretions) stood very far from an original Rāma story and approached his characters in a highly sophisticated and subtle manner. Kaikeyī is not simply an unscrupulous and ambitious woman scheming to place her son on the throne. Vālmīki sees her as honest and well intentioned, incapable of wishing harm to anyone, apparently as good and noble as any aristocratic lady could be desired to be, but too easily persuaded against her own judgment. She is led astray by her confidante, a slave belonging to Kaikeyī's family and seeing no further than its apparent interest. She likewise acts from apparently honourable motives of love and loyalty to her mistress, but is characterised as 'seeing evil' and shown as a cynical 'realist' in judging others. The development of the palace intrigue consists in the conflict of motives in principle good in intention but on one side deflected by judgments of questionable validity, though having respectable authority in political science. Perhaps there is some idealisation of human nature in these characters, except for the confidante, or perhaps they should be seen as insincere in their noble speeches. Perhaps we should regard such sentiments as sheer hypocrisy. Yet we do believe in this conflict and are greatly moved by it. It is a searching critique of the aspiration to live up to some standard or ideal, and it expresses a perennial and real dilemma of the human situation with the utmost aesthetic force.

619. For ancient India this story of the exiling of Rāma had the specific interest of bearing on dynastic struggles for succession such as often occurred in real life, where probably the contestants might seem less scrupulous and idealistic. The Mauryan Empire was rent by such conflicts both when Aśoka succeeded to the throne and at the end of his reign [611]. Moreover we have the most vivid records of the conflict in theory or ideology: on the one hand the edicts of Aśoka, on the other the *Arthaśāstra* of Kauṭalya. The old Rāma story—which was handed down in some form in the old Epic tradition, and of which a version appears in Pali in the *Jātaka* (IV.126-7)—would then be a topical theme for 'Vālmīki' to elaborate. Though that much might be said for almost any period, the fact of Aśoka's attempt to realise a truly just government, corresponding to an ideal higher perhaps than has ever been attempted elsewhere, might, we may conjecture, have suggested to 'Vālmīki', if he lived at that time or a little later, the portrayal of a conflict of sincere motives in his own version.

620. Religion is not strongly in evidence in the *Rāmāyaṇa* (except in some of the later additions). The old king Daśaratha is a tragic character, unable to resolve the conflict in his family and betrayed by his own rash promise into exiling his eldest and best loved son. Soon afterwards he dies heartbroken. This human story is not softened by other-worldly consolations nor guided by divine providence. But Rāma, whose name means 'Charming', absolutely obedient to his father's commands and true to his own promises, devoted to his stepmother as to his own mother and loving all his brothers to the point of total self-sacrifice for their advantage, was gradually elevated by later generations from the ideal hero to the incarnation of Viṣṇu. Some of the more recent versions of the Rāma story, especially in the vernacular languages, are almost purely religious writings: it is necessary therefore to stress the fact that this is entirely alien to the spirit of the *Rāmāyaṇa* of Vālmīki, though it is no doubt a most significant indication of the success of Vālmīki in making his hero the focus of the human aspiration to live in a better society.

621. In the second half of the *Rāmāyaṇa*, where the legend or myth of Rāvaṇa, probably quite independent of that of Rāma in origin, has been inserted into the period of exile of Rāma, the superhuman and marvellous predominate. Here one may speak of a religious background, of ancient mythology such as usually complements traditional epic poetry: a mythical environment, which is liable in times of disorder and crisis to irrupt decisively into the foreground of human society, or at least over the periphery of that society, on the mysterious unknown borders of the then known world (in this case the far South, the Ocean and Ceylon). It is a very different kind of religion from that of the later Rāma worship, so that one would like to have a different word for it; 'mythology', perhaps, in order to maintain the negative of the last paragraph and make clear what seems a real distinction between this mysterious and alien background, encountered most dangerously when we venture too far from the centres of civilisation, and a religion which is a positive guide to human action.

622. The Southern forests, where the exiled Rāma wanders with one brother, and Sītā his ideally faithful wife, are dominated by demons *rākṣasas*. Rāvaṇa, the demon emperor, enjoys divine powers acquired in a past life, and although he abuses them even the gods cannot deprive him of invincible strength legitimately gained. His capital, a fortress and a paradise, is established in Ceylon (Laṅkā), and from there his demons ravage and tyrannise half India. Rāma successfully encounters some of the demon patrols, and his subversive presence, and more especially the beauty of his wife, are reported to the emperor, who in person abducts Sītā by a stratagem. Rāma finds friends among the forest dwellers (monkeys) oppressed by the demons and is able to collect a large army. He crosses the Ocean and takes Ceylon by storm, killing Rāvaṇa in battle, rescuing the faithful Sītā and establishing just government. Here we have the typical hero of many ancient civilisations, whose unique physical strength overcomes animals, natural powers (the Ocean) and superhuman demons. His cause is simple and obviously just, and this straightforward purpose united with exceptional strength and heroism is irresistible.—The period prescribed for his exile has now ended and Rāma returns home in triumph to claim his heritage and rule justly over all India.

623. Evidently the heroic *rasa* prevails in the story thus outlined, but in the first part it is the compassionate which is dominant. Though we do not know to what extent this aesthetic theory had been consciously formulated by 'Vālmīki's' time, he is in fact associated with the compassionate *rasa* in the tradition of the *kavis* and critics, and in fact already in the *Rāmāyaṇa* itself (but in I.II.13ff. in the First Book, almost all of which appears to be a late addition). It was the tragic incident witnessed by him, of the shooting by a hunter of one of a pair of curlews, and the pathetic cries of the bereft female bird, which inspired him to compose the first verse in the *vaktra* metre, an outburst of feeling expressed in an improvised (cf. *paṭibhāna* in Pali) lyric (we again note the lyric tradition underlying *kāvya*). It seems to have been felt very early that Vālmīki's genius was especially attuned to the compassionate rather than the heroic, and his poetic sensibilities most fully aroused by a pathetic event such as the tragic separation of lovers illustrated by the story of the curlews, and of couse the pathetic though very different story of the exiling of Rāma. The later connoisseurs of *kāvya* usually hold that the compassionate *rasa* is in fact the prevailing one in the *Rāmāyaṇa* [103], though Kuntaka, if the edition is not corrupt, gives the calmed [284], and the unknown poet who added the Last Book to the epic (probably about +100) gave complete justification for this interpretation by making his new ending tragic. Sītā was long a prisoner in Rāvaṇa's hands, and although we have been assured earlier that she remained chaste, resisting all his advances with success, in this sequel she comes under suspicion and Rāma abandons her. She appeals to the Goddess Earth for refuge, and disappears into a crevice which opens for her. From the part of the First Book added probably at the same time we learn that Sītā was born from the Earth when her father King Janaka was ploughing; the Goddess is thus her mother and the life of this strange divine heroine is appropriately ended. Though all this seems quite new to the *Rāmāyaṇa* it may not have been unknown to Vālmīki even if he chose to ignore it. The name 'Sītā' means 'Furrow' and suggests that among the probably numerous ancient tales of a pre-Vālmīki Rāma cycle was one of the miraculous nature of the heroine.

624. The style of the *Rāmāyaṇa* is extremely simple, but rough, and sometimes awkward in expression and not immediately clear, when compared with that of later epic *kāvyas*. Yet it shows the beginnings of a transition towards these when compared with the rather abrupt manner and sometimes clumsy development, as well as the partly more archaic metre, of the Great Epic. The question of metres has been touched on above; their refinement is here accompanied by the cultivation of a more poetic language, with more of the vocabulary associated with *kāvya*. The similes are more elaborate, there is occasional alliteration and other word play and more rarely some of the more recondite figures of speech of poetic theory are seen. Thus in a remarkable description of winter during Rāma's exile (Book III canto XV) a commentator finds some 'fancies' *utprekṣās* [633]. There is at present no guarantee that particular passages thus pointed out are not later additions, but we may venture to say that 'Vālmīki' allowed himself to dwell a little on the beauties of the forest and on other scenes in his story, though without seriously interrupting the narrative as later epic *kavis* do.

625. To show the style of 'Vālmīki's' narrative we may translate some extracts as literally as possible, so that they may be compared both with the Pali poetry we have read earlier [561] and with later epics [730ff.]. From the present Second Book, *Ayodhyā Kāṇḍa*, let us read the scene where the intrigue of Kaikeyī begins, from the beginning of Canto VII:

A slave woman who had been born in Kaikeyī's family and lived with her,
By chance climbed the Moon-like palace;

From that palace Mantharā ('Slow', the slave) observed Ayodhyā:
With the entire Royal Way watered, scattered with waterlilies and lotuses,...

Mantharā, who is also described as a hunchback, finds the nurse there and asks what these preparations are for—the city being further described as decorated elaborately and Rāma's mother being seen giving presents to the people: the nurse tells her it is for Rāma's consecration as heir apparent, which is to take place tomorrow. It should be noted that the spectacle of Rāma's mother exultant, the triumph of a rival queen, is evidently the thing which most moves Mantharā, who belongs to Kaikeyī's family as a slave born in the house:

> Hearing the nurse's words the hunchback quickly became indignant,
> Descended from the palace which appeared like the peak of Kailāsa, (8)
>
> Mantharā burning with anger, seeing evil,
> Went to Kaikeyī, who was in bed, and spoke these words:
>
> Get up ! Stupid ! Why are you sleeping when danger is coming towards you ?
> Aren't you aware that you are engulfed in a flood of misfortune ?
>
> You proclaim your fortune when in a calamity of pleasing appearance,
> For your fortune is transitory like the stream of a river in the hot season.
>
> But Kaikeyī, spoken to thus with harsh words by the angry one,
> By the hunchback seeing evil, fell into the utmost despair.
>
> But Kaikeyī said to the hunchback: Mantharā, is there really no security ?
> I perceive you indeed with afflicted face, violently unhappy !
>
> But Mantharā, hearing Kaikeyī's sweet-syllabled words,
> Spoke a sentence with anger,—she who was confident of her sentence.
>
> That hunchback, becoming more afflicted, wishing for Kaikeyī's advantage,
> Spoke out causing despair and dividing the Rāghava family:

O Queen ! A very great insecurity has arisen, destroying you !
King Daśaratha will consecrate Rāma as heir apparent!

I am sunk in fathomless danger, overwhelmed in unhappiness and grief;
I have come here for the sake of your advantage, as if being burned by fire;

O Kaikeyī, through your unhappiness there would be very great unhappiness for me,
And in your prosperity would be my prosperity, there is no doubt of this.

Born in a family of kings, a chief queen, you, of a king,
How are you not aware, O Queen, of the fierce reality of royal politics ?

A false lord speaks of virtue, a ruthless one speaks smoothly,
Do you not know, in your innocence, you are thus overreached by him ?

The mildness which he is using towards you is the approach of misfortune !
—Today your lord will join Kausalyā with fortune.

That corrupt man, having carried off Bharata from among your relatives,
At daybreak will establish Rāma in the kingdom in which the 'thorns' have been struck down.

An enemy, through being reported to be your husband, is suffered like a snake in the lap
By you, my dear, who are like a mother desiring his advantage.

For as a snake would act, or an enemy, when disregarded,
So today King Daśaratha acts towards you and your son.

With evil, with false mildness, my dear, you who are always accustomed to happiness,

He will establish Rāma in the kingdom: you and your
following are ruined.

O Kaikeyī, the time has come, you must act quickly
for your advantage,
Save your son, yourself, and me, you who show surprise!

After hearing Mantharā's words that beautiful-faced
one, from the bed
Gave a beautiful ornament to the hunchback.

After giving the ornament to the hunchback, Kaikeyī,
That best of women, joyful again, said this to
Mantharā :

What you tell me, Mantharā, is most agreeable,
For you, teller of what is agreeable to me, what more
can I do?

(N.B. Kaikeyī here treats the report of Rāma's impending consecration as good news : it is the custom to give a present to a servant who brings good news.)

I do not observe any difference between Rāma and
Bharata,
Therefore I am pleased that the King will consecrate
Rāma in the kingdom.

There is nothing more agreeable to me than these
excellent words of yours, good words, O you who are
worthy of what is agreeable !
For thus you have spoken what is most agreeable:
—choose another boon which I can give you !

626. Canto VII closes with this last verse in a different metre; the narrative continues straight on in Canto VIII:

But Mantharā indignant with her and dismissing that
ornament,
Full of anger and unhappiness spoke these words:

What is this joy? Child! You are acting inappropriately.
You do not recognise that you are in the midst of an ocean of grief!

Fortunate indeed is Kausalyā, whose son will be consecrated
Tomorrow with the great heir apparentship, (when the Moon is) in Puṣya, by the greatest brahmans!

When she has attained the greatest joy, famous, her enemies ruined,
You will attend on Kausalyā, saluting her like a slave woman!

Rāma's women will indeed be most joyful!
Your daughters-in-law will be depressed at the ruin of Bharata!

Then having seen Mantharā, who was speaking what was most disagreeable,
Queen Kaikeyī praised the qualities of Rāma:

Knowing virtue, restrained by his elders, grateful, truthful, pure,
—For these Rāma, the King's eldest son, deserves the heir apparentship....

Kaikeyī continues her praise of Rāma, asking how Mantharā can be angry on hearing of his consecration. But Mantharā becomes very unhappy and sighs, rebuking Kaikeyī for her foolishness, and again warns her: Princes can't all be kings and Bharata will be pushed aside; for all to become kings would be a very bad policy, therefore kings establish their eldest sons in the kingdom: Rāma, when firmly established, will send Bharata to another country, or to the other world! Therefore let your son leave the palace and go to the forest! Your son is Rāma's natural enemy, so you must save him... And his mother is your rival wife, how can she not be your enemy? If Rāma obtains the Earth, Bharata is certainly lost...

627. Thus she gradually convinces Kaikeyī and the narrative continues in Canto IX:

Kaikeyī thus spoken to, her face inflamed with anger,
Sighing long and hot said this to Mantharā:

Today I will quickly send Rāma away from here to the forest,
And quickly consecrate Bharata as heir apparent.

O Mantharā, now I have seen this, by what means
May Bharata obtain the kingdom, and Rāma not at all?

Mantharā, seeing evil, thus spoken to by the Queen,
Damaging Rāma's fortune, said this to Kaikeyī:

Well! Now I will speak out, O Kaikeyī, let it be heard from me,
How your son Bharata will obtain the whole kingdom.

Kaikeyī hearing these words of Mantharā's,
Rising a little from her comfortable bed said this:

(Here a commentator finds an implied meaning—of respect for Mantharā: Kaikeyī rose although her bed was comfortable—)

Tell me the means, Mantharā, by what means
May Bharata obtain the kingdom, but Rāma not at all?

Mantharā, seeing evil, thus spoken to by the Queen,
Damaging Rāma's fortune the hunchback said these words:

In the battle of the gods and demons, your husband went with the royal sages,
Taking you, assisting the King of the Gods.

O Kaikeyī, standing in the Southern region, towards the Daṇḍaka (Forest),

Is the city known as Vaijayanta, where he of the sea-dragon banner,

Known as Śambara, the great demon of a hundred tricks,
Unconquered, gave battle to Śakra with the multitude of gods.

Then in that great battle King Daśaratha
Was carried off unconscious by you, O Queen, from the battle;

Your husband there was protected by you when wounded by weapons;
Pleased by that he gave you two boons, O beautiful one!

You said to your husband, O Queen, "When I desire them, then
I will take the boons,"—That illustrious one said "Yes".
I was ignorant of that, O Queen,—you yourself told me before.

—Ask your lord for those boons: the consecration of Bharata,
And the banishment of Rāma for fourteen years!

Taking refuge in anger today, O daughter of Aśvapati, in anger
You must lie on the bare ground, in dark dress;
Don't meet his gaze and don't speak to him;

You are always the beloved of your lord, I have no doubt about that,
And for your sake the King would even enter fire,

He cannot be angry with you, he cannot meet your gaze if you are angry,
To please you the King would give up his life;

The King cannot transgress your words,
O slow-natured one ! Be aware of your own strength
of fortune !

Gems, pearls, gold and various jewels,
King Daśaratha would give—don't think of them:

Those boons which Daśaratha gave in the battle of
gods and demons,
Recall them, blessed one, don't transgress that purpose !

But when the Rāghava (Daśaratha) would give you
a boon, rising up,
Depending on the King you should choose the boon:

Banish Rāma to the forest, nine years and five,
Let Bharata be king on Earth, bull among kings !

Thus Rāma banished will be no-Rāma (= 'not
charming')
And Bharata, his enemy ruined, will be your king !

And by the time Rāma returns from the forest
Your son will have grown roots...

Kaikeyī is delighted and praises and flatters Mantharā: she is a beautiful hunchback !...So they prepare, Kaikeyī lying on the ground in a state of depression as directed by Mantharā...

628. When Rāma is banished, Sītā insists on accompanying him and the canto (XXIV) in which she does this is a favourite with reciters of the *Rāmāyaṇa*:

Vaidehī (Sītā), thus spoken to, she who was worthy of
what is agreeable and spoke what was agreeable,
Angered through love said this to her lord:

My lord ! —Father, mother, brother, sister and
daughter-in-law,
Enjoying their own merits, each wait upon their own
fortune;

But a wife alone obtains her husband's fortune,
O bull of men !
Therefore I too am directed to live in the forest.

Not her father, nor her son, not herself, nor her mother
nor her friend;
—Here or in the next world her husband only is always
the destiny of a woman.

If you have started for the impenetrable forest today,
O Rāghava,
I will go in front of you, trampling down the grass
and thorns.

...

I will live happily in the forest just as in my father's
palace,
Not thinking of the three worlds—thinking of my vow
to my husband (9).

Attending on you always, constant, living the 'best
life' (as an ascetic),
I will enjoy myself with you in the sweet scented
forest, O hero.

...

I wish to see streams, mountains, pools and forests,
Everywhere fearless with you, understanding hus-
band; (13)

I wish to see the lotus pools well flowered, abounding
in wild geese and ducks,
Happy, joined with you, hero.

With you, O broad eyed, I will enjoy myself with the
utmost delight,
Thus for a thousand or a hundred years, I with you.

Even if my life will be in heaven, without you, O
Rāghava,
O man-tiger, I will not like it.

629. In the present Third Book, *Araṇya* ('Forest') *Kāṇḍa*, the exiles wander for many years in different parts of the forests South of the Ganges, gradually moving further South into Mahārāṣṭra. They visit hermitages and sages, going for example to see Agastya (Canto X):

Rāma set out in front, Sītā, whose middle was beautiful, in the middle,
Lakṣmaṇa followed behind, bow in hand;

Those two went with Sītā, seeing various wild mountain places
And forests and various delightful rivers,

Cranes and ruddy geese on the shoals of rivers,
And lakes with lotuses, with water-birds,

Spotted antelopes in herds, horned animals wild with passion
—Buffaloes, boars and elephants at enmity with trees.

After going a long way, as the Sun was setting,
They saw together a delightful lake a league in length,

Blocked up with red and blue lotuses, adorned with herds of elephants,
Crowded with cranes, wild geese and ducks living in the water.

...

630. Agastya advises them to go to the pleasant Pañcavaṭī country not far away, a forest district by the River Godāvarī :

"Go !"—Spoken to by him the son of the Raghus went
By the way indicated, looking at that forest (X.71):

Wild rice, bread fruits, palms, *timiśa* trees, canes, *dhavas*,
Parrot wood-apples, *madhūkas*, wood apples and ebony trees;

Flowery, entwined with creepers crested with flowers,
Rāma saw by hundreds there the wilderness trees;

Rubbed by elephants' trunks, brilliant with monkeys,
Resounding with flocks of wanton birds by hundreds.

631. After they arrive in the Pañcavaṭī country Rāma describes it to Lakṣmaṇa (XIV. 10ff.):

This country, level, beautiful, covered with flowering trees,
Here, dear brother, you should make a hermitage properly (for us to live in).

That lotus pool can be seen not far away, splendid with lotuses,
With sweet scented lotuses resembling the gods (or the stars).

As mentioned by the sage Agastya of developed soul,
That is the delightful Godāvarī screened by flowering trees,

Abounding in wild geese and ducks, brilliant with ruddy geese,
Not too far and not too near—pressed upon by herds of animals.

Resounding with peacocks, delightful, tall, with many caves,
Mountains can be seen, dear brother, covered with blossoming trees:

With ores of gold, silver and copper from place to place,

They appear as if windowed, like elephants highly decorated;

They are brilliant with *sāla* trees, palms, *tamālas*, dates, bread fruits, sour mangoes,
Wild rice, *timiśas*, nutmegs;

With sweet mangoes, *aśokas*, *tilakas*, *campakas* and pandanus odoratissimuses,
—Covered by these different trees which possess creepers with clusters of flowers;

With sandalwood, *syandanas*, *nīpas*, bread fruit and *lakucas* too,
Dhavas, vatica robustas, acacias, *śamīs*, *kiṃśukas*, trumpet flowers;

This is good, this is fresh, it has many animals and birds,
Here we will live, O Saumitri, with this bird (i.e. the vulture Jaṭāyus who becomes their friend).

632. When they have lived some time in Pañcavaṭī a noteworthy description of winter is given (this sets the scene for the embroilment with the *rākṣasas* and eventually the abduction of Sītā, and the commentators read hints foreboding tragic events into this Canto XV). Here Vālmīki's descriptive and poetic powers rise to their highest and foreshadow future things in *kāvya* (e.g. more particularly in Aśvaghoṣa), and the commentator Govindarāja picks out a number of figures of speech:

Whilst the illustrious Rāghava lived happily,
Autumn departed and winter, the wished for season began.

Once, in the night, the son of the Raghus, at dawn,
Went out to wash in the delightful River Godāvarī;

His heroic brother Saumitri, pitcher in hand,
Following behind him devotedly with Sītā said this:

The time has arrived which is agreeable to you,
O speaker of what is agreeable,
It appears as if ornamented, through it the year is
beautiful.

The world is rough with frost, the Earth is garlanded
with grain,
The waters are unenjoyable, the bearer of oblations
(fire) is pleasing.

('naturalistic description' [197])

Having offered reverence to the ancestors and deities
by honouring them with the new first fruits
At the proper time, those who have done their 'first
fruits' (rite) are without sin.

633. In verse 8 there is a 'fancy' [213] in personifying the Northern direction and comparing her with a woman, and similarly in 9 where the Himālaya is said to be 'rich' (in frost). In 10 the naturalistic description continues: good fortune for the Sun, now welcome; bad fortune for shadows and water. Then:

The days now appear with the Sun gentle, with frost,
With sharp cold winds, with empty forests perished
with snow.

Now the nights pass cold, increased in length,
Brought by Puṣya with frosty dawns and sleeping in the
open stopped.

His fortune transferred to the Sun; his disc red as it
snows,
Like a mirror dimmed with sighs, the Moon does not
appear clearly.

(simile; and surely 'fancy' ?
—as to the 'fortune', in warmer seasons the 'cool' Moon is welcome and not the Sun, in winter the Sun is appreciated)

The moonlight, gloomy as it snows, does not appear
beautiful at full Moon
And like ploughed land, which is dark (even) in the
sunshine, it is perceived but has no splendour.

('contrast', says Govindarāja)

By nature cold to the touch, now that it is pierced
with frost
The West wind at this time blows doubly cold.

The forests covered in mist, with their barley and
wheat
Look splendid as the Sun rises and they resound with
curlews and cranes.

Their heads full of grains, giving the appearance of date
flowers,
The rice plants look splendid, slightly bent, with a lustre
of gold.

...

With the falling dew its meadows are somewhat wet,
—The forest land looks splendid sitting in the morning
sunshine (20).

Set with the gloom of dew, covered with the gloom of
frost,
The lines of woodland are perceived as if asleep —without
their flowers.

Their waters covered with mist, their cranes recognised
(only) by their cries,
The streams appear now with banks whose sands are
wet with snow.

634. Though praised so highly by Bhavabhūti and Ānandavardhana, Vālmīki is not often quoted by the critics or anthologists. Perhaps there are not many quatrain gems which could be extracted from this continuous but rather rough-hewn narrative. From the anthology point of view, as well as from that of intensive critical analysis, the beauties here are too diffuse and the language loose. The style remains on the borderline between *itihāsa* and *kāvya*; there are plenty of stock expressions which occur frequently, repeated epithets and phrases of the old Epic manner where the rhapsode stitched together the prefabricated materials of oral tradition to carry a story. The vocabulary and phraseology are still very similar to those of Pali descriptive and epic poetry. The story is the essential element, the stream of events, and such a popular story as this remained a source for new *kāvyas*: Ratnaśrījñāna in his only reference (p. 11) to the *Rāmāyaṇa* calls it *itihāsa*, in fact, and the work is often included in the corpus of Tradition. As for the apparent quotation by Patañjali (on III.1.67), it is a line which occurs twice in the *Rāmāyaṇa* (V. XXXII.6 = Bombay Edition VI. CXXVI.2; the Critical Edition of Book VI is not yet available), where it is described as a 'popular song' : "Joy comes to a living man even after a hundred years". The reference here is to Rāma's long sorrows, but if this was a popular song Patañjali need not have gone to the *Rāmāyaṇa* for it.

635. From the point of view of the evolved and perfected *kāvya* style of the medieval period, the *Rāmāyaṇa* is rough and primitive in form and open to aesthetic criticism on grounds of content as well. Nevertheless Bahurūpamiśra (on II 47) mentions it (with Kālidāsa) for the *vaidarbhī* style [238, 242]. To some it was too realistic in its characterisations, not close enough to the ideal of heroism and chivalry they thought it ought to present. Its real subtleties of characterisation might thus be missed and an idealistic structure of consistent magnanimity imposed on it, even imposed on its own interpolated text in some recensions. From an ideal point of view, for which the ethical content predominated, serious faults were found, unfortunate incidents which later *kavis* might try to 'correct' : thus Kuntaka (p.42) objects to a scene as inappropriate characterisation [281] and says it is improved in the *Udāttarāghava* (a play by Māyurāja, +7 ?). For Kuntaka the *Rāmāyaṇa* as a whole is still a model *kāvya*, giving instruction in virtue [283]. He apparently (if the reading is right) says it produces the calmed aesthetic experience, like the *Mahābhārata* (p. 239), again underlining its instructive aspect. Ānandavardhana on the other hand contrasts it with the Great Epic, saying it is compassionate (p. 529). Both of course are discussing the enlarged version which ends tragically, whereas we have argued already that the original (pre-Aśvaghoṣa) epic was primarily heroic, though with many compassionate scenes, ending simply with the triumph of Rāma.

636. Among the few verses quoted by the critics, which may show how Vālmīki appeared to them at his best, is the one we have read above about the Moon in winter. 'His fortune transferred to the Sun...' (III.XV.13). Ānandavardhana quotes this (p. 172) simply for the word 'blind', which we have translated 'dimmed', showing that a word may lose its literal sense altogether: this illustrates the first type of *dhvanikāvya* [250]. Rājaśekhara (*Kāvyamīmāṃsā* p. 71) quotes the same verse in order to compare it with one by another poet where the simile of a mirror is borrowed but used differently, when the steam on it clears again.

637. The anthologist Jalhaṇa quotes (p. 219) two verses from the description of the rainy season in the present Fourth Book, *Kiṣkindhā Kāṇḍa*, Canto XXVII. After Sītā's abduction, Rāma has been directed to Kiṣkindhā, the kingdom of the 'monkeys' who may be able to help him to trace and rescue her. Sugrīva, brother of the monkey king Vālin, has found some ornaments dropped by the captive Sītā, a clue to the direction in which to search, and himself seeks Rāma's aid against his brother, who has oppressed him. Rāma kills Vālin and Sugrīva is consecrated, then Rāma passes the rainy season in a mountain cave, miserable because of the loss of Sītā (Canto XXVI) but encouraged by Lakṣmaṇa. In the following canto Rāma describes the rains to Lakṣmaṇa:

> The mountains are wearing clouds as black antelope skins, with waterfalls as their sacred threads,
> Their caves are filled with the wind as if they are reciting their lessons (XXVII.10).
>
> (i.e. they resemble brahman students repeating the *Veda*)

The sky with thunder in it is roaring as if in pain,
As if struck by the lightning like golden whips (XXVII.11).

('fancy')

638. The description of the rains is followed by one of the autumn, during which Sugrīva is reminded of his promise to help Rāma (this being the campaigning season). Here Rājaśekhara (*Kāvyamīmāṃsā* p. 36) quotes a verse (XXIX.48), but as *itihāsa* in a discussion on sources of subject matter for *kāvya*: Lakṣmaṇa threatens the monkey king with the same fate as his brother unless he keeps the agreement. Rājaśekhara quotes a close but more poetic parallel from Kumāradāsa's epic *Jānakīharaṇa*.

639. Bhavabhūti in his two plays on the Rāma story gives complete or partial quotations of three or four verses from the *Rāmāyaṇa*, his source. In the *Mahāvīracarita* (V. 24) we find the verse spoken to Rāma in the Third Book (LXIII.14) by the dying vulture Jaṭāyus, who had intercepted Rāvaṇa and tried to save Sītā:

Sir ! Her whom you seek in the great forest, as for a herb,
That queen and my life have both been taken by Rāvaṇa.

A little later (V.34a-b) the dramatist works in a line from the Fourth Book (IV.12a-b), where Lakṣmaṇa at the first meeting with the great monkey Hanumant explains that:

A son of Fortune named Danu, who had become a Rākṣasa as the result of a curse,

had told Rāma that Sugrīva could help him. This is just a simple but memorable epic line introducing a character, which Bhavabhūti liked and used in a different context.

640. With Bhavabhūti's *Uttararāmacarita* we come to the apocryphal Seventh Book and with it the mostly apocryphal

First Book. In the Sixth Act (31-2) of the play Rāma's son Kuśa is made to recite to his father two verses said to be from Vālmīki's *Rāmāyaṇa* (!), which as a matter of fact are excluded from the Critical Edition (at I.LXXVI.15-6) though found in some manuscripts of the Northern recension (a point of importance for dating the recensions). Then in the Second Act (5) is quoted what was reputed to have been the first verse composed in the new transformed kind of *anuṣṭubh* metre (i.e. the *vaktra*) [534]:

> O hunter ! May you not attain fulfilment for an eternity of years !
> —Since you have killed one of a pair of curlews when it was deluded by love (I.II.14).

This verse is retained in the Critical Edition, the first four cantos of which constitute an introduction giving an account of the poet, making him an ancient sage contemporary with Rāma himself. They were added perhaps in the +4, showing the reverence in which the epic was then held. Here Vālmīki is inspired with compassion to utter this verse in the new metre by the pathetic sight of a bird shot by a hunter and its bereaved mate. Having thus invented the new metre the poet then proceeds appropriately to compose in it his epic, in which there are many pathetic scenes. We are now, of course, concerned with the tragic *Rāmāyaṇa* as known to Bhavabhūti and Ānandavardhana. The latter too refers (p. 85) to this verse when arguing that the subject matter is the essential thing in *kāvya*: the form (metre) was inspired by the subject. Rājaśekhara (*Kāvyamīmāṃsā* p. 7) also quotes the verse and explains the legend of its origin: Vālmīki was inspired by the Goddess Sarasvatī. As we noted at the beginning of this Chapter, Aśvaghoṣa knew this tradition about Vālmīki in an apparently different form: he was the first to compose in verse *padya* (earlier sages such as Cyavana had used prose, i.e. in the *Brāhmaṇas*). This certainly speaks for the great antiquity the *Rāmāyaṇa* was believed to belong to already in the +1.

641. The theme of the ideal emperor recurs in *kāvya* literature. He shows his ideal character in youth in his relationships with other people, displays his physical strength and enchants the feminine world with his beauty (in the *Rāmāyaṇa*, however, the stories of Rāma's youth are almost entirely late additions). Later he makes immense conquests and rules righteously over an empire happy in peace and prosperity, his virtue repelling even natural disasters. The historicity of Rāma is doubtful: if any reality underlies his empire we must look for it in the Indus civilisation of about – 2000. But the *Rāmāyaṇa* of 'Vālmīki' was composed in the Magadhan Empire, where the question of emperors, as we have already observed of the Mauryan Dynasty, was extremely topical and frequently critical. In *c.* – 410 Śiśunāga, king of Magadha (a Licchavi usurper), conquered Avanti and established the first empire known to have reached from the Eastern to the Western Ocean. A period of great prosperity for Magadha followed her acquisition of the trade route from the Ganges to the West coast ports. Śiśunāga, who thus ruled in the earliest period of *kāvya* and undoubtedly had the means to patronise the arts, is actually recorded by Rājaśekhara (*Kāvyamīmāṃsā* p. 50) among the patrons of *kāvya*, though the record is reduced to the anecdote that he prohibited the utterance of eight harsh phonemes at his court (this can be interpreted to the effect that he preferred Prakrit to Sanskrit and perhaps Āvantī (Pali ?) to Māgadhī). The government of the autocrats who succeeded him varied between the utmost extremities of tyranny (Nanda) and benevolence (Aśoka). The succession was frequently disputed, brothers murdered one another and fought civil wars and there were several changes of dynasty.

642. A variety of political and religious theories of government competed for imperial patronage as the expanding empire met the problems of disciplining the vast and disparate populations of its far flung provinces. The mighty civil service described for us in the *Arthaśāstra* of Kauṭalya, its regulations penetrating into the finest detail of the economic life of the empire, improved communications, a census, state control and ownership of most production and supervision of all distribution, did not bring social stability. With the conversion of Aśoka to Buddhism in – 261 entirely new methods were tried, instituting universal benevolence, including a great expansion of the health service and other public utilities as well as the establishment of a new department of the civil service to publicise a code of ethics, check the excesses of the legal arm and transmit appeals direct to the emperor. Though benevolence succeeded no better than Kauṭalya's repressive discipline in producing political stability, it was effective in promoting the cultural unification of India, which thenceforward developed regardless of political fragmentation. Moreover, ideals of benevolence and justice, akin to Aśoka's though reformulated to suit a variety of secular or religious backgrounds, have since set a standard wherever Indians have ruled.

643. In such reformulation the *Rāmāyaṇa* occupies perhaps the first place, and the *kavis* of India have acted as a kind of ideal cultural administration, interpreting and advocating the ideal for those who would or could apply it despite the political disasters which have periodically desolated their country. From the founding of the Magadhan Empire, *kavis* from all parts of India gathered in the capital, Pāṭaliputra, seeking favour and fame. It was here that *kāvya* seems first to have developed, drawing probably on Magadhan folk song for new rhythms, and it was here that it acquired its main characteristics as the literature of an imperial court and a sophisticated metropolis. Combining indirect flattery with the portrayal of a longed for ideal, in the figure of a legendary past emperor, the *kavi* seeks to please the autocrat and his court with an imperial story. The ideal is magnanimous, impartial except to truth and merit, accessible and responsive to public opinion, terrible to enemies and scoundrels but gracious and affectionate to all good people, particularly to the scholars and *kavis* who share in his work. Infinite tact, however, is requisite in seeking to influence a real autocrat in the direction of the ideal, and the cultivation of such subtlety had no little influence on the technique of *kāvya*, on the development of figurative language, double meanings and the power of poetic implication.

644. It is difficult to decide whether the poet Pāṇini was the same person as the grammarian. The later Indian critics seem convinced that he was (e.g. Rājaśekhara: verse attributed to him by Jalhaṇa, *Sūktimuktāvalī* IV.45; Pāṇini through Rudra's favour created first the grammar and afterwards the *kāvya Jāmbavatījaya*). An obvious objection would be that the poet infringes the rules laid down by the grammarian in the few extant verses attributed to him. In the earliest period of *kāvya*, however, poetic licence could tolerate such deviations from the grammatical norm, so that the argument is not conclusive. It was only many centuries later that the *kavis* found an additional scope for virtuosity in complete submission to the letter of Pāṇini's 4,000 odd rules of grammar. There are chronological difficulties in placing a work as advanced in *kāvya* techniques as the *Jāmbavatījaya*, 'The Winning of Jāmbavatī,' in the – 4, though in the present state of our knowledge the date cannot be definitely excluded. It appears that in this epic the *vaktra* metre of the *Rāmāyaṇa* was dethroned from its position of being almost the exclusive narrative metre (as in the *Rāmāyaṇa*) and the *upajāti* ([585] one of the new fixed metres, used in the *Rāmāyaṇa* occasionally to close a canto) was used alongside it as narrative metre for entire cantos. For his skill in *upajāti* Pāṇini obtained a permanent place in the traditions handed down by the Indian critics (Kṣemendra: *Suvṛttatilaka* III.30): apart from their quotations (rather more than 20 verses), his *kāvya* appears to have been one of the many ancient masterpieces which perished when the main libraries of India were burned by the Turks. From Pāṇini, then, we should probably date the practice, standard afterwards in *kāvya*, of varying the narrative metres of the several cantos of an epic. We may regard this as a further step in the assimilation in technique of epic poetry to lyric, which we have noted already as an essential feature of the rise of *kāvya*.

645. The title *Pātālavijaya*, 'Conquest of the Underworld,' is sometimes given as that of an epic by Pāṇini (see Namisādhu p. 12). As the story may well be the same, it is probable that this was the same epic, which, like several others, had alternative titles. The Jāmbavatī story is well known from other sources (e.g. *Viṣṇu Purāṇa* IV.13): Kṛṣṇa invades the Underworld, and having defeated its (bear) king, Jāmbavant, marries his daughter Jāmbavatī. Some versions do not clearly mention the 'Underworld', but the bear King lived in a great cavern in the forest, in which Kṛṣṇa disappeared for many days fighting him, to the despair of his followers. The occasion of the expedition was the carrying off of a certain gem, the *syamantaka*, by Jāmbavant. Some later epics and dramas retell the story. A bear-king Jāmbavant appears in the *Rāmāyaṇa* among Rāma's allies, and may have been supposed to be the same mythical being.

646. The verses ascribed to Pāṇini may not all be authentic, but those attested by the greatest weight of evidence show a style which, though it has the stamp of fully developed *kāvya* in its compactness and careful placing of words (compared with the *Rāmāyaṇa*), is comparatively simple in construction and straightforward in vocabulary. The following *upajāti* is perhaps the best attested (e.g. Namisādhu p. 12, who points out an infringement of the rules of Sanskrit grammar in it):

> When half the night has very slowly passed
> and the dark clouds of the rainy season thunder,
> Not seeing the Moon's orb, as it were her calf,
> then the Goddess Night lows like a cow in protest.

The poetic licence here is in the form translated 'not seeing'. In the original the two words 'night' are—one might say of course—different; the vocabulary of English being so much poorer than that of Sanskrit—even before the coinings of many centuries of *kāvya* had further multiplied it—we could save the clarity and effect only by the artificial expedient of substituting 'Nox' for 'Night' in the last line. Perhaps from the same context is the following *upajāti* ascribed to Pāṇini in the *Subhāṣitāvali* (1943):

> The cloud, having observed with his lightning eyes
> the face of a woman going to meet her lover in the night,
> Thought: 'Have I poured forth the Moon with the falling showers?'
> and roared with greater distress.

This is discussed by Ruyyaka (*Alaṃkārasarvasva* p. 108) as an example of 'condensed expression' *samāsokti* [211], implying a comparison, without any punning. The *Subhāṣitāvali* (1815) has another *upajāti* ascribed to Pāṇini and related in theme, but we have moved from the rains into autumn :

> Autumn, taking on her pale clouds (breasts) the rainbow,
> its light broken by his tender nails,
> Increased the heat of the Sun,
> whilst placating the dark-spotted Moon.

Here the Sun and the Moon are rivals for Autumn's love, though it is well known that both shine more brightly when autumn clears the air after the rains. The Moon shines more brightly, is 'placated', but this also brings out his dark spot, fancied to be due to his jealousy of the Sun, whose passionate rays (hands, nails) had left scratches on her clouds. The verse is discussed by Abhinavagupta (*Locana* p. 114), Kuntaka (p. 177), Mahiman (p. 361) and Ruyyaka (p. 117), again as 'condensed expression' and as mixed with several other figures: fancy, simile, pun, 'having *rasa*' [215], etc. Then there is this *vaṃśastha* ascribed to Pāṇini in a number of anthologies (*Subhāṣitāvali* 1969, *Saduktikarṇāmṛta* 412, *Sūktimuktāvalī* 72.5, etc.), which might have stood at the end of an *upajāti* canto describing the moonrise or in a *vaṃśastha* canto describing sunset and moonrise:

> The Moon with rising passion seized
> the face of Night whose stars were trembling,
> As her whole garment of darkness slipped off even in the East
> and in her passion she didn't notice it.

This is yet another 'condensed expression', in this case with much punning and also 'having *rasa*' and metaphor, discussed again by Ānandavardhana (p. 109), Kuntaka (p. 175), Mahiman (p. 11) and Ruyyaka (p. 105), as well as the commentator on Bhāmaha (pp. 34-5: Udbhaṭa? —reading *moha* for *rāga*). Thus passion *rāga* means also 'redness', stars *tārakā* means also 'pupils' (of the eye), face *mukha* means also 'beginning', in the East *puras* means 'in front', and so on. Several more verses in *upajāti* and *vaṃśastha* ascribed to Pāṇini in the anthologies are on the same themes of sunset and the Moon (*Subhāṣitāvali* 1898, 1899, 1904, 1968), so that it seems his epic contained noteworthy descriptions of these, as well as night, the rains and autumn, in the manner approved by some of the critics, such as Daṇḍin [407] and Rudraṭa [408].

647. Some verses ascribed to Pāṇini in anthologies are in much more elaborate fixed metres, including *śikhariṇī*, *śārdūlavikrīḍita* and *sragdharā*, hardly to be expected in the period of the *Rāmāyaṇa*. Thus a *śikhariṇī* (*Subhāṣitāvali* 1765, *Sūktimuktāvalī* 61.18, etc., anonymous in Vidyākara 251) describes the clouds looking for the Sun in the rains. A *sragdharā* (Vidyākara 920) describes the Moon and Night again. A *śārdūlavikrīḍita* (*Subhāṣitāvali* 2037, *Sūktimuktāvalī* 65.10, etc., anonymous in Vidyākara 451) describes how the beauties of a young woman confuse the bees. Two gruesomely vivid *sragdharās* describe a cemetery, one with vultures and one with jackals in their own ways gleaning food from the cremations (Vidyākara 1528 and 1529). The Vidyākara verses have all been translated by Ingalls in his version of the anthology.

648. According to various traditional accounts the grammarian Pāṇini lived in the time of the Magadhan emperor Mahāpadma Nanda, consequently in the middle of the—4 (the main ancient source for these legends was perhaps the *Bṛhatkathā*; they appear in some of its later paraphrases, *Kathāsaritsāgara* I.IV.20, etc.; *Mañjuśrīmūlakalpa* LIII.404; Hiuen Tsiang, *Si Yu Ki*, translated by Beal, 114ff.). He was born in NW India, in Gandhāra, and presumably studied at the university in Takṣaśilā, which had long been one of the greatest centres of learning in India. He went, or was invited, to the imperial court at Pāṭaliputra, where he was honoured and settled (see also Rājaśekhara, *Kāvyamīmāṃsā* p. 55). A school of grammarians studied and elaborated his doctrine, and curious legends and anecdotes are told about them. One of the earliest, and a fellow student of Pāṇini under the Vedic teachers Varṣa and Upavarṣa, was named Vararuci (see also *Pariśiṣṭaparvan* VIII and *Mañjuśrīmūlakalpa* LIII. 529-35). He is also called Kātyāyana.

649. Vararuci early became a legendary figure in the traditions of *kāvya* (to the above add Daṇḍin, *Avantisundarī*, 180ff., where Pāṇini is not mentioned). The *Bṛhatkathā* legend (Kaśmīra version [675]) makes him an incarnation of one of Śiva's attendants *gaṇas*, who brings the great novel to Earth and passes it on to a *piśāca* in the Vindhya Forest. His extant grammatical work, a *Vārttika* or 'Supplement' to Pāṇini's grammar, is accepted as authentic. Though he is recorded by ancient authorities to have composed several *kāvyas*, the only *kāvya* ascribed to a Vararuci which seems to be extant is certainly by some much later *kavi*. This is the satirical monologue *Ubhayābhisārikā* [1101], which mentions philosophical concepts of a later period. Patañjali, who wrote the Great Commentary *Mahābhāṣya* to Pāṇini's grammar, in which he takes up all the Supplement of Vararuci or Kātyāyana for further discussion, mentions a *kāvya* by Vararuci without giving any details about it (on Pāṇini IV.3.101). The reference at least guarantees the antiquity of the *kavi* Vararuci,—we have no such ancient witness for the *kavi* Pāṇini—though it does not prove his identity with the grammarian. A verse ascribed to Rājaśekhara (Jalhaṇa: *Sūktimuktāvalī* IV.46) names a *kāvya* by Vararuci as the *Kaṇṭhābharaṇa*, 'Ornament for the Throat': there is a pure conjecture that it was a *citrakāvya*, a display of linguistic virtuosity (see Krishnamachariar p. 87).

650. A verse in an anthology, ascribed to Vararuci, is in one manuscript (Vallabhadeva: *Subhāṣitāvali* 1740, MS in Govt. Or. Ms. Library, Madras) stated to be from his *Cārumatī*, which from its title seems to be either a novel or a biography. A *Cārumatī* is also quoted in the *Śṛṅgāraprakāśa* of Bhoja, Chapter XXVIII (not yet printed: see Krishnamachariar p. 88), but without mentioning the author. Both verses are simple, but melodious through alliteration. There would be no difficulty in placing them earlier than Patañjali, perhaps reflecting the beginning of a trend in *citrakāvya* more fully represented by the *Kaṇṭhābharaṇa*. At the same time their alliteration is rather a poetic figure enhancing the expression than an exercise in *citra*: it may reflect Vararuci's taste in verbal music, elsewhere more elaborately indulged, but it does not exceed the limit of purely poetic expressiveness. The alliteration can be seen from the original Sanskrit:

ālohitam ākalayan kandalam iti kampitaṃ madhukareṇa |
saṃsmarati pathi sa pathiko dayitāṅgulitarjanaṃ lalitam ||

The traveller on his road seeing a reddish *kandala* flower
shaken by a bee
remembers the playful threatening by his beloved's
finger. (metre *āryā*)

kanakakuṇḍalamaṇḍitagaṇḍayā jaghanadeśaniveśitavīṇayā |
amararājapuro varakanyayā tava yaśo vimalaṃ parigīyate ||

Your bright fame is celebrated

before the king of the gods by a beautiful maiden
With a *vīṇā* resting in her lap,
her cheeks adorned with golden earrings. (*drutavilambita*, a fixed metre)

—The second verse, says Bhoja, was spoken to the hero on a journey in the cause of love by two fairies (or centaurs— *kinnara*). At present it seems this is all we know of the *Cārumatī*.

651. About twenty more verses are ascribed to Vararuci in anthologies. The *Subhāṣitāvali* in particular has besides the *āryā* (1740) discussed above sixteen such verses, of which fifteen are in the simple *vaktra* metre and stylistically appear early. Some of them might have been taken from the *Cārumatī*, as incidental verses. Some describe the rains (1719-20, 1733):

The ground shines with Indra's herdsmen [556], as if filled with drops of blood
Dripping from the hearts of those abroad, broken by the arrows of Love. (1719)

Others describe autumn (1804-8):

The Moon's Lady, Night, slender in summer as if with anger,
As if weeping in the rains,—autumn placates her. (1807)

Autumn, by placating the Moon when gloom is within him,
Makes the Sun extremely hot, as if she were Dawn with her reddish lustre. (1804)

Another verse describes moonrise (1955). Some of these verses appear to be variations on some of those ascribed to Pāṇini, discussed above. It seems almost certain that in fact these simpler verses are the more original ones, those ascribed to Pāṇini the later variations. In another verse a lady mocks her unreliable female messenger (sent to her lover):

What's the use of saying much about this ? O messenger, to accomplish my affair
Even your own flesh has been given ! —Not to mention other things. (1434)

A verse ascribed to the 'Vārttikakāra', implying Vararuci [649], in which a lover longs to be united with his lady, might seem to fit these contexts but is in the *hariṇī* metre (e.g. Vidyākara 777). A verse in the *bhujaṃgavijṛmbhita* metre, which has twenty-six syllables in each of its four lines, is surely by the later Vararuci, author of the *Ubhayābhisārikā* [1103], which begins with a verse in this same unusual metre (*Subhāṣitāvali* 1103). Another verse ascribed to Vararuci (*Sūktimuktāvalī* 96.10, Vidyākara 1171 anon.) shows instead alliteration carried much farther than those first quoted above [650]. It describes a cock fight with onomatopaeic words suggesting the noise of the birds. The author of the *Ubhayābhisārikā* shows no fondness for such sound effects.

652. It is uncertain whether the *Cārumatī* was a biography or a novel: the little we know of its content would seem to suggest the latter. On the other hand there is plenty of evidence for the cultivation of the biography in the period of the Magadhan empire [610]. Kauṭalya, who finally eliminated the sons of the usurper Nanda and placed Candragupta Maurya on the throne (–317), mentions biographies in his *Arthaśāstra* (I.5). Vararuci in his grammar mentions biographies (*Vārttikas* to IV.2.60 and IV.3.87). Patañjali explaining these Supplements names three biographies (all of women: *Vāsavadattā*, *Sumanottarā* and *Bhaimarathī*). The *Vāsavadattā* presumably told the very popular story of the princess who became the beloved queen of Udayana, shortly before the extinction of the ancient Paurava Dynasty at Kauśāmbī in the Magadhan empire (-5). Perhaps it was contemporary with its heroine [424] and the source for the numerous later *kāvyas* on her story [1162]. The other two heroines are not now well known. As to Cārumatī, Kṛṣṇa had a daughter Cārumatī by Rukmiṇī. Or, if she was a historical character of the –3, we can suggest Cārumatī, daughter of the Emperor Aśoka, recorded in very late *Vaṃśāvalī* tradition in Nepal. This tradition is so late and apocryphal (intended to connect the Kirāta kings of Nepal with Aśoka and make the latter establish shrines in the Valley) as to carry very little weight, moreover to accept it would make the author of the biography not earlier than the second half of the −3 (which is inconsistent with his being the Vararuci associated with the Nandas in the legends). In spite of the evident popularity of biography in this period, then, we have no examples extant, and indeed no examples available for many centuries to come. This situation should again warn us of our extreme ignorance concerning trends in *kāvya* in ancient times, and of the need to utilise every scrap of information and avoid any generalisation at all which rests on the mere absence of any record (for example, many modern 'historians' regard it as a commonplace that the ancient Indians had no interest in history or biography, whereas careful enquiry shows us that they were vigorously cultivated).

653. There are traditions about a *kavi* Subandhu as a minister of the emperor Bindusāra (−293 to −268) [576]. It appears that Subandhu was imprisoned and then released, and that he afterwards 'captivated the heart of Bindusāra' (Daṇḍin: *Avantisundarī*, introductory verse 6) with his drama on the story of Udayana. There are quotations from this play in the critical literature, where it is called *Vāsavadattā Nāṭyadhārā*, a *nāṭyadhārā* being a particular kind of play apparently obsolete before our present *Nāṭyaśāstra* text was finalised (Abhinavagupta III p. 172) [347]. In connection with -*dhārā* there are also references to either *vāra* or *nṛttavāra* or *nṛttacāra* elsewhere, and, as *dh* may easily be misread as *v* or *c* by scribes unfamiliar with the term, it is likely that all refer to the same *dhāra* or *dhārā* (Bodhāyana: *Bhagavadajjukīya*, prologue; Śāradātanaya p. 241). It appears the *dhāra* was a full length *nāṭaka*, in as many as ten acts, but its special characteristics are not clear. It is also recorded (Śāradātanaya pp. 238ff.) that there was a dramatic theorist named Subandhu, who is supposed to be the same as this *kavi*, that he had an idiosyncratic theory of five kinds of *nāṭaka*, called *pūrṇa*, *praśānta*, *bhāsvara*, *lalita* and *samagra*, and that the *nṛttavāra* play was in fact an example of the last variety [165].

654. From the title we see that the subject of the play was the favourite story of Udayana and Vāsavadattā. The critics who quote from this *Vāsavadattā* do not enlighten us on its nature, except to tell us that it contained an incidental dramatic device which they call *nāṭyāyita* [174]. According to Abhinavagupta this is when a piece of 'unreal' drama is inserted in another drama, like a dream intervening in real life. Thus the characters on the stage appear in the rôle of audience to a play within a play. Amongst the examples of this, Subandhu's play shows Udayana on the stage as a spectator of a play about Vāsavadattā. When the producer (of the play within the play) recites to his audience (Udayana) by way of introduction a verse praising his (Udayana's) good deeds, Udayana intervenes: 'Where are my good deeds?' and weeps, calling on his mother and his ministers to fetch the princess (i.e. Vāsavadattā). —From this we see incidentally that the main play is about the later episode in the Vāsavadattā story, in which for a time Udayana is made to believe she is dead [964]: the inserted play was presumably about the earlier episode of Udayana's elopement with her.—At this point, according to Abhinavagupta, there is another interruption, by Bindusāra. This is difficult to understand without the full text. Either Bindusāra in the audience, presiding over the initial performance (as *sabhāpati*, 'president of the hall', a rôle taken by the highest-ranking person in the audience in the ancient Indian theatre), was supposed to be so moved at this point as to cry out: 'Fortunate is she who is thus lamented by her lover! [*sighs*]', or Subandhu makes Bindusāra appear as a character on the stage, during the prologue. As Abhinavagupta cites the example for the additional complexity of a play within a play within a play, like a dream within a dream, the latter is probably the correct interpretation.

655. Thus the real audience, and originally the real Bindusāra, see the prologue, in which probably the character Bindusāra asks the producer to perform a play about Udayana. Udayana then appears, in despair at the loss of Vāsavadattā. He in turn perhaps (this is not made clear to us) asks to see a play about Vāsavadattā (he may be supposed to see the producer when he enters, and to ask for this consolation, unless we assume he calls in his own producer afterwards), whereupon the incidents given by Abhinavagupta occur.

656. If the play which Abhinavagupta had (*c.* +1000) was authentic, and there is no reason to assume it was not (Vāmana in the +8 quotes the play also, p. 38, and Daṇḍin in the +7, in the *Avantisundarī*, mentions its performance before Bindusāra), we see from this that the Indian drama had reached a high degree of sophistication by the –3, with a technique of prologue akin to, but perhaps not identical with, that later described by the *Nāṭyaśāstra*, and a theory in some respects divergent from that standardised later (Subandhu's types of *nāṭaka*). The fact that the technique and theory of Subandhu were obsolete by the time of the extant *Nāṭyaśāstra* would seem to confirm the great antiquity and probable authenticity of the *Vāsavadattā* from which Abhinavagupta quotes.

657. Vāmana's quotation is of half a *śārdūlavikrīḍita* quatrain, as an example of 'strength' as a quality of meaning [243]:

> Now this son of Candragupta, this youth whose glory
> is like the Moon's,
> Has become king, a support for men of intellect;
> luckily his efforts are satisfied...

Vāmana says that 'a support for men of intellect' hints at Subandhu's own (prospective) ministry (under Bindusāra). We may suppose that if this play was performed before the new king (as we learn from Daṇḍin) this verse, presumably from the prologue, was intended to suggest to him that he should offer a suitable appointment to the author. The use of the *śārdūlavikrīḍita* metre as early as the –3 is somewhat surprising, since it is one of the more advanced fixed metres (having 19 syllables in each line of its quatrain) [584, 587]. It may make the authenticity of the verse appear questionable unless parallels of comparable antiquity can be found [647].

658. Coming back to Patañjali, to see what else he has to tell us about the state of *kāvya* by his time (–2), we find that he adds a little to our knowledge of ancient drama by mentioning three more stories which had been dramatised: Urvaśī (on V.2.95 in the context of 'actor' *naṭa*, which is not quite conclusive), the death of Kaṃsa and the binding of Bali (on III.1.26). The actor on the stage *raṅga* is noted at I.4.29. Urvaśī is the nymph loved by Purūravas in the old Vedic story mentioned in an earlier chapter [510]. Kaṃsa is the wicked uncle of Kṛṣṇa, the usurper and tyrant who tries to murder all his nephews after imprisoning his brother (or father—Tradition varies) [526]. The infant Kṛṣṇa is saved and brought up secretly in the country: on attaining manhood—or rather youth—he reveals himself, challenges Kaṃsa and kills him. Extant plays from the +2 onwards have this story (e.g. Bhāsa [1044]). Bali was the king of the demons, possibly identical with the Vepacitti of the Pali Canon who at least once was overpowered and bound by the gods [589]. Later references to Bali make him king of the demons on the occasion when they were victorious and—as in a Vedic myth [513]—offered to leave the gods as much of the universe as Viṣṇu could cover in three steps [1074]. Already according to the Vedic myth Viṣṇu on this occasion had taken the form of a dwarf to deceive the demons. In Tradition after the three famous steps in which he covered earth, atmosphere and heaven, confining the demons to the Underworld, it was then the dwarf (Vāmana) Viṣṇu who bound Bali (*Vāmana Purāṇa adhyāyas* 50-1 and 62-6). It is not certain that this was the story of the play known to Patañjali, but at any rate it concerned the popular subject of the wars between the gods and the demons, the gods eventually getting the upper hand and the king of the demons being bound. As to the types to which these plays belonged, all may have been 'religious' plays according to our description in an earlier chapter: the Kaṃsa and Bali plays are both likely to have been 'fights' *ḍimas*, the Urvaśī perhaps a 'rape' *īhāmṛga* [1149]. If elaborated into more than four acts, of course, they would according to the *Nāṭyaśāstra* be *nāṭakas*.

659. The quotations of *kāvya* type verses by Patañjali mostly agree in the metres used with the early *kāvya* metres of the later parts of the Pali Canon (for these quotations see Kielhorn, *Indian Antiquary*, XIV, 326ff.). That they are in Sanskrit instead of Pali seems quite secondary to this similarity in style. Thus we have in *pramitākṣarā*, with much alliteration:

> The Earth is proclaimed through you as married.
> (on IV.1.32)

This evidently is a line in praise of a king, lord of the Earth, with *kāvya* figurativeness. The *pramāṇikā* is simply a special form of *anuṣṭubh* (with monotonous cadence-rhythm):

> Drums, conches and flutes sound severally in the assembly. (on II.2.34)

660. Two new metres not found in the Pali Canon occur among these quotations, the *vasantatilaka* (on III.2.26) and the *praharṣiṇī* (on II.2.34). The following line is evidently the last of an *aparavaktra* quatrain (of which we met an example above in the *Jātaka* [583]; it is a fixed metre derived from the 'musical' metres):

...slender one!—The cocks are crowing! (on I.3.48)

The situation implied here is of a clandestine lover realising it is time to part, because the night will soon end, and indirectly telling his beloved so. Whether the verse occurred in a longer *kāvya*—an epic or novel for example—we cannot say: it is equally possible, however, that it was a detached verse in a collection of sensitive lyrics, a forerunner of the Māhārāṣṭrī anthology of verses of this type made by Sātavāhana, to which we were referred by Ānandavardhana in an earlier chapter for examples of that excellent kind of *kāvya* in which the implied meaning predominates over the literal meaning and may set it aside entirely. This ancient verse in fact illustrates precisely such *dhvani*, carrying implied rather than literal meaning: 'It is time to go!' (not 'The cocks are crowing!').

661. Here is another (complete) quatrain from Patañjali (in *vaktra*):

When elders (*guru*=parents and teachers) strike,
their hands are moist with ambrosia, not poison:
faults depend on caresses, good qualities on blows!
(on VIII.1.8)

662. Before concluding this chapter we should perhaps note two further obscure figures in the traditions of *kāvya*. According to Rājaśekhara (*Kāvyamīmāṃsā* p. 55) a king Vāsudeva was one of the famous patrons of the art, in fact the first of a series of four who are otherwise in chronological order (the second is 'Sātavāhana'). Nothing else seems to have come down to us about him. In this period he may be identified as Vāsudeva Kāṇva of Magadha (*c.* –75 to –66), but the tradition may equally have stemmed from Vāsudeva Kuṣāṇa (probably +152 to 176). Even more obscure is a king Kuvinda of Śūrasena (ibid. p. 50), mentioned with Śiśunāga [641], who prohibited harsh conjunctions of sounds in his palace.

CHAPTER XIV

THE NOVEL *c.* −100 : GUṆĀḌHYA

663. As the imperial power of Magadha weakened, the temporary cultural hegemony of Pāṭaliputra was challenged successfully by other cities. Though the Māgadhī language lost its prestige, and its literature almost vanished (so that we had to study it above through Pali versions made in the reviving ancient cities of Kauśāmbī and/or Ujjayinī), the forms of *kāvya* which we have found established in the Empire, and which seem to have originated from Māgadhī lyric poetry, continued to be cultivated vigorously in a variety of languages in the different provinces formerly under Magadhan rule. The cultural unification of India endured and the free republic of letters flourished on the ruins of political centralisation. The imperial ideal, indeed, lived on in the aspiration of rulers, encouraged—and also moralised into impracticable perfection—by some of the *kavis*. The ideal universal empire, which with its perfect justice would have left the *kavis* in absolute freedom and security, was sincerely praised by poets, dramatists and novelists who in reality enjoyed the freedom of choosing a congenial home among a number of separate and politically independent centres of *kāvya*, and the security of being able to change it for another. The gradually increasing popularity of Sanskrit eventually eliminated the barriers of dialect and consolidated a pan-Indian republic of civilisation and culture, in defiance of the spread of monarchical and feudal institutions in its ever fragmenting political parts.

664. The use of Sanskrit had disadvantages as well as advantages, and evidently in any given locality the local vernacular could reach more people. If Sanskrit made possible diffusion over all India, and indefinite endurance in time, the Prakrits (as eventually the modern languages) made a greater immediate impact. The traditions embodied in Pali literature were continued in a very similar, perhaps originally identical, dialect in the region of the 'Road to the South' from Avanti (Ujjayinī) to the rising city of Pratiṣṭhāna on the Godāvarī. In the −1, and perhaps as much as a century earlier, this city was the capital of the Āndhra or Sātavāhana Empire. The Sātavāhanas subverted the Southern part of the Magadhan Empire, most probably at the time of the revolt of Puṣyamitra Śuṅga (−180), and in −30 uprooted the last effective Magadhan dynasty in a successful invasion of Magadha itself.

665. In Pratiṣṭhāna was written that wonderful novel the *Bṛhatkathā*, on which we have touched in discussing the characteristics of the *kāvya* novel [444-5]. It was apparently the first great novel produced by a *kavi*, and probably the greatest Indian novel. We shall probably be right in stressing its newness, though we have no earlier novels available with which to contrast it. There are of course plenty of short stories available, which may be subsumed under the same general form of *kāvya*, i.e. *kathā*. Some of the features of these stories were taken up in this giant fiction, and some earlier *kathās* (such as Vararuci's, if it was a *kathā*) are likely to have been of a fair length, with a succession of episodes. It was, however, very likely the *Bṛhatkathā* which for the first time boldly appropriated in a prose fiction the entire scale and scope of the epic : the grand and leisurely manner, the rich detail, the whole range of aspirations and emotions and *rasas*, but with more realism, whilst mingled among its episodes were more marvels as well. Here then was a modern Great Epic, to suit an age when commerce and art and science had replaced heroism; a Great Story of success such as all men dreamed of, to supersede the *Rāmāyaṇa* with its too high-minded hero and too unworldly idealism.

666. The original Paiśācī text of the *Bṛhatkathā* seems not to have been preserved, nor have we any other Paiśācī literature now (unless we include Pali as a Paiśācī dialect), though probably literature once flourished in this ancient language. Thus Ratnaśrījñāna in the +10 knows another Paiśācī novel, a *Ratnaprabhā* (p. 26). The outmoded dialect was no doubt largely responsible for this neglect and replacement by versions in other, later, dialects or in Sanskrit. The novel as a form of art seems also to have lost its popularity during the later middle ages, when realism, fiction and humanism were submerged in a flood of idealism, romanticism and faith. The Great Epic and the *Rāmāyaṇa* then regained their ascendancy, reinterpreted as Vaiṣṇava scriptures.

667. Our appreciation of Guṇāḍhya's novel therefore

depends on the study of several paraphrases, none of them as faithful as we would wish, in Prakrit, Sanskrit and Tamil. Among these the Sanskrit *Saṃgraha* by Budhasvāmin seems most adequately to preserve the style of the original, despite versification, but unfortunately, as we have it, it covers not more than half the original *Bṛhatkathā*. The Prakrit abridgement incorporated into the *Vasudevahiṇḍi* by Saṃghadāsa (+5? [1448]) is probably the earliest extant version. It would appear to be more faithful to the original story, in outline and in the spirit of its episodes, than any other version except Budhasvāmin's, but the narrative is fragmented and forced into a new frame. It is difficult to use because the names of the characters have been changed. It confirms that the *Saṃgraha* is true to the spirit of the original. The Tamil *Perungadai* by Kongu-Vēḻir is again incomplete as known to be preserved, containing perhaps one-eighth of the narrative.

668. It is clear that, like the *Rāmāyaṇa*, the *Bṛhatkathā* was subjected to considerable additions over several centuries. Its popularity and fame as the supreme fiction made it a central, as it were 'canonical', work round which other successful fictions collected. Some of these, whether imitations of episodes, which could fairly easily be lodged in the main text, or even quite independent narratives, were then actually incorporated within the great classic in some of its recensions. Since one of the most basic forms of presentation of a narrative in ancient Indian literature is to have one person telling a story to another, as the Great Epic was recited before kings, the incident of the telling of a story could always be made to occur as an event within another story. Thus in what is often called the Kaśmīra recension, as known to its paraphrasers Kṣemendra and Somadeva in the +11, besides unoriginal episodes added to the main narrative but dealing with the original heroes, some other quite unrelated fictions such as the *Pañcatantra* [1249] had been incorporated. The statement of Somadeva that he 'translated' the work indicates that these additions to the text had been made in the Paiśācī language of the original. To what extent the recensions current elsewhere had been similarly interpolated can hardly be investigated, since practically nothing seems to be available from them. However, Bhoja in the +11, in Avanti itself, used a recension which resembled that of Kaśmīra in having certain probably unoriginal features. Raghavan has collected the references (*Bhoja's Śṛṅgāraprakāśa*, 839ff.) : they include the legend of Guṇāḍhya, perhaps the story of Kaliṅgasenā [703] and the story of Karpūrikā, besides some presumably original parts of the *Bṛhatkathā* such as the history of Avanti after the death of Pradyota. It is quite possible that Bhoja's copies (Raghavan thinks he had a Paiśācī text and a Sanskrit paraphrase) belonged to the same recension as the Kaśmīra *Bṛhatkathā*, which in that case would be simply a Western recension.

669. The date of Guṇāḍhya is uncertain. He is recorded to have been patronised, reluctantly, by a Sātavāhana emperor in Pratiṣṭhāna, but we do not know which one. On purely linguistic grounds, as noted in Chapter I, we would wish to place a work in the archaic Paiśācī dialect at the beginning of the dynasty and close in time to Pali canonical literature. Towards the end of the Sātavāhana dynasty, in the +2, we see the rise within the Empire of a new dialect for *kāvya*, Māhārāṣṭrī, much later in its phonology than Paiśācī. The known inscriptions of the dynasty on the other hand are in an archaic dialect much closer to Paiśācī, Pali and the inscriptions of Aśoka, though far from identical with any of these. This was presumably a long standardised language of administration, unchanged since the establishment of the Sātavāhanas. The date of their establishment, however, is itself obscure. Working back from the emperors known from inscriptions to have ruled in the +2, the available chronologies (The *Matsya* and *Vāyu Purāṇas* seem the best) would carry us far beyond the conquest of Magadha in −30, although Tradition attributes this conquest to the first Sātavāhana. Probably this is wrong, it being mistakenly assumed that the dynasties of Magadha and Pratiṣṭhāna should be placed end to end without overlap. On the other hand the legend of Guṇāḍhya himself, which possibly formed part of the original work, appears to make 'Sātavāhana' contemporary with Mahāpadma Nanda (−4), unless we assume superhuman longevity for the *piśāca* who learned the story from Vararuci and later taught it to Guṇāḍhya. The versions of the length of the Sātavāhana dynasty conflict, particularly in its early reigns: the numerals have not always been accurately preserved, the number of rulers varies and we suspect some tampering with the list in attempts to clarify ancient confusions. A shorter version would place the beginning of the dynasty *c.* – 100, longer ones *c.* – 200 or even earlier—the latter implying that this part of the Magadhan empire was subverted soon after Aśoka's reign. The time of the subversion of the Mauryas by Puṣyamitra (– 180) seems more likely. One might be inclined to favour the shortest version, if only on the ground that dynasties in Tradition seem more liable to elongation than shortening, but the question will remain open until more archaeological evidence is collected.

670. Guṇāḍhya's Paiśācī being more archaic than the administrative language of the dynasty, we may assume that it was a literary vernacular of the Dakṣiṇāpatha region, the border land between Aryan and Dravidian India, before the establishment of the Sātavāhanas. The tradition that Guṇāḍhya's patron at first rejected the novel because he did not like the language possibly reflects this difference of dialects. In any case it seems we should look for this patron among the earliest rulers of the dynasty, such as Śātakarṇi I (*c.* – 139 to – 129 ?). Not to labour the point further, we may tentatively place Guṇāḍhya in the – 2, or at the latest in the – 1, whilst his legend appears to place him as early as the – 4 or at an unspecified date somewhat later than that.

671. The connection of the *Bṛhatkathā* with Pali literature is much more than linguistic. Its fictitious story is placed in the - 5 and connected with the history of that century. The famous Paurava Dynasty of Tradition gradually declined in its new capital at Kauśāmbī, where it was reduced to ruling the small countries of Vatsa and Cedi. The last king who successfully upheld the traditions of his family was Udayana, familiar in Pali literature, but his weapons were diplomacy and marriage alliances rather than military power and his successes were purely defensive. Soon after his reign his kingdom was swallowed up in the Magadhan Empire. Countering the real rise of Magadha with his fiction, Guṇāḍhya gave Udayana an imaginary son, Naravāhanadatta, endowed with all the virtues of his ancestors and rising to universal empire far wider in scope than that of Magadha. Thus perhaps some legitimist party, wishing for the restoration of the Pauravas and the extinction of upstart Magadha, imagined a miraculous renewal of the true Indian kingship. There is no nostalgia in Guṇāḍhya, however: he looks forward, not back, and summons new sciences to aid his hero. He is interested in reality, in the details of social and economic life, and particularly in technology. In some of his episodes, such as trading adventures to distant countries in South East Asia, we meet the same background as in similar Pali stories, especially in the *Jātaka* and the *Niddesa* [702]. In India itself we find the same terrain, divided into numerous independent states, as is familiar to us in the Pali stories of the time of the Buddha.

672. A passage in the *Saṃgraha* (XXI.13ff.), which is probably from the original, tells us that there are five kinds of story *kathā*, dealing with virtue *dharma*, wealth *artha*, happiness *sukha*, Nirvāṇa and health *cikitsā*. One might make a similar classification of Pali stories: 'virtue' is here defined in a very Buddhistic manner as 'helping beings by one's actions' and could be abundantly illustrated from the *Jātaka*; 'wealth' is dependent on winning friends even among those who were previously enemies and could also be illustrated from there; 'happiness' is the thoroughly Buddhistic being contented with little and avoiding anger; Nirvāṇa requires no comment and 'health', described as discrimination in food and avoiding crooked doctors, may call to mind the popular story of Jīvaka in the Buddhist Canon (Pali *Vinaya* I 268ff.), a good doctor of genius and humanity who supports the Buddhist monks.

673. Many parallels of theme and incident could be adduced between the Pali and Guṇāḍhya, but enough has been said to indicate a common tradition. To clinch the matter we can point to the common locus of this developing literary tradition. The *Bṛhatkathā* is set principally in Kauśāmbī and the states of the Ganges valley, whilst Guṇāḍhya according to the Kaśmīra tradition (Ksemendra, Somadeva) was born in Pratiṣṭhāna on the 'Road to the South' and lived there in the Sātavāhana capital. Alternatively he was born in Mathurā (Śūrasena) and then lived in Ujjayinī, the starting point of the Road lying on the direct route to Kauśāmbī, according to the *Nepālamāhātmya* (XXVII. 49, 52). His patron in the latter is called 'Madana', not Sātavāhana, but nevertheless has a Queen Līlāvatī, known from other sources as queen of a Sātavāhana.

This Nepāla legend appears less reliable than those in the paraphrases of the *Bṛhatkathā* itself. The Pali Canon equally records events in the Ganges states, but the Sthaviravāda school of Buddhists who preserved it had their original centres in Kauśāmbī and Ujjayinī—hence they used a Western language—and early spread via the Road to the South into South India. Pratiṣṭhāna is mentioned in one of their later canonical texts (*Suttanipāta* 976ff.—v.1011), which also describes the route from there via Ujjayinī to Kauśāmbī and the Ganges cities. The school was established in Ceylon in the −3 by monks from Ujjayinī who probably took the Road to the South, although the tradition is that they miraculously flew there. Finally Udayana, king of Vatsa in the time of the Buddha, is a popular figure in Sthaviravāda tradition (see especially *Dhammapadaṭṭhakathā* I 161-231). The main tradition of Indian story telling, then, which at this point creates the novel, spread from the Ganges region to Western India and South to the Godāvarī, using the Pali and Paiśācī languages, which may have been the vernaculars of Ujjayinī and Pratiṣṭhāna respectively. According to other Buddhist schools the Sthaviravāda Canon was in Paiśācī, i.e. Pali is in fact Paiśācī [13]: according to the grammarians there were a number of dialects within 'Paiśācī' and we may suppose Pali was one of them.

674. The *Bṛhatkathā* possibly opened with an autobiographical narrative of Guṇāḍhya, a form of opening sometimes used by later novelists. The object is to explain how the *kavi* came to write his story: the source of his inspiration or information (usually the latter since the stories are presented as truth). The available versions of Guṇāḍhya's autobiography vary widely and the *Saṃgraha* and *Perungadai* lack it altogether. This last circumstance does not prove that it was a later addition, since it may originally have stood at the end of the work, lost in both versions, but it certainly casts doubt on the authenticity of the autobiography.

675. The available versions agree that Guṇāḍhya attributed the original story to Śiva (but see below on this being certainly an interpolation), who entertained his consort Pārvatī with the adventures of Naravāhanadatta, one of the universal emperors (or of seven such emperors: seven stories including Naravāhanadatta's). The narrative was overheard by an attendant, who told it to a maid. When the truth of the eavesdropping came out, Śiva condemned the attendant to suffer birth as a human being. We are told either (Nepāla version) that this attendant became Guṇāḍhya, charged with publishing the story on Earth, or (Kaśmīra version) that he became Vararuci (!) and that his brother, who interceded for him, was condemned to become Guṇāḍhya. The latter version is made to account for the use of the Paiśācī language, which puzzled later critics: Vararuci had to be born in Kauśāmbī and in due course to proceed south into the Vindhya mountains, therethe would meet a *piśāca* (which later at least meant a 'goblin' or 'fairy' as well as a speaker of Paiśācī), would remember the narrative and tell it to him (Vararuci would then be freed from the curse). Guṇāḍhya must then learn the narrative from the *piśāca* in the Vindhya and write it down. In the event, we are told, he had to retain it in Paiśācī because, as a result of losing a wager, he was bound to abstain from using 'Sanskrit, Prakrit and the *deśa* (local dialect) language': he had in fact learned the language of the *piśācas* in order to regain the power of speech. This version at least looks like a later anecdote: that the novel should have been written in a 'fairy' or 'goblin' language seems absurd, but when Paiśācī was obsolete, and the inhabitants of Pratiṣṭhāna spoke Māhārāṣṭrī and eventually Marhaṭṭa (early Marāṭhī, the *deśa* language), someone may thus have accounted for the peculiarity.

676. On account of our doubts about this supposed autobiography we need not dwell on it further. We must, however, note that the connection with Śiva at least seems apocryphal: as Lacôte points out (*Essai*, 213f.), where the Kaśmīra paraphrases have Śiva, the *Saṃgraha* in corresponding places has Kuvera, the God of Wealth. This is very appropriate for a 'bourgeois' epic, the very name of whose hero means 'Given by Kuvera', and we must reject the Kaśmīra tradition here as an adaptation by a Śaiva writer. At the same time it must be noted that a Śaiva version was known already to Bāṇa in the +7 (*Harṣacarita*, introductory verse 18: Pārvatī enjoys the novel as in this legend of Guṇāḍhya).

677. The text continued, or more probably opened, with the history of Avanti from the death of king Pradyota (*c.* −480: one of Udayana's fathers-in-law—the father of Vāsavadattā).

This leads from history into fiction when one of Pradyota's successors is abducted by a 'wizard' *vidyādhara*. The emperor of the wizards, Naravāhanadatta, intervenes to give judgment in the case and to release the king. Naravāhanadatta then relates the story of how he became emperor. This introductory narrative may well be the original beginning of the whole novel: it accounts sufficiently for the story becoming known on Earth if the king of Avanti be supposed to have handed it down so that eventually Guṇāḍhya learned it, and we recall once more the affinity of the languages, Āvantī with Pali-Paiśācī. The main story being thus introduced, it is narrated in the first person by Naravāhanadatta.

678. The son of King Udayana of Vatsa, Naravāhanadatta ('Given by Kuvera') was brought up with four sons of hereditary ministers, of his own age. Their youthful characters and exploits are brilliantly described, and their wild adventures bring them by chance into contact with an unfortunate wizard. They are able to help him, and in consequence Naravāhanadatta gains a superhuman friend and will ultimately be able to learn the 'sciences' *vidyās* of the wizards, giving him superhuman powers. Having thus intervened in the affairs of the wizards Naravāhanadatta becomes gradually more involved. The decisive event is that he crosses in love a powerful wizard prince, Mānasavega, marrying a (human) heroine, Madanamañcukā, born a geisha, desired by both of them. Mānasavega then abducts Madanamañcukā. The wizard's sister Vegavatī, however, sympathises with the abducted girl and takes a message from her, then assumes her form and is 'found'. Naravāhanadatta at once wins the love of Vegavatī and consequently her aid against her brother, after discovering who she really is. Before he can develop a plan to recover his wife, Naravāhanadatta is himself carried off by Mānasavega. Vegavatī intervenes as her brother flies off with his victim, and Naravāhanadatta is dropped as they fight. Through Vegavatī's 'science' he floats down to earth unharmed, and lands in a forest not far from the city of Campā on the lower Ganges.

679. The son of the amorous Udayana surpassed even his father in the conquests of love: it is love which is the aim of all his efforts, politics and war being purely incidental. Though his object is to recover Madanamañcukā, Naravāhanadatta is easily distracted from this preoccupation by his encounters with a series of beautiful girls who fall in love with him, human or divine or mixed. From his arrival in Campā a series of incidental adventures begins as he faces these distractions, though from time to time he remembers Madanamañcukā, his greatest love, and renews his efforts to get home and to organise an attempt to recover her. At the same time his incidental affairs are really necessary to his ultimate success, for he marries all his mistresses and thereby (like his father) gains powerful allies, some of them among superhuman beings (such as the Siddhas or Genii), and especially *vidyādharī* wives endowed with the 'sciences' and bringing him allies in the realms of the wizards themselves. Altogether he acquires twenty six wives, the queens who eventually adorn his cloud-borne court.

680. Naravāhanadatta's handsome appearance, charm of character and manifold skills win him friends as well as mistresses everywhere, and usually the protection of kings. As far as possible he maintains his incognito on his long wanderings, posing as a wandering brahman. Of course Vegavatī has no difficulty—with her sciences of flight and invisibility—in discovering his residence in Campā; but finding him already in love with Gandharvadattā, a beautiful semi-divine girl but the adopted daughter of a merchant, whom in due course he wins in a lute *vīṇā* contest, she retires hurt, and for a time leaves him to his fate. In the music competition we are incidentally reminded of Naravāhanadatta's ancestry and the partly divine origin of the Paurava, or rather Pāṇḍava, dynasty. The sons of Pāṇḍu were supposed in reality to have been the sons of gods, and Arjuna, through whose grandson Parīkṣit the dynasty continued, was the son of Indra. He learned from his father to tune his *vīṇā* to the *gagrāma* gamut used only by the gods, and this knowledge was handed down to his descendants. The object of the contest in Campā is simply to accompany Gandharvadattā successfully in her singing, but as she is of semi-divine origin she uses the *gagrāma* gamut and baffles all but Naravāhanadatta. The explanation of the girl's origin brings in as a subsidiary narrative the extraordinary story of the travels of her adoptive father Sānudāsa.

681. After his marriage with Gandharvadattā, Naravāhanadatta lives for some time in great luxury, but then falls in love with an outcaste *caṇḍāla* girl. She turns out to be Ajinavatī, a Siddha girl, in disguise, and these Siddhas, inhabitants of a mythical Eastern region, are enemies of the wizards of the Southern Wizard kingdom (in the Himālaya) where Mānasavega lives. The wizard king, Gaurīmuṇḍa, has schemes afoot against Naravāhanadatta, but the latter is protected by the Siddhas into whose alliance he enters by marrying Ajinavatī. He is then conveyed by air to her mountain home. A brother of Gaurīmuṇḍa suddenly appears and abducts Ajinavatī from a park: the Siddhas fly off to fight and Naravāhanadatta is left alone. He wanders through the mountains, seeking his way back to the world of men.

682. Meanwhile his boyhood friends, the ministers' sons, lead an expedition towards Campā to find him. This is broken up by an attack of barbarian tribes from the Vindhya mountains and the friends are scattered. As he leaves the mountains Naravāhanadatta meets one of them by chance, and together they reach Vārāṇasī (Banāras). There Naravāhanadatta finds himself two more wives, one of them a merchant's daughter and the other Bhagīrathayaśas, the daughter of Brahmadatta, the king of the Kāśi Kingdom of which Vārāṇasī is the capital.

683. This is as far as the *Saṅgraha* takes us, and a sufficient indication of the way in which the story develops, skilfully combining amorous adventures with the furthering of the main plot of the struggle with Mānasavega. Among the incidents which follow we may mention that Naravāhanadatta is again abducted, but this time by a *vidyādharī* lady, Lalitalocanā, who has fallen in love with him and is determined to make him her own. She takes him by air to the Malaya mountains in South India and has no difficulty in marrying him, but she is not able to monopolise his affections. He leaves her for a time on the mountains but somehow returns with her to Kauśāmbī (the details here seem to be lost).

684. From time to time Naravāhanadatta recovers sufficiently from his series of infatuations to think again of Madanamañcukā. Yet he makes little effort for a long time: he knows her whereabouts from Vegavatī but apparently has no idea how to rescue her. Eventually a *vidyādharī*, Prabhāvatī, from compassion for her carries him off from his other wives and takes him secretly to Mānasavega's palace, though quietly marrying him herself on the way. Disguised as Prabhāvatī, he is then able to visit Madanamañcukā by stealth in her prison in the palace, but he is in the end caught and fettered. Fortunately his enemy is obliged to submit his complaints against Naravāhanadatta to due legal process in a *vidyādhara* court. Naravāhanadatta of course defends his action of visiting his own wife, and succeeds in establishing his right to a fair and equal legal contest with his fetters removed. After this Prabhāvatī uses her superhuman science to bamboozle the court and rescue him.

685. Having at length regained Kauśāmbī, our hero at last makes serious preparations for a military invasion of the realms of the wizards to settle accounts with his enemies. With his by now numerous allies, especially the superhuman ones, including some of the wizards themselves, open warfare and even an attack on regions inaccessible to ordinary human beings seem practicable. The Southern Wizard kingdom, ruled by Gaurīmuṇḍa, is located between the Himālaya and Mount Kailāsa (the summit of the latter being the abode of Śiva, in the Kaśmīra recension, but also traditionally of Kuvera, who presumably was mentioned here in the original text of Guṇāḍhya) —a region which it was believed no mortal could enter, owing to the barrier of mountains and snow and the interdiction of the gods who lived there. We may note here that there is also a Northern *vidyādhara* kingdom between Kailāsa and Meru (the North Pole, also believed to be a high mountain). The two Wizard kingdoms were in Gaurīmuṇḍa's time completely isolated from one another by Śiva's (or rather Kuvera's) presence on Kailāsa, which would not brook overflights even by *vidyādharas*.

686. Naravāhanadatta's first invasion is unsuccessful, his troops being scattered by the powers of the wizards. After seeking divine aid he then finds time to marry Sulocanā, daughter of the first wizard he had met and helped. In a second invasion of the Southern Wizard kingdom, more carefully planned, he kills both Gaurīmuṇḍa and Mānasavega in battle. Having married five more wizard maidens, who had been secretly pining for him, and taken possession of Gaurīmuṇḍa's kingdom, as well as freeing Madanamañcukā, his aim would seem to be accomplished, but Naravāhanadatta has yet to fulfil his destiny of becoming a universal emperor. To do this he must subjugate the Northern Wizard kingdom by some means, but the final attainment of the imperial power depends primarily on proving his predestined claim by obtaining the seven imperial emblems ('gems') which only a universal emperor can possess. The first of these he obtains from a place in the Southern kingdom, to which only a predestined emperor can climb, the rest from a cave in the Malaya Mountains in South India, where they are guarded by the sage Vāmadeva (they have been preserved in these places since the time of the last universal emperor). He learns how to pass Kailāsa, through a tunnel under it which is strictly guarded, especially by Pārvatī (Kaśmīra version, originally Kuvera's consort Bhuñjatī or Buddhi ?), but may be traversed by one possessing the seven gems and by his wives and messengers. In due course he sallies forth to encounter Mandaradeva, king of the Northern Wizards, overpowers him and marries his sister and her four best friends.

687. Naravāhanadatta, who has thus tasted victory in war and is inclined, contrary to his former way of life, to further martial exploits, is dissuaded from the only possible military conquest which seems still to remain: Meru, the home of the ancient Vedic gods. The North Pole, it appears, is ever beyond the reach of even a universal ruler of this world and sacred to the true gods of the other world. Naravāhanadatta is told the northward march had been attempted by Ṛṣabha, a previous universal emperor, but that the latter had met his death at the hands of Indra, king of the gods.

688. The story then concludes with the imperial consecration of Naravāhanadatta, blessed by Śiva and Pārvatī (or originally Kuvera), and universal rejoicing.

689. This great novel set a standard aimed at by almost all subsequent *kāvya* fiction. Though their views of life vary, and consequently the subjects of their interest, later novelists such as Bāṇa, Daṇḍin and Dhanapāla seem to have taken Guṇāḍhya as their model. Like him they blend realistic narrative and character study, in varying proportions, with incursions into a fanciful semi-divine world on the periphery of the ordinary human world, which enlarges the aspirations of their heroes, or rather materialises their dreams: there their true qualities are automatically given recognition, they can find means to rectify the evils of human society and the calamities of worldly existence, and of course they find partners of superhuman beauty and charm of character. Only the *nidarśanas* (and presumably *matallikās*) among the *kathā* forms exclude the superhuman altogether and develop purely the realistic side of the art of fiction, as do the comedies and satirical monologues. On the other hand the type of play called 'fiction' *prakaraṇa* sometimes admits wizards and the like in an incidental and subordinate rôle, although its main action is always strictly of the human world [1000].

690. Whilst recognising the important place of the superhuman in Guṇāḍhya's novel, and the fact that the objective of the story belongs to this superworld, the main impression left by reading the most faithful version (the *Saṃgraha*, which of course confines us to the first half) is of realism. This realism appears in the characterisation, in the somewhat technical outlook (an interest in the possibilities of science and technology) and in the scenes of worldly deceit, robbery and intrigue, such as the youthful dissipation and ruin of Sānudāsa (XVIII. 4—177). It is possible to regard the story of wizards, with its marvellous *adbhuta rasa* (noted by Daṇḍin: *Kāvyalakṣaṇa* I. 38), as a popularising framework for the serious business of the novelist. Such a distinction between frame and content, however, overlooks an important link between them. It is surely Guṇāḍhya's interest in technology and the wonders of science, for example in the possibility of flying machines, a prominent theme in his novel, which has led him from the world of the probable into a possible and even fantastic world of a kind which may be paralleled in more recent exercises in 'science fiction'. The possibility of flight is transformed into the most important of the 'sciences' of the wizards; those who possess it are located in an inaccessible part of the earth, from which they can irrupt by air into the world of men and—if not divided amongst themselves and without human allies—at times exercise empire over mankind. It should not be overlooked that there are a number of scenes where men, especially artisans, discuss the supposed actual technicalities of construction of flying machines and sometimes succeed in building them: it seems likely enough that Guṇāḍhya believed they were technically feasible without benefit of 'magic'. The modern reader, however, may prefer the more probable adventures of the young hero and his friends and be more interested in such scenes as those describing the life of a wealthy private citizen *nāgaraka* and his circle *goṣṭhī*, here as perhaps nowhere else recorded with vivid and convincing detail.

691. To convey an impression of the probable manner of Guṇāḍhya we may translate some extracts from the *Saṃgraha*. First from the youthful adventures of Naravāhanadatta with his friends (X.1ff., after they have saved the wizard Amitagati; Naravāhanadatta as usual is narrating the story in the first person):

> Then I ate some excellent food produced there by Rumaṇvant, who had organised the excursion *yātrā*, and set out to continue the excursion. I mounted a comfortable chariot yoked with the best oxen, like the Sea God mounting a celestial palace yoked with Moon-white geese. Gomukha took the sunshade which was like the orb of the full Moon, Marubhūtika the fly whisk with its handle of polished gold. Tapantaka, stationed at the front of the chariot, took the reins; Hariśikha was at my side with a ready strung bow in his hand. The remainder of our army, having eaten succulent food, bathed and drunk, went slowly along on all sides of the chariot.
>
> Whilst all this was happening, Marubhūtika, moving the fly whisk slightly, saw Hariśikha and said to him: 'The Prince through engaging in the evil sport of hunting has saved the life of a living being and acquired great virtue !' The other replied: 'What is marvellous in that ? You have spoken like this because you have not attended on good people and think that the exertion and exercise are the main thing. As between land, a friend and gold, it is a friend who surpasses the other two, because through his support one can obtain those. Therefore he has acquired a friend.'
>
> (10) While those two were thus conversing I said to Gomukha: 'Tell me which is the most important as between virtue and other things.' He replied: 'Since

virtue, friends and wealth are employed for the sake of pleasure, pleasure is the most important. Pleasure, in essence, is desire and happiness. Thus when you, my master, saw a footprint on the sandbank, first you had a desire to see who made it there. As, O Prince, you saw him and thus attained happiness, it was not a friend, nor virtue, nor wealth, which was gained, but pleasure. Now there is another and great pleasure which has not come within your experience! You are a wooden doll excluded from the company of those who enjoy all pleasures! Those who know the science of pleasure have pointed out four kinds of men: superior, intermediate, inferior and the fourth kind are nothing at all. Among these I, Gomukha, am superior. You, Prince, are intermediate. I will mention the inferior later, but you others are nothing at all!'

Angry, Marubhūtika then derided him: 'Ah! You have become a *nāgaraka* (i.e. educated, well bred, cultured [27], here spoken sarcastically of course) among us followers! Aren't you a young ox? Truly you are Bull Face (Gomukha)! Who indeed with a human face would utter this filth, that among these Gomukha is superior, the Prince intermediate? Who would describe himself in this manner as surpassing his master?' (20) Gomukha replied: 'You are invincibly stupid, you comprehend nothing at all, for it is not just by being the master that one is a superior exponent of pleasure! He who is loved and loves is the most excellent, like me. He who is loved but is not in love himself is intermediate, like the Prince. He who loves a woman who does not love him is considered inferior. Those who are neither loved nor loving are said to be nothing at all. Know this as the definition of those who are lovers, but you who lack these characteristics are nothing at all!'

This discussion leads to Gomukha revealing his hitherto secret visits to the geishas' quarter of Kauśāmbī and his discovery that Madanamañcukā loves Naravāhanadatta.

692. In Campā Naravāhanadatta goes with a party of sixty four *nāgarakas* to the magnificent house of the wealthy merchant-banker Sānudāsa, where the *vīṇā* contest is to be held. The party constitute a 'circle' *goṣṭhī* and this episode illustrates the activities of such a group [28] (*Saṃgraha* XVII):

> (60) Then in the first courtyard I saw sixty four seats which had been arranged, covered with large woollen blankets (another was brought afterwards because Naravāhanadatta made sixty five)... (68) Then a hundred and thirty geishas went out from the house, like demon girls from the great demon city. One of them, who had taken a beautiful vase, slanted the water for each (guest), one washed the feet of each. (When their feet were washed the guests entered the house)... (79) Then I entered a spacious hall with paving clear as the water of the (dark) Yamunā when unrippled and stone columns blazing with gems. That hall, with the *nāgarakas* having ornaments of varied brilliance, shone like the plain at the foot of Mount Meru with its flowering wish-yielding trees. Then a chamberlain came out, pushing away the screening curtain as a wild goose pushes aside a circle of lotus leaves. He spoke to the multitude of *nāgarakas* with a decorous bow: 'The *śreṣṭhin* (merchant-banker, president of the guild of merchants, Sānudāsa) informs you: "Welcome to the devotees of good qualities ! (This may also be interpreted 'to the amateurs of the strings of the *vīṇā*': they will compete to see who can accompany his daughter's singing.) This house is purified by you noble people full of worth, as if with golden pitchers of Ganges water. If everyone has arrived and the fatigue of the way has gone, then let Gandharvadattā (his daughter and the prize) be given your instructions." ' They looked at each other with faces seeming just roused from sleep. Ashamed, they gazed in all directions into space, their answers absent. (The fact is they have tried before, at previous contests, and failed to play in tune with her. Only Naravāhanadatta speaks up : let her come if she is ready.)

(99) Then the maiden, surrounded by chamberlains, pushed away the curtain (*javanikā*—at the rear of the stage of an Indian theatre: this hall was evidently arranged so that dramatic and other performances could be given in it), and our queen, Gandharvadattā, came out, overpowering the brilliance of the hall. How can I describe her beauty? Briefly, let me say that surely now the companies of nymphs have retired from the world as nuns. She seated herself on a square dais made of stone set with rubies, which had been prepared in the middle of the hall, like the digit of the Moon on a cloud at twilight. The *nāgarakas* closed up because of her overpowering brilliance, like beds of white lotuses because of that of the new digit of the Moon. She humiliated the *goṣṭhī*, which was emptied of understanding and speech, possessing only its visible appearance like the rows of columns of the hall.

(104) Then a chamberlain raised his right hand and said: 'Hear the words of the *śreṣṭhin*: "O best of *nāgarakas*! Here is Gandharvadattā waiting, and here is a *vīṇā* which has been tuned. Whoever is able to play —why does he hesitate to approach?" ' (Eventually the best player of the circle tries, but fails because Gandharvadattā sings in the divine *gagrāma* gamut. Naravāhanadatta notes this and offers to try, though his host Dattaka feels ashamed that he should, believing him a mere beginner and sure that he will fail ignominiously...)

(129) However, I left my seat, while Dattaka looked aside, and took the seat I was given beside Gandharvadattā. Then I looked at the *vīṇā* the chamberlain brought and said: 'Bring me another, sir. A person like me cannot play on this! Its body seems to be full of cobwebs, so that the gamut of open chords has gone dull.' The *nāgarakas* seeing me acting thus cast their glances elsewhere, showing the tips of their teeth as they smiled, and said: 'This brahman must be honoured with the top pennant for shamelessness!' (Naravāhanadatta rejects a second *vīṇā* which has a

> hair spoiling the strings and finally accepts a third brought to him by Sānudāsa himself. Then he sits on the stool covered with a new cloth:) (146) When the strings were touched only slightly with the tips of the fingers, they gave out *dhaivata*, etc. (the notes of the gamut), by themselves in the proper order.

He accompanies the girl's singing of the divine song perfectly, whereupon the chamberlain asks the assembly to say whether he has accompanied her or not. They all raise their hands and declare loudly that he has fairly won the girl. The chamberlain then draws the curtain and shows the *nāgarakas* out. Naravāhanadatta is married to Gandharvadattā and discovers that transmigration *saṃsāra* is a much better fortune than *nirvāṇa* (181).

693. The theme of flight is first introduced before Naravāhanadatta's birth, but appropriately when Vāsavadattā is pregnant with him (*Saṃgraha* V). In ancient India the feelings and dreams of a pregnant woman were usually supposed to be reliable indications of the kind of offspring about to be born, moreover they must be carefully humoured to ensure a good start to the new life. In the present case, Vāsavadattā is filled with a longing to see the whole Earth from a celestial chariot flying in the sky (190). Vasantaka, the court jester, suggests a hammock, but Udayana's other ministers take the matter more seriously and Yaugandharāyaṇa has the problem referred to the artisans *śilpins*. The latter are much afraid when ordered to construct a flying ('space' -*ākāśa*) machine (196), expecting punishment because they are unable to obey. After a long consultation they report (198): 'We know four kinds of machine, namely water, stone and earth machines and those made of assemblages of parts. It is said that the Greeks know space machines, but we have not seen them ourselves.'

694. Ancient Indian technology being an almost totally neglected subject at present, the nature of the four types of machine is for us a matter of conjecture (see Lacôte's notes, *Bṛhatkathāślokasaṃgraha* p. 462), though future research will probably clarify the matter. Meanwhile we may suggest that a 'water' *jala* machine is a waterwheel, if not a ship; a 'stone' *aśman* machine a catapult in which the fall of a heavy stone impels a missile, or else a drill for boring through stone; an 'earth' (or 'dust') *pāṃśu* machine could be a vehicle running on the earth, or even a mill; a machine made of an assemblage of parts *kāṇḍarāśikṛta* may be a more complex machine combining various principles.

695. The general Rumaṇvant then has the artisans beaten to extract from them the secret of space machines, which he suspects they are concealing (273ff.). An unknown visitor intervenes and saves them by undertaking to make such a machine if given the necessary apparatus. First he enquires the number of passengers, since kings sometimes overload space machines with disastrous results. Then he constructs one having the aspect of Garuḍa (the great bird on whom Viṣṇu rides [1440]) and invites the 'Viṣṇu' of kings to mount it. Udayana does so with Vāsavadattā and the whole court. They fly over Kauśāmbī, circumnavigate the Earth and then visit Ujjayinī, where they find King Pradyota of Avanti on an excursion for some festival, which they stop to see. Udayana drops an arrow with greetings inscribed on it.

696. On returning, Udayana honours the unknown artisan, discovering that 'he' is really a female sprite *guhyakā* who had been cursed by Kuvera, whose servants the sprites are (300). The science of flight is therefore the secret of the superhuman beings of the Himālaya rather than of the Greeks and we are not far from the world of the Wizards. This sprite had been born as the female elephant Bhadravatī, who carried Udayana when he escaped from Ujjayinī with Vāsavadattā. She had died on the way to Kauśāmbī, but seeing Udayana's affliction at her loss she has remained near him. Now she predicts that his son will become king of the Wizards (323).

697. Introducing Rumaṇvant's idea of the secretiveness of artisans, a brahman tells a story of an artisan Viśvila from Saurāṣṭra, who knew how to make flying machines and used a mechanical cock to fly home each night whilst away building a temple for King Brahmadatta of Kāśi (248). Viśvila keeps his secret, lest space machines become as commonplace and despised as beds (251-2), and later abandons his family rather than reveal it to King Mahāsena (Pradyota).

698. It may be noted that the *Vasudevahiṇḍi* [1451]

gives (pp. 62 f.) some more details about machines going in space, probably derived from the *Bṛhatkathā*. There are machines of different shapes and they have strings *tantis* and a pin *kīlikā* (or axle) which somehow supports them in the sky (on the principle of a top or gyroscope?). Unfortunately the episode of the *Bṛhatkathā* in which Naravāhanadatta himself acquired the science of flight does not seem to have been preserved in any of the versions we have. It may be appropriate to remark here that the idea of the knowledge acquired by a universal emperor *cakravartin*, such as Naravāhanadatta in this novel, derives from the same tradition as the Buddhist conception of the equivalence of an emperor and a *buddha*. In Buddhist legend the *bodhisattva* has the choice of becoming a universal emperor or a *buddha*. Here (*Saṃgraha* XXVII.85) a universal emperor is 'pure', has endless merit and is omniscient *sarvajña*, seeing things as they really are with a 'divine' eye just like a *buddha*.

699. Sānudāsa's first sea voyage from Tāmralipti, in the hope of making his fortune, begins smoothly but leads to sudden disaster:

> (XVIII.253) Was it not a celestial chariot, which with the speed of mind went a hundred leagues in the twinkling of an eye? Then a whale emerged from the water and struck the ship, which burst into planks, its joints shattered. Remembering the song: 'In whose hair the clouds...[and whose essence is water]...', through fate I supported myself on a plank and reached the shore of the ocean.

The song Sānudāsa remembers when in danger of drowning is from the Great Epic, Bhīṣma's hymn to Kṛṣṇa (Viṣṇu) (XII. 47.41). He is at length rescued, but wrecked again in South India, regaining Tāmralipti only after many turns of fortune.

700. Having had little success, he is ready to venture again on any enterprise which offers a chance of fabulous profits:

> (XVIII.428) Once I saw a merchant named Ācera

> ('Teacher', in Prakrit, and his followers obey him as an in allible authority), who was going with many merchants to the Land of Gold (Suvarṇabhūmi, the Mōn country of Lower Burma and Siam). Going with them in a big ship some distance across the ocean, we abandoned the vessel on the shore and set out on land. Then, when the Sun became red, we rested where the trees were impenetrable at the foot of a mighty mountain whose peak licked the clouds. Then, at the end of the night, as we sat on a carpet of leaves with the food we had brought, the caravan merchant (Ācera) instructed us: 'Merchants, bind your provision rucksacks on your backs tightly, three ways; fix your oil bottles round your necks. Resting your hands on these staves, supple but thick, and avoiding any with such defects as dryness, climb the mountain ! ...This is the Way of Staves *vetrapatha*, forming an obstacle to all energies but as it were leading on those who hope for gold !'

The merchants are afraid, but lured by their greed for gold they carry out the instructions. One falls, when his stave breaks, and is killed, but the rest reach the top. The next day they reach a river, in which rocks are seen in the shapes of animals. This river is said to turn everything it touches to stone (441). They must cross it by means of bamboos, namely by the Bamboo Way *veṇupatha* (446), described as seizing bamboos growing on the far side of the river as the wind bends them down within reach, then sliding over on them when the wind relents. Again one man falls when his bamboo breaks, and is petrified in the river.

701. Next (450) they come to a very narrow path ('of a snake'), with a dark and terrible, bottomless abyss into the Underworld *rasātala* on both sides. Ācera instructs the merchants to light a fire with damp fuel, to attract some mountain tribesmen *kirātas* by the smoke, who will sell them goats to carry them over this path which winds like the brow of Fate. They must also carry long bamboos as they ride. Sometimes, he says, one meets other travellers returning by the same path with gold from the gold mines—then they and our people must enter the Underworld, for there is no place to pass one another or even to turn round. Therefore we need a hero of genius, practised with the spear, in front, who single handed can kill a succession of enemies. This is the Goat Way *ajapatha* (461). After buying their goats, and saying their prayers to Śiva and Kṛṣṇa, the travellers set out:

> (464) Then the long line of goats taking the travellers set out, like a swift, steady ship in calm water. In that line of travellers I was seventh from the rear, Ācera was sixth, immediately behind me. When events had developed thus, from afar, in front, the rising noise of loud striking of bamboos was heard: shtah ! shtah !—And the sound of goats and men plunging into the murk of darkness: 'Baa ! Baa ! Aah ! Aah !'—Dismaying even the brave. In only a moment the enemy were completely destroyed except for one man; of our army the seventh (from last) was leading. Then the captain *grāmaṇī* (Ācera) berated me: 'Why hesitate ? The enemy is only one man, take him to heaven !' But the enemy abandoned his bamboo and saluted. Being without protection because his caravan of travellers was killed, he sought protection from me: 'My family is sinking, only one branch remaining: you must not annihilate it completely by cutting off that branch ! I am an only son, dear to my parents, who are blind. I am their stick for the blind, therefore, brother, do not kill me !' Then I hated my life, grey with the dust of evil: 'Fie upon gold which is to be obtained by murder ! Therefore let this poor fellow whose life is dear to him, whose life is useful to his blind parents, strike me down !' (475) Then Ācera, red and pale with rage and despair, growled at me with words harsh and gentle: 'Hey ! Foolish ox ! Ignorant of the proper times ! When the time is suitable for the sword, how is pity suitable for a wretch ? Ah ! Your compassionateness is proved, O learned in proved conclusions !—For the sake of one low fellow you want to kill sixteen ! For, if he is struck down, with his goat, fourteen will live; but if he is not struck down we shall be killed by him and you. And one should not

> sacrifice oneself, hard to sacrifice, to protect a low person. One should always protect oneself, even at the cost of wife and wealth.' And so on, he poured out a song as long as the *Bhagavadgītā*, a Viṣṇu making me, like Arjuna, do a cruel deed. Then I, excessively ashamed and taking upon myself a blameworthy action, struck the enemy's goat delicately on the feet. Then, the goat-ship plunging into the darkness-ocean, the traveller-sailor sank with his desire for wealth.

The survivors finish their deadly ride and eventually reach another river, where Ācera orders them to kill their goats and sow themselves up in the reversed skins dripping with blood. Then the yellow birds (giant vultures) of Gold Land will come and carry them off in their beaks through the sky to Gold Land. Thus they embark on a voyage through the sky, more terrible than crossing the ocean because without any means of propulsion fitted (no sails, and the birds not yoked to draw them but free to drop them as they please). Sānudāsa is separated from the others when two of the birds fight over him and he is dropped in a lake, whence he escapes to begin a new and quite different adventure.

702. These travels should be compared with a passage in the Pali *Niddesa* (I , *Mahāniddesa*, p. 155, repeated on p. 415; see p. 280 of the commentary *Saddhammapajjotikā* for explanations). The latter occurs in the midst of a long enumeration of the dangers of trying to get rich, particularly by voyages overseas in quest of wealth. After giving some itineraries of voyages to South East Asia and other places, the text notes ten means of progress in difficult forest and mountain country, which parallel some of the incidents in Sānudāsa's travels. The adventurers may have to crawl on their knees, ride on sure-footed goats or rams in the mountains, climb mountains with 'hooks' (rock climbing with ropes, etc., to get up a precipice), descend by parachute *chattra*, make bamboo bridges over rivers, be carried by birds, go down rat holes and through caves and carry staves. The *Niddesa* was a late addition to the *Tripiṭaka* (*c.* – 100 ?), but there are partial parallels in the somewhat earlier *Jātaka* (III p. 541, merchants using staves and hooks) and *Vimānavatthu* (p. 337 of edition with Commentary).

703. Though many early critics have praised Guṇāḍhya for his model of a *kāvya* novel producing the marvellous aesthetic experience, hardly any have actually quoted him, doubtless because his achievement was in the vast narrative content and not in the manner of quotable phrases. A good many presumed quotations from the *Bṛhatkathā* are just of single words to illustrate the Paiśācī language, mostly in works of grammar. At present only Bhoja is known to quote a few continuous sentences, in the latter part of his *Śṛṅgāraprakāśa* (as yet unprinted: see Raghavan's book, pp. 850ff.). The quotation occurs where Bhoja is illustrating various kinds of theft described in *kāvyas* and contains an incident in the story of the gambler Gaṅgārola (in the Paiśācī; Sanskrit form given by Bhoja as Geṇḍākarāla), where he finds some nymphs bathing and steals their clothes. They call out to him:

> O Gaṅgārola ! Give us our clothes which you have carried off while we were swimming ! We have to go to Heaven. How can we go there wearing (*parihita*) our bathing costumes ? But we are afraid not to go: through Indra's curse when the night ends at dawn we shall have to remain here turned to stone ! (i.e. if we do not return before dawn we shall be petrified by his curse).

He replies:

> I will give you your clothes if you give me one nymph as my wife !

Bhoja tells us this is from the 'Kaliṅgasenālābha', the chapter entitled 'The Winning of Kaliṅgasenā', which raises a host of problems concerning its authenticity as original Guṇāḍhya and its possible place in the *Bṛhatkathā*. Not to go too far into this discussion, let us note that Kaliṅgasenā is the name of the mother of the heroine Madanamañcukā (there is in the Kaśmīra recension another Kaliṅgasenā, apparently a duplicate derived from the original one—see Lacôte, *Essai*, p. 211). She had wanted to marry Udayana, but his minister Yaugandharāyaṇa had opposed it. The Kaśmīra recension, which alone has preserved this narrative for us, is unable to give a satisfactory explanation of this, because there Kaliṅgasenā is a princess and a perfectly respectable bride for Udayana. But, as Lacôte points out on the page just referred to, in the *Saṃgraha* Kaliṅgasenā is a geisha. How then could the king marry her? We find also that she is an incarnation of a nymph as a result of a curse. Very likely the story of Gaṅgārola and the nymphs originally belonged in the narrative about Madanamañcukā's mother, though the *Saṃgraha* has omitted it. Baulked of Udayana, Kaliṅgasenā is seduced by a *vidyādhara* who assumes Udayana's form and deceives her: from this union Madanamañcukā is born, who succeeds in marrying the Prince Naravāhanadatta where her mother had failed with his father (*Essai*, p. 81). The 'winning' of Kaliṅgasenā was thus of a somewhat provisional character, except from the point of view of the wizard Madanavega, Madanamañcukā's father.

704. We have already noted some references by the critics to Guṇāḍhya. In fact almost all who record anything of the history *vaṃśa* of *kavis* have enrolled him near the head of their list, after Vālmīki, with fulsome praise. Subandhu (II) alludes to the hero and heroine and to the division in chapters represented by their several heroines (who are 'won' in them) [1573]. Then the novel is praised by Bāṇa (*Harṣacarita*, introductory verse 18), Daṇḍin (*Avantisundarī*, introductory verse 7, where Gomukha is named also), Uddyotana (*Kuvalayamālā* p. 3) and Rājaśekhara (quoted by Jalhaṇa, *Sūktimuktāvalī* IV. 52). Trivikrama (*Nala Campū*, verse 14) places Guṇāḍhya first and Bāṇa second as giving unceasing delight. Somadeva I (*Yaśastilaka Campū* Vol. II p. 113) includes Guṇāḍhya in his list of great *kavis*. Dhanapāla I (*Tilakamañjarī*, introductory verse 21) says that 'other, Sanskrit, novels look splendid with a drop of the *Bṛhatkathā* ocean in front, on their throats' (i.e. like the central jewel of a necklace), meaning that all were inspired by the great classic, as Dhanapāla's own certainly was. Soḍḍhala (*Udayasundarī* p. 154) praises Guṇāḍhya's *Bṛhatkathā* for producing joy and aesthetic experience and places him near the head of his history of *kavis*. Guṇāḍhya receives homage again from Someśvara in the +13 (*Surathotsava* I.33). Vinaya-candra (+13) includes him in his list of sixteen great writers (IV. 188f.). This list of references might be extended, but few will be found later than the +13, when tastes changed and fiction was neglected. Up to that time, however, Guṇāḍhya's fame blazed undiminished as a source of inspiration to the greatest writers in India, for he knew how to create *rasa* and delight in his readers.

Chapter XV

THE FULLY DEVELOPED KĀVYA EPIC AND DRAMA IN THE +1: AŚVAGHOṢA

705. Though the Sātavāhanas finally overthrew the Magadhan Empire in —30 they did not succeed in establishing their own rule over Northern India. During the long decline of Magadha a series of barbarian invasions had penetrated first into Kāpiśa (the upper Kubhā valley) and Gandhāra and then further to the South and West into the Indo-Iranian borderland of Jāguḍa. From these two vantage points they pressed on respectively into the Yamunā and the lower Sindhu (Indus) valleys and at times raided even further. These invaders, whom the Indians called barbarians, were respectively the Greeks (from Bactria, Alexander's colony) and the Śakas (Scythians) who had previously crossed Iran from their nomadic homeland North-East of the Caspian Sea. Their dominion was contested by the Pahlavas (Parthians). By the time of the Sātavāhana victory over Magadha, Greek rule in India had been ended and the Śakas were the dominant power in Northern India, holding practically the whole of the Indus valley. The Parthians continued to dispute Gandhāra with them. About —100, however, the nomadic tribes of the Kuṣāṇas, a people from the region of modern Sinkiang, of uncertain ('Tokharian'?) linguistic affiliation, had overrun Bactria. At the beginning of the +1 the Kuṣāṇa king Kujula Kathphiśa defeated the Parthians and occupied Kāpiśa. His successor Vima Kathphiśa after +50 invaded Gandhāra and overthrew the Śakas, occupying the whole of the Indus valley and some countries to the East, particularly Śūrasena. It must be observed here that Kuṣāṇa chronology remains a highly controversial topic. The date most usually favoured is +78 for the accession of the Emperor Kaniṣka I, which the present writer supports for reasons stated in his contribution to *Papers on the Date of Kaniṣka* (ed. Basham, 1968), pp. 327ff., *q.v.*

706. In +78, according to our chronology, Kaniṣka (I) succeeded to the Kuṣāṇa throne and to a vast empire over

Northern India and central Asia. He established a new era, later incorrectly called the 'Śaka'. Magadha perhaps remained independent, more likely subordinate, under obscure local rulers and the 'Muruṇḍas', Śaka 'kings', perhaps under Kuṣāṇa overlordship, but at least its neighbours Kośala and Kāśi were governed by Kaniṣka's 'satrap' at Banāras.

707. After the desolation of the wars of the Greeks, Śakas and Pahlavas, and perhaps of the first Kuṣāṇa invasions, the relatively peaceful and prosperous period of the Kuṣāṇa Empire is one of the most glorious in the history of Indian civilisation. The sculpture and architecture of the Śūrasena-Gandhāra school is well known, especially for its innovations of representing the Buddha as a human figure and of elevating the Buddhist *stūpa* into a tall 'pagoda'. The achievements of the period in *kāvya* are fortunately available for us in part, through the preservation of some of the work of Aśvaghoṣa and a few later *kavis*. We know also that the drama flourished in Śūrasena in this period, establishing Śaurasenī as the basic dramatic Prakrit: as noted above [178] there is inscriptional evidence for a school of drama in Mathurā, which became the Eastern capital of the Kuṣāṇa Empire.

708. Though the Kuṣāṇa rulers were of barbarian origin, they had very early become almost completely assimilated to Indian civilisation—perhaps even before they had conquered any part of India itself. Buddhism and Indian political institutions, together with art and literature, had before the Kuṣāṇa period begun to spread into central Asia, and during that period Buddhism with its literature and art reached China from there. Political institutions were borrowed by the barbarian peoples of central Asia from both India and China, and colonies of Indians and Chinese settled among them, thus we find for example an Indian language (that of Gandhāra) used for administrative purposes in some central Asian states of the Kuṣāṇa period and after. Unlike Brahmanism, which has as a rule confined itself to India and to Indians, Buddhism repudiates racial distinctions and loyalties. It came into existence as a philosophy offering itself to all, whatever their background, and could gain adherents only by winning them from their traditional beliefs. Teaching its philosophy and hence propagating it is a major virtue, the 'best kind of generosity'. In the multiracial Kuṣāṇa Empire, Buddhism was already well established among the various peoples, Indian and non-Indian alike, and several of the Kuṣāṇa rulers adopted it. They perhaps saw in it, among other things, a philosophy, a religion and a way of life which could stabilise their great polyglot empire, and they thus followed the example of Aśoka--which was a popular theme with Buddhist teachers of their day. Having adopted the Indian heritage through its more accessible Buddhist aspect, the Kuṣāṇas patronised Indian art and literature, including *kāvya*.

709. Aśvaghoṣa was born in Kośala at Ayodhyā (also called Sāketa), which according to Tradition and the *Rāmāyaṇa* was Rāma's capital. For what is known of his life we may follow Johnston, *Buddhacarita* Vol.II, Introduction. He was probably born a brahman, but was converted to Buddhism. His *kāvyas* based on Buddhist tradition became widely known in the Kuṣāṇa Empire, and legend associates his name with that of the greatest emperor, Kaniṣka: in fact he seems to have lived about 50 years before Kaniṣka's time and possibly to have met one of his predecessors. Ayodhyā itself does not appear to have been included in the Kuṣāṇa Empire until Kaniṣka's reign, or slightly earlier. There is a story that Aśvaghoṣa was sent to the emperor as tribute, on account of his great value, which no doubt is as apocryphal as the other tales associating the *kavi* with Kaniṣka. It is in any case possible that Aśvaghoṣa visited or settled in the new empire which was propitious for Buddhism, and certain that his works were subsequently very popular there. There are possibly significant references to Gandhāra in his *Buddhacarita* (XXI.4,34), suggesting a connection of the writer with that country, whereas in reality the Buddha seems never to have visited it.

710. Of Aśvaghoṣa's *kāvyas* we know two epics in complete form (but half of one of them in translations only) and fragments of three dramas probably his; a fourth drama is known by name only. Certain lyric *stotras* in praise of the Buddha are sometimes attributed to him, but it seems unlikely that any of these are really his. In contrast to the simple style of the *Rāmāyaṇa* we have here our earliest available intact examples of *kāvya* epic in its fully developed form; it is equally important to have incontrovertible evidence for the state of the drama in the +1, showing that by then at least the methods of the *Nāṭyaśāstra* were current in the theatre in essentials and even in details. Far more important than these historical facts, however, is our fortunate possession of some of the work of one of the world's great poets.

711. Aśvaghoṣa claims to have used *kāvya* as a vehicle for the Buddhist teaching on account of the attractiveness and popularity of this literary art (*Saundarananda* XVIII. 63-4). Whatever he thought of his aim as simply didactic, for us it merely adds the salt of serious purpose to the most delicious *kāvya* dishes. Though having an ethical purpose apparently remote from the aims of *kāvya*, he seems to take pleasure in parading his strict conformity to the 'rules' of the art, and to find them absolutely congenial to him. His genius was such that he evidently could take all the intricacies of theory—of language, poetics, the science of pleasure *kāma* and other incidental props of writing—in his stride, and find the process exhilarating and productive of the most spontaneous caprices of his poetic wit. The further complexities of contending philosophical doctrines, which he brings in and for the discussion of which his works were created, equally inspired him by their intellectual challenge. For such a master the driest rules are inflammable material to catalyse the action of his genius on a story.

712. Uniting two opposites, joy *prīti* in and liberation *mokṣa* from the tyranny of attachment to the things of the world, Aśvaghoṣa has produced works full of spiritual tension, himself consciously living through the conflict of existence and writing directly from poignant individual experience. Perhaps the writing or reading of a *kāvya* could be regarded as a form of meditation, the joy found in it being perfectly acceptable in the lower stages (as in more orthodox Buddhist meditation), though transcended later. The emotional and intellectual exhilaration of poetry and drama assumes the detachment of the reader or audience from the everyday world and invites participation in a kind of spiritual exercise. Buddhist meditation begins with detachment of this kind and concentration of the mental powers: in the first stages there is intense philosophical reflection, but later this gives way to a state of profound calm. Aśvaghoṣa may have thought of his *kāvyas* as guiding people in this way to detachment and calm, and as guiding people otherwise completely inaccessible to Buddhist influence.

713. The essence of our enjoyment of Aśvaghoṣa's works, however, surely springs from the fact that he is himself involved in his drama, not detached from it. He writes with acute sympathy for every character and every aspect of human life. Thus his description of worldly pleasures and interests is always convincing. He writes most vividly and realistically of the very things he denounces as ephemeral and unreal, especially of love. We know nothing of his life beyond the sketchiest traditions, which regard him as a monk and even a patriarch. We do not know why he became a monk, but we can be certain it was not through any natural aversion to the world but rather the result of deep entanglement in it, accompanied by acute sensitivity and the self-awareness of an exceptionally clear mind. We may suppose that a sense of the ultimate futility of the worldly quest gradually overpowered his zest for pleasure. In his writings he looks back on the joys and disappointments of his own struggle, his insight deepened by later experience but the keenness of his involvement apparently undiminished: no poet has written with greater sincerity.

714. Aśvaghoṣa's most famous work is his epic Life of the Buddha, *Buddhacarita*. Of its twenty eight cantos a little less than half is now available in the original, but complete translations in Chinese and Tibetan have been preserved. The story follows the Buddha legend of Buddhist tradition with Aśvaghoṣa's habitual accuracy, whilst being articulated as an exactly proportioned epic. The poem falls naturally into four distinct parts of equal length—seven cantos each—and equal weight, corresponding to the four stages of the Buddha's life. First comes the birth and youth of the hero, culminating in his renunciation of worldly life and departure to the forest for the life of an ascetic. The second quarter of the epic culminates in the Enlightenment, after long questing and experiment, and study with various teachers, and the great 'battle' (required by the rules [405], but here purely spiritual) with Māra, 'Death' (whom we have met in Pali *kāvya* [600]). The third quarter narrates how the Buddha by teaching made his discovery available to all beings, a mission ending with the equivalent of an emperor's campaign of universal conquest, in which the hero converts the rulers and people in many countries to the new doctrine. The last quarter describes the events leading up to the Parinirvāṇa of the Buddha, his cremation and the enshrinement of his ashes, and finally the redistribution of the ashes in eighty thousand pagodas *stūpas* by the emperor Aśoka. This event more than two centuries after the Parinirvāṇa may be taken to symbolise the final establishment of the Buddhist doctrine in the world. It may be noted that the four stages are associated with the four main Buddhist places of pilgrimage, round which the legend grew: the birthplace of the Buddha near Kapilavāstu at the foot of the Himālayas (now in Nepal), the place of his Enlightenment at Gayanagarī in Magadha, the Deer Park near Vārāṇasī (Banāras) where he first taught his new doctrine and the place near Kuśinagarī where the Parinirvāṇa occurred. Within this plan various incidents are selected and enlarged according to the usage of *kāvya* epic.

715. A shorter epic, The Handsome Nanda *Saundarananda*, in eighteen cantos, is extant complete in the original Sanskrit. It is based on the humorous story of the Buddha's half brother Nanda, which is found in the Pali Canon (*Udāna* 22-3). With great difficulty this extremely worldly person is induced to become a monk, being eventually weaned away from the pleasures of love only by the promise of higher pleasures of the same kind with heavenly nymphs. The way offered him to attain these is the ascetic discipline of the Buddha's Community of monks, which he accordingly undertakes with the utmost seriousness and devotion. Only when he has made splendid progress in his monk's training, for this totally incongruous aim, are his colleagues able to make him feel the absurdity of his position and to redirect him towards true happiness.

716. In these two epics of Aśvaghoṣa we have the greater story of the Buddha winning enlightenment by his own efforts and the lesser story, but perhaps equally significant, of the Buddha's skill in bringing another person to enlightenment.

717. The *Śāriputra*, a play in nine acts, of which only a few fragments of a manuscript are known to be extant, calls itself a *prakaraṇa*, although the story of this leading disciple of the Buddha, whom we met in the earliest Pali *kāvya* pieces, is ancient and famous (see also the Life of the Buddha, Canto

17). Either Aśvaghoṣa had greatly modified it (but even so it would still count as a *nāṭaka* according to the standard theory), or, rather, the distinction between *prakaraṇa* 'fiction' and *nāṭaka*, 'play', 'history', was not yet generally recognised, *prakaraṇa* meaning simply an 'invention' by the author, whatever its basis. In most other ways, so far as the fragments allow us to see, the play conforms to later practice and theory. Thus the division into acts is standard, as is the use of various Prakrit dialects for certain characters, one of which is the jester *vidūṣaka* [31], the traditional ignorant brahman of the classical drama who here objects to being taught by a member of the warrior class (Lüders, *Sitz.* 405). There is a fragment from the prologue, with an assistant (to the producer) and the 'announcement'. The text is a mixture of prose and verse.

718. A very different play, of which still fewer fragments have been retrieved (in the same manuscript as those of the *Śāriputra*), seems on stylistic grounds also to be by Aśvaghoṣa, though the title and scope of it are unknown. The characters in the fragments are mostly allegorical: Glory, Fortitude and Intelligence, apparently with a seer and perhaps the Buddha (this is not clear). Other allegorical plays (usually *nāṭakas*) are preserved only from much later times, and no theoretical discussion of the type seems to have come down to us. This play extends our knowledge of the history of such productions back far enough perhaps to suggest a connection with the early religious types of play, but the most obvious parallel is the piece in the *Saṃyutta Nikāya* (I 124-7) which has been described above [600], in which Māra's daughters appear: Desire, Discontent and Passion—if we were right in supposing this to be intended for the stage. Allegorical characters are found already in the *Jātaka* collection [570]. For example in No. 535 we meet Fortune, Hope, Trust and Conscience as nymphs: a contest as to which of them is the best is won by Conscience, all the others having serious faults.

719. A third play, of which fragments were found in the same manuscript with these others and which is probably by Aśvaghoṣa, is apparently a *prakaraṇa* of the standard type, similar to those of Bhāsa [1011] and Śūdraka [1182]. The hero Somadatta (?), perhaps identical with the 'son of a wealthy merchant (banker)', has a geisha, Magadhavatī, as his mistress and a friend, Kaumudagandha ('Lotus Scent'—but this is a genuine brahman clan name: Lüders, *Bruch.* 25), who is the jester of the play. There is a prince, a maid, an Ājīvaka philosopher and a rogue *duṣṭa.* The story, which was probably original, can only be guessed at. There is a scene (fragment 8) between Magadhavatī and a character named Dhānañjaya, perhaps a *nāgaraka* and possibly the same as the 'prince', in which playful punishments are proposed for him for an imaginary offence. There is a scene in an 'old park' (fragments 4 and 66), vehicles are used (13, 16, 29, 41), and there is an assembly *samāja,* doubtless organised by the *nāgaraka*(*s*) as an entertainment [28], on a hill top (fragments 22, 45).

720. These plays are of particular interest for the Prakrit dialects found in them, which are more archaic than those of the better known plays of the classical repertory. In the latter we find what we have called 'intermediate' Prakrits [14], standardised between the +1 and the +4 and subsequently hardly changed but retained as 'classical' languages for the theatre. Among those, the basic or regular dialect is Śaurasenī, presumably the vernacular language of the Eastern part of the Kuṣāṇa Empire in the +2 to +4. Certain 'low' characters speak Māgadhī, the apparently discredited vernacular of the former imperial people of Magadha after they had lost their empire. In these earlier plays the regular Prakrit, spoken for example by the jester and the geisha in the presumed *Somadatta,* is an earlier form of Śaurasenī, which may be called 'Old Śaurasenī'. It is very similar to Pali and Paiśācī and ought perhaps to be identified as the 'Śaurasena Paiśācī' mentioned by some grammarians. Presumably it is the language of the pre-Kuṣāṇa kingdom of Śūrasena (which broke away from the Śuṅgas in the −2 and was conquered by the Kuṣāṇas in the +1). The rogue *duṣṭa* in this play speaks an earlier form of Māgadhī than the 'classical' Māgadhī, which may be called 'Old Māgadhī' or perhaps Māgadha Paiśācī, since it again is fairly close phonologically to Paiśācī and Pali (with the well known Māgadhī characteristics of *ś* and *l* and nominative singular masculine in *e*).

721. Another character speaks a language which Lüders (*Bruch.* 37-42) has identified as Ardhamāgadhī of an early phase ('Old Ardhamāgadhī'). It bears a strong resemblance to the language of the inscriptions of Aśoka, or rather of the Eastern inscriptions presumed to be in the administrative language of Magadha proper, and also of the Buddhist *Tripiṭaka* texts as named by Aśoka. This 'Half Māgadhī' differs from plain Māgadhī in not having *ś* (but *s* instead like Śaurasenī, Pali, etc.). According to the *Nāṭyaśāstra* (XVII.51 Baroda), Ardhamāgadhī is spoken by princes (Aśoka!), wealthy merchants (bankers) and servants. This suggests the ruling class of Magadha in its imperial period and those (servants) associated closely with them. It would be regarded as a more educated and respectable language than the vulgar, unashamed Māgadhī of the common people with its 'coarse' *ś* (a situation immediately clear to anyone who has lived in London, England). The Ardhamāgadhī of the Jaina (Śvetāmbara) Canon represents a later form of the same language (apparently because the Jaina Canon was codified only later and the language had been allowed to change into the 'intermediate' phase of Prakrit, with the loss of numerous—intervocalic—consonants). Ardhamāgadhī is extremely rare in plays later than Aśvaghoṣa, being replaced by Sanskrit or Śaurasenī (the *Nāṭyaśāstra* thus describes the earlier phase).

722. These plays are close to the standard later practice in their stage directions ('enter', 'exit' and so on), but differ from it in that those relating to Prakrit speaking characters are given in Prakrit (a perfectly reasonable arrangement, since they belong to the 'part' of the character in question; but in later plays all stage directions are in Sanskrit).

723. The +7 philosopher Dharmakīrti by chance mentions Aśvaghoṣa's authorship of a play *nāṭaka* called the *Rāṣṭrapāla*, as a way of identifying the author or describing him (*Vādanyāya* p. 67). He also quotes the first few words of the play, which are of interest for the technicalities of composition and important historically for the study of dramatic texts : *prasaṃgaṃ kṛtvā nāndyante tataḥ praviśati sūtradhāraḥ*, 'Having made the necessary connection (i.e. with the *pūrvaraṅga*, opening proceedings or ritual [310]), then the producer enters at the end of the opening benediction (and speaks as follows)'. It seems that Dharmakīrti mentions this as a peculiarity of Aśvaghoṣa's style, at least from the standpoint of the usages of his own time. We find in fact that in the +2 Bhāsa omits the first two words of this opening stage direction, and that by the +4 a different style of opening has become usual, which thereafter is standard practice: the dramatist himself supplies one or more verses for the opening benediction, which consequently stand at the beginning of his text, and these are followed by the bare 'At the end of the opening benediction: Producer:..'

724. Having noted this text-critical point we are more interested in the implication that the *Rāṣṭrapāla* was presumably Aśvaghoṣa's most celebrated work in the +7, and in its probable content. The story of Rāṣṭrapāla is well known from the Pali Canon and elsewhere (e.g. *Majjhima Nikāya* II 54ff.). When the Buddha was teaching in a town in Kuru he was heard by Rāṣṭrapāla, the only son of the leading family of the town. Rāṣṭrapāla was at once attracted to the doctrine and wished to leave the world. He asked the Buddha for permission to enter the Community of monks, but the Buddha, in accordance with a rule he had found necessary, asked whether he had his parents' consent. He had not, and had very great difficulty in getting it, as they wished him to accept his inheritance and continue the family, pointing out all the luxuries he enjoyed and adding that his renunciation would be as good as his death as far as they were concerned and would leave them miserable. Faced with their refusal Rāṣṭrapāla began a fast to death in order to extort their consent. His friends persuade them to agree now, since there is always a chance he may not like the life of a monk and return home. He then joined the Community and soon attained liberation.

725. Later, in the course of going round the town to beg alms, Rāṣṭrapāla chanced to call at his parent's house (a monk is required to be without discrimination on his begging round, and to apply to every house in turn). In his robes, with his head shaved, he is not recognised, and far from getting almsfood he gets abused—the father exclaims that it was through these shaven monks that he lost his only son. It happened however that at that moment a slave girl took out some stale barley bread to throw away. The monk asked her to give it to him, if it was to be thrown away, and as she did so she recognised him by his voice and hands and feet. She tells his parents, and his father follows him, finding him sitting against a wall eating the barley bread. He will not return to the house, but accepts an invitation to take his meal there the next day. The father makes his dispositions to receive his guest: vast wealth is piled up, hidden behind screens until the psychological moment; Rāṣṭrapāla's two former wives are told to dress up and stand by, and of course the food is excellent. The climax of the story is naturally Rāṣṭrapāla's rejection of the wealth, which he advises his father to throw away as a cause of unhappiness, and of the wives. The latter suggest that (like Nanda) he must be practising asceticism in order to attain heavenly nymphs; in denying this he addresses them as 'sisters', which causes them to faint away. Finishing his meal, Rāṣṭrapāla lectures the family on the emptiness and deceitfulness of bodily beauty and adornments, like a hunter's trap, and departs.

726. Such a story must have been irresistible to the writer of The Handsome Nanda, and have stimulated him to his best efforts. It is a pity we are unable to enjoy the result.

727. It is clear that the Buddhist drama flourished in India in the +1, despite the profound ignorance of our own times about it. Some later Buddhist plays which have survived will be described in their places below [1276]. Very indirect evidence to supplement our knowledge may be drawn from a group of plays in Kuchean and Agnean, the so-called 'Tokharian' languages of Central Asia (Sinkiang), which may be translations and are certainly Indian in theme and form (see on these Winter in JAOS 1955, 26ff.). In one play the royal chaplain *purohita* appears as the jester. Several are based on *Jātaka* stories, one *nāṭaka* tells the story of Nanda whilst another is concerned with the Bodhisattva Maitreya, who is to be the next Buddha. We do not know whether any of these are based on originals as early as Aśvaghoṣa, or earlier, but they illustrate the same tradition of Buddhist theatre. The later plays to be described below reflect a later phase of Buddhism, the Mahāyāna, though they derive from the old *Jātaka* tradition of stories of a future Buddha sacrificing himself in his former lives.

728. A native of Ayodhyā, Aśvaghoṣa not only refers to Vālmīki as the First Kavi *ādikavi* but holds the *Rāmāyaṇa* in special affection [613]. In form, style, metre and language Aśvaghoṣa's epics are remote from the simple, easy going narrative of Vālmīki, yet the *Rāmāyaṇa*, as a grand heroic poem telling an ideally noble story on a scale appropriate to its theme, is the model which the Life of the Buddha is intended to match or surpass. The Buddha, as the hero who conquered the sensual world and won Nirvāṇa, is intended to appear mightier even than Rāma. Satisfying the requirements of epic theory [405], Aśvaghoṣa introduces political consultations and intrigue and the sending of embassies: the Buddha's father, represented as a king, seeks to divert his son to the worldly ambition of kingship; after the renunciation he sends his chief counsellor and the royal chaplain after him to persuade him to return (Canto IX). There is a further political discussion between the prince and King Bimbisāra of Magadha (Cantos X and XI), developing an old tradition [561]. The central battle is fought and won against Māra, god of sensual pleasure and death, with his army of demons (Canto XIII). Another battle starts with the siege of Kuśinagarī, but peace is soon agreed when the brahman Droṇa acts as mediator and envoy between the belligerents (Canto XXVIII). The end of pleasure and the description of lovemaking are realised in the narrative of the Buddha's youth, when after his early marriage the women of the royal palace seek his love, abetted by the king who hopes to control his restless son in this way (Cantos II, III and IV). Canto III includes a famous description of the agitation of the ladies of the city when the prince drives out in his chariot. Opportunity is found to elaborate the popular theme of the birth of a son (Canto I and part of II). A hermitage is described (Canto VII). The poet displays his learning in numerous sciences (such as medicine and astronomy) and arts (such as architecture and painting) as required by convention, including grammar (Canto II especially) and lexicography but most of all, and most legitimately, in philosophy (for which he is an accurate source for his period —Cantos IX, XII, XIV, XVI, XVIII, XXVI, etc.). As in the *Rāmāyaṇa*, however, incidental and descriptive matter is strictly subordinate to the story and is never introduced merely to satisfy the theory, on the flimsiest pretexts, as in some later epics.

729. The catalogue of Aśvaghoṣa's prominent descriptions may be extended from The Handsome Nanda: a city (I), a king (II), spring (VII), the Himālaya mountains (X) and the heaven of Indra. There is a 'battle' against vicious thoughts

(XVII), leading to Nanda's liberation, in which the techniques of Buddhist meditation replace the marvellous weapons of the *Rāmāyaṇa* and other epics. However, not all the topics later favoured for description in an epic appear in Aśvaghoṣa, even in both his epics taken together, though on the other hand many are touched on in similes.

730. We can illustrate Aśvaghoṣa's style from the Third Canto of the Life of the Buddha (1ff.), in which the King seizes what he thinks is an opportunity to divert the mind of his son, the future Buddha, from the renunciation of the world which a sage has predicted for him:

> Then at one time he (Prince Sarvārthasiddha, the future Buddha) heard some songs
> composed about the parks, with their soft meadows
> And adorned with lotus pools,
> their trees sounding with cuckoos.
>
> Then after hearing of the lovely nature
> of the parks of the city, which were loved by the women,
> He set his mind on an excursion outside,
> like an elephant shut inside a house.
>
> Then the King having heard of the feelings
> of that desired object called his 'son'
> Gave orders for a pleasure trip,
> suited to his affection, fortune and age.
>
> He diverted from the Royal Way
> the distressed press of common people,
> Thinking: 'Let not the Prince, whose thoughts are delicate,
> have his mind disturbed'.
>
> Then after very gently driving away
> those who were lacking limbs and those whose senses were defective,
> Those who were disabled by age and so on, and the pitiful, in all directions,
> they made the Royal Way very beautiful.

Then, when the Royal Way was made beautiful,
the famous Prince, with disciplined followers,
Descended from the top of the palace at the proper
  time
and went to the King, being given leave.

Then indeed the King, his tears welling up,
kissed his son's head, gazed at him for a long time,
And ordered : 'Go!', with a word,
but through affection did not let him go with his mind.

Then he mounted a golden chariot,
yoked with four quiet horses
Bearing trappings of finest gold,
whose charioteer was brave, wise and true.

Then with a befitting retinue
he reached the road which was scattered with
  brilliant bouquets of flowers,
Hung with garlands, with trembling bunting,
like the Moon with a constellation in the sky.

731. Very slowly he entered the Royal Way
which was as if strewn with halves of blue waterlilies,
As he was being looked at by the citizens all around,
their eyes expanded wide with curiosity. (10)

Some praised him for his charming qualities
and others saluted him for his brilliance,
But some wished him fortune (sovereignty)
and length of life, because of his cheerfulness.

Hunchbacks and groups of mountain tribesmen and
  dwarfs
slipped out of the great houses,
And women from the little houses;
they bowed as to the banner in the procession of the
  god (Indra).

Then hearing the news from the servants:
'The Prince is going !'

Women went to the balconies of the palaces wishing
to see him,
being given leave by their elders.

Obstructed by untied girdle strings,
their eyes confused as they awakened from sleep,
Putting on their ornaments at the news,
they gathered noisily through curiosity.

—Frightening the multitudes of house-birds
with loud noise on the stairs and balconies of the
palaces,
With clamour of girdles and sounds of anklets,
rebuking each other's haste.

But the progress of some of those excellent women,
though they were in a hurry and impatient,
Was checked by the weight
of their broad buttock-chariots and full breasts.

Another, though capable of going quickly,
restrained her progress, did not go fast,
Through shame hiding the bold* ornaments
used in intimacy.

Then the windows were unextinguished
with the women's mutually crushing clusterings,
Their earrings shaken in the press,
their ornaments noisy.

But the King's foreboding of separation from his son is justified, for the gods put in the Prince's way an old man, a sight he has never been permitted to see before, and on the charioteer's explaining what old age is, and that all are liable to it, he begins to realise the impermanance of life and the futile transience of all its pleasures.

732. Eventually Sarvārthasiddha, after meeting a wandering philosopher *śramaṇa* when out riding, slips out of

(*reading *pragalbhāni* with MS A and Weller)

the palace at night on his favourite horse Kanthaka, accompanied only by the groom Chandaka, rides to a hermitage in the forest and then sends them back. Canto VIII follows, which has proved a popular one for its descriptions of the lamentations after the Prince has disappeared:

Then the groom, depressed,
when his selfless master had gone to the forest,
Made an effort to restrain his grief on the road,
yet his tears were not exhausted.

But the road which he had traversed in one night
on his master's order, with that horse,
That same way now took him eight days,
as he reflected on the absence of his master.
And the strong horse Kanthaka wandered
pained in feelings, dispirited,
Though adorned with jewellery
he was as if shorn of beauty, without him.

And returning towards the forest of asceticism
he neighed violently, pathetically, over and over
  again;
Though hungry on the road he did not approve, nor
  take,
either young grass or water.

Then gradually those two approached the city called
  Kapila,
deserted by that illustrious one who was devoted to the
  welfare of the world;
It was as if empty,
like the sky deprived of the Sun.

...

"This city destitute of him is a forest,
and that forest possessing him is a city;
For the city does not look well without him,
like Heaven without Indra when he had killed
  Vṛtra". *(13)

(*After killing Vṛtra, Indra was banished from Heaven, because it was a grievous sin according to Tradition—*Mahābhārata*, *Udyogaparvan*, *adhyāya* 10, 42ff.)

Then the women, thinking: "The Prince has come back again",
took to the rows of windows,
And perceiving the horse with no one on its back,
they shut the windows again and cried.

But the King was praying in a temple,
his mind tired with keeping vows and with grief,
Engaged in a rite for regaining his son,
and was performing various ceremonies accordingly.

Then the groom, taking the horse,
his eyes filled with tears,
Entered the palace, cast down with grief,
as if his master had been carried off by an enemy soldier.

And Kanthaka, penetrating into the palace,
looking on, his eyes streaming with tears,
Neighed with a strong voice,
as if communicating his unhappiness to the people.

Then the birds living in the palace
and the honoured horses tethered nearby
Took up the horse's cry,
apprehending the Prince's approach.

And people going in the vicinity of the King's citadel,
cheated by their excessive joy,
Thought: "As the horse Kanthaka is neighing,
the Prince is certainly entering".

Then women who had swooned with grief, from great delight,
their eyes eager to see the Prince,
Hopefully ran out from the house,
like agitated lightnings from an autumn cloud.

...

Having seen only Chandaka and the horse, without their friend,
their eyes filled with tears;
With discouraged faces those excellent women wept,
like cows in a forest abandoned by the bull. (23)

733. Other women, their splendour destroyed, their shoulders and arms loose,
were as if senseless with despair;
They did not cry, they shed no tears, they did not sigh,
they did not move, they stayed as if they were painted. (25)

This last verse is the only verse certainly by Aśvaghoṣa known to be quoted in the extant critical literature. Rājaśekhara (*Kāvyamīmāṃsā* p. 18) quotes it for an example of a 'grammatical poet' who displays both nouns and verbs. Apparently later centuries saw in Aśvaghoṣa primarily a love of language and a tremendous show of inflections, which indeed are conspicuous in his epics, where he lavishes the riches of Sanskrit grammar in an unexpectedly delightful manner. This particular verse would be noted also for its image, among other verses equally striking for clusters of verbs. Apart from critics, some other verses from Aśvaghoṣa are quoted in grammatical works as illustrations of particular points of grammar; an example is verse 13 above (for the word for 'Heaven' in it).

734. The fact that Aśvaghoṣa interested the medieval period (apart from Buddhist readers, we must note) only for his language, not for his ideas, is a significant indication of the development of taste. To a modern reader he seems full of ideas, but they are not the ideas appreciated by such a critic as Rājaśekhara. To understand their viewpoint we should compare Aśvaghoṣa with Bhāravi [1492] as a poet of ideas. The later poet is really more difficult grammatically and just as much a scholar as the earlier, but with him neither grammar nor other scholarship is displayed to be enjoyed, as it might seem, apart from the poem. Bhāravi's grammar is expressive and subordinated to the ideas. This makes the ideas stand out more distinctly for the critics. A process of integration has taken place between the means of expression and the matter expressed, marked perhaps in critical thought by Bhāmaha's definition of *kāvya* [194], laconic though that is. From Aśvaghoṣa's point of view, Bhāravi's verses have too many incidental ideas not directly connected with the narrative, though interesting as part of his general picture of life and as part of an epic having comprehensive scope. It can be argued that the earlier poet has his narrative and detailed descriptions better integrated and better balanced, his story unfolding at a fairly brisk pace for the most part, except where there are long philosophical dialogues directly comparable with the extensive dialogues of Bhāravi. Thus he packs in a great deal more narrative than later epic poets, still standing not too far from the *Rāmāyaṇa* in this respect. Bhāravi on the other hand is more concentrated, restricting his action to a relatively brief, but decisive, period in the history of his hero almost as in a drama. If, finally, we consider the aesthetic effectiveness, the *rasa*, Aśvaghoṣa is surely equal to any poet known in his portrayal of emotion, though not in his fancies so much as in the narrative itself [732]. The verses which follow (26-7) are perhaps more characteristic examples of Aśvaghoṣa's manner:

735. Other women, lacking firmness, swooning from grief
for their lord,
with their faces having eyes as springs
Splashed their breasts, where sandalwood was missing,
as a mountain its rocks with springs.

736. Then with their faces lashed with the water from
their eyes,
that palace appeared
As a lake at the beginning of the rains,
its red lotuses dripping water as they are lashed with
rain from the clouds.

737. The Handsome Nanda opens with the sage Kapila and his hermitage, afterwards the site of the city of Kapilavāstu where the Buddha was born:

With its grounds well kept,
soft, sandy, smooth,

Pale with a carpet of *kesara* flowers,
it was as if made up. (7)
<Cleared of earthy particles,
delicate, grainy, greasy,
Pale with a sprinkling of saffron>

(Here the simile comparing the grounds of the hermitage with a woman well made up with cosmetics is worked out with a series of puns, the first three lines being translatable as shown below the verse.)

738. Where sleeping antelopes appeared
among the altars
As if made into offerings
with *mādhavī* flowers and fried grain. (12)

(The *mādhavī* is a creeper which grows over the Vedic brick altars set up in the open air in hermitages: this scene, with antelopes sleeping by the altars, can be seen even today in India, for example in Assam.)

739. The 'grammatical poet' is conspicuous in the following verse:

Where *brahman* was perceived,
no one at all did harm,
The *soma* was measured out at the proper time
and none passed away untimely. (15)

(Here the four words underlined in English are all indentical in form in Sanskrit : *mīyate*. The point is that all are derived differently, so that we have a kind of punning and rhyming verse: 1) *mi* V *minoti*, 'perceive', passive *mīyate*; 2) *mī* IX *mināti*, 'injure', passive *mīyate*; 3) *mā* II *māti*, sometimes also III *mimīte*, 'measure', passive *mīyate*; 4) *mī* IV *mīyate*, 'die'. It is worth drawing attention to this kind of thing in order to show how the finer points of Sanskrit grammatical analysis inspired Aśvaghoṣa to some humorous linguistic games.)

740. In the Fourth Canto we find Nanda absorbed in lovemaking, completely unaware of the Buddha's visit to

Kapilavāstu after the Enlightenment, when he tried to bring solace to his family and of course to teach them:

Though the sage (Buddha) was there speaking of the doctrine,
and his relatives were respectful towards the doctrine,
Nanda, staying in his palace with love as his one objective,
amused himself in the company of his beloved.

For, like a ruddy sheldrake with his duck,
worthy of affection and accompanied by that beloved,
He did not think of Kuvera nor of Indra
on account of her presence, let alone of the doctrine.

Through fortune and beauty "Beauty",
through stiffness and pride "Haughty",
Through passion and anger "Passionate",
—thus she was called by three kinds of name.

She, with smiles as wild geese, eyes as bees,
full breasts as high raised lotus buds,
Shone more—a woman-lotuspool—
through Nanda as the Sun risen like his own family.

(The Buddha and Nanda belonged to a branch of the Solar Dynasty.)

..

Those two were devoted to their feelings like a pair of fairies
in a mountain waterfall,
They played and looked resplendent
as if overreaching each other's beauty and fortune. (10)

By increasing each other's passion,
that pair made each other take pleasure,
And by diverting each other in their intervals of exhaustion
they playfully made each other intoxicated.

Then he adorned his beloved,
wishing to serve her, not for the purpose of improving
her complexion;
For she was adorned by her own beauty,
she rather was the ornament of her ornaments.

Then putting a mirror into his hand:
"Hold this in front of me now
While I do my make up"
—she said to her lover, and he held it.

Then, observing her husband's beard,
she made herself up like it;
But by breathing on the mirror
Nanda countered and frustrated her.

At that playfully done villainy
of her husband she inwardly laughed,
But became as if angry with him
and crooked her forehead with a frown.

She threw her ear-lotus at his shoulder
with her left hand languid with passion,
And cancelled out his face
with the finger which had the film of cosmetic on it,
as he half closed his eyes.

Then Nanda as if afraid bowed down with his head at
his beloved's feet,
which were similar to lotuses,
On which trembling anklets were bound,
whose toes had very radiant nails.

He then appeared conciliating his beloved,
like a *nāga* tree broken down by the wind <onto an
altar>
Onto the golden bedside table, through the excessive
weight of its flowers,
with his head as the open fallen flowers.

(*vedī* means 'bedside table' and 'altar' and the description applies to Nanda and the tree; no doubt he was wearing an elaborate headdress, especially of flowers, which it was customary for men to wear [487].)

She raised him up after hugging him in her arms,
her necklace flying out from her breasts,
And laughed loudly, saying: "What is the matter?"
with her earrings hanging obliquely over her face.

741. After taking Nanda away from his wife the Buddha seeks to distract him so that he will not want to return, though he has promised her to do so. No amount of instruction in a monastery can have any effect on him, so the Buddha takes him up into the Himālayas and eventually on to Indra's Heaven, which lies further up the mountains, to show him nymphs who are much more beautiful than his Sundarī ('Beauty'). The description of the Himālayas begins like this (Canto X, 5ff.):

Those two quickly came to the Himālaya
most fragrant with deodars,
With floods of rivers, lakes and springs,
with ores of gold, with divine seers.

On that mountain frequented by celestial singers and
  siddhas [681],
happy in its upper garment made of the smoke of
  oblations,
After arriving, they stayed as if on an island of the sky
—of the homeless beyond.

As the sage (the Buddha) remained there with calmed
  senses,
Nanda looked wonderingly in all directions,
At the caves and bowers, and at the hermits,
—the adornment and protection of the mountain.

There on a very long white peak,
a peacock crouching with its tail feathers lowered
Appeared like an armlet of lapis lazuli
on the arm of Balarāma, whose arm is long and big.

Through rubbing against red arsenic and chalk,
a lion displayed a yellowish shoulder
Like a tarnished silver armlet of Kṛṣṇa (?)
inlaid with lines of pure gold.

A tiger, extended with languor and moving playfully,
wearing the sacred thread with the circle of his tail
over his right shoulder,
Appears at a mountain spring wishing to drink,
like one going down wishing to offer water to the
ancestors.

742. The crisis in this epic is reached when Nanda realises that even in pursuing the nymphs of Heaven, whom the Buddha has shown him, he is chasing a transient pleasure which will come to an end in time and leave him no better off than before, apart from the incongruity of practising asceticism for the sake of pleasure. The Buddha then begins to teach him systematically and comes to the critical point in Canto XV, where he administers some strong medicine on the subject of human relationships (verses 30ff.):

If your thought should be of the prosperity or decline
of your kinsmen,
The nature of the animate world
must be examined, to set it at rest.

In the transmigration of living beings
drawn along by their actions,
Who is a stranger? Who is one's kinsman ?
—a person is attached to a person by delusion.

(Johnston is no doubt right in translating *jana* in the third line as 'stranger' instead of 'person'—cf. the following verse—but the Buddhist critique of the concept of a person is thoroughgoing and should perhaps also be thought of here: there is no such entity as a 'person', but only transient compounds of elementary events giving rise to the illusion of a continuous personality.)

For in time past it happened that
your 'kinsman' was a stranger to you,

And in a future time a stranger
will be your kinsman.

Like the union of birds
in the evening, here and there,
So from life to life is the union
of strangers and of kinsmen.

As travellers resort
to diverse shelters,
Leave them again and return,
like that is the union of kinsmen.

In this naturally divided world,
no one is dear to anyone—
The universe is related by cause and effect,
like a fistful of sand.

For a mother nourishes her son
thinking: "He will support me",
The son is devoted to his mother
thinking: "She bore me in her womb".

When kinsmen behave
favourably towards their kinsmen,
Then these show affection;
but in the reverse case enmity.

Kinsmen are seen malevolent,
strangers are seen benevolent;
The world makes and breaks affections
according to its business.

As a painter might be attached
to a woman he had himself painted,
So a person unites with a person
having made the affection himself.

..

"That country is secure,
that one has abundant food, that one is happy"

—If any such supposition
should occur to you: (42)

You should abandon it, friend,
and not accept it at all,
Having known that the whole universe
is kindled with the fires of various disorders.

. .

Old age and disease and death
are the great dangers of this world:
There is no country where
those dangers do not apply. (46)

Where this body goes,
unhappiness follows there;
There is no destination in the world,
gone where, one is not troubled.

. .

—Or if you should have any supposition
not dependent on dying,
You should make an effort to destroy it
as a disease of the mind. (52)

No confidence is to be placed in life
even for an instant,
For like a tiger in its lair
time is the killer of the trusting.

You should not think:
"I am strong; or young"
—Death kills at all stages,
he does not have any regard for age.

743. These extracts will show that Aśvaghoṣa's epic style is intermediate between those of the *Rāmāyaṇa* and the medieval period (such as Bhāravi). The quatrains are detached, but not to the extent of interrupting the easy *Rāmāyaṇa*-like flow of the narrative: they are variegated with images and reflections, but much less figurative and less concentrated with meaning than Bhāravi's jewel-like verses.

744. It may be doubted whether Aśvaghoṣa followed in his epics the structural theory proper to the drama but applicable to epic, according to Bhāmaha [405]. We have noted in fact that the Life of the Buddha falls naturally into four parts, not five 'stages', and that Aśvaghoṣa seems to have observed this fourfold division very deliberately. However, the action of the epic can be analysed according to the five stages. If the objective is Nirvāṇa, then we can see the 'commencement' in Cantos I to IV, i.e. in the birth of the Buddha with the 'seed' idea of seeking final peace through renunciation proposed already in the first canto. The 'opening conjunction' can be seen in the third canto, where the hero is confronted with old age and begins to realise impermanence. The 'undertaking', or actual action as opposed to just the idea, clearly begins in canto V with the renunciation, the hero leaving home for the forest, and continues with his arrival in a hermitage and afterwards the arguments with his father's ministers (IX) and King Bimbisāra (X-XIII), in which the 're-opening conjunction' may be sought. The 'possibility of attainment' may be found in cantos XII to XIV leading up to the Enlightenment, which makes final Nirvāṇa possible; the 'embryo conjunction' being discoverable in the Enlightenment. From that point on the 'certainty of attainment of the fruit' seems clear, with the 'obstacle' or 'pause' in the campaign of teaching in which the Buddha engages (cantos XV to XVI), or in the attempt of Devadatta to murder the Buddha, with which Canto XXI ends. The final 'attaining of the fruit' is announced in the first verse of Canto XXII and consummated with the building of pagodas (which symbolise Nirvāṇa) in the last canto, the 'conclusion conjunction' culminating through the dispute over the distribution of the ashes in Canto XXVIII and the far wider distribution in thousands of pagodas by Aśoka. If this structural theory of stages and conjunctions had been applied to epics by Aśvaghoṣa's time, it is highly probable that he followed it, in view of his evident delight in all matters of linguistic and poetic theory and his desire to compose proper *kāvyas*.

745. The commencement of the Handsome Nanda will include the birth of the hero, and also of the Buddha, with the Enlightenment of the latter and his return to Kapilavāstu (cantos I to III). But the epic starts with a description of a hermitage on the site of that same city before it was built, suggesting the ultimate objective of liberation; only in the first canto (verse 37) the young princes, the ancestors of the hero and the Buddha, who find a refuge there in their exile from Ayodhyā, create so much disturbance that the ascetics abandon it and resort to the Himālaya. The undertaking could be traced through the Buddha's visit to Nanda's palace (Canto IV, 24ff.), where he is ignored on account of the entire household being busy serving the demands of pleasure: but one woman did recognise him as he went away and reported the visit to Nanda, who was shocked at the discourtesy and hastened to remedy it by going after the Buddha to pay his respects. The affair is now in train and the Buddha carries the hero off to a monastery (Canto V) for instruction, which at first proves futile (up to and including Canto IX). The stage of 'possibility' appears to begin in Canto X, where the Buddha takes the hero to the Himālaya and Heaven, thus inducing him to substitute the nymphs as his objective and to take up asceticism as the means to attain it. This stage then develops through to Nanda's doubts over his objective in Canto XII, where the 'embryo conjunction' could be pointed out. The 'certainty' will consist in the Buddha's systematic teaching from Canto XIII onwards up to Nanda's successful battle against vicious thoughts (XVII), where the 'obstacle' is clear. The 'attaining' and 'conclusion' come at the end of Canto XVII and in the last canto.

746. Since Aśvaghoṣa himself declares that he wrote *kāvyas* to carry the message of liberation, to give calm, not pleasure (*Saundarananda* XVIII.63), it is permissible to comment on his presentation of Buddhist doctrine. One might be satisfied to note the idea here of a 'calmed' aesthetic experience produced by narratives leading to Nirvāṇa, but there is much more than this general tendency of the works. Both epics are highly doctrinal in giving the Buddha's teaching in full detail. Aśvaghoṣa's Life of the Buddha is indeed much fuller in detailed doctrine than the earlier accounts of the Buddha's life, to be found in the various recensions of the *Tripiṭaka* itself, one or more of which constituted his source. Aśvaghoṣa has incorporated in it the content of many *sūtras* and made it a fairly comprehensive account of Buddhism. The presentation is extremely skilful, often making the points more immediately clear than does the rather heavy and repetitive style of the original *sūtras*. Though adding poetic figurativeness (but the *sūtras* provide plenty of similes and analogies themselves), Aśvaghoṣa seems not to take even the least licence with his sources in the matter of statement and interpretation of doctrine: he has simply improved the clarity and acceptibility of the exposition without—as far as one can see—modifying the content as he received it through his school (identified by Johnston as the Bahuśrutīya branch of the Mahāsaṃgha, which appears to be correct). For examples we may refer to the account of conditioned origination (XIV.52ff., as part of the Buddha's enlightenment) or, as a brief indication of a fundamental point, a verse explaining that the idea that one has a soul causes unhappiness, however subtle and refined the concept may be (XV.41): as a fire has heat as its nature, however small it may be, so the concept of a soul has unhappiness as its nature... (i.e. it is not a question of 'purifying' a supposed 'soul', because it is the very idea of a soul which is the basis of desiring things, of insatiable possessiveness, however subtle, which is unhappiness). The Handsome Nanda likewise contains extensive expositions of the doctrine, but from a slightly different point of view having regard to the nature of its hero. There is rather more of the practical matters of training and meditation and somewhat less theory. Most remarkable, however, is the exposition of the Four Truths (Canto XVI) of unhappiness and the way to end it, the essence of Buddhism, at the climax of the poem.

747. The value of Aśvaghoṣa's works as statements of Buddhist doctrine was appreciated by Buddhist philosophers, who borrow or quote from him quite often, as Johnston has pointed out (*Buddhacarita* II, xxviff.: Nāgārjuna, Harivarman, Vasubandhu, Candrakīrti, Yaśomitra, etc.).

748. Aśvaghoṣa takes full advantage of the opportunities his narratives afford for philosophical arguments between followers of different schools of thought, tending naturally to establish the Buddhist analysis ultimately as the true conclusion.

The Life of the Buddha, again the more theoretical work, contains expositions of Lokāyata philosophy (Canto IX, 55-62), appropriately by the counsellor, and of Sāṃkhya (Canto XII), put in the mouth of one of the future Buddha's teachers but said to derive from Kapila, the traditional founder of that system of speculation. Johnston has identified the particular school of Sāṃkhya here as that of Vārṣagaṇya. This is followed by an exposition of the practices of the Yoga school, said by Aśvaghoṣa to be that of Jaigīṣavya, Janaka and Parāśara: the last identified by Johnston as Pañcaśikha, apparently the earliest exponent of these practices. In Canto XVI there is a critique of soul theories which would bear on the Upaniṣadic concepts later elaborated under the name Vedānta, whilst the theory of a creator God is criticised in Canto XVIII (20ff.). There is a brief reference (XVIII.42) to the theory of Time as the cause of all things. These various speculations seem to be set out faithfully, making the Buddhist critiques which follow immediately or in later cantos appear cogent. The Buddhists of course have the last word, but Aśvaghoṣa takes care to be accurate in presenting rival views, so that his refutations may be convincing. After listening to the counsellor, the future Buddha comments (IX.73f.) that he cannot come to any conclusion about the problems of existence through another's words, but must discover reality for himself and come to a conclusion. This he does later, and the various critiques and the positive expositions of Buddhism are given gradually in later cantos, providing another structural element in this epic. In the Handsome Nanda, on the other hand, the various speculative systems are summarily dismissed in a single verse (XVI.17).

749. Perhaps the verses quoted above will indicate something of Aśvaghoṣa's power of characterisation. As examples of this one might point to the presentations of the groom Chandaka (not to mention the horse), the sketch of Sundarī with her playful passion and mock anger and the elaborate development of the character of the very ordinary, but sincere Nanda, contrasting completely with the independent and deeply reflective Sarvārthasiddha (Buddha). A minor character worthy of note is Udāyin, the son of the royal chaplain and companion of Sarvārthasiddha's youth, to be compared with Guṇāḍhya's character Gomukha, friend of Naravāhanadatta [691]. Udāyin has been appointed by the King as the Prince's companion and in Canto IV of the Life of the Buddha he first encourages the women, on an excursion to the park, in their efforts to distract the Prince, and then argues rather convincingly with the latter on the proper way to treat women.

750. There is no definite indication which of the two epics is earlier, but the reader gets the impression that the Handsome Nanda is a somewhat more advanced work in the development of *kāvya* style than is the Life of the Buddha. Its language appears slightly more polished and its descriptions more figurative; the poet seems a little freer, having a more perfect mastery of his medium, though he had more scope there to improvise and elaborate his own scenes than in the Life of the Buddha, where there was so much more narrative to be presented, faithfully following the sources. The greater popularity of the Life of the Buddha, however, was not due solely to the greater fame of its hero: it is not possible to rate it as inferior to the Handsome Nanda, for it is a deeply moving work, from the early scenes of the anxiety of the hero's father, and the pathetic episode of the renunciation, to the touching farewells as the Buddha leaves his friends and the beautiful city of Vaiśālī (XXV.34), to attain his final Nirvāṇa. To this epic the Handsome Nanda is a perfect complement with its own unique features.

751. Apart from the general conception of a Rāma-like hero and a grand epic, Aśvaghoṣa follows very different models from Vālmīki's in his epic composition. Of these unfortunately practically nothing is known to us, except the little we can discover about the poet Pāṇini and his Kṛṣṇa epic [644-6]. The pioneers of epic *kāvya* after Vālmīki had transformed it from continuous narrative into the chain of independent stanzas (quatrains), each complete with its own figure and allusiveness. We may assume that it was not primarily Aśvaghoṣa himself who was a great innovator in this respect: his avowed purpose and method presuppose the popularity of this and other *kāvya* forms. These he proposed to use for a purpose higher than merely to give pleasure, with secondarily a certain amount of education. Though he had the poetic impulse developed to the highest degree, and the genius to write splendid *kāvyas*, he could surely not have hoped to attain his purpose by sweeping innovations, which might not have proved popular, rather than by developing a well established and popular form. Genius is of course always original, but this may manifest itself in various ways: in Aśvaghoṣa we should surely seek it in his handling of the poetic vocabulary and the expressive powers of the Sanskrit language, and on the other hand in his power of characterisation and psychological penetration, not in the formal development of *kāvya*, in which as suggested above he seems rather to have delighted in his skill in outward conformity to technical rules and conventions.

752. Of Pāṇini as a model we have reported that he had the reputation of excelling in the *upajāti* metre [644]. We find in fact that this very metre is especially prominent and most skilfully handled in Aśvaghoṣa's epics. Though relatively simple in structure, it is a hard metre to use continuously as a canto metre without producing monotony, yet Aśvaghoṣa makes it capable of endless variety by his skill in setting words to it. Besides this favourite metre and a less frequent use of *vaktra*, Aśvaghoṣa uses at least four other metres as canto metres, including the uneven *udgatā* derived originally from a bar metre (*Saundarananda* III). He uses at least twenty different metres altogether. Aśvaghoṣa seems to allude (Johnston, *Buddhacarita*, Vol. II, xlvii) to an epic of which Kṛṣṇa was the hero, and this could very well have been Pāṇini's if we find his style suggests the latter as a model.

753. His models for the drama are still more obscure. Subandhu's *Vāsavadattā* was doubtfully a *nāṭaka*, of a special variety [653]. The slender evidence in Patañjali [658], for plays on such subjects as Kṛṣṇa and Kaṃsa or Purūravas and Urvaśī, does not tell us whether these were still four act plays of the *ḍima* or *īhāmṛga* types, or already elaborated into *nāṭakas* of five or more acts according to the standard of the *Nāṭyaśāstra*. It is followed by a gap of nearly two centuries before we find both of the full length types, the *nāṭaka* and the *prakaraṇa* (not necessarily distinguished exactly as in the *Nāṭyaśāstra*), exemplified in Aśvaghoṣa's plays. Roughly contemporary with Aśvaghoṣa, we know of the existence of the ancient Śailālaka School of Drama in Mathurā, the capital of Śūrasena, but not what they produced : they supported the Buddhist Community and might therefore have had some connection with Aśvaghoṣa [178]. For a possible model more immediately preceding Aśvaghoṣa's time than the plays known to Patañjali, and more tangible only in being called definitely a *prakaraṇa*, the only suggestion we can now make is that, when Māra refers in the 'battle' canto of the Life of the Buddha to the story of the princess Kumudvatī and her fisherman lover Śūrpaka, Aśvaghoṣa is thinking of the lost *prakaraṇa Kumudvatī*, mentioned much later by Śūdraka in the *Padmaprābhṛtaka* and having that story (see Johnston's translation of XIII.11) [1225, 1231]. Since the *prakaraṇa* has by definition, in the standard theory, an invented story, and since this particular story, otherwise unknown, seems to have the characteristics of a romantic invented plot, this suggestion has a reasonable probability. We know nothing of the author of the *Kumudvatī* and nothing more than the above as to its date.

754. Aśvaghoṣa's favorite figure of speech is the infinitely variable simile, so prominent in Buddhist canonical literature also. Numerous examples will be found in the passages translated above [735, 736, 741, 742]. He cultivates also the metaphor *rūpaka*, especially the 'complete' *samasta* metaphor (Bhāmaha II.22), as in the case of the great ship (of knowledge) which carries distressed people across the ocean (unhappiness) which has waves (old age), tearing foam (disease) and terrific currents (death) (*Buddhacarita* I.70). Or there is the river (the Buddhist doctrine: *dharma*) with its current (understanding), banks (firm discipline) and ducks (vows), which is cool (with concentration) and quenches thirst (passion) (ibid. 71). There are many of these [see also 740], and they can be paralleled in the Buddhist canonical literature and in the *Rāmāyaṇa*. They are very rare in later *kāvya*, where they are replaced by the complete double meaning (*śleṣa* or *śliṣṭa*), which can be seen already in Aśvaghoṣa [737].

755. Aśvaghoṣa is also fond of rhyme *yamaka*—a fondness which is part of the evidence for his delight in the sounds of the Sanskrit language [739]. Rhyme is in most Sanskrit and Prakrit literature simply a figure of speech, used occasionally to adorn a verse or a prose sentence. It belongs especially to the equipment of *citrakāvya*, as we noted in an earlier chapter [411], and the examples of *citrakāvya* in Sanskrit include a few exceptional poems in which rhyme is used throughout, just as in other *citrakāvyas* double meaning is used throughout, and which consequently are called *yamakakāvyas*. On the other hand in Apabhraṃśa and the modern Indo-Aryan languages ryhme became a standard feature of versification. Another exceptional poem (or *rāgakāvya* drama [392]) in Sanskrit, the *Gītagovinda*, also uses rhyme regularly: in this case the poem is modelled on Apabhraṃśa prototypes, being written in Apabhraṃśa metres. Aśvaghoṣa shows a greater infusion of the purely verbal effects of *citrakāvya* in his epics than most later *kavis* writing in Sanskrit allow (except that some of them allot a special canto to such writing [1543]). This is perhaps the mark of a period before *citrakāvya* had separated out as a distinct branch of poetry. Aśvaghoṣa also revels in the use of grammatical decorations, as in the different roots underlying the same verb forms, the use of the same verb in as many as nine different meanings in a single stanza (*av* in *Buddhacarita* XI.70), or the illustration of a difficult series of grammatical rules in successive verses (the last device also was later separated off as a subject for special poems, the 'grammatical' *kāvyas*). The first two cantos of the *Saundarananda*, especially, illustrate these grammatical acrobatics.

756. These features of purely verbal effect suggest the style of the Eastern or *gauḍīya* school of *kāvya* as later recognised by the critics [238, 241, 242, 937]. We lack early examples of this school for comparison, and cannot say whether Aśvaghoṣa should be included in it. At any rate he shows much affinity to it, and was an Easterner by birth. If not a fully fledged exponent of the *gauḍīya* style he certainly shows the trend towards it, or the phase of *kāvya* out of which it naturally developed. Since the style did not find favour with the most influential critics of later times it is perhaps not so surprising that Aśvaghoṣa's works were neglected, even though his genius was not surpassed. The same neglect accounts for the disappearance of almost all the early *gauḍīya kāvya* and the consequent impossibility of ascertaining its period. Aśvaghoṣa's epics actually exemplify certain types of sound-combination denounced as cacophonous by the critics from Bhāmaha (I.53—*ajihladat*: in *Saundarananda* II.30) onwards. He obviously prefers variety to the classical restraint which is the ideal of later *kāvya*, and it is evidently an essential characteristic of Aśvaghoṣa which we learn from the calculation that he uses a larger vocabulary than any other Sanskrit poet (Johnston, *Buddhacarita* II, lxxviii).

757. Aśvaghoṣa uses the figure lamp *dīpaka* [188] quite frequently, which, involving parallelism of grammatical construction, borders on these grammatical effects. A simple example is: 'He was not averse to courage and to generosity...' (*Saundarananda* II 5, c-d). Less simple is:

> He knew, by intelligence and science,
> fitness for this world and for the next;
> He guarded, by firmness and heroism,
> his senses and his subjects. (ibid. 15)

The effect depends largely on the possible collocations of such words as 'knew' and 'fitness' *kṣama* in Sanskrit. In this verse there are two lamps, in the two halves and with parallel constructions.

758. Of other figures which one might look for, there is perhaps a sufficient element of 'exaggeration' *atiśayokti* [196] in the similes about the peacock, lion and tiger, quoted above [741], to be identified as that figure mixed with simile.

759. There are a number of corroborations [208], including a whole cluster of them in *Saundarananda* XVIII, indicating that this figure was already institutionalised and consciously used. For example:

> Old age and other misfortunes of many kinds
> have power over the existing engagement of people:
> For unborn trees are not shaken,
> even when terrible winds are storming. (*Saundarananda* XVI.10)

> Previously exalted by the arrogance of wealth,
> today you are flourishing through the end of desire:
> For as long as a man has desire in the world,
> so long, though flourishing, he is always poor.
>
> (*Saundarananda* XVIII.30)

760. A probable contrast *vyatireka* [209] may be pointed out in *Saundarananda* IX.28:

A season passed revolves again,
the Moon waned waxes again:
But once they have gone these do not return—
the water of rivers and the youth of men.

761. The enumeration *yathāsaṅkhya* [212] is perhaps to be understood, though not in the precise sense of Bhāmaha, in *Buddhacarita* V. 42:

For, pure as a golden mountain,
that intoxicator of the hearts of the best of women
Stole their ears, bodies, eyes and very existences
with his speech, touch, body and good qualities.

Or again in *Buddhacarita* IX. 16:

For the action on clouds, water, dry grass and mountains
of the wind, the Sun, fire and great thunderbolts
—That action, grief is exerting on me
by pulling apart, drying up, burning and splitting.

This is perhaps rather 'equal consequence' [223].

762. Fancy *utprekṣā* [213] is quite common, though less sophisticated and in fact less fanciful than in later *kāvya*. Some examples may be found in the passages translated above, as in *Buddhacarita* III.10 [731] and VIII.25 [733]. On the whole, Aśvaghoṣa's fancy is not quite detached from simile, and the element of personification of natural phenomena, so important later, is not developed. Consider for example *Buddhacarita* VIII.26 [735], where women are fancifully compared with mountains: it is a simile, but it is almost a fancy of the later kind, in reverse. Or again *Saundarananda* I.7 [737], where the hermitage is personified as a woman, which is more like a later fancy but is mixed with a series of puns and should probably be identified as a 'partial fancy' *utprekṣāvayava* [234] (the metaphor, also required for this mixed figure, is provided by the 'carpet' of flowers). In *Saundarananda* X. 20ff. we find a series of personifications of trees (in Heaven)—they have eyes, wear clothes and jewellery and bear garlands and musical instruments, entertaining the gods, but formally these verses are not fancies, which would contain the expression 'as if'.

763. Other figures can be found, but the impression is that Aśvaghoṣa stands nearer the beginning than the end of the development of figures which led from the small group in the *Nāṭyaśāstra* to the three dozen recognised by Bhāmaha. It is not simply that the number of figures is limited, for the majority can be found if we do not make the definitions too narrow, but that most of them are not yet fully developed into the forms which became standard, as we have seen in some cases above. What is significant is that this development has definitely begun, that a series of figures unknown to the *Nāṭyaśāstra* has appeared. At the same time it is possible to identify some of the old 'characteristics' [186] of the *Nāṭyaśāstra*, such as the rhetorical question *pṛcchā* in *Buddhacarita* VIII.52ff.

764. We have seen that, in the construction of an epic, Aśvaghoṣa on the one hand follows the technique of the discontinuous chain of independent stanzas and on the other produces an overall balance in the work, through the perfect symmetry of its major parts. A further constructional feature, not much favoured by later *kavis* except in prose, is to be found in certain devices used to give formal unity to series of stanzas. These include the use of a set of parallel similes, or other figures such as rhyme or corroboration, or of a series of parallel grammatical constructions. Occasionally the ancient device of the refrain appears, sometimes a particular word or phrase is repeated in each stanza, or an argument is cast in the form of a set of parallel statements. Most of these devices used to group stanzas into paragraphs on a single subject are anticipated in Pali poetry. Like the use of the independent stanza, they may be regarded as lyric rather than epic in origin, but they offset the discontinuity of the former technique and enhance the balance of Aśvaghoṣa's works, which thus flow rhythmically in stanzas, paragraphs, cantos and groups of cantos, all matching the subject matter. The transition from the continuous narrative lines of ancient Epic (Tradition) to the series of detached quatrain-moments of later *kāvya* epic is thus facilitated.

765. There is not much to say of critics on Aśvaghoṣa, since most of the available critical works ignore him. Bhāmaha does not name him or quote any of his verses, but as we have noted above he quotes a verb form used by Aśvaghoṣa and objects to it as cacophonous. Though it is not proved that the critic had Aśvaghoṣa in mind, since others might have used the same form, it is at least clear that the type of poetry we find in the Handsome Nanda presumably did not please even this Buddhist critic in its use of sounds. There had been sweeping changes in fashion in *kāvya*, which we have to some extent indicated already, such that Aśvaghoṣa's works lost much of their interest and perhaps fell out of general circulation by about the +5. According to Johnston (*Buddhacarita* II, lxxxii) Daṇḍin knew the Life of the Buddha and utilised it, whilst we have noted [733] that Rājaśekhara in the +10 quotes a verse from it, as well as that critic's assessment of Aśvaghoṣa as a 'grammatical poet'. In some circles, however, probably exclusively Buddhist, Aśvaghoṣa continued to be better appreciated in later centuries. As noted above, Buddhist philosophers found his expositions of the doctrine valuable, but from a more literary point of view we have a note by a Chinese Buddhist critic, I-Tsing (late +7), who had a fine appreciation of *kāvya* and translated Mātṛceṭa's *Śatapañcāśatka* [890-1] into Chinese. Johnston (ibid. xxxvi) gives a translation of the relevant passage: Aśvaghoṣa 'clothes manifold meanings and ideas in few words, which rejoice the heart of the reader, so that he never feels tired from reading the poem...doctrine given in a concise form'. Also the Life of the Buddha 'is widely read or sung throughout the five divisions of India and the countries of the Southern Sea'. The Handsome Nanda also was popular in the lands of the Southern Sea in that period, for Paranavitana (*Jānakīharaṇa*, Introduction, p. lxv) has found a story that it was preferred by a king of Indonesia (Śrīvijaya) to an attempt by a contemporary poet to surpass it. Thus Aśvaghoṣa retained his Buddhist audience—perhaps also for his plays, though I-Tsing does not mention them, for, as we have seen, Dharmakīrti (also +7) mentions the *Rāṣṭrapāla*—because he provided an excellent concise presentation of their doctrine. Moreover it was an attractive presentation, so arranged and balanced that one never got tired of reading it. We have seen the truth of this judgment, for Aśvaghoṣa's narratives are always just rapid enough to keep the interest in movement, balancing the descriptions and arguments: it is this art which the Chinese critic has noted.

766. Of later Buddhist critics in India, we find that Ratnaśrījñāna (p. 61) quotes a verse as by Aśvaghoṣa, though it is not traced in the works available to us, whilst the same is true of the anthologist Vidyākara (verse 2)—it is again noteworthy that a Buddhist anthologist, of the early +12, should give only one verse by Aśvaghoṣa out of more than 1700 in his collection. Ratnaśrījñāna quotes a verse in criticism of lassitude, in support of Daṇḍin's verse (I.105) on which he is commenting:

> If lassitude were not a misfortune in the world,
> who here would not be learned or rich ?
> For through lassitude the Earth with (upto) its Ocean
> is filled with men who are like animals and poor.

This is probably taken from one of Aśvaghoṣa's plays.

767. Vidyākara's verse is also quoted, anonymously, by Vāmana (+8; p. 58) as an example of punning. It is an invocation to the Buddha, which may have stood at the beginning of one of the plays, though its authenticity has been doubted :

> Flashing with scimitars raised in their arms, with armoured breasts,
> <Having bosoms with lustre at their tips and curves reaching up to their arms,>
> warm, with wounds, tormenting the hearts of their enemies <rivals>, cruel <firm>,
> With the weight of their battalions seen extended in the sky, led by Death,
> <With the fulness of their bodies visible through their garments being loose, led by love,>
> the Deaths and the breasts of Death's women did not produce agitation in him—may the Buddha protect you !

Here the first three lines of the quatrain apply both to the Deaths (Māras, Gods of Death) and to the breasts of their women, both of whom assailed the Buddha in the 'battle' before the Enlightenment [714]. The 'wounds' are respectively those of war and of love-making with bites and scratches. The words in pointed brackets are the versions of the preceding words applicable to the breasts, where a single English equivalent could not be found to bear the double application of meaning. It is possible that this elaborate pun is really Aśvaghoṣa's, since he is fond of the figure. The metre (*śārdūlavikrīḍita*) is used in the Handsome Nanda and the *Śāriputra*.

768. Apart from these notices of Aśvaghoṣa by critics, there is the question of his influence on later poets, where they may seem to be copying points in his style or trying to improve on him. Not much need be said within the limits of the present study, but Johnston in his Introduction to his translation of the Life of the Buddha has collected a number of examples where Aśvaghoṣa's influence seems visible. The *kavis* affected include Mātṛceṭa (xiv), Śūra (xxxvi), Bhāsa (lxxxf.), Īśvaradatta (?—see the note to IV. 67 [1121]), the author of the *Ṛtusaṃhāra* (lxxxi), Kālidāsa (lxxxi) and Bāṇa (lxxxii). This suggests that his influence was considerable up to the +7, after which perhaps he was rarely read by *kavis*, who devoted their time to other models. To Johnston's collection we can now add Kumāradāsa (+8), who in his epic *Śrīghanananda* tried to surpass Aśvaghoṣa's poem on the same story, with doubtful success (Paranavitana, *Jānakīharaṇa*, lxv).

CHAPTER XVI

MĀHĀRĀṢṬRI KĀVYA IN THE +2, ESPECIALLY THE LYRIC : SĀTAVĀHANA, PĀDALIPTA, VIMALA

769. We have mentioned more than once the earliest extant Māhārāṣṭrī literature, a collection of lyrics which appears to have grown up round a kernel of folk songs. The collection is attributed to a Sātavāhana emperor, but confusion has arisen as to which one. It has in fact been doubted whether any of them had anything to do with it, since the language of their administration was—as we noted above from their inscriptions—a more archaic Prakrit [16, 669]. However, since the administrative language remained unchanged for several centuries we may reasonably assume that the spoken vernacular in Mahārāṣṭra was widely divergent from it by the +2, besides which we may reckon with the probability of a plurality of dialects in the country. Without going further into this discussion, which in the present state of our knowledge would be pure conjecture, we may for our present purpose accept the traditional ascription of the original part of the collection as probably correct.

770. The content of the lyrics relates almost exclusively to country life, the life of the villages scattered along the banks of the Godāvarī or in its tributary valleys running up into the Vindhya mountains. This life was full of hardships, but not without compensating pleasures, especially those of love. The beauty of the songs of the villagers, in which their joys and sorrows are recorded with fresh art, yet great subtlety of observation, evidently attracted poets and scholars from the capital to collect and imitate them. At some time an emperor with literary interests put his seal on a collection of such songs or lyrics, or more likely himself made the choice. Many names of authors of individual lyrics have been recorded, testifying that the collection is an anthology, 'Sātavāhana' being credited with taste in making the selection, not in composition, although one or two verses have his own name (or at least his dynastic name) attached to them.

771. For this name 'Sātavāhana' we often find the form 'Hāla' substituted, and the latter has sometimes been taken as the emperor's personal name. Tradition (the *Purāṇas*) actually includes a 'Hāla' in the dynastic list, giving him a very short reign which would fall in the +1 (see Pargiter: *Dynasties of the Kali Age*, p. 41). Probably, however, 'Hāla' is merely a Prakrit form of the dynastic name 'Sāta' (*-vāhana* means 'vehicle' or 'mount', *sāta* is a word of uncertain origin, probably not Indo-Aryan, which seems most likely to mean 'horse'). The historians have probably hypostatised the name Hāla into a separate emperor, not realising that it meant the same as Sāta, and then inserted him into the dynastic list at a conveniently obscure point, though they managed to give him only five years, or in a variant list only one year, to reign. We may assume that the collector of Māhārāṣṭrī lyrics was in fact one of the great emperors of the +2. Other literary references do not attempt to distinguish 'Hāla' from Sātavāhana, and at the same time are content, or resigned, to be historically vague as to his position in the dynasty.

772. The most interesting literary presentation of Sātavāhana now available is in a Māhārāṣṭrī novel of the +8, Kutūhala's (=Prakrit Koūhala) *Līlāvaī*. Although this romantic story of Sātavāhana is probably pure fiction (otherwise would it have been classed as a *kathā*?), the author has put in a few touches to give his hero a suggestion of historical substance. He makes the Buddhist philosopher Nāgārjuna visit Sātavāhana's court, where he meets Poṭṭisa and Kumārila —both of whom appear as poets in the anthology. An epistle of Nāgārjuna to a Sātavāhana is extant (the *Suhṛllekha*, 'Epistle to a Friend'). Several other literary sources attest this association of Sātavāhana with Nāgārjuna, including works on alchemy (e.g. *Rasaratnākara*, see Rāy : *History of Chemistry in Ancient and Medieval India*, pp. 118, 132 ff., 317 f.) and some Jaina historical works (see e.g. *Purātanaprabandhasaṃgraha*, p. 91 and Prabhācandra's *Prabhāvakacarita*, 36 ff.). We are told that at Sātavāhana's court Nāgārjuna studied under the novelist Pādalipta and then became *guru* (teacher, preceptor) to the emperor and his queen Candralekhā. Buddhist historians have recorded this traditional association (having the epistle to draw attention to it), and two of them, the Tibetans Bu-ston

(Vol. II, 136 f., of Obermiller's translation) and Tāranātha (p. 72) (following Indian sources unfortunately no longer extant), state that it was towards the end of his life that the philosopher went to the South and, most important, that he there organised the construction of additions to the Buddhist monuments in the Āndhra country (then part of the Sātavāhana dominions). There is archaeological and inscriptional evidence to confirm this, and moreover to associate a particular emperor with the operations (*A Comprehensive History of India*, Vol. II p. 316). It appears to follow that Nāgārjuna was associated with the emperor Puḷumāyi II, called also Vāsiṣṭhīputra, whose dates are either +128 to +156 or +138 to +166. The latter, then, was presumably the famous patron of Māhārāṣṭrī literature who collected the lyric anthology and patronised the novelist Pādalipta.

773. During the +1 and +2 India enjoyed great prosperity, perhaps even greater than in the time of the fabulously wealthy Magadhan emperors of the −4 and −3. At the height of this prosperity we can discern in the +2 the signs of those profound social changes which in the succeeding centuries led to the replacement of the ancient order, with its centralised governments, elaborate civil services, royal monopolies of key industries and widespread slavery, by what may be called a 'feudal' order. A better term than 'feudal' could perhaps be found to describe medieval Indian society, in which the peasants were not reduced to serfdom, but provisionally it may serve to characterise the predominance of an aristocratic hierarchy and hereditary landed gentry taking over the offices of tax collection—see below, Chapter XX [1153]. Under this new order we note the rise of numerous provincial governors to a position of semi-independence, establishing hereditary succession of their sons to their posts. Some attained complete independence from the old imperial centre, many secured full local authority as vassals bound only to supply quotas of troops to an overlord.

774. The exact relationship of this decentralising process to economic prosperity has not yet been worked out: it suggests some kind of diffusion of wealth over wider areas, and especially outside the ancient cities which had previously accumulated it. In the +1 and +2 India's overseas trade flourished as never before or since, bringing wealth which in part was used to patronise art and literature. In the North the Kuṣāṇa Empire produced new trends in architecture and sculpture (Mathurā, Gandhāra: origin of the traditional Buddha figure at Mathurā, and of the familiar 'pagoda', or many storied monument *stūpa*, at Puruṣapura), as well as in *kāvya*, and it was rivalled by the Sātavāhana Empire of the Godāvarī valley, under which a new school of architecture, sculpture and painting arose in Āndhra and Mahārāṣṭra. In the far South the +2 is the period of the Śaṅgam poets, the earliest extant literature of Tamil (for a brief account of this see K.A. Nilakantha: *The Cōḷas*, Chapter III, pp. 30 ff.).

775. It is in fact under the Sātavāhanas of the ⊢2 that modern historians have traced the beginnings of the trend towards 'feudalism' in the administrative system (see e.g. R.S. Sharma: *Aspects of Political Ideas and Institutions in Ancient India*, Chapter XIV of the first edition, cf. p. 303 of the second edition). The Kuṣāṇas appear to have been more conservative, and although their governors of West India at Ujjayinī became independent during the +2, the latter too seem to have remained faithful to the old social order.

776. It may not be pure conjecture, then, to see in 'Sātavāhana's', or Puḷumāyi II's, excursion into the folk songs of the villagers an illustration of a new outlook on society, away from the cities and into the country; away from the milieu of the merchant class—despite the continuing importance of trade—towards that of the country gentry now rising to prosperity, who might aspire to the status of *nāgaraka* [27]. If we can trust some of the commentators on Sātavāhana's anthology, the *nāgaraka* is to be found there, describing his observations of country life, though there is apparently no agreement among them as to which particular poems are supposed to be spoken by a *nāgaraka*. Thus according to Gaṅgādhara about 30 out of the collection of 700 (61, 104, 122, 161, 168, 180, etc.) are spoken by *nāgarakas*, though the other commentators so far as published offer no support for any of these identifications: Pītāmbara where available puts these poems in the mouths of women, usually of a messenger or a friend of the heroine described in them. On the other hand Pītāmbara says that poems 578 and 647 are spoken by *nāgarakas*, which Gaṅgādhara does not support. These commentators are quite late, but seem to have found in the works of their predecessors some kind of association of *nāgarakas* with the collection.

777. Verse 3 of the Sātavāhana anthology says that 'Hāla', who was 'fond of *kavis*', selected 700 songs (*gāhā*, Sanskrit *gāthā*)out of ten million (a *koṭī*, i.e. an enormous number). This work, under the title *Gāhāsattasaī*, 'Seven Hundred Songs' (Sanskrit *Gāthāsaptaśatī*), has come down to us in more than one recension, with considerable variations in content. Altogether we have more than 950 songs included in the anthology in these recensions, accepted by various commentators. Evidently connoisseurs of Māhārāṣṭrī poetry noted other verses in that language in their manuscripts of the anthology, or added new verses at the end, and these were sometimes copied out along with the more original verses when a new manuscript was needed. Later on the original number of 700, regarded as the proper total, was presumably obtained by eliminating some, probably on subjective grounds.

778. The writing of Māhārāṣṭrī lyrics in fact became extremely popular after the +2, this language being regarded as the best kind of Prakrit and as the proper language for songs even among people, or characters in dramas, who ordinarily spoke another dialect of Prakrit. From apparently the +3, as far as we know, i.e. the time of Śūdraka [1184], characters in dramas who in their dialogue speak Śaurasenī, the standard dramatic Prakrit, resort to Māhārāṣṭrī for their verses. It seems to have been only in the +4 that Māhārāṣṭrī found its way into inscriptions, in other words into official documents, though Mehendale has pointed out some of its characteristic phonological features in inscriptions as early as the +1 (*Historical Grammar of Inscriptional Prakrits*, especially pp. 62, 65, 271 ff.). It therefore replaced the older Prakrit administrative language [669] of the Deccan only after the collapse of the Sātavāhana Empire. Māhārāṣṭrī then became a standard or classical literary language alongside Sanskrit, both in a special use in dramas, as just noted, and for entire *kāvyas* in various forms, such as the *saṭṭaka* [344], epic [413, 1265, 1431], novel [436] and some of its sub-varieties [450-4] and of course lyric. It has retained this position as a classical language throughout the history of *kāvya*, though the spoken language of Mahārāṣṭra soon changed further towards modern Marāṭhī, via the Marhaṭṭa Apabhraṃśa attested in the +8 by the novelist Uddyotana. The rise of Mahārāṣṭra to political supremacy in India in the +17 and +18 seems to have encouraged the writing of Māhārāṣṭrī *kāvyas* (e.g. by Ghanaśyāma, Rāmapāṇivāda, Viśveśvara) as well as the development of modern Marāṭhī literature.

779. Weber, the critical editor of Sātavāhana's Seven Hundred Songs, distinguishes six different recensions (see his Vorwort to *Das Saptaçatakam des Hāla*, 1881, pp.XXVIIff.). These appear, however, to reduce to two main recensions, Weber's first, or 'vulgate', and his fifth, or 'Teliṅga' (T). His second and third appear to be relatively late derivatives from the first, with a number of new verses, some in common with the Teliṅga recension. The verses peculiar to them seem never to be quoted by the literary critics, whereas most of the verses in the first and fifth recensions are quoted, though usually without any mention of the source. This presumably indicates that the verses of the first and fifth recensions were well known in literary circles by the time of Ānandavardhana and Bhoja, whereas the others probably did not yet exist (Weber thinks the third 'recension' is related in orthography, etc., to the Jaina grammarian Hemacandra of the +12; which suggests it was compiled in Gujarat in or after his time). Weber's fourth 'recension' likewise appears completely unknown to the critics, its peculiar verses not being quoted. His sixth recension (W or 'second Teliṅga') on the other hand appears to be relatively old, but it consists of one hundred (more precisely, 104) verses only and is thus hardly a 'recension' of the Seven Hundred Songs. Most of the dozen verses peculiar to it are quoted by the critics (three by Ānandavardhana). Whether it really represents a selection of a hundred verses from a recension of the Sātavāhana anthology, otherwise not now available to us, is a matter of conjecture. It may instead have been a selection from the Teliṅga (T, fifth) recension, with additions from other Māhārāṣṭrī literature or composed by the compiler. The manuscripts of 'W' do not name Sātavāhana or Hāla but call the text simply *Prākṛtaśṛṅgāraśataka*, thus it makes no claim to represent a recension of the Seven Hundred Songs. The fact that at least 18 of the verses peculiar to the 'Teliṅga' or fifth recension are quoted by the Kaśmīra critics Ānandavardhana and Mammaṭa means that its circulation was far from being confined to Āndhra, where its manuscripts were found. The so called 'vulgate', which Weber found much more widely circulated in recent times, is merely another recension, which has been preferred by the later commentators. Much research remains to be done on the *Gāthāsaptaśatī* and its recensions, for there are apparently numerous manuscripts of the anthology which were not available to Weber, with several more commentaries.

780. Weber found only 430 verses common to all his recensions (allowing for the incompleteness of 'W', etc.—Vorwort, p. XLVIII). As between the Teliṅga recension and the 'vulgate', the former has about 560 verses supported by the 'first' recension or its derivatives the 'second' and 'third'. There are few clues to the relative authenticity of the Teliṅga and vulgate versions where they disagree. Here we may discuss two possible clues and then delay no longer in our study of the poems themselves. Verse 464 of Weber's edition (for convenience we shall use his numbers in the 1881 edition) mentions the emperor Vikramāditya. It is found in the vulgate but not in the Teliṅga recension. If 'Vikramāditya' here means Candra II Gupta of the +5 (which is not certain), the verse must be an interpolation, which speaks against the vulgate. Verse 490 mentions the water-wheel *rahaṭṭa* used for irrigation. It too is found in the vulgate but not in the Teliṅga recension. It has sometimes been doubted whether this machine, often called the 'Persian' wheel, was in use as early as the Sātavāhana period (e.g. R.S. Sharma, *Indian Feudalism*, p. 253). However, it is in fact mentioned in the Pali Canon (*Vinaya* II 122) as *cakkavaṭṭaka*, explained in the *Samantapāsādikā* (VI, p. 1208) as *arahaṭṭaghaṭiyanta*, which attests its existence by the —4 in India.

781. The verses translated below are all common to the vulgate and the Teliṅga recension unless otherwise stated. The numbering by Weber follows the sequence of the vulgate, in which there is no discernible order. The Teliṅga recension, on the other hand, is arranged in sections called *paddhatis*, 'paths', as it were tours through the different topics found in the anthology. The metre of the songs is the musical 'bar metre' *gaṇacchandas* [567] we met in the Pali Canon, nearly all of them being in the form called *āryā* [581]. This metre, as we have seen, is based on a musical structure of eight bars, known in musical theory as the *caturasra tāla*, which no doubt prevailed in the folk songs from which these lyrics were originally taken. We noted also in Pali *kāvya* how the new fixed metres *akṣaracchandas* developed out of the 'musical' ones through the choice of particular rhythmic structures [582]. In the variable rhythmic patterns which the musical metres could superimpose on the *caturasra tāla* it was possible to reflect emotive or descriptive associations appropriate to the subject matter. The Sātavāhana anthology beautifully illustrates the development of such a technique of using rhythms suggesting particular types of event, object or feeling (for a discussion and examples see Cappeller: *Die Gaṇachandas*, pp. 81-5).

782. The popular milieu of the Seven Hundred Songs may be compared with that of the early Pali lyrics. In the latter we met the peasants, artisans, scavengers, slaves and other ordinary people of the Ganges valley and Avanti. In the Seven Hundred we meet some of their counterparts in ancient Mahārāṣṭra. The collections differ in that, whereas the Pali lyrics were selected to illustrate the Buddhist view of life, Sātavāhana's chosen theme was love and his aim the sensitive aesthetic experience. At least, the commentators insist that love is the subject of every verse, even of the few which on the surface appear to describe something quite different.

783. In the Pali Canon, we found many verses composed by women. In the Seven Hundred it is noteworthy that, in the great majority of verses, it is women who are represented as the speakers; though we cannot say how many were authentic folk songs, which might have been composed by women, and how many were imaginatively and rhetorically cast in that form by more sophisticated poets, either men or women. The interest here is the point of view presented, which is generally that of women: it is almost always women who love in these lyrics, who experience the emotions which inspire the sensitive experience in the reader or listener to the song:

In whichever direction I look, I see you there, as if drawn,
The whole wheel of the directions is as if bearing a series of your likenesses. (531)

In the Māhārāṣṭrī the gender shows that the person seen here is masculine. The commentator Gaṅgādhara explains that a girl very much in love thus reveals her feelings to a youth.

784. Let us see how the Seven Hundred Songs illustrate the life of the peasants (explicitly in such verses as 64, 107, 317, 373):

The peasant drinks the medicine cooled by the fragrant wind from the lotus mouth of the girl who asks him how he feels,
So that although it is of a pungent nature he doesn't leave any. (317)

According to Gaṅgādhara a woman says this to her friend, showing the power of love.

785. As its etymology indicates, the word *halika*, which we translate 'peasant', meant more specifically a 'ploughman'. This work was hard:

Her husband fallen asleep, feeble from dragging the ploughshare sticking in the swamp,
The labourer's wife, deprived of the happiness of love-making, swears at the rainy season. (324)

Gaṅgādhara thinks this may be a verse composed by a *nāgaraka*, or that it may be spoken by a female messenger *dūtī* to a prospective lover, implying that this is a good time to make advances to the wife, even though her husband is at home.

786. The following description of a rice field, as the milky looking new grain starts to appear in the winter, according to Gaṅgādhara, is not found in the Teliṅga recension. It is worth quoting for its elaborate double meaning, reminiscent of Aśvaghoṣa [737] but foreign to Sātavāhana's collection, as well as for its picture of the peasant:

The peasant is delighted by his rice field as by his son—
Dark with mud, looking as if drinking only milk, going in up to the knees. (568)

The commentators Gaṅgādhara and Pītāmbara say that a woman sings this so that her lover can overhear and know that she will meet him by the rice field. This is a very typical comment and shows how a verse apparently not about love was brought into line with the assumed subject of the anthology.

787. The peasants also have sesame fields, for producing oil (8, 695 which is not in T, 769 which is in T as well as one version of the vulgate). Verse 8, where a girl describes the sesame field in the cold season *śiśira* to her mother-in-law, is again said by Gaṅgādhara to be intended to be overheard by her secret lover: the seeds have been harvested and so the field is deserted now, a safe place for lovers to meet. There are also hemp (9) and cotton (360) gardens, and saffron gardens according to Gaṅgādhara and Pītāmbara on 392, where a woman asks the plant to conceal her secret love. There are various tasks in the cotton garden (359) and the hazard that it may be trampled by a buffalo (550). The following verse, not in the Teliṅga recension but in all versions of the vulgate, shows a woman performing a ritual in the cotton garden:

As she makes the blessing on the plough, on the auspicious day for the cotton garden,
The unfaithful woman's hands tremble because of her secret wish. (165)

Gaṅgādhara explains that the cotton garden is the rendezvous with her lover.

788. Besides the peasants, the hunters in the forests of Mahārāṣṭra are described (e.g. 119-22, 173):

With an ear ornament made from a peacock's tail-feather the hunter's bride wanders haughtily about
Among her rival wives who have embellishments set with pearls from elephants. (173)

As Gaṅgādhara explains, the new bride overreaches the older

wives of the hunter, although for them he had killed elephants and made ornaments with the pearls from their temple bones. Now he is able to hunt only peacocks, but that is because his strength has been exhausted through his great love for the new bride.

789. Women are met as milkmaids:

In the forest ardent with the breezes of the honey month, bringing the jingling of the bees,
The milkmaid sings something set with words of separation, which bewitches the minds of travellers. (128)

The 'honey month' is the first month of spring.

790. Women also grind grain:

The travellers look with unblinking eyes at the peasant's daughter made pale with flour,
—With desire, as if at Fortune coming forth from the Ocean of Milk. (388)

The allusion here is to the myth of the churning of the Ocean by the gods, which produced among other precious things the Goddess Fortune (Lakṣmī), moreover Fortune is symbolised by the colour white. It is a commonplace that the gods' eyes do not blink, thus the travellers' stares would suggest that they were gods. On this verse Gaṅgādhara adds that 'some' commentators say that it was spoken by a *nāgaraka* to his companion, but the idea is not supported by Pītāmbara. We have a variation on this theme of grinding:

See ! As if they are white geese resting in the shade of her lotus face,
She bears her breasts white with the powder flying up from the grinding of the flour for the festival. (626)

Gaṅgādhara thinks a *nāgaraka* says this, but Pītāmbara holds it is a woman friend of the girl described.

791. The housewife in her kitchen is thus described:

The husband laughs at the housewife when her hand, dirty with soot sticking to it from the kitchen work,
Touches her face and leaves it in the condition of the Moon. (14)

Bhoja (*Śṛṅgāraprakāśa* II p. 416) quotes this verse as an example of implied simile, *sāmya*, defined by him as a separate figure of speech. The allusion is to the dark mark on the Moon, regarded by Indian poets as an ornament. The wife looks beautiful to her husband even when dirty from the housework.

792. Girls have the task of serving water to travellers at drinking places by the roadside (49, 161):

The more the traveller with upward glance lengthens his drink of water, his fingers wide apart,
The more the serving maid, too, makes thinner the already thin stream. (161)

793. Whatever the prosperity of the gentry or the towns in this period, the villagers are likely to live in poverty. The following verse sounds like the *nāgaraka* observing country life:

The village girls steal the hearts of sophisticated men at the Love (Festival),
With the burden of their breasts having only saffron dyed bodices as ornaments. (546)

794. If the simplest and cheapest dress enhances village beauty for a man bored with city sophistication, the more poignant and compassionate aspect of poverty is also recorded:

In the house of misfortune the housewife protects her husband from confusion;
—When asked about her pregnancy longing she says once more only 'water'. (472)

A pregnancy longing must be satisfied, according to ancient Indian belief, otherwise the baby may be deformed. The husband must therefore try to satisfy every fancy and whim of his pregnant wife, regardless of difficulty or expense.

795. The following vulgate verse is not in the Teliṅga recension:

In winter his misfortune is indicated by the sweet scent
of a dung fire,
By his being tawny with smoke and by his worn out
garment with very sparse threads. (329)

According to Gaṅgādhara this is spoken by a woman friend advising a girl not to be attached to such a hero.

796. The following verse again is not in the Teliṅga recension and with its philosophising perhaps stands a little apart:

Let him be born in a forest place, and even as a crooked
stump with feeble leaves,
Not in human society—if he is generous, sensitive—and
poor. (230)

Again Gaṅgādhara, bringing this into line with the main subject of the anthology, says this is a woman's complaint to her messenger.

797. The next verse, which is in all the available recensions, expresses a different kind of philosophy which could very well be found in a village, even with its puns:

Enjoy what is in your power! How could there be salt
in the stores of a poor village?
Handsome one! What use is salt where there is no
oil? (316)

'Salt' *loṇa* also means 'elegance' or 'beauty'; 'oil' *siṇeha* also means 'affection' or 'love'. Gaṅgādhara says a messenger from the village says this to the hero, whilst from our knowledge of other poems in the anthology we may easily suppose that, as the commentators sometimes say, the woman is acting as her own messenger. She means that here you will find affection, whereas the city beauties are fickle. As noted above [787], the villages produce their own sesame oil; they could not produce salt. Gaṅgādhara further notes this as a case of 'citation of something else' *anyāpadeśa* [418], in this case the cooking analogy. Such citations are fairly common in the anthology and the Teliṅga recension has a whole section of them as well as others scattered about in other sections.

798. General reflections on the evils of the world are found in two verses, one (704) in the Teliṅga recension and some manuscripts of the vulgate, the other (710) only in a few manuscripts of the vulgate. The first says bitterly that the deaf and the blind are lucky because they do not hear malicious words and do not see the prosperity of scoundrels. The commentator Sādhāraṇadeva reduces this to a woman's complaint about her rival. The second says that good men are as rare as wild geese, scoundrels as common as crows; which the commentators available interpret in three quite different ways as expressing the feelings of supposed heroines.

799. Of a different character is this reflection, which is much more likely to be original to the anthology:

> When, of a couple whose love has grown with time,
> increasing through sharing the same pleasures
> and troubles,
> One dies, surely that one lives—it is the other who is
> dead. (142)

The aesthetic experience here is definitely the compassionate, as Bhoja states (*Śṛṅgāraprakāśa* Chapter XXIII, p. 64 of Yadugiriyati's ed.).

800. Different again, and probably original, is the following:

> For a man who undertakes something there will
> inevitably be fortune or death;
> Now, there will be death even if he doesn't undertake
> it, —but not fortune. (42)

Gaṅgādhara says this is spoken by a messenger from a girl, urging the hero to do something.

801. The great majority of the Seven Hundred Songs deal clearly and directly with love, so let us now turn to them and see how they present this subject in all its aspects. It is possible to find here the various types of heroine classified in the *Nāṭyaśāstra* (XXIV.203 ff., etc., Kāśī), as well as the stages of love [142] and many other aspects of the emotion. The commentators and critics point out some of these themes, Bhoja in particular illustrating his theories profusely from the anthology, and the composers of the poems in fact seem to have been aware of some of the types of heroine as described in the *Nāṭyaśāstra*. The anthology undoubtedly typifies many of the aspects of love, yet at the same time its characters and situations are strongly individualised, in other words made vivid and particular. The method used here exemplifies the same principles as the figure of speech known as corroboration *arthāntaranyāsa* [208], especially the presenting of a particular case which illustrates a generalisation. As a rule the generalisation will not be stated in these poems, but the reader will feel that the character presented, or the situation, is typical.

802. There is the agitation of the girl who goes to meet her lover (the *abhisārikā*, *Nāṭyaśāstra* XXIV, 212), very simply portrayed in the following verse:

> When he comes, what shall I do? What say? How will it be?
> —The heart of the girl who acts boldly, going out for the first time, trembles. (187)

This heroine is also 'uncertain' *adhīrā* in her actions, Bhoja points out (*Śṛṅgāraprakāśa* Chapter XXIII, p. 39). A different heroine is portrayed in the same situation as follows, with humour:

> Today I have to go in the dense darkness to that handsome one!
> —The lady practises a series of steps with her eyes shut, in the house. (249)

Bhoja chooses this to illustrate an 'effect of emotion' *anubhāva* [54] (*Sarasvatīkaṇṭhābharaṇa* p. 616).

803. With reference to the sensitive aesthetic experience, the *Nāṭyaśāstra* (p. 73, Kāśī) [57] distinguishes two determining factors or positions *adhiṣṭhānas*, 'union' *sambhoga* and 'frustration' *vipralambha*. The sensitive produced by frustration is very often found in the Seven Hundred, with a great variety of situations within it. For example:

> She looks out, disappointed in her object, she sighs long, she laughs at nothing;
> Since she chatters with indistinct meaning, how much there must be in her heart! (296)

This case of frustration is during the first passion, according to Bhoja (*Sarasvatīkaṇṭhābharaṇa* p. 629). The commentator Kulanātha says it exemplifies the seventh of the ten stages of love, namely 'madness' *unmāda*.

804. A common situation in the anthology is the woman whose lover has gone abroad, of which the following is an example according to Gaṅgādhara:

> Today, without him, remembering the happiness I had experienced,
> Hearing the noise of the fresh clouds is like the drum (proclaiming my) execution. (29)

The rainy season is supposed to intensify the longing of lovers, moreover it obstructs travel so that the woman knows her lover cannot now reach her for at least another two months. Executions in ancient India were announced by a drum carried through the streets [1199]. Bhoja quotes this verse for the thunder as a 'cause of emotion' *vibhāva* (*Sarasvatīkaṇṭhābharaṇa* p. 614) [54]. Elsewhere he quotes it again for frustration in the rainy season and on the same page quotes the following verse for frustration in the spring (*Śṛṅgāraprakāśa* Chapter XXIII, p. 59). Gaṅgādhara explains that this is a woman's reply when another woman has asked her about her well-being:

> Well-being? How could there be well-being? From the head of that crooked mango tree by the gateway to the house
> Surely some misfortune has been born. (499)

The mango buds mean spring has come, which is a misfortune for her (Gaṅgādhara).

805. The heroine 'anxious through separation' *virahotkaṇṭhitā*, whose lover does not come (*Nāṭyaśāstra* XXIV.206 Kāśī), appears in the examples pointed out by Gaṅgādhara to have good cause for her concern, because it is clear that he no longer cares for her, though he may eventually feel obliged to visit her:

O helping fever ! Bringing from afar even this rare
man who asks me how I feel,
Though you are taking away my life you are not at
fault ! (50)

Gaṅgādhara says the man has been forced to come to her through fear of public opinion, not through affection, and in these words addressed to the fever which is ending her life she rebukes him. Death is welcome to her. Bhoja (*Sarasvatīkaṇṭhābharaṇa* p. 474) quotes this as an example of the figure 'praise of what is not the subject' *aprastutapraśaṃsā* [219].

806. In another verse about a woman 'anxious through separation', her friend goes to remonstrate with the man she loves (Gaṅgādhara):

I am not a messenger, you are not loved, what business
have I in this matter ?
—She dies, you are dishonoured, I am speaking the
words of duty. (178)

Gaṅgādhara says she means he will run the danger of being guilty of the crime of murdering a woman, if he does not go ('duty' *dhamma*, i.e. *dharma* virtue or law). Kulanātha thinks this refers to the tenth stage of love, dying *maraṇa*, but perhaps things were not really as desperate as that. Viśvanātha (*Sāhityadarpaṇa* p. 547) quotes the verse as an example of 'spurning' *ākṣepa* [207], i.e. denying her real nature as messenger.

807. According to Gaṅgādhara the heroine described by her messenger in the following verse is 'separated by a quarrel' *kalahāntaritā* from her lover (*Nāṭyaśāstra* XXIV. 208 Kāśī):

She says: 'Whom do you remember?' She chatters: 'Who is mine?'
By her agitated weeping I have been made to weep too. (389)

Bhoja quotes it (*Śṛṅgāraprakāśa* II p. 446) as a clear example of *rasas* being increased by the causes of emotion, etc. Here we can easily pick out her remembering him as the cause of emotion, her meaningless chatter as an effect of emotion and her agitation as a transient emotion; her tears are an expressive *sāttvika* emotion which is also a transient [59]. Bhoja should of course be understood in relation to his own theory of *rasa*, in the context of which this is quoted [113]. At this level there are many *rasas*, which at the higher level will fuse into one.

808. The beginnings of love and the effects which first reveal it are illustrated in a number of poems:

If he is really not your beloved, then when his name is mentioned, my dear, why
Does your face blossom like a red lotus at the touch of the rays of the Sun? (343)

My pen falters on its way because of the state of my trembling and perspiring fingers,
I haven't even finished writing 'Greetings'—dear friend, how can I write the letter itself? (244)

Gaṅgādhara notes here the 'expressive emotions' perspiring and trembling [59]. Bhoja quotes these two verses under his topic 'test of love' *premaparīkṣā*, or 'trial of love', 'examination of love', the way in which it is proved to be present (*Sarasvatīkaṇṭhābharaṇa* p. 637). In the following verse he finds a case of the test and the response to it (p. 635):

On the pretext of the rough descent to the Godāvarī she abandoned herself on his chest,
By him, too, innocently and out of compassion, she was tightly embraced. (193)

Bhoja (p. 347) also quotes this verse for the figure 'reciprocity' *anyonya*, known to us first from Rudraṭa [260].

809. Love is not always innocent, and the anthology includes many scenes of deceit and intrigue:

> Right in front of her husband the girl is led to the house of her lover, the doctor,
> Waving both her arms as her clever friend supports her with her hand, saying: 'She has been bitten by a scorpion !' (237)

810. After quoting this for 'secret' *pracchanna* passion (*Śṛṅgāraprakāśa* Chapter XXII, p. 40), Bhoja goes on to quote (p. 45) the following for 'unfeigned' *akṛtrima* passion, arising in this case, he says, from the combination of youth and trustfulness:

> The traveller was looked at in such a way by the daughter-in-law, her pupil slightly turned towards the outer corner of her eye,
> That, though turned away by the master of the house, he stayed on the veranda. (254)

The 'master' is obviously her father-in-law and her husband presumably away, whilst we gather that she dislikes them both.

811. It is naturally among the poems on themes such as this that the critics found excellent examples of implied *vyaṅgya* meanings insinuated by literal meanings not really intended [250]. Thus:

> Here my mother-in-law sleeps, here I, here all the servants;
> —O traveller, blindly in the night, don't go to sleep in my bed ! (669)

This means exactly the opposite of what it literally says. Ānandavardhana, the theoretical pioneer of the study of the nonliteralness of good *kāvya*, quotes it (with slight variations) as an example of an 'injunction' *vidhi* in the form of a 'prohibition' *pratiṣedha* (i.e. a literal prohibition which really implies an injunction; *Dhvanyāloka* p. 71). The implied meaning here is contained in the actual subject matter of the poem [252].

The commentator Pītāmbara remarks that by her intonation *kāku* the lady shows that this is really an invitation and not a prohibition.

812. Here is another example:

Wander on confidently, virtuous man! —That dog
has been killed today
—By the proud lion which lives in the wild arbour on
the bank of the Godāvarī. (175)

Gaṅgādhara explains that a woman says this to keep the wandering sage away from the arbour where she has arranged to meet her lover, as it looked as if he was on his way to meditate there. Ānandavardhana quotes it (p. 52) as a prohibition in the form of an injunction. Afterwards (p. 73) he quotes a verse (Weber 944) from the Teliṅga recension as an injunction which is not intended but which implies neither an injunction nor a prohibition; the girl is in fact censuring the hero for his offence of having an affair with another woman (cf. Bhoja, *Śṛṅgāraprakāśa* I p. 248). Other theoretical possibilities could easily be imagined, and Bhoja illustrates a whole series of them, largely from the recensions of the Seven Hundred (*Śṛṅgāraprakāśa* I pp. 247-8).

813. Ānandavardhana illustrated other parts of his theory from Sātavāhana's anthology. The following is for him *kāvya* where the implied meaning is subordinate *guṇībhūtavyaṅgya*, though it is present, because the literal meaning is very striking and the implied meaning not immediately clear (*Dhvanyāloka* pp. 281f.):

Aunty! The lotus beds have not been crushed and the
wild geese have not been made to fly up;
—Someone has put the open sky in the village pond!
(110)

Ānandavardhana understands this instead that someone has stretched out the clouds in the pond, but that does not affect the discussion. In either case the meaning is that the pool was undisturbed: no one had been there. Gaṅgādhara explains that a secret meeting place near the pond had been appointed by the lover of the girl who is speaking. She had returned from there at dawn under the pretence of bringing clean water (an ordinary, everyday action). She tells her aunt that she has seen a wonderful thing: someone had put the sky in the water, yet without disturbing the lotuses or the wild geese. Kulanātha adds a necessary further explanation, namely that the girl told her aunt this in the presence of other people, including her lover: it means that he failed to keep the appointment—'I went, you didn't go', he understands. This, 'Why weren't you there?', is the implied meaning as Ānandavardhana understands it. This presumably would be immediately clear to him, though not to the reader of the *kāvya*. The striking, fanciful literal meaning of someone putting the sky in the pond subordinates the implied meaning for the reader.

814. The following verse also belongs to the category where the implied meaning is subordinate, according to Ānandavardhana (p. 479). In this case the implied meaning is indicated by the intonation *kāku*, he says:

> Yes indeed! We are bad women! Go away, you
> who observe your vow to your husband!
> Your clan is not besmirched.
> But why should we, then, love the barber, like somebody's wife? (417)

This seems pretty obscure, except that it is part of a quarrel among women. It appears full of implied meanings, though they are obscure except to the initiated, and it is not easy to see what Ānandavardhana meant by the literal meaning which predominates (the second half?). The commentators Gaṅgādhara and Pītāmbara agree that the speaker is herself 'bad', i.e. unfaithful to her husband. Gaṅgādhara adds that she claims to be attached to a hero of high birth (presumably the affair would not then be a disgrace to her own clan *gotra*). But she says the other's clan is not degraded either, though her family (?—i.e., her husband's?) *kula* (originally 'tribe') is. We do not at present know enough about ancient Indian society to be certain what this means. The *gotra* is perhaps being alleged to be an inferior one, so that it could not be degraded by a liaison, even with the barber. If we turn from these unsatisfactory commentaries to Ānandavardhana and his commentator Abhinavagupta we find slightly different readings, but the essentials seem the same. Abhinavagupta says that 'Yes indeed! We are bad women!' is spoken with intonation intending ridicule. 'Go away' or its variant is meant literally. '..vow to your husband!' is sarcastic and 'Your clan is not besmirched' also intends something else, it is said 'stammeringly'. 'Somebody's wife' is blinded by love; 'we' do not love a proletarian *pāmara*: this is ridicule. A lady who had been seen misconducting herself was ridiculed by another lady 'of good family' *kulavadhū*. But this other was attached to the barber, so that the first counters her ridicule with this verse. It is the intonation which conveys the ridicule, i. e. the implications. The literal meaning which dominates can be understood as the explicit mention of the barber, which should be the decisive blow in the argument.

815. Ānandavardhana also quotes (p. 515) from the Seven Hundred for *dhvani kāvya* mixed with figures of speech. The verse he quotes is this:

> On the darkened days when the fresh rains resound
> The dancing of the peacock flocks looks splendid, their
> necks impetuously stretched out. (560)

Ānandavardhana says that simile and metaphor are mixed in this, but we have to read Abhinavagupta for an explanation. As we have it, moreoever, his reading of the text is different from that of the manuscripts of the Seven Hundred itself (both recensions), and this different reading is explained by Abhinavagupta. As for the implied meaning, some of the commentators, including Gaṅgādhara, see here an indication of a secret place of meeting, namely an arbour where the peacocks dance, also possibly the time as night, when the day is 'darkened', or that during the rains the days are dark enough for the heroine to go to meet her lover without waiting for the night. The anonymous commentator on the Teliṅga recension, on the other hand, suggests that a traveller is speaking to another, urging him to hurry in order to get home before the rains make further progress impossible. The latter is closer to

Abhinavagupta's idea, as we shall see. For the figures, we can suggest a simile in the darkened days being likened to night and a metaphor perhaps in the dancing of the peacocks or in the resounding of the rains, since both words imply musical performances. These, however, are not what Abhinavagupta finds. Whether following what Ānandavardhana originally read, or introducing new readings, Abhinavagupta has: 'On the days dark for travellers, when the fresh clouds resound...' (omitting also 'impetuously' in order to make room for 'travellers'). In the words 'dark' *sāmāia* and 'fresh clouds resound' *ahiṇaapaoarasia* he can now find double meanings, 'audience' and 'connoisseurs of performances with acting'. The implication of the first meaning is simply that these are 'gloomy', depressing days for travellers. The second meaning is 'when there is an audience of travellers who are connoisseurs of performances with acting' (for the peacock dance). Now Abhinavagupta can point out a simile in the days being 'gloomy' *like* the travellers and a metaphor in 'traveller-audience' (the travellers *are* the audience). In view of the manuscript tradition of the Seven Hundred, all this looks like misplaced ignenuity on the part of the critics, who have 'improved' the text to produce these subtleties. Such punning seems foreign to the original anthology and we should probably find a lesson in this example, that the critics are not always reliable guides to *kāvya* composed many centuries before their own time. In their analysis they tend to be too ingenious, to overinterpret a simple poem. If we wish to read here something more than simply a description of the beginning of the rains, no doubt with the emotional overtones associated with that season, and to find the poem as suggestive as the collection usually is, we may take it as an invitation, that the days have arrived when it is good to go out to meet one's lover. Some of the commentaries support this and may well preserve the original understanding of the verse.

816. Whilst discussing Ānandavardhana, we may glance back at verse 173 [788], which he quotes (p. 256). The literal meaning which implies the implied meaning may be taken by a writer direct from actual life, alternatively it may be just something fancifully imagined by him. The scene of the hunter's bride exemplifies something taken from life. We might generalise about this: in the Seven Hundred Songs the meanings are almost invariably taken from life; when we find fancies superimposed on nature, they are the fancies of the characters portrayed, part of the life, not imaginative descriptions by the poets.

817. Before discussing the figures of speech in the anthology let us quote one more example of implied meaning. Ānandavardhana himself does not discuss this, but Mammaṭa, who follows him in elaborating the theory of *dhvani kāvya*, gives it (*Kāvyaprakāśa* p. 22):

> See! Motionless and calm the female crane is beautiful on the lotus leaf,
> Like an oyster shell placed in a vessel of spotless emerald. (4)

The commentators are agreed here that a girl speaks this to her escort: over there is a secluded spot for our meetings! No people disturb the bird and we shall not be disturbed. They ignore her simile.

818. In a collection like this we shall not expect to find many figures of speech, except sometimes in the indirect expression of the characters themselves. With reference to the theory of figures one would have to classify most of the verses as 'naturalistic description' *svabhāvokti* [197] or 'realism' *bhāvikatva* [198]. However, we have already noted a few of the figures which are found by the critics, especially by Bhoja, rarely by the commentators. Thus from Bhoja we noted cases of implied simile *sāmya* [791], praise of what is not the subject *aprastutapraśaṃsā* [805] and reciprocity *anyonya* [808]. Viśvanātha has pointed out 'spurning' *ākṣepa* [806]. We can add here that Pītāmbara notes a 'fancy' *utprekṣā* in verse 626 [790], Bhoja (*Śṛṅgāraprakāśa* II p. 400) finds another case of reciprocity in verse 161 [792] and Ānandavardhana calls verse 230 an implied constrast *vyatireka* [796, 209].

819. Bhoja quotes (*Sarasvatīkaṇṭhābharaṇa* p. 400) the following as an example of simile:

Her face is like the Moon, the moisture of her lips
is like the ambrosia,
Her kiss—brilliant with the impetuous seizing of her
hair—what is that like? (213)

The ambrosia is supposed to come from the Moon; *ggaha* means both 'seizing' and 'eclipse'. The figure at the end might be compared with 'want of agreement' *ananvaya* [225], since nothing is found to compare the kiss with.

820. Kulanātha notes a 'fancy' *utprekṣā* in the following verse, whilst Bhoja sees an example of a figure which he calls 'comparison' *upamāna*, in the technical epistemological sense, however, of identifying something after having heard a description of it:

The castor oil plant, whose leaves come out of the
hole in the fence, is as if establishing for youths
That here in this house a peasant's bride lives, whose
breasts measure *this* much. (257)

Kulanātha explains that the curved leaves of the plant, like a hand with outstretched fingers, look as if they are extended to show the diameter of the breasts. This is a straightforward example of 'fancy', with the personification generally associated with that figure. Bhoja's explanation (*Sarasvatīkaṇṭhābharaṇa* p. 389) is similar, but bringing in the figure 'comparison', not found in any earlier writer and perhaps first introduced into poetics by him. In fact he introduces, as figures of speech, the six means of knowledge from Mīmāṃsā epistemology, including this. Here the 'comparison', in this sense, is enacted by the plant. Bhoja says that from its gesture the youths are able to know that the unseen breasts inside are like those previously experienced by them of such a kind.

821. The following, says Bhoja (*Sarasvatīkaṇṭhābharaṇa* p. 349), is an example of 'revolution' *parivṛtti* [228]:

Her lower lip's redness, driven away at night by her
lover,
Is surely seen at daybreak transferred to the eyes of her
rival. (106)

Gaṅgādhara says her friend is telling others of her success.

Daybreak of course implies the redness of dawn. According to Bhāmaha, however, as noted above, revolution should be combined with corroboration, of which there seems to be no trace here. In fact there are very few examples of corroboration in the anthology, which as we have said deals with particular cases without stating, though they may imply, a generalisation [801].

822. Here according to Bhoja (*Sarasvatīkaṇṭhābharaṇa* p. 336) we have a 'hint' *sūkṣma* [196, 259]:

> The beauty of the face of the dark girl, who is looking with half an eye, darkens
> As the peasant's son wanders about with a rose apple leaf made into an ear ornament. (180)

If this 'hint' (of jealousy?) is not enough we can consult the commentator Gaṅgādhara, who says the leaf indicates the rendezvous and that the girl refuses to go. Bhoja's explanation is instead that she thinks, from seeing the leaf ornament, that he probably will not go to their meeting; presumably, therefore, understanding that the ornament was made for, or by, another girl. The 'hint', for Bhoja, is in the girl's expression. For Gaṅgādhara, this is an observation made by a *nāgaraka* to his companion, as both watch the scene.

823. The following verse contains a 'fancy', or more exactly an implied fancy, according to Ruyyaka (*Alaṅkārasarvasva* p. 74); but Mammaṭa (*Kāvyaprakāśa* p. 110) and Viśvanātha (*Sāhityadarpaṇa* p. 209) give a more complicated explanation:

> Not finding room in your heart filled by a thousand women, O handsome one,
> Engaging in no other work she daily makes thinner her body, thin as it is. (182)

The messenger says this, according to Gaṅgādhara. Ruyyaka's 'fancy' is in the 'making thinner'. Mammaṭa and Viśvanātha also see implied meaning here, but in their case there are two different figures, one of which implies the other. The implying figure, which Mammaṭa calls 'cause' *hetu* [196, 259] and Viśvanātha 'literary middle term' *kāvyaliṅga*, a redefinition of the same figure which seems to be given first by Udbhaṭa (*hetu* may also mean 'middle term' in logic), implies the figure 'distinction' *viśeṣokti* [230]. Mammaṭa says that by the 'cause' —that although made thinner her body does not find room in your heart—'distinction' is implied. Śrīdhara in his commentary on Mammaṭa says here that the making thinner is the cause poetically imagined for the purpose of getting into the heart; since the effect is still not produced, 'distinction' is implied. We may recall that according to Bhāmaha this latter figure tends to involve a paradox, understanding then 'your heart is most extraordinary'. Śrīdhara says there is also 'fancy' here, probably following Ruyyaka.

824. Bhoja quotes the following as an example of 'error' *bhrānti* (*Sarasvatīkaṇṭhābharaṇa* p. 364), a figure we find first defined by Rudraṭa [261]:

> People laughed, clapping their hands, at the travellers
> who went to the dried up fig tree;
> When the flock of parrots, which looked like leaves and
> fruit, flew up. (263)

This is a pleasant picture of country life as it stands, but the commentators must explain its presence in the Seven Hundred. In the Teliṅga recension it is placed in the section of citations of something else *anyāpadeśa*, i.e. it is taken to have some implication. Gaṅgādhara also says it is such a citation, demonstrating that qualities which are not innate do not last long. He adds that 'some' (commentators) say that a messenger says this to stop a girl from going to meet her lover at a rendezvous: there are other people there. Presumably they are waiting to laugh when she goes and the 'lover' doesn't turn up. An anonymous commentary quoted by Weber says the messenger means the girl will be a laughing stock if she is devoted to such a man.

825. We have noted the importance of the 'citation of something else' in the Seven Hundred already. It is in effect the same as Rudraṭa's figure 'expression of something else' *anyokti* [261]. Let us look at two more examples. The first is pointed out by Gaṅgādhara as a citation of something else:

The peasant's son is burned internally in the house
empty of his wife,
Looking at the place of delight as at one from which
his treasure has been dug up. (373)

The commentator explains that the wife is dead. One might think that the parallel of the lost treasure was sufficient as the 'something else', but Gaṅgādhara goes further and sees here a woman telling a man that he should not show his grief over a mere mistress who had died.

826. The second appears in the 'citation of something else' section of the Teliṅga recension (the first is in a different section, that on village life) as well as being pointed out by Gaṅgādhara:

Without branches and hard to climb, my boy, do not
climb up the trumpet flower!
Climbing and falling down, who have not had their
hopes destroyed by her? (468)

This is a very clear instance of such a 'citation'. Gaṅgādhara says a woman speaks thus to stop a man from going to another woman, of unreliable and crooked character, to whom he is attached. Abhinavagupta in his commentary on the *Nāṭya-śāstra* (Vol. II p. 310) quotes this verse as an example of the 'characteristic' *lakṣaṇa* 'wish' *manoratha* [186]. In this characteristic, too, the wish is expressed by speaking of something else.

827. We have sampled the riches of this anthology, but there is much more which is noteworthy. For example, among the more usual kinds of love lyric we sometimes find descriptions of family life, including delight in children and their actions (e.g. verse 11, and 568 translated above [786]): in verse 200 the baby's first teeth appear.

828. We have seen in some of the verses above that wild nature, as well as villages and fields, forms part of the background: love responds to the succession of the seasons and lovers find opportunities on the wild banks of the Godāvarī, whilst various animals, birds and flowers are mentioned. The Vindhya Mountains to the North are mentioned several times and described as they appear in different seasons, for instance:

The Vindhya has his limbs embellished with horripilation—the shoots of fresh grass—
Being excited by the cloud-breasts of the Fortune of the rains. (578)

'Cloud-breasts' *paohara*, here is a pun, the word meaning both.

829. References to myth and legend are rare. Śiva and Gaurī are invoked in the first verse and appear again in 455. The love of Kṛṣṇa and Rādhikā is referred to in 89 and his precocious childhood in 112. The Churning of the Ocean is alluded to in 388, translated above [790], and is mentioned in 475 and 594. The Dwarf incarnation of Viṣṇu and his binding of Bali is used in a simile in 425. The contradictory properties of the arrows, made of flowers but very sharp, and so on, of Pleasure or Love *Kāma* are described in 326. The stories of the Great Epic (443) and of Rāma (35) are alluded to, whilst the following verse is perhaps developed from *Mahābhārata* III *adhyāya* 54 verse 9:

On whichever of her limbs one's glance first falls,
There it remains...no one has seen her whole body!
(234)

In the Epic the glances of the kings become stuck to the various limbs of Damayantī at her 'self-choice' *svayaṃvara* and do not move. This lyric heightens the idea with its comic inference.

830. One of Sātavāhana's introductory verses to his anthology says:

Those who do not know how to recite and listen to ambrosial Prakrit *kāvya*,
Yet practise the system of the principles of pleasure—how are they not ashamed? (2)

In this way Sātavāhana introduced the new literary fashion at his court. If it was at first a collection of folk songs, our impression is that many of the verses are no longer at that unsophisticated level of creation. It is very probable that poets at court, encouraged by this royal appreciation of Māhārāṣṭrī songs, emulated them. To go much beyond this impression would perhaps be too subjective to help in deciding the question, but we can refer to the elements of *kāvya* technique discussed above in relation to the songs, where the critics found so much to illustrate their theories of poetics. Since our choice has been largely guided by the critics, we may possibly have given a too sophisticated picture of the anthology, yet there seems to be enough surviving of popular poetry, in the verses we have translated, to allow us to suppose that much of the theory was derived from the analysis of these poems, rather than the other way about. Apart from the *Nāṭyaśāstra*, and a few passages in works not on poetics, the critical writings we now possess are much later than Sātavāhana. It seems that Ānandavardhana's theory of implied meaning owes much to a study of this anthology; it is possible that the older theory of the figures of speech also derived some of its ideas from this source.

831. The recognition of Sātavāhana's anthology by the critics as a classic of *kāvya* has been indicated above, where we found many of the Songs quoted and discussed by Ānandavardhana, Abhinavagupta, Bhoja, Mammaṭa, Ruyyaka and Viśvanātha. They do not name the anthologist, or the original authors often noted in the commentaries for the individual verses, but this is not unusual and we have no reason to doubt that they were quoting from recensions of the anthology we know. To the critics just named, we can add Dhanika, who quotes a dozen verses for the types of heroine and other aspects of dramatic theory; Kuntaka, who quotes verse 455 for lexical figurativeness (p. 36) and verse 675 for grammatical figurativeness (by using the future tense—p. 123); and Rāmacandra and Guṇacandra, who quote (p. 146) verse 161 [792] in their discussion on the sensitive experience, as portraying the desire for union. The large number of commentaries extant is further evidence of the position occupied by the Seven Hundred Songs as a standard work of *kāvya*.

832. A number of writers have been more explicit in naming Sātavāhana and expressing their appreciation of his anthology. Bāṇa (*Harṣacarita*, introductory verse 14) includes Sātavāhana's anthology of 'things well said' *subhāṣitas*, which was like a treasury of genuine jewels, in his list of great classics. He calls it indestructible and also 'not vulgar' *agrāmya*, literally 'non-village'; evidently paradoxically, with reference to the fact that it is largely about village life yet is anything but vulgar from the aesthetic point of view. Bāṇa is suggesting that King Sātavāhana here made himself a treasury which can never be exhausted, unlike a king's ordinary treasury of jewels. Sātavāhana (Sālāhaṇa) is also praised by Uddyotana (*Kuvalayamālā* p. 3), when speaking of the pioneers of Prakrit literature, and by Rājaśekhara (*Kāvyamīmāṃsā* p. 50), as a king of Kuntala who favoured Prakrit and again (p. 55) as a great patron who maintained a literary circle *kāvya goṣṭhī* and presided over its assemblies. A verse of Rājaśekhara, admiring Sātavāhana's 'series of pictures' in the anthology, is quoted by Jalhaṇa (*Sūktimuktāvalī* IV. 53). Abhinanda (+9) in verses in honour of his patron Hāravarṣa (Deva Pāla), interspersed between the cantos of his epic *Rāmacarita*, several times compares him with Hāla. 'After Hāla he collected his own anthology (treasury) to make manifest the treasuries of the *kavis*' (end of cantos 4, 7, 9 and 12). 'Pālita (Pādalipta), best of *kavis*, was caressed by Hāla with the highest honour' (and likewise Abhinanda by Hāravarṣa—beginning of canto 33). Pālita or Pādalipta is a famous Prakrit novelist, but a number of verses in the Seven Hundred are attributed to him by the commentators on the anthology. Soḍḍhala adds his tribute to Hāla in an introductory verse to his novel *Udayasundarī* (p. 2), as one of the great patrons of *kāvya*, but with nothing more specific than the grief caused by his death.

833. Virahāṅka (+7), in his treatise on Prakrit metre (*Vṛttajātisamuccaya* pp. 14 f.), mentions Sālāhaṇa (Sātavāhana) among authorities on stanza construction, though we have at dresent no clear evidence that he wrote any theoretical work. A later writer on the same subject, Svayaṃbhū (+9), quotes (*Svayaṃbhūcchandas* pp. 103 and 106) three verses (70, 75 and 197) from the Seven Hundred for examples of metrical quantities and the use of caesura. In the case of two of these verses an author's name is noted by Svayaṃbhū, 'Pādalipta' for 75 and 'Bhogin' for 197.

834. We have already noted that the commentators name such authors for many of the verses. How authentic such names may be is unknown. Nearly all of them are no more than names to us now. Some are probably of the court poets of Sātavāhana, some may be of village poets. Practically the only one whose name is significant for us now is Pādalipta (or Palitta or Pālitta or Pālita, Prakrit forms of the name). Of the dozen verses ascribed to him we have translated one above, that portraying a women's quarrrel (417) [814].

835. Jaina tradition honours Pādalipta as a monk and a great teacher and preserves legends of his life (see for example Prabhācandra's *Prabhāvakacarita* 28 ff., *Purātanaprabandhasaṃgraha* 92ff.). According to these, Pādalipta was born in Kośala but later was associated with the Muruṇḍa ruler of Pāṭaliputra in Magadha, presumably the Śaka governor of that province under the Kuṣāṇa Empire(+1 to+3). Later, he frequented Sātavāhana's court, where he produced his celebrated novel *Taraṅgavatī* (Prakrit *Taraṃgavaī*, but sometimes called *Taraṃgalolā*).

836. The legends we have, all from a much later period, are extremely fantastic. The great teacher possesses, besides the power of flight which might be regarded as a 'normal' science after the time of Guṇāḍhya and his wizards, a mystic 'preserving' *dhāriṇī* knowledge anticipating the development of Tantrism. He also meets the alchemist Nāgārjuna, who knows how to prepare the elixir *rasa* which converts stones into gold. Nāgārjuna himself is the subject of fantastic legends in some of the Buddhist sources, moreover there seems sometimes to be a confusion of the Madhyamaka philosopher of the +2 with the Mantrayāna (Tantric)teacher of the same name, who lived in the +9 (author of the *Pañcakrama*, a commentary on the *Guhyasamāja* and other works), the aim being to represent the Mantrayāna as being as ancient as the Madhyamaka. By the time of Prabhācandra(+13) it is perhaps not surprising if some of this confusion has been communicated to the Jaina legend of Pādalipta and Nāgārjuna; thus at one point in the legend (*Prabhāvakacarita* V. 114) Pādalipta visits the city of '*Mānakheṭa*' where a king Kṛṣṇa is ruling. This looks rather like a reference to the Rāṣṭrakūṭa dynasty of the+8 to +10, unless it was in origin simply an imaginary prehistory of that dynasty projected back into the Sātavāhana period as vassals of the Empire (it is not unusual for upstart dynasties to have such high ancestries invented for them). According to Prabhācandra (pp. 36 ff.), Nāgārjuna became Pādalipta's pupil, thus transferring all his celebrity to the Jainas.

837. As regards Pādalipta's contemporaneity with 'Hāla' or 'Sātavāhana', however, we have the earlier and independent evidence of Abhinanda already quoted [832], who was not a Jaina nor writing for a Jaina patron (the Pāla emperors generally supported Buddhism). This is at the same time a significant tribute to Pādalipta's quality as a *kavi*, as seen by a Brahmanical *kavi* of the +9, for the Jaina tradition reveres him principally as a scholar and teacher, the author of several learned works on Jaina doctrine as well as of a novel. On the other hand Kutūhala in his *Līlāvaī* [772] ignores Pādalipta and gives prominent parts to Nāgārjuna, as teacher *guru* of Sātavāhana (1008) and as (Buddhist) monk *bhikṣu* (1016 and 1021), and to some of the Emperor's ministers.

838. Before discussing Pādalipta's novel, it should be observed that the Prakrit form of his name as Palitta corresponds to Sanskrit Pradīpta ('lighted'), as noted by Prabhācandra (V. 39), who explains (pp. 37-8) that he got the name Pādalipta later from the anointing of his feet which enabled him to fly. His original name, given by his parents, was Nāgendra (V. 29) and he received the name Palitta after becoming a Jaina monk.

839. Unfortunately the original *Taraṃgavaī* appears to be no longer extant. Replacing it we have an abridged paraphrase, the *Saṃkhitta Taraṃgavaī*, written by one Yaśas of uncertain date, in Māhārāṣṭrī like the original but eliminating difficult dialect *deśī* words. According to the abridger (verses 5ff. of his version), no one read Pālitta's novel because of its difficulty as well as its great length. He has therefore freed it from the dialect words and shortened it so that people will again read it. It should be noted that the Seven Hundred Songs contains many 'dialect' words: the language of the *Taraṃgavaī* was thus probably similar to that of the lyric collection, but instead of being equipped with commentaries and Sanskrit translations *chāyās* to accompany the text, the long novel has suffered a fate comparable with that of Guṇāḍhya's. As far as we know, the *Taraṃgavaī* is the first novel to have been written in Māhārāṣṭrī: a contrasting counterpart, as it were, to the lyrics collected by Sātavāhana, in the same new language.

840. The action depends on the memory of former lives, especially of one extraordinary incident which inaugurated a train of suffering for the heroine and her husband. In the time of the main narrative, in which the heroine is named Taraṅgavatī, the characters have at first no recollection of the tragic end of her previous life, though they will not be able to find peace of mind until they discover the truth and rediscover one another in their present incarnations. The tragedy will then dissolve in reunion, after many obstacles have been overcome, though in the end the Jaina writer will have a sequel to add, leading his heroine towards the highest goal of his philosophy. The *Taraṅgavatī* is thus the earliest known novel (as distinguished from short stories handed down in the Jaina tradition) of a long series by Jaina writers exemplifying the working out of events or actions of a former life over a sometimes long future, during which the characters are impelled by emotions they do not understand until at last memory awakes. At the same time it is the first known *dharma* novel, since 'virtue', in the Jaina sense, is its ultimate goal and teaching, though in the main body of the story love is supreme. Taraṅgavatī at last becomes a Jaina nun, leaving the world of uncertainties and ever present death in quest of final peace. It is as a nun, now named Suvvayā (Suvratā), that Pādalipta has her relate her own story, to a merchant who enquired why she, a very beautiful woman, had left the world.

841. She was the daughter of a wealthy merchant-banker of Kauśāmbī when Udayana was ruling there (—5). The placing of the story in Kauśāmbī and mention of Udayana of course recall the *Bṛhatkathā* and take the reader back to a romantic world of legend and fiction inextricably mixed. The closeness of the time to that of Mahāvīra, the founder of Jainism, was perhaps merely a result of this choice, arising from the desire to give an appropriate and attractive setting to a fiction, though for Jaina readers it would have the happy effect of adding further 'interest'.

842. One day, being driven in a carriage on an excursion to a park outside the city, Taraṅgavatī saw some ruddy sheldrakes—*cakravāka* birds [740]—and instantly remembered her previous life as one of these, with its tragic end. A hunter had shot her mate by accident. At first she had fainted. As she had revived she had seen the hunter respectfully cremating her dead mate and performing rites to expiate his sin, for the ruddy sheldrake was not legitimate prey (not to be eaten) and, which was much worse, he had broken the hunters' rule not to shoot any birds or animals during their mating seasons. In anguish she had thrown herself into the same fire to follow her lover, had died and been reborn as the merchant's daughter.

843. She confided the story to her maid, a friend since childhood, then seemingly fell ill. In her hopeless sorrow, for there seemed to be no way of finding out what had happened to her mate, Taraṅgavatī took to painting and produced a large scroll (on cloth): a series of scenes depicting that tragic story of the two birds, their loves and their death. On the occasion of a festival, the maid hung the scroll as decoration on a balcony of the merchant's palace, clearly visible from the street.

844. Now it happened that the *cakravāka* had been reborn not far from his faithful mate, as Padmadeva, the son of a caravan merchant in that same city. Passing by the palace with some friends during the festival, he admired the painting and praised its details, then suddenly fainted. Reviving, he told his friends of the past he had suddenly remembered, then sent to find out who had painted the scroll and duly asked for Taraṅgavatī's hand.

845. Her father, however, considered himself too high and wealthy a person to become connected with a mere caravan merchant, in any case likely to be a poor husband because his trade kept him away from home so much. He rejected Padmadeva and the pair corresponded secretly, eventually eloping. Padmadeva takes Taraṅgavatī down the Yamunā in a small boat, intending to stay with his aunt at Kākandī (on the Ganges). But they are surprised on the way by robbers and carried off to a stronghold in the Vindhya Mountains. Rejecting a suggestion that they be offered for ransom, the robber general decrees that in nine days' time they shall be offered in sacrifice to his patron Goddess, Kālī.

846. Some of the robbers and their wives are dissatisfied at this fate decreed for such a handsome young pair. One of their guards, pitying them, learns their whole story from Taraṅgavatī. Then, while the robbers are feasting, he leads the pair secretly out of the stronghold towards the edge of the forest, leaving them within reach of a village. As search parties have been sent all over India to look for them, it is not long before they find friends and are taken home. Taraṅgavatī's father has relented, having been told everything by the maid, so she is married to her former mate and they live happily together for many years.

847. Long after (Pādalipta, or at least his paraphraser, does not tell us how long, beyond indicating indirectly that it was more than twelve years), the couple happen to meet a Jaina monk in a park near Kauśāmbī. They were Jaina lay followers (like many of the merchant class), so he instructs them in their religion. They ask him how he came to leave the world. He tells a strange story: he was in a former life that very hunter responsible for their deaths. He had been so affected by his sin of destroying them that, in a fit of revulsion against his hunter's existence, he had ended his own life in that same fire which he had lit to cremate the *cakravāka*. Through this good impulse he had been reborn in better circumstances, in the family of a merchant in Vārāṇasī. However, despite a good education, he took to gambling and then theft, finally joining the robbers in the Vindhya Mountains. He in fact was the sympathetic guard who had listened to Taraṅgavatī's story and then freed them. Her tale had made him recall his own previous life as the hunter. Reflecting on the world of transmigration he had determined to leave it and became a monk. Taraṅgavatī and Padmadeva on hearing this decide to leave a world of insecurity and death and themselves join the Jaina communities of nuns and monks.

848. Pādalipta's novel, so far as we can judge through the paraphrase, was shorter than Guṇāḍhya's, being much less episodical and apparently lacking the many discursive passages of his great predecessor's manner. On the other hand it brings in the extra dimension of a previous life, the unseen and generally unknown force of previous actions and experiences, still potent in the present life. This is an important element in the Jaina view of the universe here emphasised, but later novelists exploited the idea also for its purely narrative possibilities in plot construction and as explaining a great part of what appears irrational in human behaviour. Most of them probably accepted one of the various theories of transmigration widely current in the society in which they lived; as novelists they might therefore bring in this dimension without any intent to edify, in conjunction with the other resources of *kāvya* fiction—primarily those pioneered by Guṇāḍhya. The paraphrase hardly allows us to answer such questions as whether Pādalipta emulated Guṇāḍhya in characterisation, being brief and leaving us to speculate how much of the original has been cut out. The scanty impression we get is that the forces carried over from the previous life, and presumably from the whole series of former lives of each person, constitute most of the character here: people are only to some extent what they superficially appear to be in their present social relationships; what they really are can be described only by enquiring into the unseen affections embedded in their souls by past experiences.

849. A few more points can be made from the abridgement, however. The life of the young Taraṅgavatī, as the daughter of a rich merchant, is interesting (pp. 8ff.). The girl lives in great luxury and her father watches very carefully over her well-being as he conceives it. Our impression is strongly reminiscent of the youth of Sarvārthasiddha, the future Buddha, as described by Aśvaghoṣa in his Life of the Buddha [730-1], particularly the drive to the park, admired on the way by crowds of people (p. 15). The description of the park which follows (16 f.), when the ladies alight and walk through it, is elaborate even in the abridgement, with its ornamental trees and birds, its pavilions and lotus pools. The description of Taraṅgavatī's painting (pp. 30 and 36 f.) is detailed, with the different scenes of the life of the birds in the several seasons of the year, the different places where the birds fly, rest or enjoy themselves and the series of events of the final tragedy. To understand the technique here it is necessary to look at the narrative reliefs, in the form of long panels, at Caityagiri (Sāñcī) near Vidiśā, where a series of incidents is dynamically represented in a single 'composition'.

850. We have already noted some of the appreciation

of Pādalipta by later writers, both as a *kavi* in the *kāvya* tradition and as a Jaina teacher. The earliest reference (*c.* +300 ?) seems to be in the Jaina canonical work *Anuyogadvāra Sūtra* (*sūtra* 308), which merely mentions him as 'the author of the *Taraṅgavatī*' as an example of this kind of linguistic expression, along with 'the author of the *Malayavatī*'. This *Malayavatī* seems to be otherwise unknown: it was presumably another novel or a biography written not long after Pādalipta's. From this mention we gather simply that in the time of the author of this text (Āryarakṣita ?) these were well known novels. For the date of the *Anuyogadvāra* see p. 71 of the Introduction to the new edition in the Jaina Āgama Series. Other Jaina references include Jinabhadra (*c.* +600) in his *Viśeṣāvaśyakabhāṣya* (1508, with a *Vāsavadattā*) and the *Visesanisīthacuṇṇi* (as quoted in the introduction to the *Saṃkhitta Taraṃgavaī*, p. 7), the latter giving the *Taraṅgavatī* along with the *Naravāhanadattakathā* (i.e. the *Bṛhatkathā*) and a *Magadhasenā* (otherwise unknown ?) as examples of 'pleasure' *kāma* novels [446], but adding that whereas the *Bṛhatkathā* is 'worldly' the other two are 'transcendent' *lokottara* (go beyond this world).

851. Among literary critics, or rather *kavis* in this case, who praise Pādalipta we have mentioned the epic poet Abhinanda [832] (+9), significant particularly because he was not a Jaina. Uddyotana (+8—*Kuvalayamālā* p. 3) gives prominent mention to 'Pālitta' in his verses on great Prakrit writers, associating him with Sātavāhana, naming the *Taraṅgavatī* and referring also to the pair of ruddy sheldrakes in the story. Dhanapāla (+10) in his novel *Tilakamañjarī* (introductory verse 23) says that the way of the *Taraṅgavatī*, resorted to by the pair of birds, is clear *prasanna* and deep *gambhīra*, thus purifying the Earth like the River Ganges. Since the birds live by the Ganges in Pādalipta's novel this is very appropriate. By 'clear' and 'deep', Dhanapāla should perhaps be understood as alluding to the qualities clarity *prasāda* and 'exaltation' *udāratā* [189] which he admires in the novel, as qualities of style, as well as to the ideas conveyed by the story.

852. Māhārāṣṭrī was used for epic composition also from a very early date. The earliest such epic extant is again the work of a Jaina writer, Vimala or Vimalasūri (*sūri* being a title often given Jaina sages). The 'Jaina Māhārāṣṭrī' here exemplified differs slightly from that of the Sātavāhana collection (and of later 'standard' Māhārāṣṭrī writers), mainly in orthography and through the occasional use of forms borrowed from the language (Ardhamāgadhī) of the Jaina scriptures. It also tends to avoid the more obscure dialect words and to substitute forms closer to Sanskrit.

853. Vimala gives the date of composition in his epic (if we can trust the manuscript tradition) as the year 530 of the Jaina era. This would put him in the +1, but the accuracy of Jaina chronology has been seriously challenged and there is good reason to believe that, even in this relatively early period, the record of years elapsed since Mahāvīra had been interrupted and then incorrectly reconstructed. In short, it proves impossible to reconcile Jaina chronology with that which has been adopted for this book (rightly or wrongly). Jaina tradition greatly reduces the period between on the one hand the Buddha and Mahāvīra (who are generally taken to have been contemporaries) and on the other hand certain famous Jaina teachers of the +1st millennium (e.g. Haribhadra), though it does not appear to do so consistently. It would seem that confusions resulted from the use of several different eras and the conversion of dates from one to another, sometimes with wrong identifications of the particular era of a date in some document, this often not being specified. More research is needed on Jaina chronology; meanwhile, since there seems to be no tradition connecting Vimala with any contemporary rulers or historical events, but only with an obscure line of ancient teachers, we can say provisionally that he may have lived in either the +1 or the +2, and quite possibly as late as *c.* +200. He may be regarded as among the earliest pioneers of Māhārāṣṭrī literature, which, as noted at the beginning of this chapter, is usually supposed to have begun not before the +2.

854. Vimala is known to have written two epics, one on the story of the *Mahābhārata* and one on that of the *Rāmāyaṇa*, of which only the latter seems to be extant. The purpose of his *Paümacariya*, Life of Padma, is to provide a version of the story of Rāma acceptable to the Jainas. Vimala contends that the version in the *Rāmāyaṇa* is false, in various places reversing the true facts, as if making a deer kill a lion or a dog rout an elephant (II.116). The Jina Mahāvīra, however, in his omniscience, knew the true story (III.14). Vimala presents his epic by having King Śreṇika Bimbisāra of Magadha, a contemporary of both the Jina and the Buddha [561], ask the Jina's leading pupil about 'Padma' or Rāma.

855. In his introductory canto Vimala makes clear both his aesthetic and his moral intentions, saying that in one's heart one should energetically praise great men, for the aesthetic experience *rasa* of the qualities of a *kāvya* endures as long as the circle of the Sun, Moon and planets, whilst the body abounds in diseases and life is impermanent like a flash of lightning (I.17-8). The story of Rāma, then, whom the Jainas call also Padma (Māhārāṣṭrī Paüma), is to be retold as part of universal history *purāṇa*, which the Jainas regard as an important branch of study and self discipline.

856. Vimala's epic found great favour with later Jaina writers, though they honour him mostly by plundering his work rather than praising it; several later poets using his story as a basis for new versions, generally very faithful to his, in various languages suited to their own times. As for his sources, the Jaina canonical books contain only sketchy and schematic indications concerning the heroes of universal history: their stories seem implied to be well known and easily supplied from oral tradition [529]. The earliest extant work to outline universal history appears to be the *Sthānāṅga* (—1 ?). Vimala may be presumed to have collected many details from such tradition in his community, and perhaps to have invented a certain amount himself; but, despite his criticism and several fairly important alterations, to us it appears that his main source was in fact the *Rāmāyaṇa*, for his main story is very similar to that of the 'First Kāvya'. In his time we know that the *Rāmāyaṇa* was still undergoing major alterations itself [614-5] and had recently had the apocryphal Seventh Book added to it, so he might justly complain of tampering with the true story by bad poets (III.15) and feel that his revisions were perfectly legitimate, and necessary to save a fine history from the protagonists of bad doctrines (III.8). He incorporated the story of Sītā's renewed exile from the Seventh Book of the *Rāmāyaṇa*, but added a Jaina conclusion to his history: Rāma becomes a Jaina monk and attains enlightenment and *nirvāṇa*.

Jaina ethics is stressed throughout: it is violence and particularly eating meat which generates the evil and suffering in human life (e.g. XXII.83ff., XXVI.34ff.).

857. The major falsification which Vimala proposes to rectify concerns the character of Rāvaṇa. This hero, though misguided enough to be Padma's opponent and to perpetrate the abduction of Sītā, was not a demon (III.15) or monster (VII.95-6) but a wizard *vidyādhara* [677-8] who had performed many truly heroic deeds and whose religion was Jainism, despite his human weaknesses. The real demons in this world, says Vimala (XI.40-44, etc.), are those who perpetrate animal sacrifice, demons *rākṣasas* in the guise of brahmans. Among many smaller details which Vimala objects to as impossible, such as Rāma's cowardly killing of Vālin (III.10) and his shooting of a deer (such a hero could not be accused of harming animals), or monkeys building a bridge over the ocean (III.12), he insists that the so called 'monkeys' *vānaras*, who were Rāma's allies, were not actual monkeys but wizards from a Monkey Island who used a monkey emblem (VI.88-9). There is nothing incredible in wizards (Rāvaṇa's followers) being defeated by other wizards, whereas it is incredible to say they were conquered by monkeys (II.105, III.9).

858. This criticism of Brahmanical legends and myths as impossible was continued by many later Jaina writers, both in literary form and as straight philosophy. They aimed to present universal history and cosmogony, incorporating whatever mythology seemed to them acceptable, in a credible form which could harmonise with the laws of transmigration, and the working out of the moral results of actions, as understood in Jaina philosophy. Thus they produced a history which at least could be true, as they saw the world, and which in its main outlines they believed guaranteed true by the omniscience of the teacher from whom these narratives were supposed to have been handed down. At the same time Jaina writers were concerned with the ethical purpose, equally in harmony with their view of transmigration, that such great persons as the heroes, human or divine, who appeared in universal history could not be represented as guilty of very monstrous crimes incompatible with their noble characters. On the contaryr their actions must appear as good and instructive examples, if they are to satisfy Vimala's requirements for the subject matter of a *kāvya*.

859. The *Paümacariya* is a long epic, consisting of 118 cantos, comparable with the *Rāmāyaṇa* itself rather than with the epics of Aśvaghoṣa. The metre of the narrative is the *āryā* form of the *gaṇacchandas* [413] usual for Māhārāṣṭrī epics, each canto ending with a verse in some other metre.

860. Vimala begins by saluting all the 24 *jinas* of the present cycle of evolution, then declares his purpose and the difficulties, both of ascertaining the truth and of getting men to listen to it. For the first, the thread of his narrative can follow through the hole made by the diamond-needle of the omniscient one, as recorded in the scripture *āgama*, in the great jewel (the story) (I.13). For the second, men's minds are like leaves blown by the wind so that no one can catch them. Even the *jinas* could not make all men of one opinion, let alone could he, yet he will do his best despite men's attachment to falsehood (I.14-16). After some further remarks on this theme Vimala in the rest of his first canto summarises the main points of the story. To introduce this he then, as we have just noted, brings in, in the second canto, a description of Magadha in the time of Mahāvīra and King Śreṇika Bimbisāra. The story of Mahāvīra is briefly noted and his teaching a great assembly, with a summary of the doctrine of moral action and its results. The King was present, but afterwards feels doubts when he reflects on the Padma (Rāma) story in relation to what he has just heard. Thus he mentions some of the criticisms of the *Rāmāyaṇa* we have noted above. To satisfy his doubts he attends on one of Mahāvīra's leading disciples, Indrabhūti Gautama (Prakrit Goyama), and puts them to him (III). In reply Gautama relates the entire story in its correct form as he has heard it from the Jina himself.

861. This narrative begins (from III.18) with cosmology and then sketches universal history from the beginning of the present declining cycle down to the life of the first of the 24 *jinas*, Ṛṣabha, with the decline in the physical and moral stature of men, the origin of civilisation, social classes and the kingship, and an account of Nami, grandson of Ṛṣabha, from whom the families of wizards are descended. There is more of this in the fourth canto, with Bharata becoming a universal emperor and the origin of the brahman class (65ff.) and their false *Veda* (80), enjoining animal sacrifice, in his time. In the next cantos we find the main dynasties of kings in India (Solar, Lunar, Wizard and 'Hari'=Yādava), the second *jina* Ajita (V), the origin of the 'monkey' wizards and the founding of their city of Kiṣkindhā (VI). There is a list of the 'great men', *jinas*, etc., at V. 145ff.

862. In canto VII we have an account of the gods, particularly Indra, and of the birth of Rāvaṇa and his acquisition of various 'sciences'. Canto VIII includes (143ff.) the life of Hariṣeṇa, tenth of the 12 universal emperors, who had lived a little earlier, narrated to Rāvaṇa. Thus we reach the main story carefully set against the background of the entire sweep of universal history. In IX we meet Sugrīva and Vālin and learn of Rāvaṇa's fight with the latter. Vimala continues with several heroic narratives about Rāvaṇa (his wars with Nalakūbara, XII; Indra X, XII and XIII; and Varuṇa, XVI and XIX), stressing his devotion to the Jaina religion. In canto XX we have some more universal history, filling in the account of the *jinas*, universal emperors (especially Sanatkumāra, the fourth) and the series of *vāsudevas* and *baladevas*. Padma (Rāma) is the eighth of the nine *baladevas*, his brother Lakṣmaṇa (often called Nārāyaṇa by the Jainas) the eighth of the nine *vāsudevas* and their enemy Rāvaṇa the eighth of the nine opposing *prativāsudevas*. The story of Padma takes place in the period of the twentieth *jina*, Munisuvrata (XXI).

863. The main story of Padma begins from canto XXI with the two kings, Janaka of the Hari Dynasty, father of Sītā, and Daśaratha, father of Padma. The general outline of the story follows that of the *Rāmāyaṇa*, with the numerous corrections of detail required by Vimala, some of which we have noticed already. Naturally a Jaina background is substituted for the Brahmanical as far as possible. It is after fighting victoriously against the barbarians who had invaded Janaka's kingdom that Padma is betrothed to Sītā (XXVII). At this point Vimala brings in again the troublesome brahman Nārada, who in Canto XI had had a hand in the invention of the sacrifice, with its terrible consequences. Nārada goes to see Sītā, famous for her beauty, but when he enters her palace she hides and he is driven out. Enraged by this, he plans to make trouble for her by finding another suitor, himself acting as go between. He succeeds in embroiling the wizards in his plan and this leads to Janaka having to call a self-choice for Sītā, with the contest in strength which Padma in fact wins (XXVIII).

864. Kaikeyī demands Daśaratha's kingdom for her son as a boon, as in the *Rāmāyaṇa*, but she does not demand Padma's exile; he goes abroad on his own initiative (XXXI). The conflict between Padma and the wizards in the forest develops much as in the *Rāmāyaṇa* and Rāvaṇa abducts Sītā (XLIV). On the other hand the episode of the 'monkey' brothers Vālin and Sugrīva is completely changed. Vālin in not killed at all but becomes a Jaina monk, whilst the story of Sugrīva is quite different (XLVII). Though in Vimala's epic heroes are rarely killed, but only captured by their enemies, he does not find it possible to avoid killing Rāvaṇa. However, it is Lakṣmaṇa, not Padma, who takes his life (LXXIII).

865. Vimala handles the concluding episodes very freely, guided by Jaina doctrine. After her second exile Sītā in disgust becomes a nun (CIII). Lakṣmaṇa dies suddenly and goes to purgatory after Rāvaṇa, such being the reward of the violent. Rāma in grief for the loss of his brother renounces the world and finally attains *nirvāṇa*.

866. It is clear that Vimala makes all the characters in the story more moral and especially less violent. The main heroes are all more civilised and chivalrous than in the *Rāmāyaṇa*; Kaikeyī is softened into an affectionate mother. But all this reflects the Jaina conception of the way life really is, of the rule of moral law in the universe: it is inconceivable that irrational and arbitrary behaviour should prevail in such a universe. The setting of universal history is not simply an introduction, certainly not an irrelevant digression from the story; it is an essential part of the narrative because it tells us what the universe is like, as the author understands it, and it is the nature of the universe which explains the life of the hero. The Life of Padma is an artistic presentation of the Jaina view of the universe, a universe in which everything is alive and in which assault on life is the ultimate evil.

867. Though Vimala's style is simple and straightforward, it is clear that his intention is to write a *kāvya* epic. In his use of metres he is in fact richer than later Prakrit epic poets in introducing a greater variety, including occasionally fixed metres as well as the normal musical metres of Prakrit poetry. At XXVIII.47-50, which is a four verse hymn to the *jina* Ṛṣabha, he uses four different metres, evidently to produce an elevated effect appropriate for such matter. A number of the traditional epic descriptive passages are worked in, though they are relatively short. We have the rainy season (XI.111-9) and winter (XXXI. 41-7), evening twilight (XVI.46-54), cities (LXXXIX: founding of Mathurā), a palace (LXVIII.5-15), a cemetery (CV.52-61), old age (XXIX.21-8), water sports (X.36-44), battles (e.g. XXVII) and so on. Figures of speech are used sparingly, but often enough to enliven the narrative. As details, there is little which a critic might quote and admire, though occasionally we find a striking simile such as that quoted above comparing men's minds with leaves blown by the wind. It is the continuous narrative which prevails throughout, in the ancient epic manner or that of the *Rāmāyaṇa* rather than in that of Aśvaghoṣa. Vimala's narrative is rich in interest, in its flow of attractive details and rapid events. He himself takes his stand on the aesthetic experience *rasa* as the enduring effect of epic narrative, as we saw in a verse quoted above. This experience is produced by narratives of great men. Probably we should understand the heroic to be intended as the dominant *rasa* here, with its various aspects, remembering its importance in Jaina aesthetic theory [116]. The calmed, though prominent, may be considered subordinate to this.

868. Practically nothing seems to be known of Vimala's epic covering the story of the *Mahābhārata*, which was entitled *Harivaṃśa*, 'Line of Hari' (Uddyotana, *Kuvalayamālā* p. 3). From its title, and from later Jaina epics on the same matter, we infer that the central figure was Kṛṣṇa of the Hari or Yādava dynasty, whose origins are noted briefly in the Life of Padma. The Bhārata War will be a major episode in Kṛṣṇa's life, followed by the destruction of his city of Dvārakā and his tragic death [526]. In the scheme of universal history, this matter comes later than that of the Padma or Rāma story, Kṛṣṇa being the ninth *vāsudeva* and Jarāsandha his *prativāsudeva*, whom he kills as Lakṣmaṇa kills Rāvaṇa. It can be assumed that

Vimala also included the life of Nemi, the twenty second *jina*, in the introductory part of this epic.

869. According to Uddyotana this epic was the first to narrate the story of the Hari Dynasty. We can thus say that in these two epics Vimala established in literature the entire structure of Jaina universal history, that it was his genius to create and give life to this grandiose conception out of the abstract sketch offered in the Jaina canon. His work is to be appreciated as a whole, as Uddyotana indicates. Its study is also necessary in order to understand the many later *kāvyas* by Jaina authors which move within its literary universe. Vimala's influence, as remarked already, consists in his being followed in detail by so many Jaina writers, though hardly any of them acknowledge their source. Uddyotana supplies the needed acknowledgement by praising the vast scope of the matter and the *rasa* made of ambrosia which Vimala provides, probably thinking of the poet's own words on enduring *rasa* in a *kāvya* on the actions of great men. Śīlācārya (+9) in his *Caupaṇṇamahāpurisacariya* (see Kulkarni, p. 3 of his Introduction to the 1962 edition of the *Paümacariya*) refers to the Life of Padma for the story he has abridged.

Chapter XVII

SANSKRIT LYRIC AND PROSE IN THE +2 : MĀTṚCEṬA AND ŚŪRA

870. The tradition of Sanskrit poetry represented by Aśvaghoṣa continued, and we are able to trace it through a number of other Buddhist writers, some of them datable in the +2. Though usually much concerned with the ethical content of Buddhist subject matter, just as Vimala was with that of his Jaina history, they seem to show a greater interest than he had in the technical elements of poetry, in metre, figures and grammatical patterns, and in this they closely resemble Aśvaghoṣa. Of these elements, metre and grammatical structure usually hold the poets' main interest here, the figures appearing more incidental and sporadic, moreover among the figures themselves alliteration is often conspicuous. The individual poets vary, and some show a profusion of similes and metaphors, as does Aśvaghoṣa; even here the formal interest sometimes manifests itself, as in the 'complete' metaphor with its series of parallels [754]. On the whole, therefore, this is a phase of poetry whose art consists very largely in verbal or formal effects, rather than in the figurative meanings elaborated in later *kāvya*. Afterwards verbal effects will become a separate and subsidiary branch of poetry which, unlike this, relegates its subject matter to the status of a mere frame in which to hang its artifices.

871. The extant Buddhist poetry of this period includes a number of lyric 'hymns' *stotras* in praise of the Buddha, or less often of his doctrine or of the community of monks, following the example of those included in the old Buddhist Canons, such as the Pali poems we have noticed earlier [549, 569]. The content of such hymns would appear to be somewhat limited, and moreover the poets for the most part adhere to the mass of traditions about the Buddha, his deeds, his powers, his character, his well known epithets, found in their Canonical books. Even so, when a poet of genius handles this modest form of composition, exhausted, it would seem, by thousands of monks down the ages manufacturing verses for their evening ceremonial, he can find endless possibilities of bringing in new ideas. Through his originality what seemed outmoded suddenly appears completely fresh and full of new meanings.

872. A number of the *stotras* of this period have been recovered in a more or less fragmentary condition from long ruined Buddhist sites in Central Asia, one of them from a complete manuscript in Tibet. Some other *kāvya* works by writers of the same tradition have been preserved in Nepal. A whole series of *stotras* and other works has been preserved in Tibetan translations, partly overlapping these.

873. First we may look at five *stotras*, or parts of *stotras* (some may be parts of the same *stotra*), fragmentarily recovered and not available in Tibetan, which may represent the period between Aśvaghoṣa and Nāgārjuna. Nāgārjuna, whose more literary works will be noticed afterwards, is the philosopher contemporary with 'Sātavāhana', mentioned in the preceding chapter (his floruit may be +130 to +160) [772]. These five *stotra* fragments are anonymous.

874. Some verses in praise of the Enlightenment of the the Buddha (Schlingloff Fragment H) resemble Aśvaghoṣa in style, as their editor has pointed out, in their use of the 'complete' metaphor. They are in *vasantatilaka* [660], a *kāvya* fixed metre very popular later. Some broken words and gaps are supplied conjecturally (in pointed brackets) :

You have felled <the tree, grief,> whose <root,> desire,
is firmly rooted in the darkness, intoxication,
<whose branches are the various> destinies (realms of
living beings), filled with the leaves, indolence,
And whose fruit is fear <etc.>
—with the axe, intelligence. (31)

With the ship, speech (i.e. teaching), you have crossed
over the river, transmigration,
which<has its source in>the mountain, ignorance,<..>
Has birds, wrong reasoning, is full of water, intoxication,
subject to waves, desire, and crooked, having fear
and falsehood. (32)

875. A short fragment in the same metre describes the various parts of the Buddha's body, his forehead, eyebrows and so on, comparing them through different figures with many beautiful and desirable things. In *kāvya* such elaborate and detailed descriptions from head to toe are a familiar exercise when applied to beautiful women; this is an early example of the form, adapted to the content of a hymn (Schlingloff Frag. K). In the Buddhist tradition the descriptions go back to an ancient conventional account of thirty two 'characteristics' by which the body of the Buddha or of any 'great man' was supposed to have been distinguished. The origin of these is unknown. The earliest poetic expression of them is probably that found in the Pali *Dīgha Nikāya, Lakkhaṇasuttanta,* of *c.* —200, from which a verse has been quoted above [584] explaining why his skin was golden in colour. Another of the present series of fragments (Schlingloff I), in the *āryāgīti* variety of bar metre *gaṇacchandas*, is more closely related to this tradition of the 'characteristics'.

876. The remaining two pieces are in praise of the Buddha's doctrine and of the community of monks founded by him. The first (Schlingloff Anhang 1.) is apparently complete but very short (5 verses); it strings together some traditional epithets of the doctrine in the old *triṣṭubh* metre (with some *jagatī pādas*) and may be centuries older than the *stotras* among which it was found. The second (Schlingloff Fragment E) is also simple and archaic in style (reminiscent of the Pali poetry of the *Suttanipāta*), but more poetic. The Buddha himself (as if this were a canonical piece, which in fact it may have been in some recension of the *Tripiṭaka* not now known to us) is introduced as praising the community, mostly with traditional epithets arranged with a view to alliteration. A line of refrain runs through the greater part of this poem, which is in the *vaktra* metre.

877. The philosopher Nāgārjuna himself wrote, besides his purely philosophical works, some *stotras*, a celebrated epistle *lekha* in verse to 'King Sātavāhana' (probably Puḷumāyi II) and some verse tracts (*parikathās*, in a special sense apparently peculiar to the Buddhists) of which the most important is the *Ratnāvalī* addressed to the same king. All these works have been preserved in Tibetan translations but only some extensive fragments of the first and the last in the original Sanskrit (in Nepal), though more may yet come to light. It is likely that some of the minor works ascribed to Nāgārjuna in the Tibetan collection are not really by him. We noted in the last chapter [772, 837] that Brahmanical as well as Buddhist and Jaina writers make Nāgārjuna a contemporary of Sātavāhana, and may add here a similar reference in Bāṇa (*Harṣacarita* p. 398) to the monk *bhikṣu* Nāgārjuna, who obtained for King Sātavāhana a precious healing necklace from the dragons of the Underworld. Surely this is an allusion to the celebrated *Ratnāvalī*.

878. The most important of the *stotras*, and one the authenticity of which seems clearly established, was known in India as the *Catuḥstava*, 'Four Hymns', of which the four parts were also circulated separately (the Tibetan collection does not group them but mingles them among others). The four parts are entitled *Lokātītastava*, *Niraupamyastava*, *Acintyastava* and *Paramārthastava*, of which the second (25 verses) and the last (11 verses) are extant in Sanskrit (the first and third parts have 26 and 57 verses respectively). Unlike the other hymns we have examined so far, Nāgārjuna's express throughout the philosophical standpoint of his own Madhyamaka school of Buddhism, which rejected much of the traditional interpretations of the *Tripiṭaka* of the earlier schools. The apparent paradoxes of the Madhyamaka, which arise from the interplay of the 'two levels of truth' and disappear when these are discriminated, here assume their proper rôle as figurative language in a poetic expression of that doctrine:

Ultimately there is in this world no 'knower' nor any 'thing to be known',
ah! You have known nature *dharmatā* which is supremely difficult to know! (II.3)
(*dharmatā* is the real nature of the universe)

O master! You do not engage in the perception of 'beings' in any way,
yet you are very compassionate towards 'beings' afflicted by unhappiness! (II.9)

How shall I praise you, the master who has not occurred
(been in the world as a worldly phenomenon) and
has no home,
is beyond any comparison (simile) in the world and
beyond the range of the ways of speech? (IV.1)

Having praised the Well Gone (Buddha) who has
neither gone nor not gone and is without going,
may this world through that meritorious action go the
going of the Well Gone! (IV.11)

879. The 'Epistle to a Friend' contains none of this philosophy, but instead summarises Buddhist ethics with particular reference to the laity and in accordance with early doctrine practically common to all the schools. The only suggestion which is apparently Mahāyānist is that the king should emulate the *bodhisattva* Avalokiteśvara and the *buddha* Amitābha in looking after the happiness of the world he rules. There is little or nothing original in these verses, about 120 in number, most of which have close parallels in such old Buddhist collections as the *Dhammapada* [575]. Perhaps this excellent piece of advice, with a simile, was new:

Understand that men are like mangoes: some which
are unripe
look ripe, some which are ripe look unripe,
Some unripe ones look unripe,
some ripe ones look ripe. (20)

The epistle form was much cultivated among the Buddhists from this time until the +12 and the Tibetan *Tripiṭaka* preserves a selection of them. Several were written to kings by famous monks, exhorting them to rule well, others were addressed to pupils, to a son or to a teacher.

880. According to its commentator, Ajitamitra, the *Ratnāvalī* also was addressed to 'Sātavāhana'. Its title as given in the Tibetan *Tripiṭaka* version calls it a *Rājaparikathā*, 'Discourse (tract) to a King', and its second verse contains the vocative 'O king'. *Ratnāvalī* means 'Necklace of Gems' (i.e. of the Buddhist doctrine). A much longer composition than the Epistle, it is divided into five sections elaborating Buddhist ethics more fully. It is more independent of traditional Buddhist phraseology, taking up current terms used in non-Buddhist doctrines such as the Vaiśeṣika (e.g. *naiḥśreyasa*, the supreme good; *abhyudaya*, exaltation; the former meaning liberation from transmigration and the latter perfect happiness or heaven) and using them to express Buddhist ideas.

881. The first section and the fourth and part of the second are available in the original Sanskrit. Nāgārjuna here goes deeply into Buddhist philosophy, particularly the explanation of the genesis of the false conception that there is a 'soul' or 'ego', as the basis of his exposition of its ethical teaching. He even gives part of the Madhyamaka critique of certain philosophical concepts such as causality (I.47ff.). 'Sātavāhana' must have made considerable progress in Buddhist philosophy if he was expected to accept and study such an offering. There is, however, archaeological evidence for the support of Buddhism by several rulers of this dynasty, so that the situation is not at all improbable, and the Jaina tradition associating Nāgārjuna and 'Sātavāhana' is weighty evidence for the royal patronage, coming as it does from opponents of the Buddhists. The *Ratnāvalī* (I.61) brackets the Jainas with the Vaiśeṣikas and Sāṃkhyas, and with the 'Pudgala' and 'Skandha' schools (the latter including Sthaviravāda, Sarvāstivāda, etc.) of early Buddhists, in saying that the king would ask all of them in vain to expound that which passes beyond existence and non-existence (as the Madhyamaka school does).

882. The second section continues this philosophical discussion and then draws various ethical conclusions from it, going particularly into the question of politics and the proper policy *nīti* a king should follow (II .28 ff.), which is nothing but the application of the Buddhist doctrine. This is certain to please the people and also to displease the king's enemies. The virtues desirable and useful for the king are then discussed: truth generates trust and it alone is absolutely beneficial; three more excellent things are liberality, calm and understanding. Other advice follows, with exhortations to accept it and put it into practice, though it be like harsh medicine.

883. In the fourth section Nāgārjuna goes further into the difficult question of the advising of kings: even if a king conducts himself mostly contrary to virtue and propriety his followers will praise him, therefore it is difficult for him to know what to approve and what not. If it is hard for others to tell the king what he should approve, when it is displeasing; it is still harder for him, being a monk, to tell such a great emperor. Yet he alone will tell him what is wholesome, though exceedingly displeasing, because of his gratitude to the king and affection for him, and out of compassion for the people (IV.1-3). Nāgārjuna then continues his unpleasant lecture, with particular emphasis on the need for generosity and the proper use of his inherited wealth, without delay. One here begins to get some insight into the character of this king, one feels, as inclined to be stingy and probably vacillating and unreliable in carrying out promises and expressions of good will. Another sore point is the appointment of ministers in the government. After this Nāgārjuna goes on to the administration of justice and makes some interesting suggestions for prison reform, with the object of making the prisoners into worthy persons; corrupt persons and murderers, however, should be exiled from the country. There follow some more poetic verses describing the good king and good government with similes and metaphors. The king should be a tree whose wealth of flowers is honour, whose great fruits are gifts and whose shade is tolerance, visited by birds who are his dependents (IV. 40). The kingdom represents for the king an investment of capital which may produce either unhappiness as commodities or, with sufficient effort, a continuing succession of the commodities of sovereignty (IV.44-5). Having arrived at the question of 'happiness' Nāgārjuna then proceeds to enquire into the nature of this and returns to his philosophical discussion. The happiness of physical sensations is nothing but the remedying of unhappiness, he argues, and mental happiness consists in perception (including mental perception of ideas) and is thus simply imagining. As this is all the 'happiness' there is in this world it follows that it is without any significance *vyartha* in itself (IV.47-8). However, Nāgārjuna argues in the following verses, the whole universe and everything in it is similarly without any absolute significance, therefore we should extinguish our attachments in *nirvāṇa*.

884. Nāgārjuna in this 'tract' shows consummate skill in blending practical advice such as might draw the interest of a king with the highest reaches of philosophical abstraction. In fact his teaching is a comprehensive system, here set forth in such literary form as might render it accessible and appealing to a layman. We have already suggested that Bāṇa appreciated this tract: perhaps he meant also to approve its study by his own king.

885. It was a pupil of a pupil (Ārya Deva) of Nāgārjuna, Mātṛceṭa, who attained the highest art in this phase of Buddhist *stotra*, epistle and tract literature. He is known to us, and to the Buddhist tradition, simply as a poet, not as a philosopher. Historically he was indeed a poet first and a Buddhist second, for from his own words as well as from history we gather that his talents were formerly exercised in praise of 'what was unworthy of praise' (Śiva, according to the historians). After being persuaded of his error by Ārya Deva, he sought, he tells us, through his first major Buddhist composition, to cleanse himself of the stain left by the mud of those words.

886. This is the *Varṇārhavarṇa Stotra*, 'Hymn Praising what is Worthy of Praise' (also known as the 'Four Hundred Hymn', from the number of its verses), which we may tentatively date *c.* +160. In this Hymn an elaborate poetic art is applied to the praise of the Buddha. Mātṛceṭa shows himself learned in Buddhist tradition, particularly in 'Buddhology' and the practical training in meditation, but unlike Nāgārjuna concerns himself very little with philosophy. The major difference between his verses and those we have just been considering, however, is the profusion of figures of speech in Mātṛceṭa. Though he uses some traditional comparisons he brings in far more which appear to be of his own invention. Besides similes and metaphors he is especially fond of contrast *vyatireka* [209], contradiction *virodha* [231] and related figures. Having set out to praise the Buddha, he finds no one and nothing with whom or which his subject can be compared (I.8ff.), a difficult situation indeed for a poet to be in (this will be the figure *ananvaya*, 'want of agreement' [225]). He therefore proceeds by way of contrast and contradiction in attempting his 'impossible' (title of his first section) task. A student of the figures will find a rich collection of materials here representing an early period in the invention of the more recondite figure of meaning, which does not yet seem to have been investigated.

887. In his second section and elsewhere Mātṛceṭa is perhaps more conservative in making a display of alliteration, which sometimes seems again to mark the extreme difficulty of finding words to praise the Buddha by suggesting stuttering. There are also many *yamakas*, 'rhymes' (internal rhymes, however, defined as repetition of syllables or longer segments, properly with different meanings [188]), intensifying these effects of sound. For example:

sadā sadācāravidhāyineyine, kṣarākṣarāptapratisaṃvide vide;
mahāmahāyāpratimāya te yate, namo namorhāya mahārhate 'rhate.

(II.70. *yamaka*)

Hail to the Worthy One, worthy of being hailed and greatly worthy,
whose pupils always promote good conduct;
To him who knows, having comprehension reliable for what is perishable and what imperishable,
to you, ascetic, whose great festival (or great joy) is incomparable !

...samāsamasamo 'samaḥ (III. 6d) '...(you are) unequalled, being equal towards equal and unequal.'
(i. e. impartial towards friendly and unfriendly)

pūjyapūjyatamaṃ loke, lokapūjitapūjitam;
pūjārhaṃ pūjayāmi tvā, pūjābhājam anuttaram. (III.3)

Most honourable of those to be honoured in the world,
honoured by those who are honoured in the world;
I honour you, worthy of honour,
supreme one entitled to honour.

These effects, however, perhaps owe more to their period than to the genius of Mātṛceṭa, which as we shall see was capable of creating deeply moving poetry.

888. Continuing with his anti-comparisons, contradictions *virodhas* and contrasts, Mātṛceṭa describes the apparently self-contradictory qualities of the Buddha's speech (concise yet ample, brilliant yet not dazzling, and so on, in other words ideally balanced) and the impossibility of refuting it (one might wound the unresisting sky, but not pierce this doctrine with another). A curious section juggles with the sequence of conditions formulated by the Buddha in the manner of a Brahmanical mystical discussion on ritual verses and then praises the Buddha and his doctrine in Brahmanical terminology, as if the consummation of the Brahmanical tradition. This is immediately followed by a verse: 'Whatever has been well said in the world comes from your doctrine...' (VII.17). Praising the benefit conferred on the world by the Buddha in making the way to *nirvāṇa* so clear, Mātṛceṭa is able to bring in a long series of metaphors describing the evils of the world and the obstacles to knowledge which have been swept aside. He then returns to his contrasts, between the Buddha and other teachers, especially in that the Buddha helps all beings without distinction. There follows a section on the parts of the Buddha's body in the tradition mentioned above, but much richer and more original than the earlier attempts known to us. A few similes are permitted here, almost as if by oversight, but far more contrasts. We have an enumeration *yathāsaṃkhya* [212] of white or bright objects, all very different among themselves (as is proper for this figure), only to be told they do not in the least approach the whiteness of the Buddha's teeth (X.9-11). A whole section is next devoted to the Buddha's tongue, which, the word 'tongue' being feminine in Sanskrit, is described as the mother of the teaching and the queen of all the Buddha's characteristics, having proclaimed her commands (the doctrine; there is a pun here) throughout the world.

889. The concluding section is concerned with the Buddha as producing the apprehension of transmigration (of its evils, otherwise borne complacently by those in it). It is so evil, and *nirvāṇa* so peaceful, that even the powerful and compassionate Buddha was subject to them (i.e. could escape the evils of transmigration only by attaining *nirvāṇa*) (XII.7). Without the Buddha, the teaching has lost its brilliance and strength...opinions have changed through the ages: its gleam (prosperity) has altered, as the beauty (fortune) of a lake soon vanishes if its dragon is taken away (corroboration [208]). The poem ends in these sombre tones. Who would not fear transmigrations, like flaming swords, after pondering the attainment of *nirvāṇa* by the powerful *buddhas* ?

890. Most of the *Varṇārhavarṇa Stotra* is extant in Sanskrit, restored from scattered and broken manuscripts, and the whole of it in Tibetan. In the Tibetan collection it is followed by a series of short hymns ascribed to Mātṛceṭa, the authenticity of which is not certain and which have not yet been recovered in Sanskrit, and another fairly long one, the whole of which is available intact in Sanskrit, the *Prasādapratibhodbhava Stotra*, better known as the *Śatapañcāśatka* or 'Hundred and Fifty', from its length. This seems certainly authentic and is Mātṛceṭa's finest *stotra*, showing his most mature style. It has been his most celebrated work among the Buddhists and the most widely disseminated, including a Chinese translation. Here Mātṛceṭa exercises greater restraint over the use of figures of sound only (alliteration, etc.), in harmony with a general appearance of simplicity and the avoidance of any pretensions to poetic brilliance. This appearance is deceptive: the restraint of these verses is that of complete mastery of the medium, able to express rich meanings with a few carefully chosen words and without the support of any outward display.

891. In fact the *stotra* abounds in figures, though these are handled with a kind of reticence suggestive of the poet's humility and detachment, both of which are probably sincere. Aśvaghoṣa's involvement was at least equally sincere, yet here there is a complete contrast between two writers, two opposed methods of artistic expression suited to two temperaments. It must be added that the aims of the two poets were also quite different: Aśvaghoṣa wrote for those 'in the world', to persuade them to abandon worldly ambitions; Mātṛceṭa wrote for those who had left the world, to inspire them in their life of meditation and detachment. We are told by the Chinese Buddhist pilgrim, I-Tsing, who visited India at the end of the +7, that in the late afternoon or at evening twilight the monks in a monastery would assemble and pay their respects to the Buddha by walking round a pagoda (symbol of the Buddha in *nirvāṇa*), whilst one of them chanted verses from a *stotra* (Schlingloff, *Stotras*, p. 8, quoted from Takakusu's translation of I-Tsing's work). Mātṛceṭa's verses are perfectly suited to such a simple exercise, in which it would be appropriate for the participants to review the ideals to which they were dedicated, and they were probably composed for this very purpose.

Just as in the Buddhist monasteries the followers of the various schools of Buddhism, those of the Mahāyāna included, lived together and shared their life of renunciation, even though they disagreed on some points of doctrine, so Mātṛceṭa's verses contain practically nothing distinctively of the Madhyamaka or Mahāyāna, which would not be acceptable to all schools, and we have I-Tsing's testimony as well as other evidence that his two major *stotras* were admired and learned by heart by followers of the Early schools as well as by Mahāyānists.

892. The title *Prasādapratibhodbhava* means 'Produced from the Inspiration *pratibhā* of Confidence (or Favour)', i.e. in the Buddha (or possibly through the Favour of the Buddha, conferred through his teachings; *prasāda* has a wide range of meaning, with 'clarity' seemingly most original—a meaning which it retains as a technical term in poetics [189]). The sections of the *Stotra* describe the various qualities and actions of the Buddha, with special attention to his self-sacrificing actions in former lives as Bodhisattva. It is superfluous, probably, to note that this is just as acceptable to the Early schools as to the Mahāyāna, though its significance for them varies, descriptive for the former, prescriptive as well for the latter. Here again Mātṛceṭa uses contrast, this time between the nature of the *bodhisattva* and ordinary human nature:

People are not as intent on helping others who return the help,
As you are intent on helping even those intent on harming you. (119)

The joy you had in abandoning your life for the sake of another
Could not be known to (i.e. is inconceivably greater than that of) living beings who regained their lives after thinking they had lost them. (17)

You have conquered revilers by tolerance, the malicious by securing their safety,
The false by truth and the injurious by benevolence. (122)

Helpful, gracious, calm in speech and gesture,
To you, even, they are hostile: see the ferocity of
delusion ! (148)

893. The theme of the impossibility of comparison in the case of the Buddha, prominent in the *Varṇārhavarṇa*, is again taken up, but we do find a series of metaphors (the Buddha is a lake, an island, in verses 96 and 98), whilst similes are possible for the Buddha's speech (a cloud, the Sun, a thunderbolt, in 73-4). The Buddha's Compassion is personified in verse 64: she is extremely good to others, yet cruel to her own support, for she has no compassion for the Buddha himself (contradiction). The Buddha's body and his qualities engage in mutual praise in verse 57. There are some *yamakas*, but these and alliteration are much less conspicuous than in the earlier work.

894. Mātṛceṭa's vocabulary is large and he generally avoids the clichés almost inevitable with such a subject. His theme is that the Buddha's qualities are innumerable, so that the little he is able to say is totally inadequate, though worth saying as conducive to his own welfare. The variety of his expression enforces this idea of the infinity of possibilities in praising the Buddha, appearing as merely a few scattered suggestions implying that there is so much more left unsaid.

895. In Ratnaśrījñāna's commentary *Ratnaśrī* on Daṇḍin's *Kāvyalakṣaṇa* we find some verses in the *vaṃśastha* metre quoted as 'by Mātṛceṭa'. These are incorporated (pp. 60 ff.) in the discussion on the concluding verse of Daṇḍin's first chapter (on style), which points out that by diligent study people can participate in learned assemblies and enjoy them even if they have very little genius for original composition. These verses of Mātṛceṭa do not seem to be from any work of his otherwise known, whether in the original Sanskrit, like the *stotras* just examined, or in Tibetan translations, like the works mentioned below. Ratnaśrījñāna quotes twenty two and a half verses here which appear to be from a single work by Mātṛceṭa and to form a more or less continuous sequence. They develop the theme of the importance of study.

896. Briefly, study is necessary in order to be able to overcome evil men in assemblies. One must have a full understanding of both good qualities and bad ones. Then one can protect good things from the ignorant and the wicked. Honest men are caught by false scoundrels unless they understand falsity and thus know where to strike back. A good man, protected by his virtue, can, if learned and practised as well, overcome the wicked; moreover he can actually enjoy the discussions of scientific and learned subjects in assemblies. From the context in which Ratnaśrījñāna places this, it appears as an argument in favour of literary criticism and the study of the qualities *guṇas* [240] of style in writing and speaking, though it might seem at least equally to justify the study of logic. It is at present a matter of conjecture what work of Mātṛceṭa's these verses are taken from. It may have been a short tract *parikathā* on study, not much more extensive than these quotations, or it may have been a longer work on wider topics.

897. In the quotations Mātṛceṭa begins as follows:
Fallow land is broken only after first learning how to do it,
and its agriculture is revealed through labouring;
Thus the seed made of one's own thought is sown,
and the shoot grows which is the trunk of investigation.

—Thus the best grain of clarity is obtained,
the fulfilled provision, by men of swift decision...

(*Ratnaśrī* p. 61)

('clarity' *prasāda* is here taken as meaning the quality of speech so named, but particularly in a Buddhist writer it may also mean 'confidence', an appropriate overtone here; thirdly it may mean 'favour', which here would be of those listening to the speech)

898. After this Ratnaśrījñāna introduces a verse from Aśvaghoṣa, which we have translated above [766], returning to Mātṛceṭa after further discussion and quotations. Let us select some verses from the continuation of Mātṛceṭa's argument:

How can the unlearned wish to enter
the way which goes to the excellent Dragon World of the questions and answers

At the time of using the waters at the shore
of the great ocean of styles of discussion? (p. 62)

(the Dragon World is the Underworld under the Earth and also forming part of the ocean)

When the waters are relentless, he who with pure valour
forcibly penetrates the river
Goes the way either of the grass or of the stones
from the banks swept away by the power of the new waters. (p. 63)

(this is a 'citation of something else' *anyāpadeśa* [418], here evidently to be applied to the man with virtue but without training in discussion)

For a good man engages in an assembly full of good men
with circumspection, even if he is well read;
But a base fellow everywhere coolly vomits up
his speech-poison as if he is an authority. (p. 63)

899. Besides the various *stotras* attributed to him, the Tibetan collection of Mātṛceṭa's works contains two short 'tracts', one on the evils of the present age, *Kaliyugaparikathā*, including advice on government, and one somewhat longer on the four 'reversals' of Buddhist ethical teaching, namely seeking happiness in what is in fact unhappiness, etc., *Caturviparyayakathā*. There is also an 'Epistle to the Great King Kanika', *Mahārājakanikalekha*. None of these seem to be available in Sanskrit.

900. The epistle is believed to be his last work, written in old age. It was presumably addressed to Kaniṣka III (distinguished in Tibetan tradition from Kaniṣka I simply by the variant spelling, about which the Tibetans were very careful), who succeeded to the Kuṣāṇa Empire in or soon after +176 (see *Papers on the Date of Kaniṣka*, pp. 333 ff.). The epistle begins with Mātṛceṭa's apology for not visiting the King in response to his invitation, since old age and illness prevent him, and afterwards makes it clear that the King was young.

The contents and tone are suited to this circumstance: after a respectful beginning Mātṛceṭa warns of the dangers of youth, recommends study and moreover in his injunctions is a good deal briefer (there are 85 verses) than, for example, Nāgārjuna was when writing to Sātavāhana.

901. There is in fact a great contrast between the epistles of Nāgārjuna and Mātṛceṭa. Nāgārjuna sticks closely to standard Buddhist expositions of morality and apparently aimed simply to summarise these for the convenience of one assumed to be in general agreement with the Buddhist position, adding practically nothing new. Mātṛceṭa, whether through the superiority of his art merely, or also because his aim was different, is entirely original in his presentation, takes little account of the systematic Buddhist teaching (though the principles expressed are Buddhist), uses many similes and other figures and generally makes his message easy, obviously related to practical affairs and attractive. These are straightforward maxims, fully expressed, whereas Nāgārjuna's verses are concise notes bristling with technical terms of Buddhist doctrine, requiring a commentary, or at least a good deal of previous study of the subject. Mātṛceṭa assumes nothing and seeks to encourage his young ruler to adopt wise policies. Whether as a result of this advice or not, we may note that Kaniṣka III enjoyed a reasonably long and prosperous reign of more than thirty years, though in the time of his successor the Empire suddenly declined. Mātṛceṭa had recommended him to abdicate when he grew old and pass the autumn of his life in a community of monks.

902. Mātṛceṭa makes a special plea for compassion towards animals (64ff.) and begs the King to give up hunting, especially as he can find sufficient practice in the use of arms on the battlefield. Animals need compassion even more than human beings, since they suffer more and are defenceless. Concluding, he asks the King to be like the Moon (i.e. gentle; no doubt with flattering allusion to the claim that the Kuṣāṇa Dynasty was a Lunar Dynasty), not like the Sun (fierce, and a rather popular symbol of kingship).

903. Perhaps a contemporary of Mātṛceṭa was Ārya Śūra; indeed one Tibetan tradition stated that they were the same person, though the Tibetan and all other extant texts of their works keep the names of the authors quite distinct. Practically nothing is known of Śūra, assuming him to be different from Mātṛceṭa. Ratnaśrījñāna quotes (p. 34) from his *Jātakamālā* (No. 8, verse 41) as an example of *kāvya* by a 'Southern' *dākṣiṇātya* (i.e. *vaidarbha* style) writer, making him a pioneer of the style championed by Daṇḍin [240]. The traditions indicate that he belonged to about the same period as Mātṛceṭa. This indication is confirmed by his style, which has much in common with the great hymn writer; so much, indeed, that their identification does not appear at all impossible (statistical analysis with a computer would probably settle the question, but it has not yet been performed). On an impressionistic reading we here assume tentatively that Śūra is a different person from Mātṛceṭa but was very nearly contemporary with him, perhaps a younger contemporary strongly influenced by his style. The comparison is made more difficult by the fact that their extant works belong to different genres, Mātṛceṭa to lyric and Śūra to narrative and largely to prose. A verse by Dharmakīrti (+7), however, quoted by Tāranātha (Schiefner, p. 181), says that Śūra is supreme in metrics. In fact he uses a great variety of different metres, unlike Mātṛceṭa, so that even here comparison is difficult.

904. Three works by Śūra are available in Sanskrit, his masterpiece the *Jātakamālā* and two tracts called the *Subhāṣitaratnakaraṇḍakakathā* and *Pāramitāsamāsa*. They are also preserved in Tibetan translations, along with several other works ascribed to him, including another tract, the *Supathadeśanā* or *Supathanirdeśa parikathā*. It is reported that the chapters of the *Subhāṣitaratnakaraṇḍakakathā* are also found appended to the stories of the unpublished *Dvāviṃśatyavadāna*, a collection of traditional Buddhist stories thus presented as illustrating them (S. Lévi according to D.R.S. Bailey, *Śatapañcāśatka*, Introduction p. 12). Presumably Śūra was not the author of this *Avadāna* collection and the combination is secondary.

905. The *Subhāṣitaratnakaraṇḍaka*, 'Casket of Gems of what has been Well Said', consists of 190 verses divided into 27 chapters. In content it belongs to the category of the ethical lectures of the Buddha which are summarised in the *Mahāparinibbāna Suttanta* [610], sometimes delivered to laymen (e.g. *Dīgha Nikāya* II 85-6, 95) and sometimes to monks (e.g.

ibid. 91) and there called doctrinal 'discussion' *kathā*, from which perhaps the idea of a literary tract *parikathā* later originated. In form it is poetic, using a great variety of metres and much imagery, the latter mostly derived from the *Tripiṭaka*.

906. Śūra begins with exhortations to meritorious action *puṇya* as the 'one friend' we have in human existence (5), stressing the difficulty and rarity of attaining birth as a human being, a rarity which he takes up and develops further in his third chapter. In the first chapter (6) we find that this tract is addressed to a king, like the *Ratnāvalī*. Perhaps he was one of the last Sātavāhanas (Yajñaśrī?). Still rarer is it to have been born at a time when it is possible to hear the words of the Buddha (second chapter), therefore you should seize this opportunity which may not occur again for hundreds of ages.

907. After these introductory chapters Śūra sets out the various topics of Buddhist ethics for the laity, starting with generosity *dāna* (IV) and describing some of the desirable results of meritorious action (V). A great variety of specific kinds of action follows, with their results such as attaining heaven or future kingship. Some of the actions are specific types of gift, such as providing food, buildings, heating and so on for communities of monks, but others are of a more ritualistic kind such as commissioning statues of the Buddha, providing lamps for pagodas (shrines), honouring the Buddha with music, etc., and bathing statues of the Buddha.

908. After all these topics have been briefly treated, Śūra adds a miscellaneous chapter (XXII), which is by far the longest, with a mass of other suggestions and some duplication of what has already been touched on. Here it is of interest to note a number of public works recommended, such as planting parks with trees and flowers, building a causeway *setu* (this can also include bridges), providing drinking places for travellers, constructing reservoirs, wells, rest houses and protection from sun and wind (on roads)—the result of these actions being that you become a god. This chapter also goes beyond the general topic of generosity by recommending the avoidance of taking life, of theft, of another's wife, of untruth, of malice and of harshness, following an ancient list of Buddhist social principles of good conduct or virtue *śīla*. Violent passion and continual pursuit of enjoyments should also be avoided in order to obtain future happiness, and benevolence should be cultivated.

909. After a final verse extolling generosity as saving one from all kinds of dangers, it is then natural to devote a chapter (XXIII) specifically to virtue *śīla*. Since virtue has been briefly described already, this more poetic chapter praises it in its general aspect: a person averse to virtue is like a lake which is inaccessible or a tree which is covered with thorns, and so on:

> It would be better to be poor but very virtuous,
> rather than rich but not adorned with good qualities;
> For a good man is praised even when poor,
> —the taste of good qualities excels ambrosia. (159)

910. This topic is followed by chapters on tolerance (which is opposed to hatred *dveṣa*, the greatest evil), energy, meditation and understanding, thus completing (with generosity and virtue) the six 'perfections' *pāramitās* of men (190). This tract is a relatively simple and straightforward work, following the *Tripiṭaka* and its vocabulary closely and making few demands on the literary education of the reader. It is primarily the elaborate metres which stamp it as *kāvya*.

911. The *Pāramitāsamāsa*, 'Synopsis of Perfections', is a longer work (about 360 verses) in six chapters, one on each of the six 'perfections' just mentioned. Again the metres more than anything else make this work a *kāvya*, but a few figures, such as rhyme (e.g. III.1) and simile, are used. The style is more elegant and studied than in the 'Casket of Gems', not following the *Tripiṭaka* so closely but rather at a distance, amplifying selected expressions. This Synopsis differs fundamentally from the 'Casket' in advocating, not the ordinary virtues and perfections of lay life, but the perfections as cultivated by a *bodhisattva* aiming to be a future *buddha*. Thus it proposes the Mahāyāna or 'Great Vehicle', though not in an aggressive or controversial manner (I.1: those who wish to become *buddhas* should...; cf. I.20, V. 36, VI. 65). Only III.29 seems to suggest a philosophy resembling Nāgārjuna's Madhyamaka as theoretical background. In the Casket, generosity is made attractive by such results as kingship and heaven, aspirations now (I.41) called the 'inferior' vehicle; here the same gifts (e.g. I.28) may be given to obtain (facility in) meditation, knowledge on the doctrine, etc., i.e. to make progress towards enlightenment. The advocacy of the perfections here is poetic, not systematic as in the regular treatises of the Mahāyānists on the way of the *bodhisattva*.

912. The chapter (III) on tolerance is perhaps the most interesting.

Never being aware of the faults of others,
agreeably depending on the virtuous,
This name, beautiful because it turns always towards
good qualities,
'tolerance' is compassionate and lives for the well-
being of the world. (2)

This world deluded by attachment to the 'soul',
considers the rest as 'aliens';
With thoughts ruled over by that provocation,
through separation from tolerance it gets into a state
of torment. (16)

913. Meditation:

Knowledge becomes clearer
through meditation in a spotless mind,
Like the Moon's disc in the sky
when in autumn the clouds have been driven away.
(V.2)

914. The importance of understanding (VI) is stressed in relation to the other perfections, which may become perverted without it. For example virtue *śīla* without it may acquire the fault of indignation *amarṣa* (11).

915. The *Jātakamālā*, 'Garland of Births', is a *campū* narrative [433], with roughly equal amounts of prose and verse, retelling thirty four of the most popular *Jātaka* stories [570, 579]. The critic Ratnaśrījñāna (p. 23) gives it as an example of the *campū* form. Śūra is here a fastidious stylist, so far successful as, despite the Buddhist content of his work, to have commanded the respectful mention of Brahmanical critics (tradition recorded by Rājaśekhara in his *Kāvyamīmāṃsā*, p.

55: 'Sūra') among the foremost Sanskrit poets. His prose is as elegant and compact as his verse. Both appear simple in construction, which they are not, and restrained and laconic in statement, being in fact often elliptical though frequently expanded by poetic figures. The vocabulary is exceedingly rich, as any student can testify who has had to cope with its difficulties.

916. Śūra's stories are selected to illustrate the virtues of the Bodhisattva (the future Buddha), and thereby Buddhist ethics generally. They are not necessarily Mahāyānist and were perhaps intended primarily for the edification of the laity, as were Aśvaghoṣa's works. They are more insistently ethical than those in all their details, though both writers use the full technique of *kāvya* writing, including many metres, many figures of both meaning and sound, rich poetic descriptions and so on. Śūra in fact is more polished in his style, which would be a natural result of a gradual perfecting of the *kāvya* mode of expression during the period between them, and he is also more restrained, less liable to be carried away by enthusiasm for the sheer technicalities of language.

917. Each story is introduced by a brief statement of the virtue to be illustrated. For the most part they describe the marvellous acts of self-sacrifice performed by the Bodhisattva. His life is as nothing to him except that by giving it up he may be able to make progress towards his ideal of saving the world from unhappiness, in other words towards becoming a *buddha* who will be able to promulgate the saving doctrine effectively in the world. As mere Bodhisattva he is not yet fully 'enlightened' and therefore not able to do this, but only to do individual good actions consonant with the varied walks of life in which he successively finds himself. Similarly, wealth, when he has any, is of use only in that it can be given away to the poor or to ascetics, thereby improving his character through the exercise of the virtue of generosity. In general, all opportunities, even painful ones, to exercise virtues are to be welcomed. The virtues chiefly illustrated are compassion, generosity, tolerance and purity of conduct despite all incitement to depart from it. Speaking the truth and constancy are also emphasised. Good conduct means avoiding theft, anger and intoxicating drink. Avoiding pleasures and retiring from the world is also praised. Compassion in its many aspects is the most general theme and is described in various ways as an affectionate nature, as considering all beings as like oneself, as not recognising the existence of any unhappiness except that of others, as grief at the unhappiness of others, even of injurers, and so on. Good acts can win over even enemies.

918. Running through the stories is the specific 'emotion' or 'inspiration' *saṃvega* recognised by the Buddhists, and expressly mentioned by Śūra in various places as well as being made the subject of one story (No. 32, 'Ayogṛha Jātaka'), which inclines a person to virtue despite such distractions as wealth and power. The term is equivalent to 'idealism' in its moral sense, perhaps to the 'moral sense' some philosophers have attempted to define. Here it is not defined but is exemplified and glorified. The acts of self-sacrifice which seem incredible, not to say ridiculous, to our amoral society, and which sometimes appear as clumsy exaggerations in the ordinary literature of edification produced by Buddhist monks, are here narrated with such art as to be convincing. The contrast with ordinary worldly prudence is stressed, but the acting directly contrary to worldly advantage appears natural to a 'moral' character; moreover we are given to feel the lively contentment and real happiness of the inspired hero who disregards the worldly stream in the exercise of his quest for the good. This is a delightful book for all those weary of our world.

919. Let us read a short excerpt from Śūra's Jātaka (No. 2) on the famous King Śivi [527], hero of generous self-sacrifice, concerning whom more than one tale of the giving of the limbs of his own body to save others is recorded in the Great Epic and the *Tripiṭaka* (*Mahābhārata* III *adhyāyas* 130-1 gift of his own flesh to a hawk by Uśīnara, Śivi's father, a story afterwards told of Śivi himself by writers such as Somadeva *Kathāsaritsāgara* I.7.88ff.; *Jātaka* IV 401ff. gift of his eyes by Śivi, as here). We begin with verse 6 describing Śivi:

The fragrance consisting of his fame (mud) produced
from generosity (rut juice),
was scattered by the wind of the speech of his beggars
(bees);
It removed the arrogance of other kings,

as that of a 'scent' elephant that of other elephants.
(6)

(the words bracketed here are double meanings of those preceding, appropriate for the elephant simile: the rut juice from the 'scent' elephant, or finest elephant, drips down to form a fragrant mud over which the bees buzz, fanning the scent in all directions, which removes the arrogance of other elephants)

(prose) Then at one time that King, going the rounds of his alms halls, observed that the concourse of suppliants was attenuated, in consequence of the beggars having been satisfied, and because the virtue of his generosity was thus not ascending he was not pleased.

The beggars came to him and appeased their thirst;
but he, intoxicated with generosity, did not his when
he met the beggars:
For no beggar could, by the measure of a request,
conquer the resolution of his generosity. (7)

He understood: 'Most fortunate are those, distinguished among good men, who are begged, with confidence and with unrestrained entreaties, even for their own limbs, by the beggars. To me, however, the beggars, as if threatened by harsh-syllabled words of refusal, come with timid entreaties merely for money.'

Then the Earth shook like a woman whose husband
is dear,
knowing that reasoning of the King,
Very exalted and based on generosity,
with attachment ceasing even for his own limbs. (8)

Then Śakra King of the Gods, when Sumeru king of mountains, radiant with the lustre of various gems, shook with the trembling of the Earth's surface, was flustered with doubt: 'What's this?'—he understood the excellent reasoning of that King, the cause of the trembling of the Earth's surface, and his heart inclined to astonishment as he thought:

'Has this really been reasoned by that King,
his mind uplifted by surpassing joy in generosity,
His constant purpose being the gift of his own limbs,
after girding his loincloth with the resolution of his
generosity? (9)

Then I shall now investigate him.' Then while the King was sitting in the assembly, attended by the company of his ministers, the customary proclamation of invitation—'Who desires what?'—being made to the beggars; the treasurer standing by with the collections of jewels, gold, silver and money opened, packages whose interiors were filled up with various garments being broken open, beautiful kinds of carriages with yokes fixed on the shoulders of well-behaved and various animals being led near; when the beggars had begun their concourse, Śakra King of the Gods created the appearance of a blind old brahman and became visible in the line of sight of the King. Then as if the King's glance rose to meet him and as if it embraced him, impregnated with compassion and kindness, firm, clear and gentle, when invited—'With what object.. ?'—and admitted near the Lord of Men by the followers of the Protector of the Earth, he began with expressions of victory and benediction and said to the King...

We have deliberately made this translation as literal as English can well endure in the hope of transferring some indication of Śūra's style, including the long sentences, though not the compounds which make the original compact.

920. Several of the stories in the *Jātakamālā* are illustrated among the Ajaṇṭā murals, though the painters were not always following Śūra's book. Thus when they illustrate the Śivi story, showing the gift of eyes to the brahman (in the excavated monastery, No. XVII, on the right as one enters the main hall), they follow the original *Tripiṭaka* version rather than Śūra's (see Yazdani IV pp. 96 ff.). But in two cases the Ajaṇṭā frescoes actually bear inscriptions, still partly preserved, consisting of verses from the *Jātakamālā* itself, showing that here at least the painters were supposed to be illustrating

Śūra's narratives. These narratives are the Kṣāntivādin (No. 28; cf. Yazadani II pp. 57ff., Allan's Appendix on the inscriptions) and the Maitrībala (No. 8).

921. In the former (depicted in the small hall on the left of the portico of monastery No. II), the Bodhisattva is the ascetic Kṣāntivādin, 'Tolerance-Speaking', living in a beautiful forest full of flowers. During the summer heat, the King of that country set out on a pleasure excursion with his wives, to enjoy water sports in a lake in the forest, near the hermitage of Kṣāntivādin. While the King sleeps after heavy drinking, his wives wander off picking flowers and find the ascetic. They are attracted by his bearing and gather round: he welcomes them and discourses to them on his favourite subject of tolerance. Here the fresco shows Kṣāntivādin on a cane seat with the women listening, and its inscription quotes his words in several verses from Śūra, including this:

> Trees are ornamented by flowers,
> clouds, slow with rain, by the qualities of lightning,
> Lakes by lotuses with intoxicated bees,
> but men by good qualities discovered by discrimination.
> (19)

Meanwhile the King comes up and is filled with jealous rage on seeing his wives admiring the ascetic. He rushes on Kṣāntivādin with his sword, despite the appeals of the women, and hacks off his limbs, accusing him of hypocrisy, the ascetic calmly accepting the blows and feeling no anger. Over its painting of this scene the fresco inscribes this verse of Śūra:

> Though his limbs were cut off, the thoughts of the good man as he watched
> were firm with uninjured tolerance,
> He did not feel the pain, but as a consequence of affection
> looking at the King fallen from virtue was a torment to him. (56)

As he goes off, the King is swallowed up by the Earth, a flaming chasm opening at his feet. After a final speech on toleration, Kṣāntivādin dies and goes to heaven.

922. In the latter Jātaka, King Maitrībala, 'Whose Strength is Kindness', offers his own blood and flesh to some man-eating demons, protecting his people. This is painted on another wall of the same hall, and a verse from Śūra is partly preserved there, describing Maitrībala as he cut off pieces of his own flesh to feed the demons:

> Through delight in generosity again and again
> his mind did not allow
> An opportunity for being ashamed—
> for the pain of cutting to penetrate it. (44)

The demons are overpowered by this extraordinary act and beg his forgiveness, promising to live harmlessly afterwards. Śakra is again shaken from his mountain, comes down and heals the King's wounds. It is interesting that Ratnaśrījñāna (p. 34) quotes a verse from this same Jātaka to illustrate 'Southern' style *kāvya*, as we noted above, and particularly to show that it can be 'soft' *mṛdu* in quality without being 'loose' *śithila* (the reference is to the sounds and grammatical construction of the original, which can hardly be translated). The King has had his veins opened so that the blood runs out and the demons can drink:

> The King, whose blood was being sought*
> by the demons, seemed to have a golden body,
> Like Meru embraced by clouds
> borne down by their load of water and reddened by the
> sunset. (41)

923. Śūra's work was probably widely circulated in India when in the +5 the Vākāṭaka emperors sponsored the building and decorating of these monasteries at Ajaṇṭā, so that there need be no special significance in his narratives being quoted and illustrated in these Māhārāṣṭrian frescoes. But 'Southern' or *vaidarbha* in Indian criticism means of Mahārāṣṭra or part of it (Ajaṇṭā lies among the mountains on the South West border of Vidarbha, and Vatsagulma is not far from it), thus it is possible that the Vākāṭaka officials and painters

(*so Ratnaśrījñāna reads; Kern's edition has 'drunk')

were consciously honouring a famous writer of their own country.

924. Ratnaśrījñāna quotes two more verses from the *Jātakamālā*. In explaining (p. 59) Daṇḍin's remark (I.104) that inspiration *pratibhāna* results from qualities which are 'traces' *vāsanās* of previous lives, he adduces this by way of authority:

> For as a consequence of practice, good and bad actions are innate in men,
> Such are they indeed that effortlessly
> they act in another life, as in a dream. (15.1)

This is the first verse of Śūra's Matsya Jātaka (also illustrated in Ajaṇṭā monastery XVII, Yazdani IV 78f., but not necessarily from this version).

925. To illustrate Daṇḍin's argument (III.179) that a 'fault' *doṣa* may sometimes be transformed into a 'quality' *guṇa*, Ratnaśrījñāna quotes (p. 274) this from the Śreṣṭhin Jātaka of Śūra:

> Then through the power of his merit
> there was produced there a 'lotus' which was not 'mud-born';
> Which was as if laughing with contempt at Death
> with its white row of stamen-teeth. (4.19)

The 'fault' in question would be a contradiction of place, since 'lotus' here is literally 'mud-born' and is immediately contradicted, for this lotus was produced in purgatory among flames. But Śūra has used the contradiction with good effect (cf. the figure contradiction [231]).

926. The anthologist Vidyākara quotes from Śūra in his collection of verses on bad men (1292 in the Asant Vrajyā):

> A scoundrel is lifted up with shriller arrogance towards those who are gentle with compassion,
> he proceeds to the utmost excitement, for he sees no danger from them;
> But where he touches even a very little apprehension of danger,

> there he carries on with this uplift calmed, as if
> well-behaved and humble. (33.4)

This is from the Mahiṣa Jātaka, also illustrated in Ajaṇṭā monastery XVII (Yazdani IV 81). Vidyākara also has a verse (1698) of unknown authorship which praises several famous writers, including Śūra for *viśuddhokti*, 'pure (or clear) expression'. Tāranātha as noted above quotes a verse by Dharmakīrti on Śūra as supreme in the use of metres.

927. As a further example of Śūra's prose we may read the beginning of the Mahākapi Jātaka (No. 24), again illustrated in Ajaṇṭā XVII (Yazdani IV 53f.):

> The good are not tormented as much by their own suffering as by their injurers' loss on the good side. As it is handed down:— The Bodhisattva, they say, was a monkey of great size living alone on the beautiful side of the Himālaya, which had brilliant and surprising cosmetics consisting of various ores, with a beauty of forest thickets as if a cloak made with a mantle of dark silk, with compositions of many colours and shapes as if arranged deliberately with the edges of its slopes adorned with line paintings of dangers, it had waters rushing forth from many springs, it was confused with precipices within which were deep caves, it resounded with very shrill bees, its trees with varied flowers and fruits were fanned by pleasing breezes, it was a pleasure garden of the wizards.

The monkey saves the life of a man who has lost his way in these mountains, but the ungrateful man, after a casuistic argument with himself in justification, tries to kill him as a ready source of meat. The monkey escapes with a wound in the head and, full of compassion, still helps the wretch to find his way back towards the nearest village, grieving only over the man's evil life and probably worse future.

928. The style of the prose parts of the *Jātakamālā* represents for us that of a whole period from which very little has survived to show the development from the generally simple and unadorned style of traditional story telling to the later *kāvya* prose style; which latter not infrequently is as fastidious, in selection of vocabulary, balancing of rhythms and lacing with figures, as any verse. Indeed, to some tastes Śūra represents an ideal mean between barely adorned narrative and barely narrative adornment. The narrative of early Pali prose, for example, is usually simple and in everyday language, occasionally elevated in vocabulary when particularly momentous events are described (e.g. in the *Mahāparinibbāna Suttanta* [610]). Śūra is always elevated, an effect carefully maintained, even in the tersest bits of dialogue, by the exclusion of all unnecessary words and the inclusion of an occasional unexpected word bringing an idea of high purpose or a figurative allusion appropriate to nobility of character. In some prose texts earlier than Śūra, on the other hand, we find the use of extremely long compound words, a feature often regarded in later theory as especially characteristic of prose and as giving 'strength' to it. Early examples are the *Kuṇāla Jātaka* [611] and (nearer Śūra's time) the inscriptions of Puḷumāyi II (whom we have provisionally taken to be 'Sātavāhana' himself) at Nāsikā, in Prakrit, and of Rudradāman (a Śaka governor of Ujjayinī, nominally subordinate to the Kuṣāṇas) at Girinagara, in Sanskrit. Both these inscriptions were written round about +150. In all three texts we find very long sentences as well as long compounds, the two features generally going together. The royal inscriptions clearly belong to the style of *kāvya* rather than to everyday prose. The Rudradāman inscription actually praises the style of this royal *kavi* for the qualities *guṇas* of being clear *sphuṭa*, sweet *madhura*, gracious *kānta*, etc.

929. Now Śūra must have been very familiar with this kind of inflated prose which, moreover, remained popular for many centuries after his time. But he exercises great restraint in his own prose: he uses many compounds but they are always of very moderate length (frequently of four members but very rarely of more); his sentences are quite short everywhere. His descriptions are short and to the point, yet sufficiently full to give distinct and circumstantial pictures. Later prose writers cultivate the long, digressive description for its own sake and for the opportunity afforded for brilliant displays of enchained figures, and they enjoy piling up clause on clause in long, rich sentences. None of this is to be found in Śūra:

perhaps it was only much later that the writing of such long sentences and descriptions, with fairly long compounds, was developed as a true art, with mastery of the technique, rather than as a merely quantitative accumulation of words and images, with the longest possible compounds, of which we can find examples in some of the earlier prose before, and even after, Śūra's time.

930. The verse and prose parts of this *campū* are about equal in amount and seem mixed more or less indiscriminately (closer analysis might elucidate criteria of differentiation): any part of the narrative, descriptions and dialogues may be in either medium, the alternation of the two being apparently a matter of formal balance and rarely corresponding to any content. However, the verse medium seems to be regarded as more elevated in that moral reflections, and discourses on morality spoken by the Bodhisattva, are usually in verse. In the verses Śūra uses a very great number of different metres, thus adding further to the variety in his forms of expression. In his language equally he generally aims at variety of expression and at unexpected turns of phrase, avoiding monotony and anything commonplace.

931. Śūra uses many different figures, probably more than any previous writer we have met, and in their choice he is markedly closer to the standard practice modelled by the 'classical' poets of about +400 onwards than is Aśvaghoṣa. Comparison and contrast generally underlie his figures of sense, as with Mātṛceṭa, and especially the surprising contrast, sometimes the equally surprising comparison:

> As was the sight of him (the Bodhisattva when a rich
> merchant) to the beggars,
> so was the sight of the beggars to him
> ——A special cause of the awakening of joy,
> because it destroyed any uncertainty as to the
> accomplishment of their desired objects
> (No. 5, verse 1).

The identity of the effect of seeing each other on both parties is here insisted on further by the identity of wording of the first two clauses ('as ..' and 'so...') in the Sanskrit, an ambiguity in the grammatical construction which can be understood either way, literally: 'As of the beggars the sight was of him, so of the beggars the sight was of him'. The figure here may be described as 'equal consequence' *tulyayogitā* [223], since the effect is the same on both parties.

932. The simultaneous word play is characteristic of Śūra, who is fond of repeating a word in different senses or with a different significance, in fact of the internal rhyme *yamaka* used freely (i.e. not necessarily at definite points in the verse or clause). Yet he is much less addicted to word play than Aśvaghoṣa or even Mātṛceṭa, keeping it entirely subordinate to the meaning, as incidental decoration. A good example of applied ambiguity is the speech by Death (Māra) (No. 4, 5ff.), criticising the virtue, generosity, as a vice leading straight to hell and a sin inimical to the three ends of life (virtue, wealth and pleasure). Death's language is exactly that of a preacher of morality, but disguises a hollow sophistry that wealth is the basis of virtue and therefore should never be given away. The Bodhisattva's reply is equally equivocal, thanking Death for this kindness and compassion in pointing out the proper way, but regretting that his fault had not been checked earlier, since now the disease is too far advanced to respond to treatment. In fact Death's pointing out the dangers has now only increased his desire to risk them, since he is not seeking his own advantage. Death maintains to the last his pose as a benefactor giving good advice, ending with the warning that afterwards he will remember him with respect, whether he takes his advice or not. Let us leave Śūra with a warning from one bird (wild goose) to another about the falsity of the human heart, advising him to keep away from men:

> In general beasts and birds express what is in their
> hearts by the sounds they make,
> But human beings alone are clever at expressing the
> opposite of that. (No. 22, verse 19)

933. We have now to note four more anonymous *stotras* perhaps a little later than Mātṛceṭa's time, recovered in a fragmentary state from Central Asian manuscripts. Fragments from a hymn of a hundred or more verses in praise of the

Buddha are chiefly remarkable for being in the extremely complicated *udgatā* metre [752] (after which Schlingloff has named them: Fragment F), which, however, is used already in the Pali Canon. It occurs there alongside the even more complicated, but similar in having a different structure in each line of its quatrain, *upasthitapracupita* [584]. We are inclined to see in this kind of thing a metrical tour de force, but we really know little of the use of this highly musical prototype of the medieval *tālavṛttas* of Apabhraṃśa, which perhaps was very familiar at one time and flowed naturally and liltingly from the tongue of the poet:

> In this world a man crosses the (...) ocean in a ship—
> or (he may be unlucky and) not;
> But those who have joined this ship made of hymns
> infallibly cross the ocean of existence (transmigration).
>
> (8 contrast *vyatireka*)

934. We at least know the title of the *Munayastava* (Schlingloff Frag. C), though not the name of its author, which is simply its first word *munaye*, 'To the Recluse' (the Buddha). It consists of 23 simple *vaktra* verses, simpler and also much less polished stylistically than Mātṛceṭa's. The epithets by which the Buddha is praised are mostly in the dative case('hail *to*...') and the hymn ends with the author's exaggerated remark that he has used 'hundreds' of them (perhaps he wrote many more such hymns). They are all conventional and old and about the only ornament is a sprinkling of alliterations. Nevertheless this appears to have been one of the more popular hymns in Central Asia, to judge from the number of manuscripts of it of which bits have been found. It is not for the connoisseur of literature.

935. We return to literature with a few surviving verses in the rare *krauñcapadā* metre (Schlingloff Fragment G) praising the Buddha's successes in persuading the most unlikely persons to give up their vicious ways of life and follow him. These include the celebrated robber and mass murderer Aṅgulimāla, a fierce demon, a dragon and a maddened elephant (all from traditional legends). The *krauñcapadā* is one of the more imposing fixed metres, a quatrain having twenty five syllables in each line. There is a verse for each villain and the expansive metre allows scope for colourful descriptions of them.

936. Lastly, the hymn whose title Schlingloff restores as *Rāhulastava* (Fragment D) is again in *vaktra*, but a little more original in wording than the *Munaya*. The theme is the wonderful nature of the Buddha and it is contrast and contradiction which provide most of the ornamentation, along with some alliteration; the Buddha-nature stands out against the evils and miseries of the world. The significance of the title 'Rāhula' is not clear: perhaps the verses were supposed to have been uttered by the Buddha's son.

937. In the preceding chapters we have from time to time attempted to characterise the styles of various writers, sometimes suggesting a relation to the styles recognised and defined by later critics. Thus Aśvaghoṣa could perhaps be regarded as a forerunner of the *gauḍīya* [238] style, which from its name should have originated in Magadha (perhaps including some surrounding countries), though he was born in Kośala, North West of Magadha [733, 756]. We might look in the Seven Hundred Songs for a Māhārāṣṭrī origin of the other widely recognised old style, the *vaidarbha*, Vidarbha being a province of Mahārāṣṭra [830]. Śūra seems to be the earliest writer known to us (except Vālmīki [635]) who is positively called 'Southern', in a context implying *vaidarbha*, by an old critic, Ratnaśrījñāna [903, 922-3], though his date is only approximately known. It is not unlikely that Śūra was a writer of Mahārāṣṭra.

938. However, as was noted in Chapter IV in discussing the styles *rītis* [238], the first great *kāvya* known to have attained recognition as a model of this style was the *Aśmakavaṃśa*, 'History of Aśmaka' (or 'Dynasty of Aśmaka'), Aśmaka being another province of Mahārāṣṭra (South of Vidarbha). We are given this information by a much earlier critic than Ratnaśrījñāna, Bhāmaha. This work, probably an epic poem, is lost and its author is unknown. We can attempt to date it, and with it the development of the *vaidarbha* style, by the early reference to it, probably as a pioneering work, and by considering what its subject might have been. A Dynasty of Aśmaka could have described the Sātavāhanas, or it might have celebrated the Ābhīras, since there is a tradition that Śūdraka was born in Aśmaka (Krishnamachariar p. 572). It would probably not have been composed after the fall of the dynasty it celebrated. 'Sātavāhana' ('Hāla'), whom we have provisionally identified as Puḷumāyi II, is in the Māhārāṣṭrī novel *Līlāvaī* called King of Aśmaka (the editor, A.N. Upādhye, interprets Prakrit Āsaya in verse 46 as Aśmaka—p. 329). The evidence is slight, but the *Līlāvaī* reference may perhaps incline us to accept the identification with the Sātavāhanas. In this case we may conjecture that what was regarded as the first great *kāvya* in the *vaidarbha* style was written in the +2. Our conjectural date for Śūra, late +2, agrees with that period for the origin of the style.

CHAPTER XVIII

DRAMA IN THE +2 : BHĀSA

939. The plays which perhaps the prevailing, but not the unanimous, opinion of modern readers ascribes to Bhāsa have been preserved for us in a few manuscripts in Kerala in the far South of India. Their manuscript tradition does not name any author and the ascription rests essentially on the fact of Bhāsa being known from old critics to have written a play bearing the title of one of these plays, together with the fact of the apparent uniformity of style running through the whole collection of plays. A prominent feature of these plays is their opening words (a stage direction) : if we compare them with the practice of Aśvaghoṣa as reported by Dharmakīrti [723] we find the first two words, indicating that the author's text is to be connected with the *pūrvaraṅga*, are omitted, otherwise the first sentence is the same; on the other hand, if we compare them with the manner of opening usual in plays datable from the +4 onwards, we find that sentence preceded there by one or more verses and reduced to two words only. It appears those verses constitute the opening benediction, now supplied by the author in place of some traditional benediction received as part of the *pūrvaraṅga*.

940. For our present purpose we follow the hypothesis that the practice in the plays ascribed to Bhāsa represents a phase intermediate in date between Aśvaghoṣa and the later 'standard' plays, which harmonises with the known period in which Bhāsa lived. This hypothesis has been challenged by suggesting that the deviation from the 'standard' represents not a historically earlier usage but a geographical variation, the custom of the Southern theatre. The plays might then have been written in the South, perhaps as much as a thousand years after Bhāsa, by some anonymous dramatist. Our hypothesis, however, receives strong support from the Dharmakīrti quotation of Aśvaghoṣa, which was not known to the challengers, bearing in mind further that the text of Dharmakīrti's *Vādanyāya* was preserved in Tibet. Certainly the older practice may have continued longer in the South, but this does not conflict with its being the older.

941. We must note finally in connection with the manuscript tradition of these plays that what is available to us is the tradition of a living theatre in Kerala. The texts we have are those used by actors. For this reason, if there are any discrepancies between these and the scanty quotations of Bhāsa in the old critics, which are not the fault of the critics, we need not at once dismiss our texts as not coming from Bhāsa but must consider whether, apart from the slips and interpolations of scribes, we should not suppose the actors or producers to have been responsible for cuts or other modifications made in what may probably be characterised as 'acting' versions. In one instance which has been urged against the ascription to Bhāsa, for instance (*Svapnavāsavadatta*, *sthāpanā*), the two sentences quoted by a critic (Sāgaranandin, *Nāṭakalakṣaṇaratnakośa*, 1205-6, as from *Svapnavāsavadatta* and being words of the producer), though not found in the extant text, fit very neatly and satisfactorily before the bare exclamation 'Very well! I know' which the manuscripts give the producer before verse 2. Other missing quotations may have been lost by the perhaps severe cutting of acting versions, which may be the correct explanation of the fact that these plays are very short by the usual standard, though this may also be due simply to their being early. Linguistically the plays suggest an early date, before the grammatical norms formulated by Pāṇini became accepted as rules absolutely binding on any self-respecting writer of Sanskrit and before the use of Māhārāṣṭrī [178, 769] in the drama. The Prakrits used appear intermediate in date between those of Aśvaghoṣa [720-1] and those of Śūdraka [1184], Kālidāsa, etc.

942. Bhāsa, the famous dramatist mentioned by a series of classical writers and critics from the +5 onwards, lived some time before Kālidāsa, the first known to name him, in whose day he was a classic whose works held, perhaps dominated, the stage [1377, 1386]. Śūdraka (+3? [1156-8]) seems in his *Mṛcchakaṭika* to have enlarged the *Daridracārudatta* of our collection of plays, with new subsidiary action [1182]. The reference by Kālidāsa might put Bhāsa's date at least as long before his own time as we may think necessary for the acquisition of a reputation as the leading classic of the theatre. An estimate of this would be rather subjective. Assuming that Bhāsa was the author of the *Daridracārudatta*, there would be no difficulty in placing him about the +2, to satisfy all the various indications. Śūdraka is a problem himself, to be discussed below. Since an Ābhīra king was perhaps intended by the name, and an Ābhīra Dynasty flourished in the +3, the author of the *Mrcchakaṭika* might be placed in that century, nevertheless it has been suggested that 'Śūdraka' was a figure more of legend than history and that we should doubt the ascription of plays to his authorship. In view of persisting ascriptions, however, and the absence of any evidence pointing at any other author, we seem obliged to accept his authorship on a provisional basis, awaiting further research, whilst unable to rely on it as a very firm limit for the date of Bhāsa as a predecessor.

943. As to the question of Bhāsa's precise date, only one suggestion appears to have been made, that of Konow (*Das indische Drama*, §61). It appears likely from the plays, and from Kālidāsa's reference, that Bhāsa worked in Ujjayinī. In that case he presumably lived under one of the Śaka governors, who were established by the Kuṣāṇas, became an independent dynasty and ruled until they were overthrown by the Guptas in the last decade of the +4. Konow has conjectured that the word *rājasiṃha*, occurring in the final benedictions of several of the plays, referred not just to any 'king-lion' but alluded specifically to the Śaka Rudrasiṃha I, who ruled during the last quarter of the +2 (as to other Śakas with names ending in —*siṃha*, we have Viśvasiṃha *c.* +280, Rudrasiṃha II in the early +4 and the ill-fated Rudrasiṃha III briefly at the end of that century). This is no more than a plausible conjecture. The date, end of the +2, thus suggested for Bhāsa harmonises with such other evidence as there is, which has been sketched above, and for the lack of anything more definite or more probable we may here adopt it as a working hypothesis. In view of Bhāsa's importance as perhaps the greatest Indian dramatist (such is the quality of these plays, whoever wrote them, and such would seem to have been the fame of his name), it has seemed proper to devote a little space here to an outline of the problem.

944. The chief characteristics of the plays ascribed to Bhāsa are that they are short, full of incidents and seem to have an eye to the stage rather than to a reader. Even if we assume severe cuts in the texts this characterisation will not have to be greatly modified. The contrast will still be strong with the later plays, from the +5 onwards, which are very long, full of polished lyrics and careful development of the causes and effects of emotion and designed to please readers who are connoisseurs of lyric poetry as well as an audience. In Bhāsa description is always brief, the lyric verses few, unpolished and simple. Incidents follow rapidly one upon another, conflict and dramatic change in fortune are everywhere prominent and there is hardly ever a case where the action halts whilst a series of verses develops the portrayal of emotion. Surely these were originally conceived as stage plays only, with a view to the effects which good actors can there produce. The later connoisseurs of poetry outside the theatre, and especially of the lyric, understandably found little here for their anthologies or for elaborate linguistic comment and appraisal of figures. This will explain the complete neglect of Bhāsa in Northern India since the +13, when the Turks conquered the main cities and suppressed the theatre on religious grounds. Such tradition of *kāvya* scholarship as survived the Muslim persecutions in the North was confined to private reading and study: it was natural that the *paṇḍitas* who were the sole guardians of literature in that dark age should concentrate on what was most rewarding in minute textual analysis and on lyric gems—for many generations they might never see a play actually acted. Thus we may understand the failure to preserve excellent plays by Bhāsa, and by other early dramatists, in the North. Where the theatre survived, mainly in the South, stage plays could survive.

945. The Bhāsa collection illustrates several of the types of play recognised by the *Nāṭyaśāstra* [320]. There are histories *nāṭakas*, fictions *prakaraṇas*, heroic plays *vyāyogas*, a tragedy *utsṛṣṭikāṅka* (perhaps two) and a light play *nāṭī*. A three act play is difficult to classify under the standard theory, but should be a cooperation *samavakāra* or more probably a contention *sallāpa*. Here then we have a broad view of the ancient Indian theatre, which can be supplemented with plays from approximate contemporaries of Bhāsa, to be discussed in the next chapter, including the types satirical monologue *bhāṇa* and comedy *prahasana*. An old street play *vīthī* which one modern scholar has suggested might be by Bhāsa is discussed at the end of this Chapter [1074]. The later repertory in our possession rarely goes outside these types, which remain the standard dramatic forms, except that the tragedy is neglected and excepting also the popular and ephemeral secondary types and 'ballets'.

946. The stories used by Bhāsa for his heroic plays and tragedies are all taken from episodes in the Great Epic *Mahābhārata* [518, 525]. Two heroic plays deal with the sending of envoys by the Pāṇḍavas, or by Kṛṣṇa, to their enemy the Emperor Duryodhana: one to propose a peaceful settlement of their claims, the other to threaten vengeance after a supposedly unfair incident in the Battle. Kṛṣṇa here is already the incarnation of Viṣṇu (Nārāyaṇa): when sent, in the *Dūtavākya*, 'Speech of the Envoy', as the peaceful envoy of the Pāṇḍavas, he shows his supernatural power over the kings attending Duryodhana's court. The Emperor, in council selecting his commander-in-chief, will hear nothing of peace and assails the messenger with harsh words. Kṛṣṇa tries to propitiate him with words of conciliation *sāman* [141], but Duryodhana rejects the idea that the Pāṇḍavas are his kinsmen—they are sons of gods [1500] and his kin are men (verse 30)! After an exchange of abuse the enraged Duryodhana tries to seize Kṛṣṇa, but the god appears everywhere at once and cannot be touched. Kṛṣṇa thinks of killing Duryodhana with a supernatural weapon, but restrains himself because his mission on Earth would then not be fulfilled. There are only five parts in this play, the other characters being imagined. Essentially it is a lively dialogue between Duryodhana and Vāsudeva (Kṛṣṇa), framed within the rapid incidents of the council and Vāsudeva's arrival and of the violent attempt to seize him.

947. Duryodhana had intended to receive Vāsudeva with contempt, but instead is at first somewhat overawed by the envoy's divine power and speaks politely:

DURYODHANA. Sir envoy ! —

The son of Dharma, Bhīma son of the Wind,
my brother Arjuna son of Indra of the Thirty Three
(gods),
The disciplined twins, sons of the Aśvins:
are they and their dependents all well? (19)

VĀSUDEVA. This is befitting in Gāndhārī's son! Indeed yes, all are well. Yudhiṣṭhira and the Pāṇḍavas enquire about the well-being and health of your kingdom and person, external and internal, and inform you:

'We have experienced great unhappiness
and the agreement has been fulfilled,
So let the legal
inheritance be shared.' (20)

DURYODHANA. How now? Inheritance?

My uncle (Pāṇḍu) as a consequence of hunting in the
forest
caused offence and met with a sage's curse:
Since then, not desiring his wife,
how can he become a father to others' sons? (21)

VĀSUDEVA. Let me ask you, who are learned in the past:

Vicitravīrya the sensual met with calamity
through consumption—however on Ambikā
Vyāsa begat Dhṛtarāṣṭra:
how did he, your father, obtain the kingdom? (22)

No sir!—

Thus by increasing their mutual opposition
the Kuru family will quickly become nothing but a
name, O king!

Therefore you ought to cast away your anger
and do what Yudhiṣṭhira and the others affectionately
request you. (23)

DURYODHANA. Sir envoy! You do not know the usage of the kingdom:

The kingdom is enjoyed by courageous princes after
conquering their enemies;
it is not begged for among the people, nor given to one
who is wretched;
If they desire to obtain kingship let them soon use force
—or else, as they fancy, let them enter a hermitage for
calm, frequented by those with calmed thoughts!
(24)

948. In the second play, the *Dūtaghaṭotkaca*,'Ghaṭotkaca as Envoy', Ghaṭotkaca in the midst of the battle, but during a lull, is sent to Duryodhana by Kṛṣṇa. The envoy exchanges threats with the Kauravas and is ready to fight the whole court single handed, but at last keeps to his proper task and retires after securing the Emperor's promise to meet Kṛṣṇa and the Pāṇḍavas and give his reply with arrows. Here we have some more heroic dialogue, but among several characters (there are nine parts in this play). Duryodhana has heard of Arjuna's promise or vow *pratijñā* [199] to avenge the death of his son Abhimanyu, and Ghaṭotkaca brings Kṛṣṇa's message confirming this and concludes:

Understand that the destruction of the nobles has been
decided!
may the Earth have contempt, strewn with hundreds
of kings!
For, because of the destruction of his son, loosing fierce
weapons which he has prepared,
nothing at the head of the battle will be too great at ask
for Arjuna. (45)

ŚAKUNI.

If this Earth could have been conquered
merely by speeches
If it could be, in many speeches
the killing of the nobles has already been done ! (44)

GHATOṬKACA. Oho ! He has changed his nature !

Give up the dice, O Śakuni ! Make ready for the arrows
a chequer board, proper object in the business of war !
For here there is neither taking of wives nor system of kingship
—here the stake is life and love is with arrows of fierce strength ! (45)

Here the 'nobles' are the aristocracy or vassals of the Empire, fighting in the Kaurava service. Śakuni, king of Gandhāra, is Duryodhana's uncle who organised the deceitful gambling match in which Yudhiṣṭhira lost his share of the Empire.

949. In a third heroic play, the *Madhyama*, 'Middle One', we have the earlier incident of Ghaṭotkaca in the forest meeting his father, the 'middle' Pāṇḍava brother Bhīma. The two do not know each other and Bhīma intervenes to save a brahman family from the half-demon Ghaṭotkaca. Then Bhīma recognises his son but tests him in fight. Finally Bhīma agrees to go to Ghaṭotkaca's mother, the demoness who craves human flesh, and all ends happily, Bhīma being pleased with his newly discovered son's prowess. This meeting in the forest is not found in the available Great Epic and was perhaps invented by Bhāsa, as a happily dramatic means of uniting the unknown son of a demoness *rākṣasī* with his father (who had encountered her in a previous episode, described in the Epic). In the Epic, Ghaṭotkaca fights alongside the Pāṇḍavas in the final battle and dies heroically. It is noteworthy in this heroic play that the fight takes place on stage.

950. The tragedy *Ūrubhaṅga*, 'Breaking of the Thighs', known also as the *Gadāyuddha*, 'Mace Fight', shows Duryodhana's death [329]. It is the climax of the great battle. Let us see, by way of example, how Bhāsa introduces his play [310-4, 723]. An incidental point about our translation, which may be noted, is that the word (with various synonyms) 'kings' frequently met with in connection with the battle should possbly be understood as meaning 'warriors' generally, or 'nobles'. The play begins with the prologue *sthāpanā* as follows:

PROLOGUE

Then the producer enters at the end of the opening benediction.

PRODUCER.

With Bhīṣma and Droṇa as its banks, Jayadratha the water, the King of Gandhāra a lake,
Karṇa, Aśvatthāman and Kṛpa the waves, crocodiles and sharks, Duryodhana the current,
Arjuna crossed the river of his enemies, with arrows and swords as its sand, by the boat
—the Lord Kṛṣṇa: may he be a boat when you are crossing over your enemies ! (1)

So I inform you, ladies and gentlemen...Oh ! Now just as I was intent on my announcement I seemed to hear someone speaking. Well let me see—

Off stage. 'It's us, sir ! It's us !'

PRODUCER. Very well ! I know....

Having entered:

ASSISTANT. Your honour, where are they coming from ?

With oblations of bodies prepared at the battlefront for attaining heaven,
with their limbs made rough by hundreds of arrows and javelins,
With their bodies torn by the tusks of wanton kingly elephants:
men surge about, touchstones for each other's heroism. (2)

PRODUCER. My friend, don't you understand? Of Dhṛtarāṣṭra's party, devoid of a hundred sons and his plans, only Duryodhana remains. Of Yudhiṣṭhira's party only the Pāṇḍavas themselves and Kṛṣṇa remain. (The field of) Samantapañcaka being covered over with the bodies of kings:

This battle with slaughtered elephants, horses, kings
and soldiers,
like a painting crammed with mixed together figures;
—Now the fight between Bhīma and Suyodhana*
has started
the soldiers have entered this one house of death for
kings. (3)

[*Exeunt.*

END OF THE PROLOGUE

951. SUPPORTING SCENE *viṣkambhaka* [126]

Then enter three soldiers.

ALL. It's us, sir! It's us!

FIRST.

This is the sanctum of enmity, the touchstone of
strength, the house of firmness of pride,
—in battles, the heroes' home of men is the hall for the
self-choices of the nymphs;
This is the hero's bed for kings at the last time, the
sacrifice with the fire-oblation of life,
—we have arrived at the hermitage called 'battle', the
transit to the sky for kings. (4)

SECOND. You speak properly.

The mountains of the earth are bodies of kingly ele-
phants, made rough by stones,

(*Duryodhana is often more auspiciously called 'Suyodhana' in direct speech.)

in all directions vultures' nests have been made,
chariots have had their excellent warriors destroyed,
The kings have reached heaven in the battle with dying
as its rite,
they have done such things as will long make them seem
present—they are struck down but not destroyed ! (5)

After some more verses of general description of the battle, the three soldiers report the decisive duel between Bhīma and Duryodhana.

SECOND.
When Bhīma's chest, big like a beautiful golden rock,
reverberates,
when Duryodhana's shoulders, hard as the trunk of
Indra's elephant, are torn,
When the weapons are taken up against each other,
guided between their pairs of arms;
then the uproar rises, produced by the striking of the
fierce maces. (16)

THIRD. The King (Duryodhana)—
His diadem prancing with the agitation of his head, his
face with eyes inflamed with anger,
has made his body small in the attacking posture, with
hands raised anew;
His mace, wet all over with his enemy's blood, shines
in his fingers,
like Indra's thunderbolt, with meteors, ready on the
peaks of Mount Kailāsa. (17)

FIRST. Now the Pāṇḍava is seen with his limbs watered with blood from many blows:

With blood pouring forth from the pierced front of his
forehead, with the points of both shoulders broken,
his chest made wet with copious blood from crushing
blows;
Bhīma shines with deep wounds wet with blood from the
striking of the mace,

like Mount Meru with its rocks smeared with streams
of ore-water. (18)

It looks as if Bhīma is beaten: he falls (verse 20), Yudhiṣṭhira thinks all is lost and Duryodhana mocks the 'miserable' enemy whom he has struck down, proudly disdaining to hit him again while he is down. At this critical point Kṛṣṇa, who is watching, makes a sign to Bhīma by slapping his thigh. Reassured by this, Bhīma pulls himself together (verse 23), then:

FIRST. Oh! The mace fight has started again, for he (Bhīma)—

Rubbing the palms of his hands on the ground,
vigorously and repeatedly wiping his arms,
his lips compressed from the strength of his valour,
roaring with increased anger,
Abandoning virtue and pity, setting aside convention,
according to Kṛṣṇa's sign
Pāṇḍu's son has hurled his mace at Duryodhana's
thighs. (24)

Duryodhana falls mortally wounded. This is an unfair blow. Elaborate rules of war are recognised in the Epic, but it is remarkable that the final battle is won through a series of underhand tricks: Duryodhana himself, however, had seized the Pāṇḍava's kingdom by deceit, so that this may be regarded as poetic justice. The Pāṇḍavas retire in confusion at having acted contrary to the warriors' code. Here the three soldiers go to stand by the Emperor and the supporting scene ends. Now the play proper begins.

952. Duryodhana with both his thighs broken drags himself out of the line of battle. The divine Baladeva (Kṛṣṇa's brother, but friend of Duryodhana, though he takes no active part in the battle) comes to him and offers to take vengeance, but the dying Duryodhana has accepted his fate from Kṛṣṇa's intervention, as the end of the quarrel he himself provoked. He desires the war to end: there is no reason for further slaughter, so he will not accept Baladeva's offer:

Today for the first time this head of me thrown on the ground
has fallen down at your feet; give up anger!
Long live the libation-clouds of the Kuru family!
—enmity and talk of war, and myself, are destroyed. (31)

Duryodhana continues as Baladeva complains of the unfair trick '...if you comprehend that I was beaten by deception, then I have not been beaten (34)...it is Hari (Kṛṣṇa) who has taken my life, entering Bhīma's mace' (35).

953. Duryodhana's aged parents and very young son now arrive on the scene, with his two queens. The characteristic atmosphere of an *utsṛṣṭikāṅka* as required by the theory is then developed, with the weeping of the women and grief of the blind old father:

Hearing that my son has been struck down
in the battle today by a trick,
My blind face, with hidden tears in its eyes,
is made still blinder. (37)

O Gāndhārī, are you there?
GĀNDHĀRĪ (Dhṛtarāṣṭra's Queen). I am alive through my wretched fate.
TWO QUEENS (of Duryodhana). O King! O King!
KING (Duryodhana). Ho! Alas! My women weep—

Before, I knew no pain from the striking of the mace,
but now I am made aware of it,
Since my womenfolk have entered
the battlefield with their hair dishevelled. (38)

The little boy tries to sit on his father's lap, as is his habit, but Duryodhana holds him off, explaining that he is going away to join his brothers (all previously killed in the battle). He tells his two wives not to weep, for he has died heroically.

954. The Emperor now prepares to die, telling his family to seek reconciliation with their enemies, but his brahman general Aśvatthāman swears to take a terrible vengeance and make the boy emperor. Duryodhana, dying, then sees his ancestors and brothers, and others who have fallen in the battle, and the nymphs, Urvaśī and others, coming towards him. A flying palace, vehicle for heroes, drawn by a thousand geese, comes for him. The curtain (at the back of the stage) is extended as he 'goes to Heaven'. Dhṛtarāṣṭra and Aśvatthāman have the last words, the former expressing his contempt for kingship and going off to an ascetic grove, the latter swearing vengeance. Baladeva pronounces the final benediction.

955. The *Karṇabhāra*, 'Karṇa's Task', or *Kavacadāna*, 'Gift of Armour', seems also tragic and might perhaps be classed as a tragedy, alternatively it is simply a heroic play. It stands near the border line between the two types. Karṇa, fighting on Duryodhana's side, is sent to fight Arjuna, who in fact is his half brother. He feels his weapons cannot be used successfully against his 'younger brother', moreover he remembers that there is a curse on them because he learned their use by deceit. He therefore resigns himself to death, that is to Heaven. Then the god Indra, disguised as a brahman, appears and asks Karṇa for a boon. When the hero agrees to give anything he wishes, Indra chooses to take his armour from him. In return he reluctantly accepts a magic weapon and commands his charioteer to drive where Arjuna is. The play ends on this note of foreboding and its whole spirit is that of resignation. In the Epic the magic weapon will be expended in killing Ghaṭotkaca and Karṇa will be killed by Arjuna, as no doubt Bhāsa's audience would know.

956. In all these plays Bhāsa has altered the details of the Epic stories (at least as we now know them, but there is no reason to suppose they were greatly different in his time) in shaping his dramatic episodes. The aim appears to be extreme simplicity and brevity of action and the result is always forceful and brilliantly suggestive. A few short phrases of Karṇa's indicate his conflicting, hopeless feelings and heroic resignation. With similar economy Duryodhana's implacable hatred and fatal obstinacy and blindness are sketched in the two episodes with the envoys.

957. The three act play *Pañcarātra*, 'Five Nights', possibly intended as a 'cooperation' (the *Nāṭyaśāstra's* only type having three acts), otherwise a 'contention' [346], is also based on an episode from the *Mahābhārata*. The Pāṇḍavas at the end of their exile are living incognito at the court of the King of Matsya, a kingdom adjacent to Duryodhana's realms. Duryodhana engages in a cattle raid on Matsya territory, confident of easy success, but his troops are unexpectedly beaten by the disguised Pāṇḍava heroes, primarily Arjuna, in Matsya service. Bhīma captures Arjuna's son Abhimanyu, who had been left with the Kauravas.

958. The dramatic tension is increased by Duryodhana's vow *pratijñā* in Act I, on the occasion of an important sacrifice, to give back half his realms to the Pāṇḍavas if news is brought of them within five days. The whole of this act is an argument among the Kauravas, and their brahman advisers and teachers, over whether to give the Pāṇḍavas their share of the inheritance. The wise old Kaurava Bhīṣma, Duryodhana's great uncle, eventually proposes the cattle raid, in the secret hope of bringing the Pāṇḍavas to light within the stipulated time, after hearing news which leads him to suspect their whereabouts. In Act II the cattle raiders are defeated and in Act III their suspicions about the nature of their mysterious foes are confirmed when an arrow bearing Arjuna's name is brought to Duryodhana. The five days have not yet elapsed and Duryodhana when finally convinced agrees to fulfil his vow (III.15).

959. Thus as required by the description of a cooperation a number of heroes attain their ends: the party in favour of conciliation at Duryodhana's court, who had persuaded him to make the vow; the Pāṇḍavas who will benefit from it; the Matsyas whose cattle are saved; Duryodhana himself is satisfied; finally Abhimanyu is married to the Matsya King's daughter, thus consolidating the friendship between this King and the Pāṇḍavas. All this, including the subsidiary 'sensitive' interest, the arrangement in three acts, of which the third is extremely short, and the use of disguises is strikingly consonant with the theoretical requirements for a cooperation [330-1].

960. On the other hand the cooperation of the *Nāṭyaśāstra* appears to be much more a religious and mythical play than this, requiring the heroes to be divine. We could still regard the five Pāṇḍavas as the joint heroes, since they were supposed to be divine incarnations. Perhaps this play was rather an experiment by Bhāsa to adapt the narrow, and probably already obsolete, *samavakāra* form to wider applications, not restricted to the properly religious field but extended to cover the epic. The Vedic metres, prescribed by the *Nāṭyaśāstra* (Kāśī XX.80; Baroda XVIII.76) and presumably found in the ancient *samavakāras*, are missing in Bhāsa's play, though a fair number of relatively elaborate fixed metres are used. Later theorists (e.g. Udbhaṭa quoted by Abhinavagupta, II p. 441) recognise specially complex metres as a permissible substitute here. The prominent theme of the sacrifice, with which the play opens, does nevertheless point at religious and specifically Vedic associations. The description of this in the supporting scene prefixed to Act I is elaborate, with long metres such as *śikhariṇī*, *śārdūlavikrīḍita* and *suvadanā*. For example:

> Their feet have been touched by the turban silk of
> kings, their great learning being praiseworthy;
> their restraint is still advancing in advanced age,
> their faces being heroic with study;
> —The brahmans go by, feeble with excessive years,
> their crooked hands resting on the shoulders of
> their pupils;
> stepping with three legs because of their sticks, they are
> like lordly old elephants. (I.5, *śārdūlavikrīḍita*)

We do not in fact know Bhāsa's intention in the form of this play, whether he meant to adapt an old type, simply disregard the rules, or even follow some since forgotten type or model.

961. It is possible, alternatively, that we have here to recognise a *sallāpa*, 'contention', a secondary type unknown to the *Nāṭyaśāstra* but described by later theory [346] and mentioned by an early dramatist, Bodhāyana, who may not have been far removed in date from Bhāsa [1085]. Bodhāyana puts the *sallāpa* among the main types, the number of which he raises to twelve, adding also the *vāra* [347] (*Bhagavadajjukīya, sthāpanā*). The requirements for a *sallāpa* as known to us are fairly free, but include fighting and deception, so that there would seem to be less difficulty in classifying Bhāsa's play here than as a *samavakāra*. There seem to be no other *sallāpas* extant for comparison.

962. Here in the *Pañcarātra* Bhāsa has again greatly altered the *Mahābhārata* episode in working out his plot. In the Epic there is no question of Duryodhana agreeing to give up half his empire to the Pāṇḍavas: when negotiations are attempted he refuses to relinquish even five villages, hence war becomes inevitable (Bhāsa's two envoy plays reflect more closely the character of Duryodhana as depicted in the Epic). Yet here he is brought to accept the division of his empire, the events being set in train by the sacrifice (not in the Epic), and the whole Epic story seems concluded without the Great Battle, with the situation before the gambling match and Duryodhana's seizure of the Pāṇḍava's kingdom happily restored. Presumably we have to understand that the terms of this agreement were not in the end carried out and the quarrel reopened.

963. Woolner and Sarup have suggested (in their translation of these plays, Vol. I p. 107) that the play was written for the celebrations attending the ending of a feud in the royal family (presumably of the Śakas). It was Konow who first sought such links between this and other plays of Bhāsa and the events of the reign of Rudrasiṃha I (*Das indische Drama*, §61). In fact there was a feud between Rudrasiṃha and his nephew Jīvadāman, with the temporary ascendancy of the latter in +188 to +190, after which Rudrasiṃha regained the supreme authority (as *mahākṣatrapa*). Though topical allusions to the royal fortunes and appropriate choice of theme are likely enough in a theatre patronised by kings, all this linking of Bhāsa with Rudrasiṃha I remains in the realm of conjecture.

964. The remaining plays in this collection are more substantial. The most famous is the Dream Vāsavadattā *Svapnavāsavadatta*, a *nāṭaka* in six acts elaborated from the Udayana legend. It in fact deals with the same part of that legend as Subandhu's *Vāsavadattā Nāṭyadhārā* [654]. Where several plays had been written on the same subject matter, it was usual to name a new one after some special feature or incident invented by the author. Here Udayana at the Magadha court dreams of his lost Queen Vāsavadattā, or thinks he does, hence this is the 'Dream' play on Vāsavadattā. However, it was she herself, staying near him incognito, who had been present in the room where Udayana had by chance wandered: she was to have waited on the Princess Padmāvatī there (the sister of the King of Magadha). She slips out of the room, he sees her going and jumps up, yet is afterwards persuaded it was only a dream, for he believes she had died in a fire. The whole situation is in fact the extraordinary contrivance of Udayana's ministers, when his kingdom of Vatsa is invaded at a time of weakness and only alliance with Magadha can save it. Vāsavadattā has to 'die' so that the King can be brought to marry Princess Padmāvatī and thus form the needed alliance. The unhappy Vāsavadattā secretly remains near and thus has to watch her husband drawn into marriage with the beautiful Padmāvatī. The play is a fine study of Vāsavadattā's emotions in this situation of self sacrifice, in which she is consoled by Udayana's inability to forget her even in the midst of a new love affair. It appears that this play was acclaimed as Bhāsa's masterpiece by the critics (see Rājaśekhara's verse quoted by Jalhaṇa, IV. 48); modern readers have agreed with them.

965. In the Prologue, the producer about to announce the play is interrupted by voices off stage, as is usual in Bhāsa's dramas. Someone is shouting 'make way !', and the producer looks and then tells the audience that it is the escort of Padmāvatī, clearing the way for her to enter the hermitage. He retires and two soldiers appear, crying 'make way !' Udayana's minister Yaugandharāyaṇa and Vāsavadattā, both disguised, enter at this moment and are surprised to be told to make way in a hermitage. As the text stands, this leading in from the Prologue to the play seems to be an example of parallelism *avalagita* [139], the producer being driven back and these two characters meeting with the same treatment. Sāgaranandin, however, quotes (1205 ff.) from what seems to be simply a fuller version of the same Prologue, where the producer before withdrawing tells us that Yaugandharāyaṇa, who wishes to restore the kingdom of the King of Vatsa (Udayana), is being driven away by Padmāvatī's people. The critic quotes this as a case of direct announcement of an actor *prayogātiśaya*, indicating what he is doing, another form of leading in. The variation is a minor one but a useful indication of the state of the available manuscripts of the play. As these stand, it will be some time before the audience learn who these two major characters are, which is contrary to the usual convention of the Indian theatre. Sāgaranandin's text would therefore seem to be more original, preserving two sentences which have been lost in the manuscript tradition.

966. A stage direction in the play states that Yaugandharāyaṇa is disguised as a wandering ascetic, Queen Vāsavadattā as simply a lady in the dress of the Avanti country. Vāsavadattā forgets that she no longer appears as a queen and is indignant at being driven away without ceremony, and Yaugandharāyaṇa has to remind her discreetly of their plan: 'The gods are disregarded like this, if not recognised'. Vāsavadattā says she finds the humiliation more exhausting than her exertions. Now Yaugandharāyaṇa speaks a verse which indicates the seed *bīja* [123] of the objective:

> Previously you had agreed to this:
> by the victory of your husband you will again attain honour;
> In the course of time the series of fortunes of the world
> goes revolving round like the series of spokes in a wheel. (I.4)

967. Again they are told to make way and now Yaugandharāyaṇa sees a chamberlain *kāñcukīya* (a palace officer whose title derives from the peculiar tunic of his uniform; in plays he is always an aged brahman), whom he can approach for information. Thus he learns that the royal visitor causing all the disturbance is the very princess he hopes will become a future queen of Vatsa. It is simply a coincidence that she is visiting the hermitage where he is hiding with Vāsavadattā, after causing Udayana to believe that both of them are dead. Yaugandharāyaṇa is reported to have died in the fire trying to rescue the Queen, so that he can disappear with her and protect her while the other ministers proceed with the plans for the alliance with Magadha. Now he thinks this is a splendid opportunity to find a secure place for the disguised Queen, relieving himself of a rather difficult charge,—as a lady-in-waiting of this princess who, if all goes according to plan, will eventually bring her back to Vatsa. The opportunity offers when Padmāvatī expresses the desire to mark her visit by gifts to the ascetics: Yaugandharāyaṇa asks for a boon, that his 'sister', i.e. Vāsavadattā, whose husband, he says, has gone abroad, should be protected by the Princess. The chamberlain suggests that this trust *nyāsa* will be difficult to protect, but Padmāvatī insists on honouring her proclaimed wish to give the ascetics whatever they desired.

968. Now a young ascetic arrives who has been in Vatsa. The chamberlain offers him hospitality and he brings the latest news. He has been in the village of Lāvāṇaka, where the disastrous fire took place, and reports the death of the Queen and the ensuing despair of Udayana, which Vāsavadattā is not displeased to hear though she must try to conceal her feelings. From Yaugandharāyaṇa's point of view the plan is developing well, not least in that Padmāvatī's interest in Udayana is being aroused, and the minister Rumaṇvant is reported to be taking good care of the despairing King. Everything now depends on Rumaṇvants' successful carrying out of his share of the ministers' secret plan. Yaugandharāyaṇa withdraws and the chamberlain concludes Act I with a verse describing the sunset.

969. Act II takes place in the gardens of the palace of the King of Magadha (Darśaka), near a pavilion with *mādhavī* creepers (the *mādhavī*, literally 'spring', is a variety of sweet scented white jasmine). Padmāvatī is amusing herself with a ball; Vāsavadattā and a maid are in attendance. They tease her about her expected marriage, the maid revealing to Vāsavadattā that Padmāvatī loves Udayana. Vāsavadattā of course is not supposed to know anything of Udayana, unless by hearsay, and almost gives herself away when the others speculate about him. A nurse enters and confirms that the marriage is really arranged. Udayana is believed to have come to Magadha for some other purpose (no doubt contrived by Rumaṇvant), but King Darśaka likes him and has therefore offered his daughter to him. Vāsavadattā is upset and forgets herself again at this 'bad' news, but is able to pass her displeasure off as a general reflection on the inconstancy of men and on Udayana, who was supposed to have loved his late wife so much. She is comforted by being told that Udayana took no initiative in the matter: it was Darśaka's idea. The Act ends with the appearance of another maid, coming from the Queen of Magadha to ask Vāsavadattā to assist in the preparations for the Princess' wedding. Vāsavadattā aside expresses the darkness in her heart, increasing with the haste of the preparations.

970. In Act III Vāsavadattā has escaped into a pleasure grove in the same gardens and reflects on her unhappiness. Her husband now belongs to another. Why live on? Only in the hope of seeing him again. But a maid finds her: the Queen wishes her to make a garland for the Princess at the wedding. Even this she must do: the gods are pitiless! For the sake of covering her misery and saying something to the maid, she asks about the son-in-law, first encouraging her to speak about Udayana, then again checking herself to hide her feelings, breaking off the discussion on the pretext that it is improper to listen to praise of another woman's man. At length the garland is ready, she hands it over and decides to go to bed in the hope of escaping.

971. In an introductory scene to Act IV the jester and a maid discuss the wedding, the jester happy because of the feasting. The jester goes to find Udayana. Padmāvatī enters the pleasure grove with her train, including Vāsavadattā, the main ceremony apparently having been completed. As usual the maids talk about Udayana. One suggests Padmāvatī ask him to teach her the *vīṇā* (everyone knows that he taught Vāsavadattā). Padmāvatī says she has already spoken of it to him, but he said nothing. She infers that he was remembering Vāsavadattā and only restraining his tears in front of his new bride. If that were true, Vāsavadattā reflects aside, she would indeed be fortunate!

972. Then Udayana and the jester enter the grove, looking for Padmāvatī. Respecting the supposed delicacy of Vāsavadattā, who of course must avoid being seen by Udayana and achieves this by adopting an attitude of extreme punctilio about not setting her eyes on another's husband, Padmāvatī withdraws into the Mādhavī Pavilion. The jester notices that the *śephālikā* flowers have been picked from some clusters and infers that Padmāvatī has passed that way. Udayana decides to sit on a stone bench and wait for her. Here there is another instance of a quotation by a critic indicating a missing passage, or a cut, in the present text of this play. Rāmacandra and Guṇacandra quote (*Nāṭyadarpaṇa* p. 74) as from 'Bhāsa's *Svapnavāsavadatta*' a verse which belongs here. Udayana says the bench is warm: someone was sitting on it and has suddenly gone on seeing him. This is an example of the limb 'inference' *anumāna* in the embryo conjunction [148].

> The flowers have been crushed underfoot
> and this stone bench is warm,
> Surely some lady has been sitting here:
> seeing me she has suddenly gone.

The first half of this logical verse provides the 'middle term' *liṅga*, the second half the inference.

973. Next, the jester wants to go into the neighbouring pavilion, where the ladies in fact are, since it will be cooler. A maid checks him by shaking the creepers, which are full of bees: they fly out angrily and the jester gets stung. Udayana tells him to stay where they are and now a conversation ensues between the King and his jester, which the ladies overhear. The fool proceeds to ask Udayana whom he loves best, Vāsavadattā or Padmāvatī. Udayana is very reluctant to discuss this, but eventually admits that, though he esteems Padmāvatī highly, he still loves Vāsavadattā. At last Vāsavadattā is really consoled: she has received the wages for her exhausting part. We understand that this guarantees her complete restoration, if Udayana is victorious. Even Padmāvatī approves this 'amiability' *dākṣiṇya* of Udayana. A good woman, no doubt, approves such tenderness in a man even if it seems on the surface to contradict her own interest: she admires him more for it, thinking him worthy of love. As a result of the further chatter of the jester, Udayana momentarily imagines Vāsavadattā is still alive, thus preparing the way for the Dream scene in the next act. This is a noteworthy point of dramatic construction: the audience learning of Udayana's character and feelings is made ready to appreciate and believe fully in his confusion in the later scene.

974. Now Vāsavadattā suggests that Padmāvatī should

join Udayana, herself retiring. When Padmāvatī goes to Udayana there are tears on his face, the cause of which she knows from the conversation just overheard. He of course must offer her some explanation. The critic Vāmana quotes (IV.3.25) his verse, as it is still found in the text (with an insignificant variation: 'Moon's rays' for 'Moon'), as an example of his figure 'sham expression' *vyājokti* (not found in any available earlier critical work, though Vāmana notes that others have described it under the name 'deceitful expression' *māyokti*):

Through the pollen of the *kāśa* (grass) flowers
pale as the autumn Moon,
Blown into it by the wind, O passionate girl!
—tears are running down my face. (IV.7)

The jester reminds Udayana of the afternoon reception being given by King Darśaka and the importance of increasing the affection of his friend, and they leave, Udayana adding:

Creators of abundant good
and of unfailing hospitality
Are common in the world,
but appreciators are rare. (IV.9)

975. In an introductory scene to Act V some maids report that Padmāvatī has a headache and that the 'Avanti Lady' is to be fetched to tell her stories as she rests. A couch is prepared in the 'Sea Room'—probably a room cooled by running water like the 'stream rooms' we hear of in later Indian literature. The jester appears and is told to inform Udayana. After this introductory scene Udayana enters. When the jester arrives with his message, the King goes to the Sea Room to see Padmāvatī. She is not yet there, so Udayana himself lies down on the prepared couch to await her. He is tired and dozes, whereupon the jester takes the opportunity to go for his cloak, since the room is chilly.

976. Then Vāsavadattā appears, brought by a maid who at once goes off to accelerate the preparation of a headache lotion. Vāsavadattā goes to the couch, thinking Padmāvatī is lying on it, and sits on it beside the sleeping figure. Udayana as if dreaming mutters 'Alas, Vāsavadattā !'—and she realizes who it is. She lingers by him, though afraid of upsetting Yaugandharāyaṇa's task of carrying out his promise or vow (to restore Udayana to his kingdom). She touches Udayana and even talks with him a moment as he speaks to her, slowly awakening from his dozing. He imagines she is angry with him, because she is reluctant to speak—perhaps she suspects an infidelity? He asks her to pardon him and stretches out his hands. Vāsavadattā knows she must go at once: she replaces his hand on the couch and rushes out. Udayana suddenly rises and runs after her, but knocks into the doorway and stops, dazed, not knowing whether what he saw was real. The jester returns and declares he has been dreaming, when told Vāsavadattā is alive. They argue; Udayana says:

> If indeed this was a dream,
> it would be fortunate not to wake up again;
> Or, if this should be error,
> then may I long be in error ! (V.9)

The jester takes him out into the quadrangle, where they meet the chamberlain, who brings a message from Darśaka to Udayana that the armies are deployed to fight Āruṇi (King of Pañcāla, Lacôte, JA 1919, 511) and that he is urged to come out: Vatsa will be reconquered. Udayana goes to fight his enemy.

977. Bhoja in his *Śṛṅgāraprakāśa* (II p. 502) summarises the Dream scene just as we still have it, as an illustration of the 'other conjunction' *sandhyantara* 'dream' *svapna* [141]. Even if it was not really a dream, he argues, this must in any case count as an example.

978. Introducing Act VI, a chamberlain and a portress *pratīhārī* (her office is to admit or bar visitors from a royal presence), in a 'mixed' supporting scene [126], make it clear that we are in Kauśāmbī, the Vatsa capital, after the victory ('mixed' means that there is a 'middle', Sanskrit speaking character, namely the chamberlain, as well as a 'low', Prakrit speaking character, the portress). The scene is the Golden Gate of the Suyāmuna Palace. King Mahāsena of Avanti (Vāsavadattā's father) and his Queen have sent a chamberlain and the nurse (who had nursed Vāsavadattā) to Udayana with congratulations on his victory. In the Act proper, Udayana and Padmāvatī prepare to receive these emissaries, Padmāvatī expressing her deference to the memory of Vāsavadattā. After the congratulations, over which the 'death' of Vāsavadattā casts a shadow, the nurse presents to Udayana, from Queen Aṅgāravatī, portraits of himself and Vāsavadattā. These she had had painted in order to celebrate with them a formal wedding, in the presence of the fire, of Udayana and Vāsavadattā, who had eloped from Avanti. Now she sends them in memory of Vāsavadattā.

979. Padmāvatī at once sees that Vāsavadattā in the portrait closely resembles her 'Avanti Lady' and tells Udayana. He asks for her to be brought. Yaugandharāyaṇa still disguised enters, with trepidation, for it is time to reveal the truth. Udayana hearing Padmāvatī's explanation asks her to return her trust to this supposed 'brother'. The nurse, acting as a witness of the transaction, immediately recognises Vāsavadattā and Yaugandharāyaṇa reveals his own identity. Compliments are paid all round and Udayana decides to go in person to Ujjayinī to take the good news to Mahāsena.

980. If we analyse this play according to the *Nāṭyaśāstra* principles outlined in Chapter III we appear to get the following quite straightforward results. The objective *kārya* is the restoration of Vāsavadattā as Udayana's Queen, as we see at the end of the play. The seed *bīja* as already noted suggests this at the beginning of Act I (I.4). The continuity *bindu* is provided by Udayana's continually remembering Vāsavadattā through the acts of the play (I: his despair at her 'death'; II: he took no initiative in the Padmāvatī intrigue, thus hinting at his continued love for Vāsavadattā; III: the apparently fatal interruption of the wedding with Padmāvatī, Vāsavadattā hearing no comforting news, at least as we now have this Act in an extremely short form, though still sustained by hope; IV: Udayana reveals through the jester that he still loves Vāsavadattā; V: the culminating Dream scene; VI: the actual reunion, sealed by the approval of the King and Queen of Avanti and news of the formal wedding ceremony of Vāsavadattā, since until then Udayana apparently had believed that his old enemy Mahāsena was hostile to the match). All this is presented through Vāsavadattā's experience, her sufferings, though her own rôle in the action is only to remain hidden. The sub-plot *patākā* is the securing of the alliance with Magadha through the marriage of Padmāvatī. This bears fruit in the victory of the united Magadha and Vatsa forces between acts V and VI, reported in the supporting scene of the latter. This subsidiary action is decisive in that Udayana is restored in his kingdom. Yaugandharāyaṇa can bring Vāsavadattā out of hiding. Moreover the victory brings the congratulations from Avanti, along with the news of the formal wedding which had been carried out there with the portraits of Udayana and Vāsavadattā: thus Vāsavadattā's honoured status as Udayana's first consort is made clear. An instance of an intervention *prakarī* might be seen in the appearance of the young ascetic in Act I bringing Yaugandharāyaṇa news of the development of the plan.

981. In an analysis by 'stages' or 'situations' *avasthās* we find the commencement *ārambha* depending on the seed (I.4), the undertaking *prayatna* where the marriage with Padmāvatī is agreed on which will lead to the restoration of the kingdom (Act II), the possibility of attainment *prāptisambhava* where Vāsavadattā learns that Udayana still loves her (Act IV), the certainty of attainment of the fruit *niyatā phalaprāpti* perhaps in the Dream scene (Act V) and the attaining the fruit *phalayoga* where Vāsavadattā is united with Udayana in Act VI.

982. The opening *mukha* conjunction *sandhi* occurs with the production of the seed (I.4) and perhaps with it the appearance of Padmāvatī as the means of producing Udayana's victory. The re-opening *pratimukha* would be the simultaneous arrangement of the marriage of Padmāvatī and report that Udayana himself did not initiate this, indicating his real love for Vāsavadattā. The embryo *garbha* will be when Vāsavadattā hears from Udayana himself that he still loves her (Act IV). For the obstacle *avamarśa* or pause *vimarśa* it is difficult to make a definite suggestion as we look at the events between this and the final success. This latter has to await the military victory concluding the sub-plot, whilst the pause continues until Yaugandharāyaṇa makes his revelation in Act VI by asking for the return of his 'sister'. The hazard of the Dream scene, the danger which Vāsavadattā saw, in her fear of upsetting Yaugandharāyaṇa's plan by a premature disclosure, might also be picked out as part of this conjunction. The conclusion *nirvahana* is of course the final reunion.

983. The more we study this play the more we find all its parts knitted together in an inseparable whole. The analysis shows that the parts are all integral to the total action and do not fall apart as unassimilated constituents. Learning this is the value of analysis, not finding a mechanical scheme.

984. Śāradātanaya (238ff.) gives as Subandhu's a classification of *nāṭakas* into five kinds, one of which is the 'calmed' *praśānta* [165]. This has a set of conjunctions peculiar to itself, though there are still five (the 'full' *pūrṇa* kind has the regular *Nāṭyaśāstra* conjunctions). The 'calmed' play is said to have mostly 'calmed' aesthetic experience *rasa* and the 'expressive' *sāttvatī* mode *vṛtti* of stage business [181]. Śāradātanaya then gives the Dream Vāsavadattā as an example of the 'calmed' kind (Subandhu being apparently very ancient, the illustrations seem to be from a theorist Drauhiṇi also named by Śāradātanaya here). An analysis of this play is then offered according to the conjunctions of a 'calmed' play. These are called 'trust' *nyāsa* (or 'deposit'), 'germination of the trust' *nyāsasamudbheda*, 'expression of the seed' *bījokti*, 'showing of the seed' *bījadarśana* and 'non-mention of the consummation' *anuddiṣṭasaṃhāra*. The last of these refers to the limb consummation of the *kāvya*, *kāvyasaṃhāra*, in the conclusion [150], where in many plays a character asks the successful hero what further wish he can satisfy for him, receiving the answer that there is none, all his wishes have been fulfilled. A 'calmed' play therefore ends without this, as is in fact the case in the Dream Vāsavadattā.

985. In the analysis of the Dream Vāsavadattā reported by Śāradātanaya, Vāsavadattā's separation from Udayana on account of the disaster and being entrusted to the Magadha Princess is the 'trust', which is said to correspond to the opening. The 'germination of the trust' is said to be when Padmāvatī has been seen specially adorned (presumably anticipating her marriage in Act III); it corresponds to the re-opening. It is possible that this refers to something missing from the modern text of the play: if Udayana recognised the garland made for Padmāvatī at her wedding, as being like those made by Vāsavadattā, he might be struck by the idea that she was still living or at least be reminded of her. Such a scene could have occurred at the end of Act III. Śāradātanaya's text is not at all clear as regards the connecting of his references to the play with the conjunctions these exemplify.

986. The 'expression of the seed' is Udayana's agitation, apparently when the jester in Act IV brings out his feeling for Vāsavadattā (IV.5). The 'showing of the seed' is when Udayana sees, touches and talks with Vāsavadattā in the Dream scene. Finally, verse VI. 3 is quoted:

> My love long asleep
> has been awakened by the *vīṇā*,
> But I do not see that Queen
> to whom Ghoṣavatī was dear.

Ghoṣavatī is the name of the *vīṇā* on which Udayana gave lessons to Vāsavadattā before their elopement. Udayana has it with him during his first appearance in Act VI, after the return to Kauśāmbī: he has long neglected it, but brought it out perhaps at Padmāvatī's suggestion (cf. Act IV). It is not clear, but seems to be intended, that this represents the final conjunction according to this analysis. Soon he does see Vāsavadattā.

987. A 'calmed' play is further required (Śāradātanaya p. 241) to have five particular limbs of the opening conjunction (judgment, attainment, concentrating, performing and surprise [146]), others being evidently optional. This is still more obscure: they should presumably be looked for in Acts I and II. It is not at all obvious why this play may be said to have mostly the calmed *rasa*. The main *rasa* is surely the sensitive; it is only that Vāsavadattā has renounced her happiness by going into hiding for the sake of her husband's restoration to his kingdom. In this sense her renunciation dominates the action, since without it the marriage with Padmāvatī could not have been brought about.

988. Very different is Abhinavagupta's adducing of the *Svapnavāsavadatta* (I. p. 39) as an example of a drama which is playful in content (has *krīḍā*). He may have been thinking of the fourth act in particular, with Udayana in the pleasure grove overheard by the ladies in the Jasmine Pavilion in his conversation with the jester. Act II also has a considerable element of play in it. On the other hand Abhinavagupta may merely have had in mind the traditional idea of Udayana as a 'playful' *lalita* hero [99], contrasting with the stern and 'exalted' *udātta* Rāma and other types.

989. Sāgaranandin (2826f.) has a further note relevant to the Dream Vāsavadattā. The sensitive experience may stand in relation to any of the three ends of life, virtue, wealth and pleasure (2821f.). Udayana marries Padmāvatī for wealth, in order to recover his kingdom. He marries Vāsavadattā for pleasure, simply for the sake of being united with her. With this note we may compare Bhoja's theory of the sensitive in the four ends, including liberation [115].

990. Yaugandharāyaṇa's Vows *Pratijñāyaugandharāyaṇa* brings us another Udayana story, the extremely popular one of his capture by Pradyota, King of Avanti, and of his escape from Ujjayinī, the capital, with his enemy's daughter, Vāsavadattā, with whom he forms a liaison during his captivity. Udayana's minister Yaugandharāyaṇa is the hero of Bhāsa's play on this story. Feeling responsible for the King's ridiculous capture when hunting elephants, since he had failed to get intelligence in time of Pradyota's trap (a dummy elephant filled with warriors), Yaugandharāyaṇa takes a solemn vow to release his master. To carry this out he goes to Ujjayinī in disguise, with numerous other ministers, officers and soldiers of Vatsa, including the court fool, all disguised and all in addition to the regular establishment of spies in an enemy capital. It seems indeed that "All Kauśāmbī (the capital of Vatsa) is here except the wall and the gateway". Meanwhile Udayana has started his intrigue with Vāsavadattā and the minister has to take a second vow: to carry her off as well. Yaugandharāyaṇa himself, disguised as a lunatic, is captured in the final affray, but Udayana escapes with Vāsavadattā. The captive minister, filled with pride and glory in his success, is carried to Pradyota's palace expecting death: however, Pradyota acquiesces in the marriage of his daughter and all ends harmoniously with honours bestowed on Yaugandharāyaṇa.

991. In this play there are four acts, so we should presumably regard it as a *nāṭī* (or *nāṭikā*), 'light play' [339]. The elopement theme might indeed suggest that Bhāsa is here bringing the 'rape' *īhāmṛga* [334], likewise a four act type, into a less religious subject matter, but it is probably a more accurate judgment to classify Yaugandharāyaṇa's Vows as a forerunner of the later *nāṭikās*. In fact the secular *nāṭikā* of palace intrigue very likely displaced the old *īhāmṛga*, with its mythical stories of goddesses and nymphs, in popularity. The romantic Udayana appears in some later *nāṭikās*. There would be plenty of scope for interludes of music and dance in Yaugandharāyaṇa's Vows, if that were requisite in the production of a *nāṭī*, as described in the *Nāṭyaśāstra* (XX.61-2 Kāśī) and as one of the secondary types of drama. For example Udayana and Vāsavadattā do not actually appear in the text of the play, but their meetings in Ujjayinī, contrived under the pretext of Udayana giving the Princess music lessons, he being a brilliant *vīṇā* player (this is the traditional story, Bhāsa does not give these details in his play), would offer ideal material for such interludes.

992. The four acts are arranged as follows. The Prologue leads into Act I by parallelism *avalagita* [139]: an actress asks the Producer to send a man to obtain news of her relatives and he hears off stage Yaugandharāyaṇa likewise preparing to send a man. The scene is Kauśāmbī and Yaugandharāyaṇa, who has just heard of the scheme of one of Pradyota's ministers to capture Udayana when out hunting, is sending a man with a letter to warn the King. It is too late: Haṃsaka, a survivor from Udayana's guard, is brought in before the letter is ready. He reports at length how Udayana, in an elephant forest far away beyond the Narmadā River, was decoyed away from most of his army and ambushed in front of the dummy elephant. Most of the men with him were killed and he was captured after being wounded. The Avanti minister Śālaṅkāyana himself sent Haṃsaka back to report in Vatsa. Most of this act is taken up by the long report, with Yaugandharāyaṇa's comments making it more dramatic. The critic Bhāmaha possibly refers (IV.39ff.) to this play when criticising an account of the fighting similar to Haṃsaka's. He thinks it inevitable that Udayana would have been killed in such a fierce struggle, his enemies enraged after he had killed a brother, a son, a father, etc. Of course there were other early versions which the critic may have had in view, including the *Bṛhatkathā*. The Bhāsa version is perhaps not utterly impossible: Udayana fell wounded, the Avanti soldiers tied him up, then this talk of their lost relatives started and one soldier decided to kill him but slipped on the slimy ground as he swung round to deliver a blow with a mace. At this moment Śālaṅkāyana came up and ordered them to stop.

993. When the report is concluded Yaugandharāyaṇa makes his first vow, to free Udayana (I.16). At the end of the act there is a report of a wonderful happening at a meal for brahmans who, it was hoped, could save the King by their spiritual efforts. Someone appeared in the dress of a lunatic, predicted the success of the royal family and then disappeared, leaving the lunatic's dress behind. The brahmans think it was Kṛṣṇa Dvaipāyana himself [532]. The dress is brought to Yaugandharāyaṇa and he thinks he has received instructions. This again is a case of hinting at future events at the end of an act; it is a kind of 'introduction to the (future) act' *aṅkāvatāra* [126], in fact to Act III. Yaugandharāyaṇa ends Act I with this verse:

> Fire is produced from a stick when twirled,
> the earth gives water when dug;
> Nothing is impossible for men of energy,
> all efforts bear fruit when started in the right way.
> (I.18)

994. With Act II we are in Ujjayinī: Mahāsena is concerned about the marriage of his daughter Vāsavadattā. Various suitors have sent emissaries but he has not made up his mind. He discusses the problem with his Queen (Aṅgāravatī). Then the chamberlain enters and reports the capture of Udayana by Śālaṅkāyana—which at first he refuses to believe. Udayana is an enemy and had therefore not sent any emissary. He is proud of his Bhārata ancestry and his knowledge of music. The Queen thinks such qualities are desirable but Mahāsena does not like his independence. He gives orders that the wounded Udayana is to be carefully looked after, nevertheless, and begins to feel some sympathy for him.

995. Act III brings us Yaugandharāyaṇa in Ujjayinī disguised as the lunatic, with Rumaṇvant disguised as a Buddhist monk and the jester disguised as a beggar. The lunatic pretends to run off with the beggar's coconut shell, in which he had some sweets, in a wild scene which attracts the monk: they all run into a (Vedic) fire temple (with an altar for rituals). It is noon and the temple is deserted. Yaugandharāyaṇa wants the jester to take a message to Udayana that the plan for escape is ready. It is two weeks since he was captured and he is now recovering from his wounds. The plan is that the mighty elephant Nalāgiri will be made wild, so that Udayana, an expert with elephants, will be asked to assist in calming him—then he will escape on the elephant. The jester comments in an offhand manner that the attempt will miscarry. Pressed to explain, he reports Udayana's affair with Vāsavadattā and brings a message from him to Yaugandharāyaṇa that the plan does not please him. As Udayana puts it, this is not just a love affair: he wants to show his contempt for Mahāsena, i.e. to abduct his daughter. Yaugandharāyaṇa remarks that they will grow old in their disguise, but the jester thinks it is time to give up: they have demonstrated their devotion sufficiently. The minister will hear none of this and makes his second vow (III.8): he will arrange for Udayana to abduct her. They disperse, resuming their wild behaviour.

996. In an introductory scene to Act IV a drunkard appears, who turns out to be the man responsible for looking after Vāsavadattā's elephant. A soldier finds him: the elephant is wanted. After a long rigmarole the man explains that he has pawned the elephant to buy liquor. But in reality he is one of Yaugandharāyaṇa's secret agents, who has insinuated himself into Mahāsena's service. He has taken the elephant to Udayana. As the two argue, there is a sudden uproar: Udayana is escaping and all the Vatsa agents are in the streets fighting off the Avanti troops; the man rushes off to join them. In the Act proper Yaugandharāyaṇa is brought in a prisoner: his men have been overwhelmed but his vows are accomplished and Udayana with Vāsavadattā is far away. The Avanti minister Bharatarohaka enters and takes charge of the prisoner, finally the chamberlain brings the news that Mahāsena has decided to approve the marriage of his daughter to Udayana. It will be celebrated with paintings (the exact agreement with the Dream Vāsavadattā is important as confirming a common authorship: some of the other plays in the collection are similarly linked).

997. Though a 'light play' has only four acts, the later critics disagree over whether it can have all five conjunctions, like a full length (five or more acts) *nāṭaka*. Thus Sāgaranandin says (2757f.) it has four conjunctions, omitting the obstacle (it will thus resemble a four act rape). Abhinavagupta on the other hand thinks it has all five conjunctions and illustrates (III pp. 52ff.) the limbs of the obstacle from a light play, the *Ratnāvalī* of Harṣa (+7). Bhoja (*Śṛṅgāraprakāśa* II 505ff.) manages to illustrate all 64 limbs from this same light play. Bhaṭṭanṛsiṃha in his sub-commentary on the *Daśarūpaka* (p. 157) attempts a compromise by saying that, since there are only four acts, the pause will be very small in a light play. In Yaugandharāyaṇa's Vows we may find the obstacle conjunction in Udayana's affair with Vāsavadattā, reported in the second half of Act III and leading to the second vow. The other four conjunctions seem to occur precisely in the four successive acts.

998. The *Avimāraka*, 'Sheepkiller', is a *prakaraṇa*, 'fiction', in six acts. Its plot is perhaps adapted from an incidental story in the *Bṛhatkathā* (*Kathāsaritsāgara* XVI, but there is no guarantee this is from the original *Bṛhatkathā*). The hero and heroine are mentioned in the *Kuṇāla Jātaka* [611], the latter as a faithless woman with several lovers (*Jātaka* V 424f.). There is no trace of such a story in this play. The hero, Sheepkiller, is the bastard son of a Queen Sudarśanā of Kāśi, his father being Agni, the God of Fire. The boy was secretly substituted for a stillborn child of that Queen's younger sister Sucetanā, who is Queen of Sauvīra (modern Gujarat, W. India), and brought up as if a son of the King of Sauvīra. He was named Viṣṇusena, but acquired the nickname Sheepkiller in childhood, when his divine power (derived from Agni) enabled him to kill a demon who had taken the form of a sheep as a disguise. As the result of a curse the Sauvīra King and Queen, with Sheepkiller, have to live as outcastes for one year in Vairantya, the capital of King Kuntibhoja. This seems to be the same city as Verañja mentioned in Pali literature, whose exact position is at present uncertain but somewhere in or near the Kuru country. There Bhāsa's play begins.

999. In this complex situation Princess Kuraṅgī, daughter of Kuntibhoja, is rescued from an elephant by Sheepkiller, thus apparently by an outcaste. This outcaste will not reveal his true identity to Kuntibhoja's ministers, but he and the Princess are already in love and soon establish contact through a messenger. Sheepkiller climbs the palace wall at midnight and reaches Kuraṅgī. In the scene leading to this meeting we have a fine description of the city at night, as its various inhabitants pursue their nocturnal pleasures or business and Sheepkiller makes his way cautiously to the palace. This descriptive monologue by the hero is reminiscent of a *bhāṇa* with its setting in the streets of a great city. Here also it is appropriate to note that the Indian stage with its rare use of scenery is not static: as in a film, but with descriptive verses and mimicry of walking or riding in place of scenery and movement, the actors may pass from place to place, going about a town with perfect ease or moving from room to room; even aerial journeys present no technical difficulty.

1000. Sheepkiller is discovered with his mistress but escapes to the forest. Wandering about disconsolate he attempts suicide: first his divinity saves him when he throws himself into a fire, then, about to throw himself down a precipice, he is interrupted by a wizard and his sweetheart flying on their way from the Himālaya to South India, who chance to descend for a rest on the mountain Sheepkiller has climbed. Thus we have here, enacted on the stage, Sheepkiller's wanderings in the forest and climbing a mountain, and the wizards' flight and descent, through gesture language accompanying the speeches of the characters. The wizard (we are now in the world of the *Bṛhatkathā*) gives Sheepkiller a magic ring which can make its wearer invisible. The hero at once returns to his princess. He finds arrangements have been made to marry her to the legitimate son of the King of Kāśi, but by this time the supposed outcastes are released from the curse, all is explained and the clandestine marriage recognised. In this fiction much comic relief is provided by Sheepkiller's friend, the jester in this play, who accompanies the hero in some of his escapades.

1001. In the Prologue of Sheepkiller an actress desires the producer to take her to the park, but he hears voices off stage indicating that it is closed because Princess Kuraṅgī is driving there. The play proper then begins with King Kuntibhoja and his Queen, discussing the question of the marriage of their daughter Kuraṅgī. They are interrupted by the minister Kauñjāyana, who reports that an elephant has attacked the Princess' carriage, but some youth has saved her. This minister is characterised as rather an old fool, unable to pick out essentials, incompetent and overapologetic. Bhūtika, the officer who actually escorted the Princess, then appears and reports having tried to find out who the youth was, without success as yet except that he has traced him to his house. The discussion about the marriage is then resumed. Kauñjāyana remarks that the kings of Sauvīra and Kāśi are both distinguished by having married Kuntibhoja's sisters. The former, King Sugṛhīta (supposed to be Sheepkiller's father, as we find out later), had sent an emissary on behalf of his son, but according to the reports of spies this king and his son have mysteriously disappeared. Bhūtika adds that Sugṛhīta is the brother of the Queen, a further recommendation. The King of Kāśi has also now sent an emissary on behalf of his son Jayavarman.

1002. The jester in an introductory scene to Act II informs us that his friend seems to be in love with Kuraṅgī, then Sheepkiller himself appears sitting in his house and thinking of her. Kuraṅgī's nurse Jayadā and a maid Nalinikā arrive: their mistress is desperately in love and they think she will die unless they do something to bring about the lovers' union. They suggest to Sheepkiller that he visit the palace secretly and explain its plan so that he can find the way to Kuraṅgī's apartments. After they leave the jester returns, giving a ridiculous description of the sunset, which reminds him of various kinds of food. He wants to accompany his friend on his escapade, but Sheepkiller is determined to go alone, though the jester can escort him as far as the city.

1003. In Act III Kuraṅgī is spending the evening on the roof terrace of the palace with her maids, lovelorn. While they sit, Sheepkiller enters dressed as a robber, carrying a sword and a rope. He is still outside the palace walls and his ensuing monologue describes in detail how he cautiously approaches, overhearing the sounds of the city at night, avoids a real thief and some police, hides in the parasites' hall and finally climbs the palace wall with his rope. Now he follows his instructions and finds Nalinikā, who takes him to Kuraṅgī. Before he takes the decisive step of climbing the palace wall, Sheepkiller recites the following verse, which afterwards passed into Indian popular lore, with variations (e.g. Introduction of *Hitopadeśa*) :

> When an effort has been made, if there is no success,
> what fault is there ?
> or who, thinking: 'There is no success for me', does
> what ought to be done ?
> The manliness of men in this world is through good
> efforts:
> the disposition of fate follows success in what ought
> to be done. (III.12)

1004. Act IV opens with an introductory scene in which the maids inform us that after Sheepkiller has spent a year in the palace the King has found out about his daughter's secret love affair : Sheepkiller just manages to escape. Now we have the changing scenes of Sheepkiller wandering through the country, attempting suicide and meeting the wizard couple. On his way back with the magic ring he meets the jester. He can make the jester invisible too by holding his hand when wearing the ring on the right hand. They return to the palace together.

1005. In Act V Sheepkiller and Kuraṅgī are again united, Nalinikā taking charge of the jester. It is the rainy season, time for lovemaking.

1006. In an introductory scene to Act VI we learn that plans are under way to marry Kuraṅgī to Jayavarman, who has arrived in Vairantya with Queen Sudarśanā. Kuntibhoja's Queen still hesitates, however, hoping for news from Sauvīra of the missing Viṣṇusena (Sheepkiller), whilst the King himself has heard from the Sauvīra ministers that Sugṛhīta and his son are living in disguise in Vairantya. Enter Kuntibhoja with Sugṛhīta whom he has discovered, but whose son is missing. Sugṛhīta tells Kuntibhoja about the curse, laid on them by an angry sage. Its duration has now ended and he is free, only he is grieving for his son. He also tells Kuntibhoja the story of how Viṣṇusena came to be known as 'Sheepkiller'. Up to this point, we note, Sheepkiller's identity and relationship to the other characters has been a mystery for the audience except for a hint by the jester in Act IV. The dénouement is brought about by the intervention of the divine sage Nārada, a friend of Kuntibhoja's father, whom we shall meet again in the *Bālacarita* of Bhāsa. First Nārada calls for Queen Sudarśanā, to remind her that Sheepkiller is really her son. He explains to Kuntibhoja that his daughter is already married to Sheepkiller. Jayavarman will have to look upon Kuraṅgī as his elder brother's wife, but Nārada suggests he be married to Kuraṅgī's younger sister. Sheepkiller is brought in, dressed as a bridegroom for a formal wedding ceremony, with Kuraṅgī.

1007. It is not quite clear whether Sheepkiller was familiar to the old critics whose works we have [1062]. M. R. Kavi, claiming to follow old critics (unidentified), quotes from the play twice in his explanations of characteristics *lakṣaṇas* (chapter XVI *anubandha* of his edition of the *Abhinavabhāratī*). As 'admonition' *upadiṣṭa* [187] he quotes (II p. 357) the last verse of Act I, where Kuntibhoja, worried by the discussion on the problem of marrying his daughter and under the pressure of various demands on his time, complains of the difficult task of being king :

> Let alone that virtue must be thought of, what is in the thoughts of the ministers must be observed by his own understanding;
> passion and anger must be concealed, the qualities of gentleness and harshness must be produced according to the proper times;
> The mood of the people must be known, the surrounding states must be observed through the eyes of others as spies;
> his life must be protected with effort here, but again at the head of the battle it must be disregarded. (I.12)

1008. As an example of 'excuse' *leśa* [187] M. R. Kavi

quotes (II p. 362) from the first conversation between Sheepkiller and the nurse, in Act II (p. 126) :

NURSE. Sir ! What are you thinking ?
SHEEPKILLER. Lady ! Of a science.
NURSE. What is this attractive science called, which you are thinking of in seclusion ?
SHEEPKILLER. Lady ! It is the science of union *yoga*.
NURSE [*smiling*] Your auspicious words are accepted! Let it be only the science of union !
SHEEPKILLER [*aside*] What is the meaning of this speech ? Because of my longing for one thing I am interpreting it differently....

1009. The +8 playwright Vijayā mentions Sheepkiller and Kuraṅgī in her play *Kaumudīmahotsava* (II.15 repeated at V. 9) as famous lovers. She may have had Bhāsa's play in mind but of course there may have been other versions of the story.

1010. We seem to have no old analysis of the construction of this play. It seems clear that the opening conjunction is in Act I and the re-opening in Act II with the actual undertaking. The rest is less obvious. If the objective is the wedding of Sheepkiller and Kuraṅgī, that is their ceremonial public wedding and not just their private *gāndharva* union by mutual agreement, then in Act III we may see the embryo. The obstacle will begin with the King's discovery and Sheepkiller's flight, extending up to the beginning of Act VI where Kuraṅgī is still threatened with Jayavarman as a bridegroom. It should be noted that, in accordance with Sheepkiller's verse III.12, his efforts are followed by 'fate' (if that is a correct translation of *daiva*, 'divine') in the shape of Nārada's intervention. A sub-plot can perhaps be discerned in the curse on Sugṛhīta, terminating with his freedom from it before the end of the obstacle conjunction, when he joins Kuntibhoja and matters are forced to a head. In view of the mystery surrounding the hero of this play until its conclusion, it is worthy of note that this is a structural feature of Indian novels [458] : the play is almost a novel presented visibly and without long descriptions.

The conspicuous monologues and rapidly changing scenes add to this impression. We are indeed not far from the *Bṛhatkathā* here, nor on the other hand from the less chronological novels of Bāṇa and Dhanapāla.

1011. Another fiction, Impoverished Cārudatta, *Daridracārudatta*, is of a very different character, realist instead of romantic. Unfortunately we have only four acts of this play; the torso of a masterpiece. Either the remainder has been lost or perhaps Bhāsa died before completing it. However, Abhinavagupta (III p. 8) and Rāmacandra and Guṇacandra (p. 47) name the Impoverished Cārudatta as an example of a play in which the 'fruit' (objective) depends on fate (rather than human effort), which appears to prove that they knew the play entire. In this work Bhāsa brings on the stage a crowd of new characters. Cārudatta is a merchant who is generous, so much so that all his wealth has now gone and he lives in abject poverty. His wife is perfectly devoted to him. Nevertheless he has a mistress, the geisha girl Vasantasenā. The jester in this play is his good-natured and loyal friend Maitreya. Then we meet an ex-servant of Cārudatta's, originally a merchant of Pāṭaliputra who suffered adverse fortune, who has now turned professional gambler because Cārudatta could not afford to keep him. There is Sajjalaka, who makes a thorough study of the science of burglary with a view to stealing the means to buy the liberty of his beloved (one of Vasantasenā's maids). A most contemptible character is Saṃsthāna, the king's brother-in-law *śakāra*. In the latter's company we meet the parasite *viṭa* [30]. We thus have three stock characters of comedy, though all are brilliantly individualised, the jester, the parasite and the *śakāra*. This last is the brother of a barbarian girl who is one of the king's possibly numerous queens. Trying to make the most of his exalted position he is bombastic, bullying, cowardly, licentious, coarse and half-educated (or rather he has no education but pretends to much). He is extremely stupid and a complete scoundrel. This play invites comparison with the fragments of Aśvaghoṣa's presumed *Somadatta* [719], which has several of the same classes of character, including a 'rogue' *duṣṭa* instead of the *śakāra*. No doubt there had been a long tradition of such fictions about bourgeois life, very few of which have survived through the medieval period with its increasing preference for royalty.

1012. There is nothing supernatural or superhuman in the four available acts of this play. The hero being of the merchant class, we see the life of a great city (Ujjayinī, the metropolis and emporium of Western India, when it was the capital of the Śakas) from the viewpoint of a private citizen: the fringes of the court with its hangers on; the sophisticated geishas; honest citizens mixed up with scoundrels and intermediate types, all needing money and caught in a variety of predicaments, and engaged in various transactions to improve their fortunes; servants of differing characters but generally agreed in hoping to escape from servitude into a private fortune.

1013. The prologue of this play is entirely in Prakrit (Śaurasenī), except for the stage directions. This is most unusual, perhaps an archaic feature. Also there is no preliminary verse, which is again exceptional though consistent with the opening stage direction implying that the usual benediction has been provided in the *pūrvaraṅga*. It is worth studying this prologue and seeing how it leads into the first act.

PROLOGUE

Then the Producer enters at the end of the opening benediction.

PRODUCER. Why, my eyes are like two drops of water fallen on a lotus leaf, unsteady with hunger as a result of leaving the house at daybreak today. [*Walking on*] Now I will go to the house and find out whether the victuals are prepared or not. [*Walking on*] Here is our house. Now I will go in. [*Entering and observing*] As the ground has black streams from the cauldrons being turned round on it, there is a smell as if fragrant from frying in oil, the servants are rushing about like a good omen, it may be that the victuals are prepared! But rather through hunger I think I see the world of the living made of boiled rice! Now I will call the lady. My lady! Come here!

ACTRESS. Sir! I'm here. Sir! I'm glad you've come.

PRODUCER. My lady! Is there any breakfast in our house?

ACTRESS. There is...

PRODUCER. Long life to you! Thus may you continue to be a giver of good food!

ACTRESS. Sir! I have been waiting for you.

PRODUCER. My lady, do you need something?

ACTRESS. I do.

PRODUCER. So may the gods gratify you! My lady, what then?

ACTRESS. Ghee, molasses, yogourt and rice.

PRODUCER. All this in our house?

ACTRESS. No! No! In the central market.

PRODUCER [*angrily*] Ugh, wretch! Thus may your own hopes be cut off. And may you become nothing! I am thrown down after being raised high, like a bucket on a pole on a mound when caught up by a fierce wind.

ACTRESS. Never fear! Never fear! Wait a moment, sir! Everything will be ready. We have got it. Today you must be my companion when I am fasting.

PRODUCER. What is your fast called?

ACTRESS. It is called the 'Congenial Husband'.

PRODUCER. In your next life?

ACTRESS. Yes.

PRODUCER. Never mind that. Who told you to have this fast now?

ACTRESS. Him—our servant Cūrṇagoṣṭha.

PRODUCER. Well done, Cūrṇagoṣṭha! Well done!

ACTRESS. If you are in favour, then I wish to invite some brahman suitable for people like us.

PRODUCER. A most holy commission! And then I will have breakfast. In that case you must go in. I will look for some brahman suitable for people like us.

ACTRESS. As you command, sir! [*Exit.*

PRODUCER. Now where can I find a poor brahman? [*Observing*] There is the brahman Maitreya coming this way, the honourable Cārudatta's friend. Then I will invite him. [*Walking on*] Sir! You are invited! Don't despise me because you think I'm too poor to ask you. There will be perfect things to eat. There is ghee, molasses, yogourt and rice. Also there will be the offering money.

Off stage. 'You must ask somebody else, sir ! I am not free now.'

PRODUCER.

Very rich with ghee, molasses, yogourt,
combined with aromatic curry and relishes,
This food, the acceptable hospitality which is given,
should be enjoyed by you. (1) [*Exit.*

END OF THE PROLOGUE

Then enter the jester.

JESTER. You must ask somebody else, sir ! I am not free now.—Am I not saying that I am not free ? What do you say ? 'There will be perfect things to eat' ? But I know. The stone of a very sweet mango is not eaten because it is not suitable. Why are you repeatedly coaxing me ? I tell you I am engaged. What do you say? 'There will be the offering money'? —With my words I refuse this, with my heart I am attracted to it. Ah ! It is too bad ! I am thinking of the invitations of others..

The jester is on his way to Cārudatta's, where he can expect little to eat, but he wants to share his friend's poverty. So he resists this invitation and at once takes us with him to Cārudatta.

1014. Perhaps this Prologue can be compared with that of the Dream Vāsavadattā, but the union of the prologue to the play is even closer: the hungry Producer makes himself a contemporary and neighbour of the hero Cārudatta, competing with him for the merit of entertaining a brahman. Thus we are taken right into the world of the play. In addition, the poverty and hunger of the Producer prepare us for the poverty of the hero, which is presented at the beginning of Act I. The continuity of the Prakrit language of both the Producer and the Jester enhances the quality of concentration is this transition which seems not to be a transition at all. Indeed it even seems possible that the producer himself takes the part of the jester, for the actors who appear in prologues are normally some of those who appear in the play itself. Finally we may observe that the situation of the Producer, kept in suspense as to whether he will get any breakfast or not, again prepares for the suspense in the play.

1015. Cārudatta enters engaged in performing his domestic ritual. With a long sigh he deplores his poverty, a living death. This last remark is quoted by Vāmana (after IV. 3.23) to illustrate the figure 'distinction' *viśeṣokti* [230], of the paradoxical variety where simply the essential quality of something is denied. Cārudatta's first verse, which follows immediately, is also quoted by Vāmana (after V.1.3, on a point of metre and as an example of a standard verse which the critic presumably admired) :

> On the thresholds of my house the offering
> had its flowers divided* by geese and flocks of cranes:
> Just there, shoots of barley have grown from the old
> offerings
> —a handful of seeds falls which was chewed by the
> mouths of insects. (I.2)
> (*Vāmana 'formerly carried off')

This nostalgic verse seems to suggest that he can no longer afford to make offerings as he used to : even the insects appear richer than he is because they seem to make an offering by scattering seeds as they eat the ears of barley grown by chance. Perhaps it suggests also that the insects are helping him by performing this ritual at his house: the poor help the poor, which is a major theme in this play.

1016. In the course of this Act we have to understand that the whole day passes. It is then night and Cārudatta is still lamenting with Maitreya over the evils of poverty, which are different from what he might have expected :

> Truly my reflections are not on the loss of my riches,
> for in the course of luck riches come again,
> But this burns me, that since losing my riches and for-
> tune,
> friendships become less for a good person. (I.5)

His relatives no longer respect his words because he is poor, his generosity is made ridiculous, he is presumed to have committed evil deeds which were in fact done by others (I.6).

1017. They are interrupted by a commotion in the street outside Cārudatta's house: it is Vasantasenā trying to escape from the importunities of the *śakāra* and the parasite. Cārudatta, we learn, has fallen in love with the beautiful Vasantasenā, whom he has seen at the Festival of Love. She has loved Cārudatta, too, since seeing him at the Festival. At this point, then, the 'seed' is indicated (after I.17, by the *śakāra*). The *śakāra*, in his chatter, drawing Vasantasenā's attention to the fact that they are near Cārudatta's house (which apparently she did not know), she manages to slip in in the darkness. During the pursuit in pitch darkness the parasite utters a famous verse (quoted by Daṇḍin, II.224, as an example of 'fancy' *utprekṣā* [213]) :

It's as if the darkness anoints my limbs,
as if the sky rains black antimony;
Like service of a bad man
my sight is rendered fruitless. (I.19)

The *śakāra* expresses himself less poetically:

I hear her scent with my ears. With my nostrils
full of darkness I can't see well. (prose before I.22)

Abhinavagupta quotes this (III p. 175, with slight variations) as an example of incoherent chatter *pralāpa* indicating the foolishness of this character.

1018. The scoundrel meets Maitreya, demands that Vasantasenā be handed over and threatens otherwise to use his influence to destroy his rival (after I.26). It is obvious that he and the parasite have their eyes as much on Vasantasenā's jewellery as on her person, so she leaves the former at Cārudatta's for safe keeping and is then escorted home by the Jester.

1019. In the second act Vasantasenā confesses her unprofessional love to her maid: Cārudatta's poverty especially attracts her, but it also separates him from her. This scene sketches the heroine's character. When the inquisitive maid asks if he's some prince of 'rather high esteem' she replies: 'I wish to love, not to serve'. Cārudatta's ex-servant, the gambler, now enters her house to elude his creditors: she pays them out of affection for Cārudatta. The gambler, finally disgusted with the world, decides to become a Buddhist monk.

1020. In Act III the philosophical Sajjalaka, with meticulous attention to the details of the science of burglary and taking great pride in his work (he anticipates the morrow's discussions of his skill, or mistakes, as a modern criminal sometimes anticipates his press), breaks into Cārudatta's house and steals Vasantasenā's jewellery. In monologue form he discusses his work as he proceeds, choosing a suitable place to breach the wall and the right shape of hole to form in the bricks. His sacred thread (he appears to be a brahman) serves him as a measuring line. He carries a kind of tuning fork, to check whether the residents are asleep, and moths to let loose in order to extinguish lamps. In fact Maitreya is half awake, worried because he has been given charge of the jewellery. Talking in his half sleeping state, he tries to give the jewellery to Cārudatta to get it off his mind. Of course Sajjalaka hears him and takes it from him—there is nothing else to take anyway and the burglar, realising that as a newcomer to the city he has chosen the house of someone no longer rich, is sorry to cause distress to a man in the same condition as himself: but he must go through with it for the sake of his love. He had hoped he was robbing :

> A greedy, wealthy merchant who despises good people
> and is extremely cruel in his own business,
> —If I get into his house
> I shall not be afflicted with unhappy thoughts ! (III.7)

This scene with the half asleep Maitreya, who actually sees the burglar breaking in and talks with him, thinking he is Cārudatta and anxious to get rid of the jewellery, then sleeps on, should be compared with the Dream scene in the Dream Vāsavadattā. The portrayal of this strange half awake state, though ending differently, is part of the evidence for a common authorship of the two dramas (here the critics have not helped us, for no mention has yet been found in their works of the name of the author of the Impoverished Cārudatta).

1021. It is just Cārudatta's bad luck that the burglar picked on his house—perhaps this is an effect of 'fate'. Cārudatta is dismayed at failing in his trust, but his devoted wife gives him her pearl necklace to replace the jewellery.

1022. In Act IV the wretched Sajjalaka offers Vasantasenā her own stolen jewellery to buy her maid's liberty. Vasantasenā forgives him, sympathising with a man so much in love as to do a reckless deed, frees the maid and presents her with a dowry of jewellery. She then decides to take the opportunity of visiting Cārudatta in order to return the necklace he has sent her, taking another maid with her. Meanwhile a storm is blowing up....

1023. —That is all we have of the play. For the rest, we can imagine that the *śakāra* will attempt to make trouble for Cārudatta before the happy dénouement when Vasantasenā will become his second wife, recommended to the first wife by her virtues. There will also be the problem of releasing Vasantasenā from her status as geisha, a profession controlled by the state and therefore offering the *śakāra* an opportunity of intervening, and perhaps of trying to require her 'by law' to accept himself as her lover. From Śūdraka's *Mṛcchakaṭika* [1182], which appears to be simply an expansion of Bhāsa's play, with a great deal of new matter inserted and the old paraphrased and sometimes copied almost verbatim, we might try to extract the missing acts of the original. At the end of Act IV of the Impoverished Cārudatta the maid remarks to Vasantasenā that the bad weather is appropriate for a woman going to meet her lover and they discuss this possibility. It is clear that she will go and probably her visit took place in Act V as in the later play. The parasite there accompanies her (though employed by the *śakāra* in Act I he showed his contempt for that character; in any case parasites always try to be on good terms with everybody as a basis for their profession), but is dismissed on arrival at Cārudatta's house. After this we expect the *śakāra* to carry out his threat, probably by bringing some false accusation against Cārudatta as well as trying to coerce Vasantasenā. In the later play the *śakāra* intercepts and strangles her, leaves her for dead and then accuses Cārudatta of the crime, though the scenes leading to this episode were perhaps peculiar to the new version. She is found and revived by the Buddhist monk, Cārudatta's ex-servant—the man whose fortunes have changed so many times and who perhaps serves here as the instrument of 'fate'. After this there is the trial and Cārudatta is sentenced to death. In the last act, on his way to be executed, Cārudatta is saved by the monk bringing Vasantasenā to prove his innocence. She is released from her service to the state by royal intervention and becomes Cārudatta's second wife. All this, or something very similar to it, may have been completed by Bhāsa in about seven acts.

1024. From the references and quotations by the critics this appears as the most famous of these plays after the Dream Vāsavadattā. In this play Bhāsa has realistically portrayed the society in which he lived, with its vices and problems. In a later chapter we shall see how Śūdraka produced a new version of the drama of Cārudatta and Vasantasenā and further elaborated the picture of the society which tried to keep them apart.

1025. Besides the Great Epic and the Udayana legend, Bhāsa also took well known stories from the *Rāmāyaṇa* and the *Harivaṃśa* (the story of Kṛṣṇa, a supplement to the Great Epic) for dramatic presentation. Whereas the Great Epic offered a mass of episodic material suitable for dramatic adaptation, the *Rāmāyaṇa* offered a rather less complex main story of a great hero. Countless *kavis* have adapted this for the stage: Bhāsa is the earliest known to us but probably very far from being the first. As in his *Mahābhārata* plays he treats his subject matter with great freedom. It is indeed often overlooked by modern students of *kāvya* that dramatists chose the Rāma story for the sake of showing their originality, not because they lacked any. Probably Bhāsa had many predecessors in the staging of the *Rāmāyaṇa*: his aim would be not simply to put Rāma on the stage but to develop new insights into the story and into the various characters in it. If it could be taken for granted that the audience would know the general outline and background of the story, the dramatist would be freer to concentrate on the details that interested him, and if there were controversies over the interpretation of the actions of the characters [854-8], he would have a good opportunity to present and advocate his own views.

1026. The Consecrations, *Abhiṣeka*, a *nāṭaka* in six acts, deals with the climax of the Rāma story, the victory over Rāvaṇa. It begins with Rāma's killing of Vālin and the consecration of his ally Sugrīva as King of the Monkeys and traces the war with Rāvaṇa to victory and Rāma's own consecration. The first consecration can be regarded as the turning point in Rāma's fortunes, the gaining of a reliable ally for his campaign. Perhaps the most interesting and sympathetic character in this presentation, however, is Rāvaṇa in his vain courting of the captive Sītā and his increasing anguish as his armies are defeated, his beloved son killed and his citadel overwhelmed by irresistible foes.

1027. In the Prologue the Producer overhears Rāma and Sugrīva making preparations to kill Vālin and explains their alliance for mutual assistance, both having been deprived of their wives by their enemies. Thus, as far as the controversy about Rāma's character in killing Vālin is concerned, Bhāsa is firmly convinced that nothing need be altered and the action is justified. Here already we appear to have the seed *bīja* of the plot, the objective being the recovery of Sītā. In Act I Rāma and Sugrīva return to Kiṣkindha, Sugrīva challenges Vālin, they fight and, when Vālin seems to be getting the upper hand, Rāma shoots him. As Vālin lies dying and reproaching Rāma, the latter justifies himself (verses 19 and 20). There is a double parallel here with the Mace Fight. In both incidents a fight is won by means of an unfair blow. Then the vanquished hero dies on stage: here the death of Vālin and his being taken to heaven are described in almost the same words as the death of Duryodhana in the tragedy. This scene also foreshadows the death of Rāvaṇa later.

1028. In a supporting scene to Act II some monkeys explain that Hanumant, the son of the Wind God, has passed over the ocean to Laṅkā in search of Sītā. Then in the Act itself Sītā is found by Hanumant in a beautiful pleasure grove, at night. He sees Rāvaṇa making futile efforts to win her. Here the tragedy of Rāvaṇa might be said to begin, with the reference to his having taken the wrong way despite his royal fortune (3) and a demonstration of his pride (10). When he retires, Hanumant reveals himself to Sītā, explains his mission and identifies himself by showing her Rāma's ring (after verse 22). After promising to bring Rāma, he goes off to make his presence known to Rāvaṇa.

1029. This he does by breaking down the Aśoka Grove, which is reported to Rāvaṇa at the beginning of Act III. Hanumant successfully fights the demons sent to seize him, then allows himself to be caught and brought before Rāvaṇa.

Hanumant threatens Rāvaṇa and then returns to Rāma with Rāvaṇa's challenge. Rāvaṇa's brother Vibhīṣaṇa, who has advocated making peace and restoring Sītā, is banished.

1030. In Act IV Vibhīṣaṇa comes to Rāma, who is about to cross the ocean, for protection. It is at his suggestion that Rāma threatens to fire a divine missile into the ocean if a passage is not granted. At this threat, Varuṇa, God of the Sea, enters in agitation and begs protection from Nārāyaṇa (Viṣṇu, Rāma). They exchange greetings, Rāma asks for passage and Varuṇa disappears, whereupon the ocean becomes still and divided in two. Hanumant leads the way to the other side.

1031. In Act V the battle is going badly for Rāvaṇa. He makes final efforts to seduce Sītā, bringing a false report of Rāma's death to induce her to give up hope in him. Sītā holds out. The death of his son Indrajit is reported to Rāvaṇa.

1032. A supporting scene to Act VI describes the fight between Rāma and Rāvaṇa through the eyes of three wizards. Rāma kills Rāvaṇa with a missile. Then in the Act proper Rāma enters. He shows himself aloof and harsh towards Sītā because of the sin of her contact with the demon, despite the pleadings of Vibhīṣaṇa and Lakṣmaṇa. Let her enter the fire (of purificatory suicide)! Hanumant reports that she has done so but not been affected by it, proving that she is pure. The Fire God himself leads her in and Rāma receives her from him, being told she is sinless, also that she is the Goddess Fortune (Lakṣmī) in human form. Rāma is satisfied now that the world will be convinced of her purity. The Fire God consecrates Rāma and announces the approach of Bharata, Śatrughna and the ministers. The play ends with the regular 'consummation of the *kāvya*' and final benediction.

1033. The Statue, *Pratimā*, a *nāṭaka* in seven acts, treats the main Rāma story more comprehensively and in the main from a totally different point of view, that of Bharata, Rāma's stepbrother who has been made heir apparent through the intrigue of his mother, Kaikeyī. Bharata returns from abroad to find his father's statue added to the series in the ancestral gallery at Ayodhyā. From this the play takes its name and reminds us also of the Kuṣāṇa gallery of emperors believed to have been excavated in the ruins of Mathurā, which might have suggested this remarkable scene to a contemporary playwright. Learning thus that Daśaratha is dead, Bharata, a noble character who loves his stepbrother, refuses to become king and instead tries to persuade Rāma to return from exile. Rāma, however, is determined to observe their father's commands strictly. During the episode of Sītā's abduction and the attack on Laṅkā, Bharata makes his peace with his mother, on hearing her excuses, and then sets out with an army to support Rāma in the war. He arrives too late to join in the battle, but meets the victorious Rāma and arranges his consecration.

1034. In the Prologue the Producer asks an actress to sing something about the autumn, which she does though we are not given the song itself but merely a stage direction 'sings' (she is a Prakrit speaking character and there are, for unknown reasons, very few Prakrit verses in the texts we have of Bhāsa's plays). Then the Producer himself recites a verse about autumn, describing a female wild goose. He is interrupted in the middle by a voice off stage, which he recognises as that of a portress, whom he promptly introduces in a simile as the concluding part of his verse.

1035. The portress then enters, bringing a chamberlain orders from King Daśaratha concerning the consecration of Rāma. He goes. (This seems to be a supporting scene.)

1036. Sītā enters and in due course learns from a maid of the impending consecration of her husband. Then Rāma enters and dramatically describes how everything was ready, he was seated on a throne and the consecrating water was about to be sprinkled on him when suddenly the King dismissed him :

> The drum had begun to roll, the elders were waiting,
> over the throne
> the pot to pour the water on my face was being tipped
> to discharge, near my shoulder;
> When I was called and dismissed by the King—people
> wondered that I remained firm,
> but is it wonderful if a son carries out the words of his
> own father? (I.5)

In this extraordinarily compact verse Rāma concentrates a vivid picture of the scene with a telling suggestion of his outraged feelings and a declaration of the theme of obedience to his father's commands. This latter theme being a main one in the plot, we have here part of the indication of the 'seed'. Explaining the situation to Sītā, Rāma says that Mantharā [625] whispered something in the King's ear and—Rāma is not king. Then the chamberlain appears and informs them that Kaikeyī is responsible for the unworthy act—he should not attribute his own sincerity to the affected intelligence of women—and that she has asked for Bharata to be consecrated. This presumably completes the presentation of the 'seed' : the sons are to carry out their father's wishes and settle the affair as well as they can. Bharata himself is away, he will play his part later. Lakṣmaṇa enters, angry, but Rāma persuades him to submit : it makes no difference to them which brother will be king. Rāma leaves at once for the forest with Sītā and Lakṣmaṇa, not waiting to let his father see him first.

1037. In Act II Daśaratha remorsefully laments the loss of Rāma. The minister Sumantra, who has been sent after Rāma to bring him back, returns with the report that he refuses to come. The King wants to hear if they have sent him some message, the minister says they started to but :

After meditating long on what to say,
with trembling lips,
Since their throats were choked with tears,
they said nothing and went into the forest. (II.17)

Daśaratha, shocked at the report, collapses and dies. Once more we have a tragic scene in Bhāsa. Again the dying man sees his ancestors and goes to join them. The chamberlain extends the curtain and there is a general lamentation.

1038. In Act III Bharata, who has been staying with his uncle all this time and knows nothing of what is going on except that the King's health is failing, returns to Ayodhyā. The charioteer driving him knows the truth but reflects that no one could tell him such things as his father's death, his mother's greed for sovereignty and his brother's going abroad (verse 4). Instead, the charioteer drives him near the temple where the statues of the imperial ancestors are. Bharata enters it, to rest until the time is opportune to go into the city, sees Daśaratha's statue and understands, the charioteer now telling him the whole story. The queens visit the temple and find him there: he angrily rebukes Kaikeyī. He refuses consecration and goes to find Rāma. Perhaps we should identify the 're-opening' here.

1039. In Act IV Bharata drives with Sumantra to Rāma's hermitage. Rāma refuses to return and asks Bharata to rule, but agrees to take over after the fourteen years which have been specified for his exile. Here we may find the 'embryo' conjunction.

1040. In Act V Rāvaṇa, provoked by the killing of the demon Khara and the mutilation of his sister Śūrpaṇakhā (by Lakṣmaṇa : she was attracted to and rejected by Rāma), disguises himself as an ascetic, manages to get Rāma out of the way and carries Sītā off. This must be the beginning of the 'obstacle'.

1041. In a supporting scene to Act VI two old ascetics describe the fight between Rāvaṇa and Jaṭāyus [631]. The vulture is killed and the ascetics go to inform Rāma. The Act itself is in Ayodhyā. Sumantra reports that on visiting Janasthāna to see Rāma he found the hermitage deserted. After Sītā's abduction Rāma has gone to Kiṣkindhā and joined the monkeys. Again Bharata goes to reproach his mother. Now she asks Sumantra to tell Bharata about the curse on Daśaratha, of which he had not known. Daśaratha out hunting had accidentally shot and killed the son of a blind sage, who cursed him to die of grief for his son. Thus she is really the innocent instrument of the curse, moreover she had meant to demand only fourteen days' exile for Rāma but in her confusion had said fourteen years. Bharata is reconciled to her and prepares to march with an army to help Rāma.

1042. In Act VII we learn in a supporting scene that Rāma has killed Rāvaṇa and returned to Janasthāna with Sītā. Bharata arrives with the queens to meet him and they at once have his consecration performed, the play concluding with their congratulations.

1043. In this play Bhāsa has shown all his skill, presenting a very complicated story clearly through a series of striking and rapid scenes.

1044. There remains one more play in this collection (we shall discuss below four other anonymous plays, found separately, which also have been assigned to Bhāsa by some writers, simply on the basis of a supposed similarity of style). It is a *nāṭaka* in five acts, the Life of the Boy *Bālacarita*. The boy here is the young Kṛṣṇa, the story being based on the *Harivaṃśa*, probably in an earlier version than the one we now possess as a supplement to the *Mahābhārata*. The plot concerns Kṛṣṇa's birth, his escape from the murderous hands of his uncle Kaṃsa and return to kill Kaṃsa when he grows up. This is known to have been a very ancient subject presented in dramas, since Patañjali in the −2 already mentions a Death of Kaṃsa [658]. Several deaths occur in this play and not off stage, an infringement of the usual rule which is worthy of investigation. Probably the rule was not yet strictly observed and was so far merely a recommendation, to be followed scrupulously only later. In the Bhāsa collection we have met other examples: Duryodhana translated to Heaven, the death of Daśaratha and Vālin apparently dying on stage after being shot down by Rāma (he too is said to go to Heaven). Possibly a translation to Heaven, or a transformation (as in this Life of the Boy), was accepted, perhaps also in some traditional plots a death which had from time immemorial been presented on the stage gave no offence.

1045. Here we are in the world of mythology, supernatural powers, mysteries and divine retributions. The wicked uncle is an incarnation of a demon : he imprisons the old King Ugrasena of Śūrasena and makes himself king. Kṛṣṇa is an incarnation of Viṣṇu, born to kill the demon. The demon knows of a prophecy that he would be killed by a son of his sister and therefore has all her offspring destroyed. Her seventh baby, Kṛṣṇa, is concealed and taken out of Mathurā (the capital of Śūrasena) to a herdsman, to be brought up in safety. As a child, known to the herdsmen as Dāmodara, he displays the qualities for which he is celebrated to this day by his worshippers: his strength is extraordinary, he kills several demons, he is a naughty child and steals the butter and other produce from the dairy and he flirts with the milkmaids *gopīs* and dances with them (a *hallīśaka* dance [368]: as noted in Chapter V the *hallīśaka* was later recognised as a kind of ballet, *nṛtya*, which could be performed independently). A girl baby had been substituted for Kṛṣṇa in the palace in order to make possible his removal. Kaṃsa takes her as his sister's baby and kills her on the stage by smashing her against a rock, but she turns into the Goddess Kārtyāyanī, who had assumed the baby's form to assist Kṛṣṇa. The boy Kṛṣṇa later kills a bull-demon on the stage, crushing it in his arms : this demon recognises Viṣṇu by his strength and expects to go to Heaven if killed by the God. In the last act Kṛṣṇa is brought to Mathurā by Kaṃsa, who has heard of the young herdsman's strength. Fearing this, the demon usurper plans to trap and kill 'Dāmodara'. His two best gladiators are killed on the stage as he watches from his palace (the stage sometimes had a gallery which would presumably be used for this scene), then Kṛṣṇa leaps up to where Kaṃsa is and hurls him down. Kṛṣṇa triumphantly describes the shattered body of his enemy in a verse. The people are pacified when the situation is explained and the old King is restored to his throne.

1046. The Producer in the Prologue announces the approach *prayogātiśaya* [139] of the divine sage Nārada [863]. Nārada then appears in what apparently is an opening to the act *aṅkamukha* [126], by one character. He describes himself (I.3) as a lover of quarrels *kalahapriya*. Since the wars of the gods and demons have ended (I.4), he is flying down to the Earth. He wants to see Nārāyaṇa (Viṣṇu) born in the Vṛṣṇi tribe in order to kill Kaṃsa for the welfare of the world.

1047. He exits and the baby Kṛṣṇa is carried in by his mother Devakī. His father, Vasudeva, joins them. It is night: Devakī is taking her seventh baby out to save it from being killed by Kaṃsa as the others have. Vasudeva takes the baby from her, goes out through the gate of the city of Mathurā. He prepares to swim the River Yamunā but there is a miracle: the waters divide (cf. the Consecrations). Reaching the other side, he decides to entrust the baby to a cowherd he knows, Nandagopa, at the cattle station *ghoṣa* there. He waits for morning in order to avoid a sensation and greater danger of discovery, but Nandagopa himself comes out, also carrying a baby. Vasudeva recognises and intercepts him. Nandagopa explains that he is carrying a stillborn baby girl which his wife, Yaśodā, has had. Yaśodā fainted and he has removed the baby before she knows what has happened, wanting also to avoid spoiling a festival to take place in the morning. Vasudeva orders him to give him the body and then gives him his own son to look after, with a brief explanation. Garuḍa (Viṣṇu's mount) and Viṣṇu's five weapons enter, intending to disguise themselves as cowherd boys in order to accompany their master. Vasudeva returns to Mathurā. The baby girl comes to life and he takes her to Devakī to deceive Kaṃsa, who knows a baby is expected.

1048. In Act II King Kaṃsa is awakened in the night by portents: a storm with earthquakes and meteors. When he sleeps again the Curse of the sage Madhūka comes to him and orders his Royal Fortune to leave him. She obeys. Kaṃsa awakes, makes enquiry about the portents and learns that Devakī has a daughter. He calls Vasudeva, orders the baby to be brought and when the nurse brings it dashes it against a stone to kill it. From it the Goddess Kārtyāyanī (Caṇḍī, Pārvatī) appears with her retinue: she was 'born' here for the ruin of Kaṃsa and now disappears to visit the cattle station.

1049. In an introductory scene to Act III some herdsmen describe the cattle station. Since the birth of Nandagopa's supposed son all has gone well. They have named the boy Dāmodara because of his great strength and courage and he has killed several demons; his naughtiness is also described. Now he is going to dance a *hallīśaka* with the dairymaids here in Vṛndāvana. The girls enter, followed by Dāmodara, his elder brother Saṅkarṣaṇa (born to Rohiṇī, another of Vasudeva's wives) and other boy herds. Dāmodara asks the girls to dance the *hallīśaka* group dance *nṛttabandha* and they do so. The bull-demon appears, intending to kill Dāmodara: he fights and kills it. Then he is called to fight the dragon Kāliya, which has occupied a lake by the Yamunā, and goes.

1050. In Act IV Dāmodara enters the lake and drags the dragon out. They fight, the dragon breathing fire; Dāmodara overpowers him and sends him away. Now a soldier brings an order from Kaṃsa for Nandagopa's son to come to Mathurā for a bow-bending tournament. Dāmodara knows it is the secret time appointed by the gods and goes.

1051. In Act V Kaṃsa has heard of Dāmodara's heroism and is planning to have him killed by one of his champions at the tournament. Dāmodara behaves wildly and kills Kaṃsa's men, then climbs Kaṃsa's palace, seizes him by the head and throws him down. There is chaos as soldiers rush in. Vasudeva appeals to the citizens for peace, explaining what has happened. The old King Ugrasena is freed and restored as King of Vṛṣṇi (the old name of Śūrasena, or rather of its people at that time). Nārada enters to honour Viṣṇu.

1052. This play seems somewhat more primitive than the other works of Bhāsa. Perhaps this is due to the nature of the story, from the traditional incidents of which the playwright has not cared to depart. There is no scope for subtle characterisation here: all is violence, divine or demonic fighters, a usurper and straightforward retribution. The strange scene of Kaṃsa, the Curse and his Fortune is perhaps the most interesting and the most characteristic of Bhāsa. It is a variation on his favourite theme of dreaming. One might suggest that this is his earliest play and the least original. In the absence of the ancient play on the killing of Kaṃsa which Patañjali knew, this one may give us some idea of the early phases of the Indian drama, in which the city of Mathurā itself was a leading centre. A long development is comprised between the violent excitement and supernatural marvels of the Life of the Boy and the sophistication of the Dream Vāsavadattā.

1053. In these plays ascribed to Bhāsa the dramatic interest and rapid action so much overshadow any lyric interest that it seems almost irrelevant to examine his style from the point of view of figures, vocabulary, metres, the 'qualities' of language, or other features. As a rule in fact the style is very simple, much easier than Śūra's, for example, and seemingly entirely free from the preoccupation with elegant expression which marks that writer, probably a near contemporary. There is generally little ornamentation of any kind and compounding is severely restricted. On the other hand Bhāsa uses a full range of *kāvya* metres, whilst avoiding too heavy a concentration of the longer ones and keeping the language of the verses simple, so that they are much easier to follow than the verses in most later plays. On occasion, too, he does produce a series of descriptive verses, with fairly long and colourful compounds, or even much longer compounds in a descriptive prose passage. The most noteworthy example of this is in the Breaking of the Thighs. Elsewhere there are only very limited approaches to such fulsome description, which in the tragedy was perhaps called forth by the strong emotions to be represented, as well as by the theory that the 'eloquent' mode was appropriate for the compassionate aesthetic experience (*Nāṭyaśāstra* XXII.66 Kāśī).

1054. We have noted already a number of references and quotations by the critics. There are other references to Bhāsa of a more general character praising his work. We find his fame reflected in all periods of creative and critical activity in the *kāvya* tradition, even though his plays tended for a time to be overshadowed by those of the period +3 to +10. It may be uncertain whether Bhāmaha's critical reference to a scene of the capture of Udayana is in fact to Bhāsa's play. In any case there are points of affinity between the views of this early critic and Bhāsa. In particular the prominence given by Bhāmaha to the 'vow' or 'promise' *pratijñā* [199], as corresponding to a kind of logical thesis on the basis of which the 'argument' of a *kāvya* may be developed, reflects a method of which Bhāsa is a great exponent. There are many 'vows' in Bhāsa's plays. For example the two which give its title to Yaugandharāyaṇa's Vows, Duryodhana's vow in the Five Nights (I.47, etc.), Yaugandharāyaṇa's vow to restore Udayana in the Dream Vāsavadattā (indicated at the beginning, actually so called by Vāsavadattā in the Dream scene), Arjuna's vow in Ghaṭotkaca as Envoy, though it is not fulfilled in that play, the fulfilment of Bhīma's vow in the Mace Fight (verse 33), which is followed by Aśvatthāman's vow of revenge (verse 64) and the implied vow of Hanumant to bring Rāma to Sītā (end of Act II of the Consecrations).

1055. Among the *kavis* themselves, Kālidāsa [1386] seems to be the first known to name Bhāsa, though protesting that he and similar playwrights dominate the theatre when a new *kavi* would like to produce a modern play. Bāṇa (*Harṣacarita*, introductory verse 16) praises Bhāsa among the great writers and in doing so mentions specific features of his *nāṭakas*, though perhaps somewhat constrained by a double meaning involving the construction of temples. Saying that the commencements *ārambhas* are effected by the producer probably means more than simply that the producer starts the plays, since there is nothing distinctive in such a feature of all dramas. What would be more characteristic of Bhāsa would be that the 'commencement' stage or situation is indicated already in the prologue and not left until the play proper has begun. Bhāsa does not allow the dramatic tension to lag but starts at once by introducing the action. Bāṇa says further that there are 'many parts' in Bhāsa's plays, which is certainly characteristic of most of them (there are 36 characters in the Life of the Boy, 27 in the Consecrations, though the Dream Vāsavadattā might be regarded as more 'classical' and restrained in having 17). Bāṇa further notes the sub-plots, in which he could be supported by pointing out both their richness and fullness of development and their closeness to the main action. The possible allusion to Sheepkiller by Vijayā has been noted above.

1056. Daṇḍin as critic in his *Kāvyalakṣaṇa* quotes from the Impoverished Cārudatta for a 'fancy', as we have seen; as *kavi* himself he enthusiastically praises Bhāsa (*Avantisundarī*, introductory verse 11). He fancies that the great dramatist, though departed, remains in the bodies of his *nāṭakas* [cf. 951 (5) for the idea]. In these plays the limbs of the opening and other conjunctions are very distinct (or 'well divided' *suvibhakta*) and the characteristics and modes are clear. We have to some extent indicated the dramatic construction of Bhāsa's plays above. We have noted also that M. R. Kavi quotes from the Sheepkiller to illustrate the two characteristics 'admonition' and 'excuse'. It would be a valuable exercise to identify more characteristics in this collection of plays, since these are essential to dramatic expression as conceived in the *Nāṭyaśāstra* [182, 185] and are surely responsible for much of the effectiveness of Bhāsa's dramas as 'theatre'. It is the characteristics and not the figures of speech which are the means of dramatic expression, producing lively stage business, hence Bhāsa offers relatively little to the student of the figures. Abhinavagupta (*Locana* p. 344) indeed quotes a 'Dream Vāsavadattā' for a verse in which a figure is introduced, he says, to the detriment of the *rasa*. This verse is not found in Bhāsa's play as we have it and it does not seem at all in Bhāsa's manner. Probably either Abhinavagupta has made a mistake or there was another play with the same title (a thing not unknown in the history of *kāvya*: thus there was another play entitled the Life of the Boy, besides the one we have). Among the modes of stage business we have already found the 'expressive' *sāttvatī* noted in connection with the Dream Vāsavadattā by Śāradātanaya. The 'violent' *ārabhaṭī* may be identified in the heroic plays and the Life of the Boy, the 'eloquent' *bhāratī* probably in the Mace Fight, as appropriate for a tragedy [181]. The 'tender' *kaiśikī* mode might be appropriate for a production of the Impoverished Cārudatta.

1057. Vākpatirāja (+8, *Gauḍavaha* verse 800) appears to call Bhāsa 'friend of fire', though it is possible that Jvalanamitra was the name of a writer, now unknown. In any case the Prakrit poet includes Bhāsa in his short list of favourite authors. 'Friend of fire' would be appropriate enough for Bhāsa on account of such incidents in his plays as the false burning of Vāsavadattā and Yaugandharāyaṇa in the Dream Vāsavadattā, of the latter again in Yaugandharāyaṇa's Vows, as Sītā's ordeal in the Consecrations, where the Fire God himself appears on the stage, and as the sacrifice scene at the beginning of the Five Nights (where there are sixteen verses describing the sacrificial fire), whilst Sheepkiller himself is a son of the Fire God and cannot commit suicide by walking into a forest fire.

1058. Vāmana's quotations from the Dream Vāsavadattā and the Impoverished Cārudatta have been noticed. He also quotes (V. 2.27) a verse found in Yaugandharāyaṇa's Vows:

> May he not have the new vessel filled with water
> well consecrated and covered with the sacred grass,
> Who would not fight for the sake of his master's board:
> may he go to purgatory! (IV.2)

The allusion in the first lines is to the funeral rite for a fallen soldier. Vāmana's point here is purely grammatical: he defends the verse against possible criticism. It is curious that this verse occurs in the *Arthaśāstra* (X.3.31), though it seems to be an interpolation there (see Kangle in his translation at that point).

1059. A verse from Rājaśekhara (via Jalhaṇa, IV. 48) has been referred to already, which says that when Bhāsa's collected plays were submitted to the fire of criticism the Dream Vāsavadattā was not burned. In other words no fault was found in it, whereas presumably some faults were found in the other plays. We note the 'fire' motif again. There is another verse in Jalhaṇa (IV.111), which Śārṅgadhara, who also quotes it (188), ascribes to Rājaśekhara, placing Bhāsa first in a list of the great writers (the order appears to be chronological). Somadeva similarly includes Bhāsa in his list of *kavis* (*Yaśastilaka* II p. 113), but afterwards (p. 251) quotes this verse as Bhāsa's :

> Liquor should be drunk, the face of the best beloved
> should be looked at,
> and new clothes should be worn which are graceful
> in nature;
> —By whom this kind of way to freedom was seen,
> long may he live, the Lord Pinākapāṇi !

This of course could be a drinking song in a play, like the simpler one found in Yaugandharāyaṇa's Vows :

> Fortunate are those who are drunken with liquor !
> fortunate are those who are anointed with liquor !
> Fortunate are those who are bathed in liquor !
> fortunate are those who are sacrificed in liquor !
> (IV.1)

Somadeva's verse, however, is found in Mahendravarman's *Mattavilāsa* (+7), where it is recited by a Śaiva devotee (Pinākapāṇi = Śiva) of a tantric school. Either Somadeva made a mistake or Mahendravarman borrowed the verse from a Bhāsa play not now available.

1060. Most of Abhinavagupta's references to the Bhāsa plays have been noted above. In addition to the Dream Vāsavadattā and Impoverished Cārudatta, he appears to refer to the Mace Fight. The reference for the characteristic 'establishing' *prasiddhi* (II pp. 360f.), however, is only by M. R. Kavi (or his unknown source), who names the tragedy and quotes from the dialogue between Duryodhana and Baladeva [952], beginning after verse 34 :

> BALADEVA. Shall Bhīma remain alive now after tricking you in the fight ?
> DURYODHANA. Was it Bhīma by whom I have been tricked ?

BALADEVA. Then who did this to you?
DURYODHANA.

By whom with equal honour the Pārijātaka Tree was
    taken from Indra,
who slept at ease in the water of the ocean for a
    thousand years of the gods,
Suddenly entering Bhīma's mace with brilliance*,
    the lover of genuine fight,
it is Hari, lover of the universe, who has given me to
    death. (35)
(text of the play : 'violent mace')

1061. Abhinavagupta's own reference is less clear (III p. 21). The play is not named and there is no exact quotation, but the breaking of the thighs is mentioned and its report is discussed under the third kind of injection of subsidiary matter *patākāsthānaka* [143], where equivocal words indicate a new situation between the main characters, and as equivalent to a variety of the speech with a double meaning *gaṇḍa* as a limb of the street play [326]. The basis of Duryodhana's cause is lost, therefore one must follow the Pāṇḍavas. Abhinavagupta also quotes, as by Bhāsa, a verse on Rāma (I p. 319). Here he calls Bhāsa a 'great *kavi*', a status he allows very few writers. The verse is not found in either of the two Rāma plays in our Bhāsa collection, but one line of it occurs in a play called the *Yajñaphala*, which has been ascribed to Bhāsa by its editor. This ascription does not seem very probable: we shall examine the play later in this chapter. The verse in Abhinavagupta shows anger as the essence of the furious aesthetic experience. As printed it is corrupt and three syllables are missing completely, but it expresses the spirit of insatiable revenge. Perhaps it originally belonged to the Consecrations.

1062. Sāgaranandin's references to the Dream Vāsavadattā have been discussed. Though he mentions 'Cārudatta' (e.g. 294f., 970ff. with a quotation) he may always refer to the *Mṛcchakaṭika*, which he names elsewhere (despite variations in the quotation). Soḍḍhala (+11, *Udayasundarī* p. 154) simply mentions Bhāsa (so read for Māsa in the edition) in discussing the 'history of the *kavis*'. We have noted Bhoja's reference to the Dream scene in the Dream Vāsavadattā. According to Krishnamachariar (p. 568) he also refers to the story of Sheepkiller, but it has not proved possible to trace the reference in the printed parts of the *Śṛṅgāraprakāśa*. The analysis of the Dream Vāsavadattā given by Śāradātanaya, probably from an earlier critic, has been discussed above.

1063. The anthologist Vidyākara (*c.* +1100) attributes one of his selected verses (138) to Bhāsa. It is a benediction invoking Lakṣmī's smile and might have stood at the beginning of a play. Other anthologists name Bhāsa as the author of a number of verses, though they are rarely in complete agreement about the ascription. None of these verses seem to have been traced in our collection of plays. In view of the lack of unanimity among them it might be supposed that these anthologists are unreliable, but their evidence has been used to question the authenticity of the plays we possess. What we have found in the dramatic critics seems stronger as evidence. At least it would appear that in the period of these anthologists (+12 onwards) Bhāsa's works were much less familiar than those of many other dramatists, so that mistakes in ascription could easily go uncorrected. Vidyākara's benediction being Vaiṣṇava, like those in our plays, might be by the same author, though its vocabulary seems to suggest a later period. Of the verses sometimes ascribed to Bhāsa in anthologies, we may quote one, which Vidyākara (276) gives anonymously, as perhaps the nearest in style to our plays. Five anthologists agree in this case that the verse is by Bhāsa (including Śārṅgadhara and Śrīdharadāsa) and none seem to offer any other ascription. Autumn is being described :

The Sun burns sharply like a low person newly rich,
the deer abandons his horns (affection) like an
ungrateful friend;
The water is clear like a sage's thought of *dharma*,
like an impoverished lover the mud becomes dry.

1064. The references of Rāmacandra and Guṇacandra to the Dream Vāsavadattā and the Impoverished Cārudatta have been given above. In the first canto of his epic *Pṛthvīrājavijaya* (p. 4), Jayānaka mentions Bhāsa in explaining that the *kāvyas* of good writers escape burning by the criticism of villains. The Fire (God) himself released Bhāsa's *kāvya* from his mouth, like quicksilver, because of the religion of Viṣṇu (this seems to be the meaning of *viṣṇudharma*). Thus the fire motif persists in the +12 in connection with Bhāsa (probably Jayānaka knew the work of Rājaśekhara). Since the plays we have stress the religion of Viṣṇu, with the incarnations as Kṛṣṇa and Rāma, and have Vaiṣṇava benedictions, it might be thought that this served as a protection for them. In the Prologue to his *Prasannarāghava* (I.22), Jayadeva (+13) names a series of *kavis* as qualities or ornaments of the Goddess of Literature (Sarasvatī). Bhāsa is her laughter *hāsa* (which no doubt owes something to the rhyme, as do the others).

1065. Of later critics who refer to Bhāsa's plays we may note first Bahurūpamiśra, who names the Dream Vāsavadattā, following Śāradātanaya, as a 'calmed' play (Krishnamachariar p. 747; unfortunately this important commentary on the *Daśarūpaka* has not yet been printed—the reference is at III.38). Also unprinted is an anonymous commentary on Daṇḍin's *Kāvyalakṣaṇa*, in which the first verse of Yaugandharāyaṇa's Vows is quoted (Krishnamachariar p. 732).

1066. A very important work on dramatic criticism, the *Naṭāṅkuśa*, also anonymous and also unprinted, seems to have been written in Kerala. It criticises the methods of production of dramas in Kerala, which is practically the only part of India in which the classical theatre has been preserved, and is therefore essential for tracing back traditional practices from the surviving theatre to its classical predecessors. Krishnamachariar has found in it a reference to Kuraṅgī and Sheepkiller (p. 568, also 854) and a discussion on Yaugandharāyaṇa's Vows. Kunjunni Raja has reported more of the latter ('Kūṭiyāṭṭam', *Samskrita Ranga Annual* II, 1961, pp. 20 and 46 ff.). The author criticises the productions by the Kerala actors for introducing extraneous matter contrary to the *rasa*. For example there are dances, which ought to be confined to the *pūrvaraṅga*, and accounts of the previous actions of the characters who appear. Then the local language is used as well as those used by the dramatist. In the case of Yaugandharāyaṇa's Vows the production of Act III is discussed. The jester speaks the language of Kerala (instead of that of ancient Śūrasena), but there are also additional Sanskrit verses which detract from the *rasa*.

Above all, superfluous discussions on political theory are inserted (on the pretext that the ministers discuss their practical plans to free Udayana), which distract the audience from the action.

1067. Finally we may glance at the anonymous *Abhijñānaśākuntalacarcā*. In the course of this commentary the author refers to about thirty different plays when explaining technical points of construction and production. Seven of these are from the collection ascribed to Bhāsa, including Ghaṭotkaca as Envoy, Karṇa's Task, the Five Nights and the Life of the Boy as well as the three most famous plays. They are discussed mainly in connection with the form of the Prologue, a controversial matter on which the author is extremely full. Through works like these we can see how this collection of plays has been handed down in the Indian theatre until modern times. It should be noted here that commentaries on some of the Bhāsa plays themselves exist in Kerala, but none appear to have been printed yet.

1068. Whether these plays were written by Bhāsa or not, this collection is unsurpassed in the entire repertory of *kāvya* drama. Other dramatists have produced plays equal in quality to some of these, Śūdraka and Viśākhadatta along somewhat similar lines (though on a larger scale), Bhavabhūti along totally different lines, Bodhāyana in a different type (the comedy); they have greatly enriched the repertory but they have not given us a drama which we can say is better than the Dream Vāsavadattā or Impoverished Cārudatta.

1069. Among the other plays which some have suggested are Bhāsa's, the most likely to be his might seem to be the Fruit of Sacrifice (*Yajñaphala*; or simply *Yajñanāṭaka*, 'Sacrifice Play'). The two known manuscripts, however, were not found with the Bhāsa collection or in the South, but apparently in Gujarāt or Rājasthān. This is a *nāṭaka* in seven acts covering the early life of Rāma, from his birth to his marriage to Sītā. In style it approaches the Bhāsa collection, though sometimes the vocabulary, the ideas and a certain diffuseness form an obstacle to assigning it to the same author. A more serious obstacle is a reference to the Yoga System of Patañjali (p. 116), apparently a writer of about the +4, whereas a parallel passage in the Statue (p. 296) names Maheśvara. The Fruit of Sacrifice resembles the two Rāma plays in departing widely from its original and freely retelling the story, keeping only the basic essentials, the main characters and their relationships, unchanged whilst showing no respect for events. The reader gains the impression that the author knew the Bhāsa plays and imitated them with modifications of an ideological character (Brahmanical Dharma). Against Bhāsa's authorship might be urged the absence of fighting from the stage and even from description; moreover some clashes in the story are softened from violent encounter to peaceful confrontation. A fight with demons, to protect Viśvāmitra's sacrifice, is merely hinted at; Rāvaṇa appears threateningly but thinks it wise to retire quietly and makes no attempt to intervene in the marriage preparations; the meeting with Paraśurāma (Rāma of the Axe) begins with apprehension but is immediately made harmonious.

1070. However, the whole spirit of this play about the merits of sacrifices (of which there are three, dominating the play in turn) is peaceful: it could be said to have the 'message' that whoever performs Brahmanical sacrifices will get everything desirable and ensure the triumph of good over evil on Earth. It might be seen as an attempt to meet Buddhist and Jaina criticisms of Brahmanism. If the Bhāsa plays are violent, they also take opportunities to uphold the Brahmanical and especially Vaiṣṇava ideal: where Kṛṣṇa is concerned as an emanation of Viṣṇu sheer force predominates, with bloodshed; with Rāma the strength, still insisted on, is tempered with the peacefulness and benevolence of a restrained and modest character. What seems to distinguish the Fruit of Sacrifice from any of the thirteen Bhāsa plays, however, is the lack of the lively incidents which in these maintain the tension of the action, of the skilful use of the dramatic characteristics *lakṣaṇas* to add piquancy to the presentation. The poetic imagery is dull also. On the whole, this play is full of arguments rather than of events. The aesthetic experience is the calmed *śānta*. The Fruit of Sacrifice is surely not by Bhāsa but by an imitator whose propaganda motives were stronger than his dramatic skill. Since we have no suggestion about the date we may as well describe the play here.

1071. The first sacrifice in the Fruit of Sacrifice is that of Daśaratha to get sons, the birth festival of whom is being celebrated at the time of Act I. In Act II they have already reached the age of fifteen and Daśaratha and his three queens discuss, and harmoniously resolve, the tricky question of the succession to the throne. Bharata will be given the kingdom, as promised, but will then in turn give it to Rāma. This is a rather crudely done scene, dramatically, straining the probabilities of human reactions more than is easily acceptable. It is made possible by a drastic change in the source story—Daśaratha had already promised the kingdom to Kaikeyī's son when he married her. Only Kaikeyī's confidante Mantharā remains dissatisfied, as we see in Act III: she feels Kaikeyī, Bharata and herself are looked down on and she quarrels with the other maids, claiming superior status for herself (having nursed a queen) though all are slaves, for which pretension the others ridicule her. She afterwards eavesdrops on a conversation of the princes with their teacher, Vasiṣṭha, and learns of Rāvaṇa's threatening visit which has taken place in this Act. This suggests a plan for eliminating Rāma, but we hear no more of it in this play. We are not told that it was Mantharā who instigated the demons to interfere with Viśvāmitra's sacrifice, which follows, but perhaps we are to understand that. There is absolutely nothing about any pretensions of Rāvaṇa to marry Sītā.

1072. Rāma successfully guards Viśvāmitra's sacrifice, and in return is taught new weapons, and also in Act V we have the discussion on the 'fruit' of sacrifice which presumably gives the play its title. Security is stressed, and a peacefulness which will not be provoked into active defence without a strong reason (this will be Rāvaṇa's abduction of Sītā, in fact, but the forces upholding virtue are to wait quietly for the attack). Viśvāmitra however has his own ideas which he does not mention to Rāma and Lakṣmaṇa: King Janaka of Videha is about to perform a long sacrifice, at the end of which he will marry off his daughter, Sītā; Viśvāmitra will take the princes to it and the marriage to Rāma will be another highly satisfactory fruit of sacrifice to all concerned (including the alliance between Daśaratha and Janaka). Rāma's proficiency in weapons is a necessary prerequisite, since Janaka has offered his daughter only to whoever can bend an ancient bow in his possession, which had belonged to Śiva. Viśvāmitra has the princes admire the peasants at their productive labour. In Act VI Rāma and Sītā see each other in a garden and fall in love.

In the final act Janaka's sacrifice ends, Rāma has already broken the bow (for which he is amusingly apologetic, it was childish thoughtlessness on his part not to realise it was so old) and everyone is assembled to approve and witness the marriage. Then Rāma of the Axe suddenly appears, angry at not having been informed of what was to be done. There is general consternation, but he is quickly pacified by Rāma when he learns that the bow (which no ordinary hero could bend) has really been broken. He gives Rāma his own bow to handle and at once recognises him as an emanation or incarnation (a 'part') of Viṣṇu: he can now hand over his own unfinished task, of destroying the enemies of *dharma* and of the brahmans, to a fit successor. Sītā is now brought in as bride and Daśaratha has all his wishes accomplished. Just before the end the assembly has a vision of all the gods headed by Brahmā, Viṣṇu and Maheśa (Śiva), with their consorts, enjoying the occasion: an affirmation of syncretistic Brahmanism with harmony between the Vedic, Vaiṣṇava and Śaiva traditions, promising a peaceful and stable society. The reference in the final benediction to the classes *varṇas* is significant of the author's outlook.

1073. A striking feature of this play is that its generally serious atmosphere is several times interrupted by the jester, a character here appearing in its crudest form. The jester is here the vulgarly greedy brahman grabbing all the food he can get on the occasions of sacrifices, his own 'fruits' of religious observance. He absolutely disregards the interests of his king, unless they affect his own. He pokes fun at Kaikeyī (because she is not generous to him), mocks the minister Sumantra, is terrified of Rāvaṇa, fools the court bards with a description of Viśvāmitra as having two faces and four arms and during the final dramatic confrontation with Rāma of the Axe makes disrespectful remarks aside: 'Why doesn't the old bear go away quickly?' (interrupting Rāma of the Axe's speech about the eternal Brahman), afterwards wondering why everyone praises the old bear when at last he has gone.

1074. A very short one act piece entitled *Traivikrama*, The Three Steps, describes the scene in which the demon king Bali is overcome by Viṣṇu as the Dwarf and confined to the Underworld. M.R. Kavi suggested it was by Bhāsa (Krishnamachariar p. 568). The story is the one that we have supposed to have been the subject of a play mentioned by Patañjali, along with one on Kaṃsa [658]. Bali after performing a horse sacrifice proudly offers gifts to all, including a boon to the Dwarf, who asks for as much territory as he can cover in three steps. A minister points out that the Dwarf is Viṣṇu, but Bali remains firm until the God reveals his power and hurls the demons down below the Earth, whence Bali cannot escape. In the argument with his minister Bali hopes to gain by magnanimously giving the Earth (only):

> Misfortune enters him who says "Give!"
> she comes to him who says "There isn't" too;
> Therefore I am giving the Earth to Viṣṇu:
> let Fortune resort only to me and Misfortune enter
> him!

1075. The whole piece is like a mere prologue, only the producer and one actress (specified as his beloved, or wife, it perhaps regularly being the case that the producer and the leading actress in his company were husband and wife) appearing and a dialogue ensuing: the producer shows his wife a painting of the scene and then describes to her the events depicted. Probably the piece is an old street play *vīthī*, since it is a dialogue between two actors only [322]. In fact the producer himself relates, and possibly enacts, the whole story. He first invites his lady to look at a 'third' painting, whilst at the end she asks him to show her another. Thus it appears that this Three Steps was one of a series of such scenes, perhaps on the incarnations or introductions *avatāras* of Viṣṇu into the World. There is no scope in this short piece for the 'limbs' or rhetorical devices which theory names after the street play, nor for humour, nevertheless the little we know of the *vīthī* type suggests that it could be very varied in content. There is really nothing to indicate that this play was written by Bhāsa except that it is a very old play, in simple style, preserved in Kerala along with other plays now ascribed to him; moreover the fact that it celebrates an incarnation of Viṣṇu harmonises with the tendency of the other plays, though it is hardly a positive indication of authorship. In the Speech of the Envoy (verse 7) there is a description of a painting supposed to be brought on the stage.

The Three Steps is named and quoted from in the *Abhijñāna-śākuntalacarcā* (pp. 12f., 25).

1076. About equally short is the *Dāmaka*, which concerns Karṇa and has been found in association with the play on that hero ascribed to Bhāsa. M.R. Kavi thought this too might be by Bhāsa (Krishnamachariar p. 568). Since Dāmaka, the friend of Karṇa, appears in a major role as jester, the play has been taken as a comic episode and classed as comedy *prahasana.* Nevertheless the basic story is the serious one of how Karṇa went to the hermitage of Rāma of the Axe and secured instruction in weapons by concealing the fact that he was of the aristocratic (warrior, *kṣatriya*) class (Rāma of the Axe being a brahman well known as hating all aristocrats). Discovering the truth afterwards, Rāma of the Axe utters a curse that Karṇa's weapons may fail him in time of need (which of course happens in the Bhārata Battle, after the scene presented in Karṇa's Task). The piece could be classed as a heroic play, or else under one of the secondary types (as *prekṣaṇaka* [351]) or *nṛtyas* (as *pārijātaka* [355]). The style is again such as might be ascribed to Bhāsa, but it has several verses and phrases apparently lifted from other *kāvyas*, including the Impoverished Cārudatta, suggesting a kind of pastiche.

1077. We may disregard the suggestion that the three plays usually accepted as Harṣa's (+7), on the evidence of their manuscripts, are Bhāsa's, which seems totally improbable stylistically. This leaves us finally with the *Kiraṇāvalī* (Krishnamachariar p. 554), which has been described as a *nāṭikā*, though there is a reference to a play of that name with nine acts (which of course could be a different work). As it does not seem to have been printed yet, and even its existence has been doubted, we must await further reports.

1078. Besides all these plays, Krishnamachariar notes (pp. 553f. of his *History*) a tradition which would ascribe to Bhāsa a lyric poem. This tradition is reported as from the +12 critic Hemacandra, though the quotation given cannot be found in his extant works. It is not supported, though not contradicted, by the manuscripts of the lyric. The poem is called the Broken Pot *Ghaṭakarpara* and its author likewise is most widely known as Broken Pot, which is recorded to have been his nickname. As great a critic as Abhinavagupta (*c.*

+1000), in his commentary on the poem, accepted a tradition that Kālidāsa was the author, but this seems stylistically improbable. A great many anonymous works have been ascribed to Kālidāsa as a legendary great poet, especially when strange stories were handed down about them. The tradition said to be from Hemacandra is that formerly Bhāsa was extremely poor. He had vowed to fetch water only in a broken pot and did not forget his former state even after becoming successful and getting to the top. Other poets could not tolerate his vow and ridiculed him, nicknaming him Broken Pot. This former poverty of Bhāsa is also recorded in a verse quoted as Rājaśekhara's, *c.* +900 (Krishnamachariar p. 554). Now in the last verse of the poem itself the author swears that if any poet can surpass him in rhyming he will fetch water for him in a broken pot. This verse could very well be the basis of the entire story of the poet's humble origin as well as of his nickname. However, the tradition does, whether as mere conjecture or for good reason, give Bhāsa as the real name of the author. The poem is generally agreed to be ancient and its style, in so far as we can compare such a lyric with the dramas, seems to offer nothing against its being by Bhāsa. We may consider it here as a work probably of this period and possibly by Bhāsa. The use of rhyme *yamaka* and of rare words to achieve it does not go against a date in this period, since we have met with rhymes in the lyrics of Chapter XVII. Otherwise the style is simple and the metres also, though varied, are the earlier and simpler kinds of fixed metre.

1079. The Broken Pot is an example of the rhymed poem as a distinct type, since every line of it ends in a rhyme, a feature not usual in Sanskrit verse. As the rhyming syllables embrace whole words and more, the effect is complex, requiring systematic ambiguity of the cadences of lines. This short poem of a little over twenty lines therefore counts, as its author claimed, as a tour de force: it is a *citrakāvya* [411], not pure lyric. In fact later poets have far surpassed the Broken Pot in rhyming: in the length of their works, the intricacy of their rhyming patterns and the proportion of each line embraced in the rhyme; this is further confirmation of early date.

1080. As a lyric, the Broken Pot is an early example of a poem on the subject of separated lovers. A woman whose husband is away from home on a journey is described as tormented by love and is herself made to utter her feelings. Her loneliness is increased by the onset of the rainy season, which, as we noted in connection with the Seven Hundred, has always been regarded by Indian poets as the time when the desires of lovers are at their highest pitch [804]. All the phenomena of nature then conspire to enhance the anguish at the absence of the lover. After the prostrating heat of summer the rains are cool and refreshing, the birds respond with their poignant cries, the rain and the thunder and lightning impel everyone to seek shelter—and what shelter more natural than a lover's arms ? The sounds of the season, the aroma of the refreshed earth, the typical flowers of the season, the cessation of much human activity and drowning out of human noises by the heavy rain: all remind the lonely woman of the same romantic season in the past when she was happy in union with her lover, at the same time as they excite her sensibilities.

1081. In this poem the lonely woman talks to the clouds which have brought the rain, blames them for having come at the wrong time, then asks them to tell her lover to return home quickly, pointing out to him that the wild geese are not yet on their way to Lake Mānasa and the *cātaka* bird (supposed by poets to live on raindrops) is thirsty in anticipation of the rains (i.e. there is still time). But the rains have really come. Her tears flow like the rising ('muddied') rivers through the groves of flowering *kuṭaja* shrubs :

In the groves of flowering *kuṭajas*,
on the impatient faces of women without their lovers,
The muddied river water flows :
—why do you not regard poor me ? (8)

She points out to a girl friend that the roads are now impassable after the heavy rain, whilst the arrows of Love are sharper; the woods with their flowers, scents and breezes invite lovemaking, she can no longer bear the sight of the flowers which mock her—she names various kinds, each affecting her more than the last—and must surely die suddenly. The bee kisses the white jasmine in spite of the raindrops that fall on him, making him laugh :

Beautiful with white flowers
which cause laughter through the raindrops which fall
heavily from them,
The jasmine creeper is kissed by the bee
aware that it is time for the honey. (14)

Only the memory of her lover's good qualities keeps her alive.

1082. A dialogue on policy *nīti*, between a Boar and a Lion, consisting of twentyone verses and called the Essence of Policy *Nītisāra*, is also ascribed to Ghaṭakarpara.

CHAPTER XIX

DRAMA : BHĀSA'S CONTEMPORARIES, ESPECIALLY BODHĀYANA, VARARUCI, ĪŚVARADATTA (COMEDY AND SATIRICAL MONOLOGUE)

1083. We possess a few other early dramas generally similar in style to those ascribed to Bhāsa, whose authors are known from the manuscript tradition but concerning whose dates we have no evidence except their style and an occasional reference to current philosophical ideas. As they seem to be not far removed from the Bhāsa collection in time, either earlier or later, we may review them here in order to complete our survey of what is known of the ancient theatre in the period before Śūdraka, who appears to have inaugurated a new phase. Taken together, the plays of Bhāsa and his approximate contemporaries, with whom we might also associate Aśvaghoṣa, presumed to be a century and a half earlier, bring us a respectable repertory representing this period. We may add a few touches to this picture by gleaning some information about plays not now available to us, to which we have references, which probably formed part of the same repertory or in part were time honoured pieces inherited from the early traditions of the actors. The *Nāṭyaśāstra* as we now have it was probably not finally codified until the end of this period, and should therefore be related to it as summing up the ideals and aims of the theatre at this time. In general we may characterise the repertory of this period, as distinguished from the phase which followed it, as essentially of the theatre, of the stage. The plays are short, the action is rapid, the language clear and not burdened with literary as opposed to dramatic effects, the aesthetic experience is produced by action and events and not by description. Lyric poetry is rare and the theatre is permeated by the sense of being close to the epic, to Tradition, from which indeed its main stream seems to have flowed. Bhāsa is of course the supreme representative of the drama based on Tradition, though he wrote fictions as well.

1084. The more purely secular stream in this period is

represented, apart from these fictions, by one comedy *prahasana*—we discount the *Dāmaka* mentioned at the end of the last chapter—and two satirical monologues *bhāṇas*.

1085. The Master-Mistress, *Bhagavadajjukīya* or *Bhagavadajjuka*, is a comedy, in one relatively long act, by Bodhāyana. There is no evidence whether this Bodhāyana was anything to do with the Bodhāyana known as the author of a *Vṛtti* on the *Mīmāṃsā Sūtra*, probably to be dated in the early +3. The printed, rather recent (*c.* +1600, by a pupil of Nārāyaṇa), commentary on the Master-Mistress appears to assume that the author was the philosopher, and chronologically the identification is easy, but this seems no more than a conjecture (suited to the rather special aims of this commentator) and the name is hardly a unique or even personal one, being presumably a form of the clan name Baudhāyana (i.e. the form it would have in the vernacular language). The style and technique of the play are similar to Bhāsa's. Referring to the Sāṃkhya philosophy, a character in the play quotes, as does Aśvaghoṣa, from the old system of Vārṣagaṇya (probably −2; see Johnston, *Early Sāṁkhya*, 9, 25, 35, 82 f., etc.), not from the system later popularised as 'classical' Sāṃkhya, which originated in the +3 (*Ṣaṣṭitantra*). In the prologue the producer refers to a theory of the types of drama different from that standardised in the present *Nāṭyaśāstra*. According to Bodhāyana the *nāṭaka* ('play', history) and fiction are the basic types and ten other main types are derived from these (the eight of the standard theory plus the *vāra* [347] and *sallāpa* [346], 'turn' or 'series' and 'dispute' or 'contention'). These non-standard references agree with the date indicated by the style though they are not conclusive proof for it. The purpose of the reference to dramatic theory is simply to say that among all these types the comic aesthetic experience is the best, therefore a comedy ought to be performed.

1086. The humour of this play depends on an absurd situation and its satire is directed primarily at vanity (later Indian comedies usually ridicule primarily hypocrisy, which is in evidence here only as a secondary feature, mostly in the character of the jester). The 'Master' *Bhagavant*, a brahman 'wanderer', is actually a genuine *yogin* (not the stock impostor of later comedy), whose weakness is that in displaying his powers he forgets his own rule of proceeding carefully in this dangerous world (verse 4). He also appears ridiculous in being fussy about who touches him though he has himself entered the body of a helot girl. The Master *yogin* appears with his student, a stupid brahman who rejoices in the venerable name of Śāṇḍilya. Śāṇḍilya in the *Upaniṣads* is the originator of the momentous doctrine of the identity of the *ātman*, soul, with *brahman*. This aged 'student', unable to make a living in any other way, has tried the different schools of wanderers: he had become a Buddhist monk in the hope of a punctual breakfast, but left the Community in disgust on finding they have only one meal a day; he is now studying *yoga*. Though Śāṇḍilya, like many others, is in the ascetic business simply for the sake of a livelihood, he is not a bad character, rather an 'everyman'. In this play he is the jester *vidūṣaka*, and he is always hungry, very timid whilst very friendly and over-familiar with his master, like the usual jester or fool with his king in other types of play. Śāṇḍilya discusses philosophy and the techniques of *yoga* with his Master but is hopelessly mixed up, for which he excuses himself by saying he is hungry and can think only of food.

1087. Breakfast is possibly the objective *kārya* in this play, though deferred till the evening when the student can at last return with his Master from the day's unexpectedly practical and prolonged lesson. Or is it the accomplishment of the lesson, the demonstration of the advantages (?) of *yoga*? This is suggested by the Prologue, where the Producer proposes to teach the jester comedy. Meanwhile the Master and his student wander into a park, where the 'Mistress' *ajjukā* (respectful address to a geisha) with two maids awaits her lover. She sends one maid, Little Bee, to look for him. Śāṇḍilya is now much more interested in the girl than in *yoga*, or even food, but suddenly she is bitten by a snake and dies. An Officer of Death has arranged this in accordance with his instructions to collect her soul, now due to enter the next world.

1088. The other maid, Little Cuckoo, runs off to find the girl's mother. Seizing the opportunity for a practical demonstration of his yogic accomplishments, the Master projects his soul and enters into the dead body, reanimating it. The Mistress gets up and speaks to the terrified Śāṇḍilya, who now sees his teacher apparently dead. The maids return with the lamenting mother and the lover Rāmilaka, the latter apparently a *nāgaraka* [27] fetched from his 'circle' *goṣṭhī*. They are baffled at the girl's strange behaviour: she refuses to be embraced by her mother and abuses her; the lover touches her dress but is angrily rejected. They attribute her peculiar actions to the effects of the snake bite and the mother sends a maid for a doctor while the lover tries to soothe her. The doctor arrives and begins his treatment with some magic, but his patient calls him a fool. Urged on by the anxious lover, the doctor continues his absurd efforts. At this point the Officer of Death returns, finding he has made a mistake: the victim should have been another girl of the same name ('Vasantasenā', probably a stock name for a geisha). Unable now to rectify the mistake, since he finds the girl's body already occupied, he does the next best thing and deposits her soul in the vacant body of the Master, who is thus disastrously trapped in her body.

1089. The Master, that is his body, now jumps up, again terrifying Śāṇḍilya, and at once asks for the lover. Śāṇḍilya remonstrates with him, saying he is not the Master, nor the Mistress, but the 'Master-Mistress'. Nevertheless the Master persists most improperly in trying to embrace the lover, to everyone's consternation, especially the horrified Śāṇḍilya's. The uproar increases as the Master tries to embrace her maid and greet her mother and cannot understand their sudden estrangement. The doctor and his patient meanwhile are arguing about medicine, of which the former evidently knows very little and after a heated exchange retires discomfited. Finally the Officer of Death returns again to restore order and invites the beleaguered Master to release the Mistress's body, which he is by now very willing to do. The souls are switched back and the Master leads his appalled student home, putting off explanations till later.

1090. Some extracts will show the manner of this comedy better than any discussion. First, after the girl has fallen down dead from the snake bite (Achan pp. 69-71; Veṭūri pp. 22-3; our translation does not exactly follow either edition but collates both):

MAID. Alas, Mistress !

ŚĀṆḌILYA. Master ! This geisha girl is abandoning her life !

WANDERER. Fool! Life is the dearest thing to living beings. You should say: 'The body is being abandoned by the life'.

ŚĀṆḌILYA. Ugh! Go away! Pitiless! Devoid of affection! Hard heart! Depraved intelligence! Broken character! Cruel and faithless! Shaved in vain!

WANDERER. What do you mean?

ŚĀṆḌILYA. I am going to complete your hundred and eight names.

WANDERER. By all means.

ŚĀṆḌILYA. Sir! Master! I am unhappy!

WANDERER. What for?

ŚĀṆḌILYA. She is our kinswoman.

WANDERER. How can she be our kinswoman?

ŚĀṆḌILYA. She too is like one who has left the world and has no affection for anyone.

1091. After the maid brings the Doctor (Achan pp. 83-93; Veṭūri pp. 28-33):

DOCTOR. It must have been a big snake which injured her.

MAID. How do you know, sir?

DOCTOR. By its making a big change in her. Bring all the instruments so that I can begin the treatment of poison. [*Sits down and draws a circle*]. O coiling one going crooked! Enter the circle! O son of Vāsuki! Stop! Stop! Shoo! Shoo!—Just let me do a head incision—where's the axe?—

GEISHA. Fool of a doctor! That's enough exertion now!

DOCTOR. Oh! There's bile too! I'll destroy your bile, wind and phlegm!

RĀMILAKA. Make the attempt—we shall not be ungrateful!

DOCTOR.—I'm fetching the charming tablets, the snake medicine. [*Exit.*

Then enter the Officer of Death.

OFFICER OF DEATH. Woe! I am rebuked by Death:

'This is not that Vasantasenā!
—take her back at once!

It's that other Vasantasenā
whose life is expended—fetch her here !' (30)

—Before her body is taken to its meeting with the fire I must make her alive—[*Looking at her*] Oh ! She has got up ! Woe ! How's this ?

Her soul is in my hand,
but this lovely woman has got up !
It's the greatest wonder in the world !
never seen before on Earth ! (31)

[*Observing all round*] Ah ! His lordship the *yogin* Wanderer is playing about ! What can I do now ? Very well, I see. I will deposit this Geisha's soul in the Wanderer's body and when my work is finished I will do what is proper. [*Doing so*]

This woman's life is set
in the brahman's body :
—Generally they change
according to the soul, according to its character. (32)

[*Exit.*

WANDERER [*getting up*] Little Cuckoo ! Little Cuckoo !
ŚĀṆḌILYA. Oooo ! The Master has returned to life ! Ugh ! I suppose those doomed to unhappiness do not die !
WANDERER. Wherever is Rāmilaka ?
RĀMILAKA. Master ! I am here.
ŚĀṆḌILYA. Master ! What's this ? Your left hand, which was accustomed to holding the waterpot, seems to me as if loaded with shell bracelets !
WANDERER. Rāmilaka ! Embrace me !
ŚĀṆḌILYA. You go and embrace a *kiṃśuka* tree !
WANDERER. Rāmilaka ! I'm drunk !
ŚĀṆḌILYA. No ! No ! You're mad !
RĀMILAKA. Master ! This talk is contrary to your station in life !
WANDERER. I'm going to have a drink.

ŚĀṆḌILYA. Go and drink poison ! Very well, I will find out on the authority of the joke : this is not the Master. Nor is it the Mistress. Therefore the Master-Mistress has happened !

WANDERER. Little Cuckoo ! Little Cuckoo ! Embrace me !

MAID. Go away !

MOTHER. Daughter ! Vasantasenā !

WANDERER. Here I am, mother ! Hallo !

MOTHER. Master ! What's this ?

WANDERER. Mother ! Don't you recognise me ? Rāmilaka ! You are late today !

RĀMILAKA. Master ! I am not a servant !

The Doctor enters.

DOCTOR. I've got eight tablets and some herbs.—Every moment she will live or she will die ! [*Approaching*] Water! Water !—

MAID. Here's the water.

DOCTOR. Let me rub in a tablet. Oooo ! She's not bitten ! She's possessed !

GEISHA. Fool of a doctor ! Grown old in vain ! You don't even know when living beings are dead ! Tell me : which kind of snake was she killed by ?

DOCTOR. What's so strange in this case ?

GEISHA. The science.

DOCTOR. There are a thousand sciences !

GEISHA. Well, tell me about medical science.

DOCTOR. Listen, lady :

The windy and the bilious
and the phleg—phleg—

—Oooo ! My book ! My book !—

ŚĀṆḌILYA. Ah ! Just like a doctor ! He's forgotten at the first word ! Very well, he's my friend ! —He's got the book.

DOCTOR. Listen, lady :

The windy and the bilious
and the phlegmatic are the big poisons;

It's three snakes—
no fourth is found. (33)

GEISHA. That's an incorrect form. It should be : 'They are three snakes'. 'It' is neuter.

DOCTOR. Oooo ! She must have been bitten by a grammatical snake !

1092. The Indian critics have generally neglected comedy, presumably seeing it as a minor and episodic form offering limited scope for analysis and few quotable verses. The Pallava emperor Mahendravarman (+7), himself the author of a comedy, names the Master-Mistress in an unfortunately badly damaged inscription (Mamandoor; see Krishnamachariar p. 148, *Epigraphia Indica* IV 152, etc.). We gather from this only that the work was well known in his day. Among the actual critical writers whose works we possess, Sāgaranandin (2903) names the Master-Mistress as an example of a 'mixed' comedy, since it contains a geisha. His other type of comedy, the 'pure', contains simply the basic laughing stock of wanderers, ascetics, brahmans, etc.

1093. The +14 dramatist Sukumāra, in the Prologue to his Rāma play *Raghuvīracarita* (Trivandrum MS), includes Bodhāyana among his chosen few exemplary writers :

Those who have made ear ornaments from the flower
buds of Bodhāyana's sentences,
whose throats are ornamented by what Bilhaṇa has well
said as their chief necklace,
Who have tasted the delicious words of Murāri, the
only sweetness on the Earth;
they alone are contented with our words as new braids
of ambrosia.

('braid' *veṇī* is used metaphorically for 'stream', but, since ambrosia is supposed to arise from the Moon, Sukumāra may also have intended a hidden comparison of the faces of his appreciative audience with the Moon).

1094. In the Āndhra edition of Śiṅgabhūpāla's *Rasārṇavasudhākara* (+14) we find a different definition of 'pure' and 'mixed' comedies, together with the 'transformed' as a third type [pp. 228-9]. Here the Master-Mistress is said to be 'pure', because the mixed should have all the limbs of the street play [325-6], as well as a rogue *dhūrta*. This is not found in the Trivandrum edition (p. 297) and the manuscripts will have to be re-examined in case there is some confusion. However, we can say that the Master-Mistress hardly shows all the kinds of 'limb' evolved for the street play, though there are exchanges of 'outwitting' *adhibala* between the Master and Śāṇḍilya. Nor, probably, should any of the characters be classed as a 'rogue' : the Doctor is the nearest, but he is portrayed as a simple charlatan whilst a rogue would be clever and deceitful. On the other hand Śiṅgabhūpāla describes ten special 'limbs' of comedy (Trivandrum edition pp. 290ff.), which do not seem to be found in any earlier critic. This writer in fact devotes more space than any other to the comedy. After remarking that a comedy should resemble a satirical monologue in its subject matter, in having (only two) conjunctions, (one) act, in using the limbs of the *lāsya* [363] and the (eloquent) mode, whilst having the comic aesthetic experience predominating, he elaborates these limbs of comedy with illustrations. One may note in passing that application of the *lāsya* limbs, which might seem unexpected here, could be found in the Master-Mistress particularly where the actress taking the Geisha part has to impersonate having the soul of the Wanderer, and vice versa.

1095. Though Śiṅgabhūpāla illustrates his limbs of comedy from another comedy, the *Ānandakośa*, most of them can probably be seen in the Master-Mistress too. Thus 'parallelism' *avalagita* in Śiṅgabhūpāla's sense, involving degrading behaviour unsuitable for the assumed station in life, is shown in Śāṇḍilya's behaviour or, of course, in that of the Wanderer when ensouled by the Geisha. 'Transaction' *vyavahāra* might be seen where the Wanderer (in the Geisha) teases the Doctor about his science. The logical 'application' *upapatti* may be seen in Śāṇḍilya's use of the joke as an epistemological authority *pramāṇa* or means of knowledge, in the excerpt which we have translated above. 'Fear' *bhaya* is shown by Śāṇḍilya when he imagines there is a tiger in the park as he and his Master enter. Śiṅgabhūpāla perhaps intends the more comic effect of groundless fear as this 'limb', not the emotion in general. There is plenty of 'untruth' *anṛta* in Śāṇḍilya's speeches and several cases of 'confusion' *vibhrānti* of one thing with another. 'Stammering' *gadgadavāc* is exemplified by the Doctor unable to remember his text and there are several instances of incoherent 'chatter' *pralāpa*, as when Śāṇḍilya tries to expound the principles of Buddhism. If we could find the remaining two limbs as well, which is mainly a matter of how broad Śiṅgabhūpāla intended them to be, then we might conclude that the Master-Mistress is a very typical example of comic action as understood by this critic, or even that whoever first described these 'limbs' had this comedy very much in mind. These two are 'jumping in' *avaskanda* (of several characters from different standpoints but all with fallacious arguments) and 'frustration' *vipralambha*, here rather 'deception' as when pretending to be possessed by a spirit [1168-70].

1096. Bahurūpamiśra refers to the Master-Mistress (Krishnamachariar p. 747—on III. 54 ff., he calls it 'mixed'). Various commentaries and works on the production of plays in Malayālam and Sanskrit, handed down in the surviving Kerala tradition of the classical theatre, discuss and explain the production of the Master-Mistress. Some notes from these will be found in Kunjunni Raja's 'Kūṭiyāṭṭam...' The *Kramadīpikā* on the production of this play (p. 30) describes a procedure which occupies thirty five nights, though only the last three of these present the play proper. It appears that in the recent Kerala practice three nights is the normal time required to perform one act of a play, or a one act play. The preliminaries include more than seven nights' discussion by the jester of the doctrines of the various schools of wanderers, such as the Lokāyata and Buddhism. Kunjunni Raja also refers to the Malayālam version presented with the play in Kerala, for the benefit of audiences who cannot follow the Sanskrit and Prakrit (the jester speaks Śaurasenī in the original). The Malayālam speeches are generally far longer than the originals, adding explanations and further discussions. According to Kunjunni Raja (p. 40) the printed Sanskrit commentary has followed this Malayālam version in its own explanations of the original text. The version also notes the musical modes *rāgas* to which some of the verses of the original are sung (p. 39). Kunjunni Raja further quotes from an unprinted manuscript a number of additional Sanskrit, and one Prakrit, verses used in the production of the play as theme *dhruvā* songs [306] for the entrance of the jester Śāṇḍilya (pp. 26-7). Some of these suggest the Vedāntic interpretation of the play which is elaborated in the printed Sanskrit commentary.

1097. The description which Kunjunni Raja gives of the appearance of the jester on the Kerala stage probably can be applied to Śāṇḍilya in this play. He gives a reference to Dāmodaragupta's *Kuṭṭanīmata* (65), written in Kaśmīra in the +8, for a parallel description, suggesting that this Kerala practice is fairly faithful to the classical tradition :

> Rice flour is smeared roughly over his face, chest and arms; over that red marks are made on the forehead, nose, cheeks, chin, chest and arms. The eyes are smeared over thickly with collyrium [black antimony—AKW], even over the eyelids extending on either side as far as the ears. Prominent moustache is made, one side raised up and the other side hanging down. He has a *kākapada* [crow's foot] tuft of hair; but he wears a kind of head-dress. On one ear he has a red garland made of *tecci* flowers, and on the other ear a roll of betel leaves, reminding one of the description of Bhaṭṭaputra in the *Kuṭṭanīmata*: *ekasmin dalavīṭakam aparasmin sīsapatrakaṃ karṇe.* The dress is also ludicrous; the portion covering the hips is made very thick and bulging. Besides the sacred thread, he has an upper garment *uttarīya* which is spread out, but kept rolled up. He acts as if he has in his mouth something to eat and is chewing it now and then. Playing with the sacred thread is a frequent occupation of the hands. Others [occupations of the hands] are: to arrange the tuft of hair and tie it; to take the *uttarīya*, fold it and squeeze it to remove water out of it, and use it as a fan all over the body. He normally speaks in the *indala svara*, but changes the tone to suit the context. He has a stick with him; he can keep it on his lap while he is sitting ('Kūṭiyāṭṭam...' pp. 41-2).

It is not clear whether the *Kūṭiyāṭṭakrama* referred to by Achan in the Introduction to his edition of the play (p. xvii) is the same as any of the texts referred to by Kunjunni Raja. Achan dates it not later than the +12 on the grounds of the archaic

Malayālam language. It includes an explanation of the acting of the Master-Mistress.

1098. The author of the printed commentary *Diṅmātradarśinī* given in Achan's edition bore the same name Nārāyaṇa as his famous teacher, who was the writer of the great lyric *Nārāyaṇīya* and numerous *campūs* intended to be performed by jesters [434]. The pupil's name appears only in another of his commentaries, the *Bhāvārthadīpikā* on Bhavabhūti's *Uttararāmacarita* (see Kunjunni Raja, *The Contribution of Kerala to Sanskrit Literature*, p. 149, this commentary seems not to have been printed yet). The hidden meaning of the play, according to the *Diṅmātradarśinī*, is to show how Śāṇḍilya is instructed in the nature of the *brahman* as taught in the *Veda* and so led on the way towards the liberation of his soul. In other words an allegorical interpretation is proposed (see particularly pp. 2-3 of the commentary). All Śāṇḍilya's errors and vices are due to his state of ignorant involvement in transmigration and consequent unhappiness (hunger, etc.). This aspect of the play, his joining the wanderers simply for the sake of food and with no desire for any kind of virtue *dharma*, is the 'external', apparent meaning. The supposed real quest of the jester for liberation, his instruction by his Master, is the 'internal', hidden and allegorical, meaning. The internal meaning is thus frequently in absolute contradiction to the external meaning, a fact which would make this interpretation seem all the more convincing to Vedāntins holding that the external world is illusory, false. Elsewhere the allegory is simpler. Thus when Śāṇḍilya is afraid to enter the park because his mother had once told him there was a tiger there, his cowardice, typical of the jester character, and asking the Master to go first, is the external meaning. The corresponding internal meaning is that the beauties of the park are dangerous because they excite the emotion of love and attachment to the objects of the senses, disastrous obstacles to the wandering life in quest of liberation. The meeting with the Geisha naturally seems to bear out this interpretation. Rather different and completely anachronistic is the explanation (p. 55) of the climax of the drama, the entry of the *yogin* into the body of the Geisha, along the lines of tantric *yoga*.

1099. According to this commentator (p. 56) the action of the Master-Mistress takes place in Pāṭaliputra. This, however, is impossible, since the Officer of Death in describing his way to the South from the scene mentions that he crosses the Ganges. Pāṭaliputra is on the South side of the Ganges and it is presumably only ignorance of North Indian geography, on the part of a Southern commentator, which led to this supposition. If we accept the +1 to +3 as the probable period of this play, then we may conjecture that any city North of the Ganges which flourished at that time may have been the scene intended. It may also have been the place where the play was written, since comic and satirical literature in India tends to be local in reference. At that period most of Northern India was ruled by the Kuṣāṇas and their Śaka vassals: there were Śaka *kṣatrapas* at Vārāṇasī and Vaiśālī, at whose courts the play might have been produced (the Producer in the Prologue refers to his having been directed to produce a play at court).

1100. At least two other commentaries on the Master-Mistress are extant but do not appear to have been printed as yet.

1101. The first satirical monologue, which is probably the earliest Indian play now available intact, is the Both Go to Meet, *Ubhayābhisārikā* (more freely Both Give Way), attributed to a Vararuci. In Chapter XIII we have discussed the little evidence available concerning the work of a poet Vararuci who lived about the —3 and may have been identical with the grammarian of that date [649]. We noted also that, besides the mere mention by Patañjali of this ancient Vararuci as the author of a *kāvya*, there are much later references to or quotations from two *kāvyas* by 'Vararuci' : the *Kaṇṭhābharaṇa*, which has been conjectured to have been a *citrakāvya*, and the *Cārumatī*, probably a novel (otherwise a biography, but one quotation suggests fiction). These references are of *c.* +900 or later and the quotations are hardly enough to decide whether the work in question would be of the —3 or much later. There are also some other verses in anthologies ascribed to 'Vararuci' [651]. Among these, *Subhāṣitāvali* 1103 is surely by the author of Both Go to Meet, being in the same unusual *bhujaṃgavijṛṃbhita* metre of 26 syllables in each line as the first verse in the satirical monologue. What seems certain is that the Both Go to Meet cannot be as early as the - 3, since it mentions the Vaiśeṣika philosophy and its categories, which probably were not fully elaborated before the −1. Beyond this we have only the internal evidence of style and the small scale of the piece when compared with the other satirical monologues available. Thus we find repetitions of expressions, which later writers might avoid. The other early monologues are also of uncertain date, one being by Śūdraka [1218] and another by an unknown writer conjectured to have been a contemporary of Bhāsa [1115].

1102. The best estimate possible for this Vararuci's date, therefore, is between the − 1 and the +2. His work may represent a period when the Vaiśeṣika philosophy had just become well known, perhaps after Aśvaghoṣa but still in the +1. The scene of Both Go to Meet is laid in Pāṭaliputra and this may well have been the city where it was written, as a satire on the manners of its day. There is a reference to the king ruling there, but it does not give the kind of imperial titles one might expect of a ruler of one of the major dynasties. This would suit the period indicated: after the Sātavāhana conquest in the −1, which presumably left such vassal rulers as Bṛhaspatimitra in Magadha, we have a Śaka conquest resulting in a line of rulers known as the Muruṇḍas (*muruṇḍa* means 'king' in the Śaka language), who became vassals of the Kuṣāṇas probably in the time of Kaniṣka [835].

1103. After the opening benediction, the producer enters and recites a verse wishing that the audience may be successful lovers, causing jealousy in beautiful women to whom they are not sufficiently faithful. He is interrupted, before he can announce the play, by the entrance of the parasite *viṭa* in low spirits because, just at the height of spring, he has to perform an errand for a patron instead of indulging his own inclinations. A merchant's son has commissioned him to conciliate his angry mistress, offended because he praised an actress at a public performance. The parasite has already delayed, being stopped by his distrustful wife, and now he runs into a series of acquaintances, which further impedes his progress and gives us a delightful series of pictures of wickedness, intrigue, hypocrisy and folly in a great city.

1104. First he meets Anaṅgadattā, obviously on her way home after having enjoyed a bout of lovemaking. Clearly she has not slept (the time is morning), her ornaments are in disorder and her lips bear the marks of love bites. The parasite takes this encounter as a portent of success in his errand. Anaṅgadattā passes by, disregarding him, but turns round as he is about to speak, saying she had not recognised him (no doubt she had hoped not to be recognised herself). He compliments her on her evident success and she tells him she is returning from the house of the son of some bureaucrat. The parasite remarks that this son is no longer wealthy and so her mother will not be pleased. The girl smiles, ashamed: she is in fact in love, infringing the conventions of harlotry. He promises to conciliate her mother for her and continues on his way.

1105. He next meets Mādhavasenā, in great distress because her mother, in order to make money, has forced her to visit a very rich merchant's son, a 'modern Kubera (the God of Wealth [676])'. He very well understands her predicament and comforts her, but starts to explain the science of her profession. She cuts him short, as having just the same views as her mother, and goes off without saying goodbye.

1106. After this he meets a supposed Vaiśeṣika ('Discrimination' School) nun, Vilāsakauṇḍinī, walking flirtatiously and heavily scented. He is not acquainted with her, but, full of curiosity, he introduces himself, mentioning his name as Mr. Vaiśikācala (Mr. Steady Harlotry). She rebuffs him: we have no use for Steady Harlotry, though we might have for a Steady Vaiśeṣika ! He agrees she needs this, teasing her with the unsteadiness of her eyes and languid appearance of her body : evidently her lover has been demonstrating her Discrimination in the topics of lovemaking. She is most annoyed and says that such words are fitting for a slave like himself (a parasite might well be sensitive to such an insult). He is not to be put down: her slaves are indeed fortunate and of course a person like himself, of no merit, could not aspire to that position. She checks him again: we are not supposed to talk to people outside the Six Categories (School, i.e. Vaiśeṣika), perhaps hinting that as he is outside the six categories, which embrace the whole of reality, he is just nothing to her. He agrees this is proper, for her body is 'substance'; the 'qualities' are her beautiful appearance and everything else lovely about her; the 'universal' (common property !) is her youthfulness; hers are the 'actions' praised by young men; 'combination' is desired by people with her, because she has 'distinction' (*viśeṣa*, the particular). In other words all the six categories are found only in her. She laughs and continues the punning: 'I know Sāṃkhya too : The soul (this man) is stainless (unanointed, unkempt), without qualities (without good qualities) and the subject who has experiences (a libertine)'. He replies with a final pun: 'Well, I have no answer (=Then there is no one superior to me !)', and takes his leave saying he does not want to be an obstacle to the love-making of young people. This passage, from the point where Vaiśikācala introduces himself, is quoted by M. R. Kavi (*Abhinavabhāratī* II pp. 349-50) to illustrate the characteristic 'ambiguity' *akṣarasaṃghāta* [186].

1107. Next, Vaiśikācala encounters one of the 'mothers', in fact the grandmother, it is implied, of Anaṅgadattā, namely Rāmasenā, who is on her way to fetch back her daughter Cāraṇadāsī (Anaṅgadattā's mother) from a lover who has no money left. This marvellous old lady is walking along with all the smiles and flirtatious glances of a young woman. Having enjoyed the pleasures of love herself and drunk up the substance of those devoted to her qualities, causing rivalry and enmity among young men, she is surely now on her way to milk her daughter's lover.

1108. The parasite tries to avoid the next encounter, with Sukumārikā, one of the 'third sex' (i.e. neuter) evidently very inauspicious for a parasite to meet. He flatters her with her pretensions to buxom womanhood, with the intention of escaping quickly. She claims to be returning from the King's brother-in-law after a lovers' quarrel. We may note that having brothers-in-law is traditionally a characteristic of Śaka kings and probably was noticed by the people ruled by them as a prominent and unpleasant feature of a Śaka court. This tends to confirm that this satirical play was written in the time of the Muruṇḍas. We remember also from Bhāsa's Impoverished Cārudatta that a bullying brother-in-law of a king would be the least desirable of 'lovers' (and hardly easy to 'milk'). She complains that this prince has been fooling with a maid, though claiming that afterwards he forcibly made love to her again, yet she enjoyed it and now that he has gone off again to the maid she wants the parasite to fetch him back. We have to take the description by this retarded girl of the way the prince put her on the couch, and of her climax of love and consequent fatigue, as entirely imaginary. Nevertheless the parasite expresses concern, deplores the aberration of the prince in abandoning the 'festival of love', namely her special qualities—since she does not suffer from the inconveniences of being a woman,—and promises to bring the haughty prince prostrate at her feet as soon as he has finished his present errand. He then quickly escapes.

1109. The next case is a merchant's son, Dhanamitra, now appearing destitute. Though formerly a 'teacher of villains' he has been so foolish as not merely to fall in love with a harlot but to believe that she reciprocates his passion, blaming only her greedy mother for his present predicament. He has handed over his whole inheritance to the girl, whereupon, on the pretext of an excursion to bathe in the pool in Aśoka Park, she has left him there stripped to his bathing costume, the park gates closed, and has then had the keepers pitch him out through a side door. Thus a rich man is turned into a tramp, yet he persists in believing that the girl loves him but is unduly influenced by her mother. The parasite promises to help him and hurries on his way.

1110. The last encounter is with the actress Priyaṅgusenā, about to perform in a musical play *saṃgītaka* entitled Indra's Victory *Purandaravijaya*. The performance will take place at the King's palace and she has accepted a bet with another actress that the play will be a success, that the acting will produce the desired aesthetic experience in the audience. This is why she has approached the parasite: to ask him to arrange the success (presumably to mobilise a claque in the theatre). He says this is quite unnecessary in her case: she herself will be the instrument of success. However, as a matter of fact he has already been solicited by Rāmasena (apparently the same as the King's brother-in-law) in this matter. She looks elated at hearing that her intrigue has produced the desired effect. After flattering her that she need only appear with her graceful gestures, to make the eyes and hearts of the people dance after her, without bothering to dance, he takes his leave.

1111. At last he approaches the house of his patron's mistress, but meets her maid. The maid reports that her mistress was unable to hold out in her separation, affected by the spring and eventually by hearing someone singing to the accompaniment of a *vīṇā*, that life is useless to those who do not conciliate those whom they love. She had set out with the maid for the patron's house, but he too, his firmness softened by the spring, had not waited for the parasite to return (in fact the parasite hadn't started at that time !) and had set out for her house. Hence the title of this play. They met half way, by the gate of a *vīṇā* teacher's house. As they stood there, both at a loss, the musician happened to come out. He invited them in and they spent the rest of the night there. In the morning the mistress sent her maid to look for Vaiśikācala. There is nothing for him to do but follow the maid along and pay his compliments to the couple. They are extremely polite, returning his compliments by saying that their love, which had forestalled him, was originally engendered through his efforts. He quickly takes his leave, and recites the final benediction to the audience.

1112. This summary of the content of a satirical monologue will perhaps make clearer than any comment the brilliance of Vararuci's description of the follies of Pāṭaliputra and of the consummate social skill of the parasite. It will also serve to explain the way of life of the parasite, one of the principle stock characters of the Indian theatre [30].

1113. Besides the quotation illustrating ambiguity mentioned above, M. R. Kavi (*Abhinavabhāratī* II p. 354) quotes from this play a verse from the Dhanamitra episode for the characteristic 'illustration' *nidarśana* [187]:

The poison of snakes may gradually be neutralised by
the strength of great herbs,
it is possible to save oneself in the forest from a king
of elephants whose temples are bursting with rut,
Sometimes release is possible from the mouth of a shark
in the waters of the great ocean,
never is one seen escaping after getting into the sub-
marine fire of the women of the geishas' quarter. (25).

1114. Like comedies, the satirical monologues are rarely given much appreciation by the critics. A verse found at the end of some manuscripts of Śūdraka's Lotus Gift [1218] gives the names of the authors of four satirical monologues: Vararuci, Īśvaradatta [1115], Śūdraka and Śyāmilaka [1444]. 'These four spoke satirical monologues, what power had Kālidāsa ?' In other words this was something the great poet Kālidāsa could not equal. Presumably, then, there were connoisseurs of this form who relished it above all kinds of literature and established this 'canon' of four classic works which fortunately has been preserved for us. As a rule, such monologues are topical and ephemeral. There are scores of examples from the last six centuries or so, since the form has continued very popular, few from earlier times and only these four to tell us something of Pāṭaliputra and Ujjayinī in classical times. Among the later composers of satirical monologues, the anonymous author of the *Viṭanidrā*, The Parasite's Sleep (+14), written in Mahodaya (Cochin), pays tribute to the four great classics of his form :

> May there be happiness for the four creators of satirical monologues,
> who are Suns refreshing the lotus hearts of all the intelligent,
> —For the ancient writers who possessed all aesthetic experiences flowing in words rich in meanings,
> who knew whole cities.

(Quoted by Schokker in his edition of the *Pādatāḍitaka*, p. 13; the *Viṭanidrā* has not yet been printed.)

1115. The second satirical monologue is by the otherwise unknown Īśvaradatta. It is most unlikely that he was identical with a usurper who temporarily ejected Rudrasiṃha I from Ujjayinī. His play in fact is set in Pāṭaliputra. As it appears older than Śūdraka's play of the same type, however, it may be supposed to be no later than the time of Bhāsa and to have been written during the Muruṇḍa regime in Magadha. The play is entitled The Dialogue of the Rogue and the Parasite *Dhūrtaviṭasaṃvāda*.

1116. It is the rainy season, but a fine day. The parasite Devilaka has time on his hands and wants to go out, so he considers how to amuse himself. There are two possibilities: gambling and women. As he has already lost almost all his possessions in gambling he has no choice but to go to the geishas' quarter. On his way he praises the city of Pāṭaliputra as the best place in the world with the best people in it. There are other prosperous cities, but Pāṭaliputra has uncommon qualities:

Generous men are easy to find, the arts are highly esteemed, the women have a wealth of amiability,
the rich are not intoxicated, educated men are not envious,
All the people talk with learning, appreciate each other's good qualities, are grateful,
ha !—it is possible even for the gods to abandon heaven and find happiness in the city ! (p. 4).

We may read this and his other remarks as a claim to sophistication on behalf of the old metropolis, a claim to know how to live and pursue happiness, certainly not to the pursuit of virtue as an end. The Royal Way is crowded with people :

Someone who sees me, though in a hurry, does not interrupt the conversation and go off elsewhere,
all these glad people, even in the crush, give way,
No one delays me long, through fear that business will lapse;
ah !—the reputation acquired by the best of cities is marked by men who know the world. (p. 6)

1117. He runs into Kṛṣṇilaka, the son of a rich banker, who complains that his father obstructs his enjoyment of life, being afraid of him spending money on women: as he is on his way back from one, he fears for his life if his father finds out. The parasite sympathises with him and reviews all the pleasures of youth, deploring the attitude of fathers. It is a long list of negations and in the end the parasite says he wishes he could rid the world of fathers with an axe, as Rāma of the Axe set out to rid it of aristocrats. This discussion is a long one, much longer than any in Vararuci's play.

1118. The parasite describes the geishas' quarter at some length as he enters it. The palaces are like the peaks of Mount Kailāsa, but there is so much smoke from the fragrant aloe wood (used for scenting the hair as well as rooms) that it is like bad weather. Of course there are flowers at the doorways, the sound of anklets and beautiful servant girls of the harlots hurrying to and fro in the streets. There is music of all kinds coming from the houses and the harlot girls are seen wandering here and there, beautiful, elegantly dressed and always smiling. The parasite accosts one of the servant girls, Vāruṇikā, but she is very shy and he gets only a monosyllabic giggle out of her (pp. 8-9). He stops for a moment to talk to Bandhumatikā, sitting in the courtyard at the entrance to her house trying to do up her girdle : it is a very difficult task to clasp the ends together round the swelling curves of her youthful figure. She too is shy and will only say 'It won't go on !' At Rāmadāsī's house he hears weeping and goes in. Her lover has left her because she feigned anger on seeing his lips marked by (the bites of) another girl. He advises her to choose a suitable time and go to him. Next he passes Ratisenā enjoying the breeze at her window in trying to overcome a hangover. He speaks to her, but she just laughs and shuts the window (p. 11). Then he runs into Pradyumnadāsī on her way home from the house of Rāmilaka, a *nāgaraka*, obviously having enjoyed herself there, and teases her about her appearance. She remarks that she has not seen him for a long time, for which he blames the bad weather (p. 12).

1119. Now (p. 13) he comes to the house where the 'rogue' Viśvalaka lives with Sunandā (they are described as a 'rogue-couple'). The gate is always closed, evidently because no one visits them and they have no servants. Viśvalaka has run through all his money and has nothing left but his body, like a naked ascetic; only the aged harlot Sunandā stays with him, preventing him from keeping any money, because she is like a dried up river and no one else wants her. The parasite, whose name is revealed in the following dialogue as Devilaka, thinks it improper to pass by without greeting the couple. He shouts to find out whether anyone is at home; listening, he hears someone walking in wooden shoes, making a noise like hoofs on setting out on a journey, and breathing heavily. It must be Viśvalaka. Someone calls out: "Who's there carrying out the donkey-vow ?" (braying like a donkey). Devilaka replies that he is Death's Messenger come for Sunandā and, feigning extreme anger at not being recognised and admitted at once, he utters a curse, that Viśvalaka's head may be separated from the left foot of his charming beloved through a quarrel. Viśvalaka opens up at once and lets him in, asking if he doesn't love them and saying that such a curse is proper. Of course, all this conversation is performed in the usual monologue manner, the parasite repeating what the rogue is supposed to have said. Devilaka thinks his curse must have shaken the World of Brahmā, let alone Viśvalaka, nevertheless it can be counteracted by a suitable expiation, namely an offering of strong drink. He sits down. Viśvalaka offers him water for his feet, as is the Indian convention, which Devilaka remarks is unnecessary because the main street of Pāṭaliputra is free from mud, surpassing even the roof terrace of a palace.

1120. The main part of this satirical monologue now begins, the dialogue on the philosophy of love. Viśvalaka introduces the subject, saying that in Rāmilaka's Circle *goṣṭhī* (i.e. club; cf. Chapter II above [27-8]) the members *goṣṭhīkas*, Viṣṇudāsa and others, have been arguing about some doubtful points in the system of pleasure. As they could not solve these problems, Viśvalaka has been requested to put forward his own views and has done so. However, he would like to hear Devilaka's opinions, which he regards as authoritative. In fact he had been thinking of going to Devilaka's house to ask him, but now he has appeared himself. Now if he can spare the time he would like to ask him about these points.

1121. Devilaka suggests that, as it is windy near the house, they go into the club hall and walk up and down and converse and he will say what he can. They do so, the parasite getting up and walking about, and Viśvalaka puts a long series of questions about how to deal with women, especially geishas: what they really like in a man (the best like courtesy), how to know when they are really in love, how to make up a quarrel (some say by joking, Devilaka recommends only kissing; as for the 'modern' method of throwing oneself at a woman's feet, he doesn't think much of it, it reminds him of having to touch the crab-like, rough and smelly feet of old priests annointed with rancid butter—p. 16), and so on. There are two dozen questions in all. Towards the latter part of their discussion they take up the more philosophical, the basic theoretical, problems as distinguished from the practical tactics of the game. The answer to the twelfth question might offer a kind of transition, with its generalisation from experience:

He who quickly delights a woman in a deserted place
after dragging her away as an elephant (drags)
a creeper,

or who, knowing she is drunk, gradually overcomes her,
arousing her with suggestive words,
Or plays some other trick and deceives her, or hides his
feelings:
this action of his will not be fruitless, sir!—For women
are perverse. (p. 19)

M. R. Kavi (*Abhinavabhāratī* II p. 357) quotes this for the characteristic 'admonition' *upadiṣṭa* [187].

1122. But it is the eighteenth question which really breaks away from the practical problems of knowing what is in a woman's mind: which is more delightful, a beautiful woman or an amiable one? (p. 23). The ideal would of course be both: amiability *dākṣiṇya* (or courtesy or kindness) in an ugly woman is futile, like a ballet performed in the dark; beauty without amiability gives no joy, like moonrise in the forest (in a wild and dangerous forest, *aṭavī*, the 'jungle'). But Devilaka considers amiability more important, for it is an ornament even in an ugly woman, whereas beauty merely spoils an unamiable woman. It is observed that men abandon even beautiful women and become attached to amiable ones, though these may be ugly. Beautiful women inevitably become hard *stabdha* (or arrogant or coarse), and hardness is the enemy of love. If you want only beauty a painting will do, but all other good qualities are contained in amiability alone: pleasant speech, dressing well, quietness, appreciativeness, compatibility, not being angry for long, absence of greed, willingness, are all found in an amiable woman.

1123. Should one spend money on women (or specifically on geishas—p. 24)? Even Dattaka, an ancient authority who wrote a book on harlotry for the use of the geishas of Pāṭaliputra (—4 or —3?), states that pleasure *kāma* destroys the wealth of men. According to Devilaka there are three operations with wealth: you can give it away, you can enjoy it or you can save it. Giving and enjoying are more important and saving is blameworthy. The point is that hoarded money is useless, fruitless, gives no satisfaction. One should certainly enjoy the delights of making love to the geishas: for the sake of this one would sacrifice one's life, let alone wealth. As to the question of virtue *dharma*, one should appreciate the geishas and be grateful to them, for then heaven lies in one's hand (p. 26).

1124. The topic of heaven, finally, is discussed at length. Devilaka can see no reason why one should not be attached to women. Moreover he sees no one who is not subject to such attachment: even Indra (the King of the Gods) suffered mutilation for the sake of Ahalyā (M. R. Kavi—*Abhinavabhāratī* II p. 352—quotes this as a case of the characteristic 'example' *dṛṣṭānta* [186]). Those who abandon the geishas in order to seek heavenly pleasures have been deceived. The pleasures of this world are visible and immediate and must therefore be taken more seriously than what lies unseen (and doubtful) in the future. He then reviews the special delights of love in each of the six seasons. What is heaven to one who enjoys the delights of love now? It is like the *dharma* (nature or virtue) of ants when poor wretches follow one another, risking their lives, for a heaven which they have not seen themselves; like a mirage when they are enticed by some untrue words to throw themselves over precipices, immolate themselves in fire and so on with horrible tortures (asceticism), prayers, oblations, vows, rules and uniforms in the hope of heaven (p. 29). Even the descriptions of heaven with golden houses, golden trees, etc., do not offer anything very special—what would one use for ornaments? This world is better. Moreover we have liquor to overcome the shyness of women; how would one do this in heaven where there is no drink? Devilaka would rather stay here with old priests than go after Sanskrit-speaking nymphs, who are said to be long lived and majestic. They have given birth to ancient sages such as Vasiṣṭha and Agastya: who would have any confidence in them? They are false, untrue, arrogant, envious, contemptuous and quarrelsome in love. Therefore enjoyment should be sought in this world, especially with the geishas.

1125. At this point Devilaka sees Sunandā, who says she has heard everything (apparently she has followed them)—so he finds his 'commodities have been sold'! They go into the house but the parasite refuses to stay for a drink, because it is late and his wife will suspect him. However, they seize hold of him and refuse to let him go, Sunandā promising to conciliate his wife. With this the play ends, the parasite reciting a final benediction.

1126. Bhoja (*Śṛṅgāraprakāśa* II p. 469) names a Rogue and Parasite as a *nidarśanakathā* [452], which of course must be different but perhaps was an imitation of this play's discussion.

1127. We possess one other play which is likely to belong to the period before Śūdraka, though the evidence, which is purely that of style, scale and the simplicity and rapidity of the action hardly interrupted by descriptive verses, is less clear than in most of the other plays we have considered so far. This play is a *nāṭaka* in six acts, the Jasmine Garland *Kundamālā* by Dhīranāga, a dramatist otherwise unknown to us. In general this play resembles those ascribed to Bhāsa and may be thought to belong to about the same period, though in some particulars the language seems a little more polished than Bhāsa's, a little closer to the later classical standard. The subject matter of the play is the tragic last book of the *Rāmāyaṇa*, the apocryphal story of Sītā's renewed exile and disappearance [615]. Dhīranāga has considerably altered the story and freely invented variations and new events, just as Bhāsa had in his Rāma plays, but above all he has converted the ending from a tragedy into a happy reunion of Rāma and Sītā. He thus conforms to the requirements of theory for a *nāṭaka*. When Vālmīki finally brings Sītā back to Rāma and declares her purity, instead of the Goddess Earth receiving her into her depths, Earth personified, the Goddess of the Earth, comes up out of the Underworld to give final confirmation of Sītā's perfect faithfulness to Rāma, sees this accepted by all present and Sītā reunited with Rāma and then disappears.

1128. Despite this ending the whole play is dominated by the tragic aesthetic experience, right from its beginning where Rāma's brother Lakṣmaṇa sets Sītā down in the forest on the bank of the Ganges and suddenly breaks to her the news that she is exiled. It happens that she is not far from Vālmīki's hermitage and she is seen by ascetic boys and reported to the sage, who takes her under his protection. He is at that time engaged in composing the *Rāmāyaṇa*, it being the tradition by now that Vālmīki was a contemporary of Rāma and lived through all the events of the story himself, being thus enabled to record them. It is after several years, when Rāma performs a horse sacrifice and invites Vālmīki to participate, that the sage takes the opportunity to effect the reunion, rebuking Rāma for listening to gossip. Whilst in exile, Sītā worships the divine river Ganges by daily floating a garland of jasmine flowers on her waters. Rāma walking along the banks of the river before performing his sacrifice finds a jasmine garland washed up at his feet and recognises the manner and skill of the weaving of the flowers as Sītā's. This is the first intimation he has of her presence and from it the play takes its name. Rāma continues until the last act in a state of uncertainty and remorse.

1129. The Jasmine Garland begins in a manner similar to the Bhāsa plays: 'Then the producer enters at the end of the opening benediction'; except that in this case a verse precedes these words, namely an invocation to Ganeśa. Quite possibly this is a later addition by a scribe. Otherwise it is to be taken as the opening benediction itself. In the Prologue the author, in this case, is named and said to be of the city of Anūparādha (variant reading Arārālapura). The city has not been certainly identified and the readings are probably corrupt (Anurādhapura, capital of Ceylon in this period, has been suggested, but this is only a guess; there is a lake Aravāla in Kaśmīra—*Samantapāsādikā* I p. 64). The leading in is by direct announcement of the actors *prayogātiśaya* (*Sāhityadarpaṇa* p. 270), though with parallelism *avalagita* also between the Producer's action and that of Lakṣmaṇa. The technique is reminiscent of the Dream Vāsavadattā [965].

1130. According to Sāgaranandin (153) the Producer's verse here (I. 3) contains a hint *upakṣepa* of the seed *bīja*:

"She stayed a very long time in the palace of the King
of Laṅkā"
—Rāma, confused by fear of this scandal among the
people,
Has exiled Sītā from the country though she is preg-
nant*:
—here is Lakṣmaṇa leading her through the forest.

(*so the text; Sāgaranandin has the inferior reading, at least as we have his work, '...from her husband's house to this deserted forest')

This implies that the objective *kārya* must be the rehabilitation of Sītā through some generally acceptable establishment of her chastity when Rāvaṇa's prisoner. Moreover, if we follow what appears to be the better reading, comparing it with the actual conclusion of the play, establishing the legitimacy of the twins whom Sītā will bear as Rāma's sons is also an essential part of the objective.

1131. Śāradātanaya declares (p. 223) that the Jasmine Garland has its five conjunctions very closely joined *suśliṣṭa*, though unfortunately we find no further explanation in his work. The opening *mukha* must of course include this end part of the Prologue, together with Act I, in which Lakṣmaṇa leaves Sītā in the forest and Vālmīki finds her. The re-opening *pratimukha* can be located in Act II, where (after several years have passed) it is reported that Sītā bore twin boys, whom Vālmīki is teaching, and where moreover the impending horse sacrifice by Rāma is announced. This is indeed closely joined to the opening in that Vālmīki's finding Sītā in Act I might be regarded as already part of the re-opening; however, the essential matter of the re-opening is rather the teaching of the *Rāmāyaṇa* to the boys, which equips them spiritually with their heritage as well as with the means to claim it practically by being introduced to Rāma as bards. The setting going of the sacrifice, which will bring him to the meeting with Vālmīki, might be described as constituting the re-opening from Rāma's side. The embryo *garbha* must be coextensive with Act III: Rāma sees the jasmine garland and supposes that Sītā may be in the vicinity (III.7 and the following dialogue between Rāma and Lakṣmaṇa). He also sees, and thinks he recognises, Sītā's footprints in the hermitage where the sacrifice is to be performed (III.11). In the same scene, Sītā, hidden (women are not supposed to be seen by men at a hermitage), overhears the conversation between Rāma and Lakṣmaṇa about herself. This of course develops the action from her side, since it inspires her with hope of eventual reunion, proving, what she all along believed but must obviously desire reassurance of, that Rāma has not forgotten her and will not supplant her with another queen. This scene is strongly reminiscent of Act IV of the Dream Vāsavadattā, which surely gave Dhīranāga the idea for it. The incident of recognising the garland also was perhaps imitated from Bhāsa's play, if the suggestion [985] that its text originally included a scene with Udayana recognising Vāsavadattā's garland is correct.

1132. The obstacle *avamarśa* appears to be the irruption of the nymph Tilottamā in Act IV. Her idea is to assume Sītā's form and appear before Rāma to see how he responds. Such escapades by the nymphs are not unusual in Indian legend. The jester hears of her arrival from the girls of the hermitage and tells Rāma. The effect of this is that Rāma thinks he has been deceived already by the garland and any other supposed signs of Sītā's nearness, any of which the nymph would have the power to imitate (IV. 22, etc.). At the beginning of Act V Rāma still thinks Tilottamā is making fun of him (V. 3). She does not actually appear on the stage: in the last act Vālmīki brings the real Sītā to Rāma, so that there is no opportunity for the nymph.

1133. According to Rāmacandra and Guṇacandra (p. 43), the 'intervention' *prakarī* is very important in this play, dominating the action because it brings about the attainment of the main 'fruit'. This intervention, in their analysis, is that of Vālmīki, who protects Sītā and her children and then unites them (with Rāma). This is an unusually extensive intervention, reaching from Act I to the last act, but the two critics point out that Vālmīki has no interest of his own in it. In other words it is a true 'intervention' [122], not involving a 'sub-plot' *patākā* in which a subsidiary hero would gain some end of his own. It can likewise presumably be said to be without development of its own, in that Vālmīki gains nothing, simply acting as a kind of trustee until Rāma unwittingly provides an opportunity for the reunion by inviting Vālmīki along with other sages to participate in his great sacrifice. In Act V Vālmīki sends the twin boys to Rāma on the pretext of providing an epic recitation appropriate for the occasion. They do not know their parentage, not even that their mother is the 'Sītā' of the story they have learned. At this first meeting Rāma is strangely impressed by them: he knows Sītā was pregnant when sent away and they seem about the right age. By the end of Act V he begins to think they may be his sons (V. 15). Thus the intervention here begins to lead into the conclusion *nirvahaṇa*.

1134. In Act VI the twins, Kuśa and Lava, recite the *Rāmāyaṇa* to Rāma and Lakṣmaṇa (this is presented on the stage, in bare outline, the audience imagining the familiar narrative enclosed), until they reach the episode of Sītā's exile, which is as far as they know the story. The sage Kaṇva then supplies the continuation that Sītā has been looked after by Vālmīki and has given birth to twins, finally explaining everything. Now Vālmīki brings in Sītā herself, angrily rebukes Rāma for his action and declares her pure character. This is followed by the appearance of the Goddess of the Earth, which we have noted already. After the Goddess disappears, Vālmīki, at Lakṣmaṇa's request, consecrates Kuśa as heir apparent and finally Rāma himself consecrates Lava also as heir apparent, presumably in succession to Kuśa. Thus the play ends with the legitimate succession of the dynasty restored.

1135. A further point bearing on the structure of this play may be gleaned from Sāgaranandin. He says (386) that the Jasmine Garland is an example of a drama whose title is taken from the subject *vastu* (or story), instead of from the main characters. This draws our attention to the jasmine garland which Sītā floats in the river as an offering each day of her exile. According to our analysis the recognition of one of these garlands by Rāma is central to the development of the plot, or rather it is the 'embryo' of the action: Rāma begins to think of Sītā as perhaps not utterly lost. It is this which is then interrupted by the 'obstacle' but eventually made real. Sītā makes the vow to offer a daily jasmine garland to the Ganges near the end of Act I (after verse 29): the river has already refreshed her with its cool breezes and she promises to make this offering if she has a safe delivery. This theme of the garland is repeated from the opening right through to the end of the obstacle (V. 3) and so is presented as a major element in the story. It is a thanksgiving for the safe birth of Kuśa and Lava, whose consecrations will conclude the action of the play, and it serves towards the reunion of their father with Sītā and his union with them.

1136. Sāgaranandin makes two other references to this play, quoting from it. First (1644) he points out a dramatic characteristic 'garland' *mālā*—in the figurative sense of a series of things. In this characteristic several ways of establishing what is intended are adduced: "Of equal family", "Congenial", "Possessing good qualities"... (I.12). The other quotation (3089-90) is for lassitude *ālasya* as a limb of the *śilpaka* [348]. It is odd that the quotation should be given in this connection and not rather as the transient emotion lassitude [56]. It is a speech of the pregnant Sītā in Act I (pp. 9-10), finding the climb down the bank of the Ganges in the forest difficult:

> Dear Lakṣmaṇa, my feet are not able to bear me further with the excessively heavy burden of the embryo. So go on ahead and find out how far it is to the Lady Ganges.

1137. M.R. Kavi quotes the Jasmine Garland for two characteristics. Doubt *saṃśaya* [186] is illustrated (II p. 351) from the point where Kuśa and Lava break off their *Rāmāyaṇa* recitation, their last verse telling how Sītā was abandoned by Lakṣmaṇa in the forest (VI.13). When they fall silent Rāma and Lakṣmaṇa wonder if the poet suppressed the rest of the story through being afraid to narrate what was unpleasant, namely that Sītā, without hope, has ended her life (VI.14). Attainment *prāpti* [186], which is a kind of inference, is shown where in Act III Lakṣmaṇa sees a woman's footprints (verse 10) and points them out to Rāma, who recognises them as being like Sītā's (*Abhinavabhāratī* II p. 353):

> As a consequence of playfulness or of fatigue
> or being by nature secretive, slowly
> These footprints of some woman on the sandbank
> set out to resemble the coquetry of the grey goose.

1138. Bhoja quotes (*Śṛṅgāraprakāśa* II p. 309) a verse from the Jasmine Garland (IV.20) to illustrate one of the 'qualities of a sentence' *vākyadharmas* of Mīmāṃsā and other linguistic theory. This particular quality is that of a word (here the verb 'found') being a 'pervader' *vyāpaka* of several other words in the sentence (cf. *Vākyapadīya* II 86, *vyāpin*) :

> A stake in gambling, a noose for the neck in love-play,
> a fan to take away the fatigue of frolic at the end of
> making love,
> A bed for midnight quarrels,—through the power of
> fate
> I have found the upper garment of the deer-eyed girl.

—Rāma has found a garment which he recognises as Sītā's in the hermitage. The verse is a somewhat surprising one for the usually austere Rāma to utter. No less a connoisseur than Vidyākara, however, selected it for his anthology (764), almost the only verse of Dhīranāga so distinguished.

1139. Vidyākara also quotes (55) the complex but striking benedictory verse (I. 2) with which the Producer begins the play :

> Like the flame serpenting upwards, of the ripe ascetic heat within;
> like the lustre of an anthill which is the dwelling of snakes, namely the high waves of the Ganges;
> Like twilight, with the Moon whose body is soft as a tender lotus-fibre;
> brown as a ray of the young dawn, may Śiva's mass of matted hair protect you !

This mythological benediction is rather typical of those popular henceforth in dramas. Śiva is the great ascetic, the celestial Ganges descends on his head [1150], he also wears the crescent Moon as a crest jewel. His hair is tawny and is therefore compared with various reddish things.

1140. One or two other verses are ascribed to Dhīranāga in the anthologies but not found in the Jasmine Garland (see e.g. Krishnamachariar p. 604). It is very likely that he wrote other plays not now available to us.

1141. Our information about other, now lost, plays of this period is scanty. We have already mentioned [753] the fiction *Kumudvatī* (the princess who loved a fisherman) referred to by Śūdraka [1225] and probably known already to Aśvaghoṣa. It could be compared with Bhāsa's Sheepkiller on a somewhat similar romantic theme.

1142. Another early lost fiction, of unknown date, had as hero the legendary king of thieves, Mūladeva, 'Whose God is Capital' (*Abhinavabhāratī* II p. 430). This popular hero was anciently known in the Buddhist (Pali, e.g. Commentary on the *Majjhima Nikāya*, Vol. III p. 222) tradition (as a famous bandit) as well as the Brahmanical. He is supposed to have been the author of the standard textbook (now lost) on the science of burglary. Whether the tradition goes back to any historical person is uncertain. The stories now known about him suppose him to have been a prince of Pāṭaliputra, apparently in the time of Bṛhadratha, the last emperor of the Maurya Dynasty in Magadha (—187 to —180). He was banished for his wickedness (and went to Ujjayinī) but was restored to favour with the assistance of his mistress, the geisha girl Devadattā. Afterwards he is supposed (*Avantisundarī* p. 184) to have been killed in battle by Puṣyamitra, the general who killed or deposed Bṛhadratha and usurped the throne (—180 to —151), founding the Śuṅga Dynasty. He would thus have been a Maurya prince seeking to overthrow the usurper and eventually failing. To Puṣyamitra (and consequently to posterity, since Puṣyamitra won) he was a rebel and a bandit, and perhaps he had been one before, against his own relatives. Probably also there were different versions of the story, making it still harder to arrive at any possible historical account. That the play (likely to have dealt with the banishment and restoration) is referred to by later critics (e.g. Abhinavagupta) as a 'fiction' (Abhinavagupta says the story was in fact drawn from the *Bṛhatkathā*: a fiction may draw on a novel) suggests the hero was not historical, though in the field of popular legend the distinction is thin [1367]. Udayana also appears in the *Bṛhatkathā*, linking that novel to history, was he too eventually supposed to have been a fictitious hero?

1143. In Chapter V we noted the traditions of the *Nāṭyaśāstra* concerning the earliest plays, which were of the religious types cooperation [330-2] and fight [333]. These are supposed to have been composed by Brahmā himself and it may well be doubted whether these plays ever existed in reality. If they did, they were presumably ancient pieces whose real authors had been forgotten; or indeed they may have formed part of an ancient repertory of plays handed down by oral tradition, having been freely varied and recreated extempore by actors familiar with mythology and legend, which had no authors other than successive generations of actors: they would be the common property of the actors as the Epic was of bards, or as the classical music remained long after and on the whole still remains to this day (and continues to change). In the case of an oral tradition of a group of plays, it is easy to understand that they could be regarded as primaeval creations of gods and sages, just as the Epic was ascribed to an ancient sage (a shadowy figure) with further elaborations by other sages. Later works on dramatic theory mention several other plays having this kind of authorship, along with Brahmā's cooperation Churning of the Ocean *Samudramathana* and his fight Burning of the Three Cities *Tripuradāha.*

1144. Some such plays are ascribed to 'Bharata', the supposed sage who composed the *Nāṭyaśāstra*, which itself is rather the elaboration of many generations of actors *bharatas* (Krishnamachariar p. 533, but the source of this information has not been traced). We may infer that these plays likewise were really traditional plays handed down by the actors. They were a rape entitled Victory of Kusumaśekhara *Kusumaśekharavijaya*; a heroic play Victory of Jāmadagnya (i.e. of Rāma of the Axe) *Jāmadagnyavijaya* and a tragedy Śarmiṣṭhā and Yayāti *Śarmiṣṭhāyayāti*. The identity of the hero of the first does not seem to have been ascertained; the name must be an unfamiliar epithet of some well known hero or god such as Kṛṣṇa or Kāma or probably Pradyumna (the play is named by Śāradātanaya, p.253, Bahurūpamiśra on *Daśarūpaka* III. 72 ff., see *JOR* VIII p. 328, and others; in Sāgaranandin, 2842, we read *Kundaśekharavijaya* instead). The second play described the killing of Kārtavīrya Arjuna (*Daśarūpaka* p. 75, *Nāṭyadarpaṇa* p. 109) [527] and produced the 'furious' experience (Bahurūpamiśra on IV. 75).

1145. It is not clear how the story of Śarmiṣṭhā and Yayāti could become a tragedy (*Sāhityadarpaṇa* p. 340) [524]. Perhaps Yayāti's loss of his youth was the main episode, whether or not followed by his restoration. Śarmiṣṭhā was the daughter of a demon, who quarrelled with her friend Devayānī, daughter of the demons' teacher Śukra, and threw her into a well. Devayānī was rescued by the Lunar emperor Yayāti, who married her, and in punishment Śarmiṣṭhā was made her servant. Afterwards Yayāti fell in love with Śarmiṣṭhā and secretly married her (this is usually the central theme of plays on the story). Devayānī discovered this and left him, returning to her father, who punished him by the infliction of premature old age. However, he succeeded in gaining the favour of Śukra, who allowed him to transfer his old age to one of his sons. Pūru, the youngest (born of Śarmiṣṭhā), sacrificed his youth to his father (and thereby became the eldest son), who enjoyed it for a thousand years, but at last renounced the world and restored his youth to Pūru, making him his successor (from whom were descended the Pauravas, the main line of Lunar rulers). At least five *nāṭakas* were later written on this popular Epic story of the rivalry of two women (see e.g. Krishnamachariar p. 649). There is an absurd tradition (or at least one which conflicts with the usual Tradition of the Lunar Dynasty) that when Nahuṣa, the first human being to see a drama, saw the gods' theatre in heaven, it was Bharata's tragedy Śarmiṣṭhā and Yayāti which was the first play performed before him. Now in Tradition Yayāti is the son of Nahuṣa... Of course it is even more an anachronism to suppose this ancient 'Bharata' to have composed a play on Rāma of the Axe, who lived many generations later still.

1146. Sarasvatī, Goddess of Learning and Literature, is supposed to have composed a *nāṭaka* called the Self-choice of Fortune *Lakṣmīsvayaṃvara*, which would have been on the same story as the Churning of the Ocean, since Fortune, Lakṣmī, was one of the products of the Churning and was immediately married by Viṣṇu (Krishnamachariar p. 533, but the source is perhaps the imagination of Kālidāsa [1405]).

1147. There were other cooperations which may have been ancient (*Abhinavabhāratī*, II p. 440). They presented stories about Indra and his union with Ahalyā as well as about the killing of Tāraka by Kārttikeya, which liberated the gods (cf. Sāgaranandin 2810: *Śakrānanda*). Śiva and Umā appeared in others, which presented the destruction of Tripura and the marriage of Himālaya's daughter.

1148. There were fights on the killings of the demons Vṛtra (by Indra—Sāgaranandin 2804, Śāradātanaya p. 248), Tāraka (by Kārttikeya, the son of Śiva—Śāradātanaya p. 248, Bahurūpamiśra on III. 57 ff. —JOR VIII p. 328—perhaps followed Sāgaranandin on this, whose text is now corrupt—2805 ff.—but mentions 'brilliant' *rasas*, illusions, deception, magic, gods, demons, goblins, sprites, dragons, etc., and the fall of a meteorite) and Naraka (by Kṛṣṇa—Sāgaranandin 2803: 16 heroes in this). One on the story of Vīrabhadra, created by Śiva out of a lock of his hair, is quoted by Siṅgabhūpāla, 272 ff., but may not be very ancient. Vīrabhadra was sent to destroy Dakṣa's sacrifice after routing the gods present: Śiva's consort

Satī had not been invited to the sacrifice and when she went she was insulted and committed suicide; in some versions of the story Dakṣa himself was killed, but afterwards restored to life by Śiva; Dakṣa was a son of Brahmā and a creator god.

1149. There was a rape of which Urvaśī was the heroine (Sāgaranandin 2839-40 *Urvaśīmardana*, which looks like a corruption: read rather *Urvaśīmadana* with Bahurūpamiśra on *Daśarūpaka* III. 72 ff) and perhaps resembled the rape by Veṅkaṭabhūpati (+18) *Urvaśīsārvabhauma* [658]. The *Māyākuraṅgikā* presumably has nothing to do with Kuraṅgī, but rather had an illusory deer in it (Śiṅgabhūpāla p. 298).

1150. Some early tragedies referred to are likely to be rather later than the period we have been concerned with in this chapter, but may be mentioned here. The 'death' of Lakṣmaṇa was the subject of the <*Śakti*> *rāmānuja*, with the hero's subsequent resurrection agreeably to the convention of not acting the slaying of a hero (Śāradātanaya p. 252). A tragedy *Gaṅgābhagīratha* dealt with the legend of the Solar emperor Bhagīratha, who succeeded in bringing the River Ganges (the Goddess Gaṅgā) down from heaven (in which she appears as the Milky Way) to Earth, an extraordinary feat looked upon as the supreme achievement of human effort. Śāradātanaya (p. 252) indicates that again here death was followed by resurrection. Bhagīratha's aim was to redeem his ill fated ancestors, the sons of Sagara, who lay in a pit in the Underworld, burned to ashes by the wrath of the sage Kapila. It appears their death was described in an introductory scene, just as in Bhāsa's Mace Fight the actual fight is described in a supporting scene [951]. The pit was filled by the waters of the Gaṅgā as she passed over the spot on her way to the ocean; the sons of Sagara were thus purified and enabled to proceed to heaven. Bhagīratha achieved his end by propitiating Śiva as he sat in his abode on the Himālaya Mountains (properly on Mount Kailāsa, which may be regarded as one of the Himālayan peaks): the Goddess descended on Śiva's head [1139] and then flowed down the Himālayas and across the plain to the ocean. This myth, with Gaṅgā's presence on Śiva's head and the consequent jealousy of his consort Pārvatī, is often alluded to in later *kāvya* literature.

1151. For the street play *vīthī* in this period we can supplement the example of the possibly untypical Three Steps, very doubtfully ascribed to Bhāsa, only from references to lost plays which may have belonged to a rather later period. Such examples as the *Indulekhā* (*Śṛṅgāraprakāśa* II p. 494, Śāradātanaya pp. 231 and 251, *Nāṭyadarpaṇa* p. 126 [326] and Bahurūpamiśra on *Daśarūpaka* III. 16 and 68 ff.) and the *Mālatikā* (Bhoja [326] and Bahurūpamiśra on III. 13 f. and III. 68 ff.), and some others named after their heroines, indicate a fair antiquity for the type of street play with a fictitious story. Probably they were similar to some of the very late street plays now available, by Rāmapāṇivāda and others, in that the main action described is the acquisition of an additional wife by a king, involving a palace intrigue. These stories are similar to those of the 'light plays', *nāṭī* or *nāṭikā*, and like these may sometimes be more or less 'historical', as is Bhāsa's Yaugandharāyaṇa's Vows. The *Rādhā* (Sāgaranandin 3025 [326]) is likely to have been on the well known intrigues of Kṛṣṇa. Unlike the Three Steps, these street plays appear to have had regular prologues leading to the introduction of the two characters of the play proper, who seem usually to have been the king and his jester. The action of the intrigue would then be represented through the dialogue between these two. Professor Raghavan's extract from the *Mālatikā*, however, shows three parts: the heroine Mālatikā in addition to the King and Jester (*Bhoja's Śṛṅgāra Prakāśa* p. 888). Another type of street play known later (particularly in Āndhra) agrees with the Three Steps in having a painting of some historical or legendary subject displayed as part of the props (Krishnamachariar p. 688; Somasekhara, *History of the Reḍḍi Kingdoms*, pp. 512-3). The technique of having two characters proceed through the streets of a city, describing what they see, may be a late imitation of that of the satirical monologue.

INDEX TO VOL. II

(The numbers refer to paragraphs)